My Three Lives

To Ginger Becker, — because we love you. Happiness

Mary Carey

9-9-81

Mary Carey

This book is being made into a movie.

EAKIN PRESS 🜏 Austin, Texas

FIRST EDITION
Copyright © 1997
By Mary Carey
Published in the United States of America
By Eakin Press
A Division of Sunbelt Media, Inc.
P.O. Drawer 90159 ⌨ Austin, Texas 78709-0159
email: eakinpub@sig.net
💻 website: www.eakinpress.com 💻
ALL RIGHTS RESERVED.
1   2   3   4   5   6   7   8   9
1-57168-125-6

Library of Congress Cataloging-in-Publication Data

Carey, Mary (Mary Latch)
    My three lives / by Mary Carey.
      p.   cm.
    Include index.
    ISBN 1-57168-125-6
    1. Carey, Mary (Mary Latch) 2. Alaska — Biography. 3 Texas — Biography.
4. Fugitives from justice — Texas — Biography. 5. Adventure and adventurers —
Texas. 6. Adventure and adventurers — Alaska. 7. Frontier and pioneer life —
Alaska. I. Title.
CT274.C357A3   1997
811'.52--dc21
[B]   96-29630
                                       CIP

Contents

Preface

Despite the fact that my name has appeared in the Obituary columns three times recently, and that I will be eighty-four years of age when this book appears, I ain't dead yet!

The first time it appeared in the Obit it was about a Mary Carey, about my age, who was charge nurse at a Fairbanks hospital. I'll never forget meeting her. I was in the kitchen, at my lodge, baking peanut butter cream pies, as usual. One of the waitresses came back and delivered a puzzling message, "Tell Mary Carey her daughter is here."

"How could she be?" I asked the waitress who smiled and walked away as I washed my hands and walked toward the front of the restaurant, all the way, without seeing her at all. Then a young lady stood up smiling, extended her hand. "I'm Mary Carey's daughter," she quipped, "and this is my mother, Mary Carey." Soon we became good friends and I was always happy to see them. Now she is dead. What a void it left in my heart. But I'll tell you one thing, if I can do as much good for others as that Mary Carey did, I have not lived in vain.

When the name Mary Carey, who was a writer graced the Obit, my daughter started receiving sympathy calls. Frantically she called from Texas to Alaska and before I could say a word came her plea, "Mom, please say it is you answering. A friend who you once taught in the writer's conference thought it just had to be your Obituary."

"Well, Darling, I am glad to report this Mary Carey still enjoys good health; but if I can do as much good for my readers as you and the other Mary Carey have done for children through your books, I will die happy. Just keep writing. Grown-ups enjoy your books too!" I went to reread a book the other Mary Carey wrote about how an orphaned girl finally found happiness through her own ingenuity. I wonder how many lonely and unhappy children this book has helped.

The third assumption of my death came through a front page news story which went out over the wires. This time I was fortunate enough to see the story first, and called my only chick immediately. "Jeannie," I reported happily, "I will be in Texas next week as planned. I will still be a little black and blue, but don't let any news story frighten you by saying I am in the hospital. I told them I really didn't believe I had any broken bones, but because I looked a little battered, they insisted. Lenora is O.K. too. Just badly bruised."

"Mamma! What in the world are you talking about?"

"Oh, nothing much. I didn't think it so unusual for a couple of Senior Ladies to tackle a shoplifter and hold him there until the police arrived."

"What?" she stammered. Then I knew I had to tell her all about it before she saw the news report.

It happened during the Iditarod dog mushing race from Anchorage to Nome. I was in Kodiak Furs, which your cousin Lenora Preston owns. Like usual, I was helping with sales when not autographing books. The race was just starting, less than a block from her shop. Even though it's February, there was not enough snow to make a good path for the mushes, so the snow had to be hauled in. All the streets near Fourth Avenue, where the race starts, were blocked by ropes and snow berms. No traffic was allowed until all the racers were started, one at a time in single file. Usually this takes until near noon because there are seventy or more to get going and they are spaced about 100 yards apart. The fur and craft shop was never very busy as the racers were started, yet the news stand and temporary bleachers were always completely filled. Often one of us from the shop would walk down and watch as a favorite musher was started. A few people were in buying, but most of them just warming up between starts, when a tall, dark and handsome walked in. He made his way toward the artifact case and a table where I was autographing books. He hesitated, stopped to look at some delicately carved ivory, until I finished with a customer. "Could I help you?" I asked.

"I came to look at artifacts for a buyer," he reported. As I began to show him some of our prized possessions I noticed that his eyes were traveling around the shop. When I realized that he didn't know the difference in a wing bone, a hollow bone that the natives sometimes used as a straw and an "oosik," penis bone of a walrus, I began to wonder why any one would send him to purchase artifacts.

I took a closer look at him. He was dressed in a dark business suit, but there was something different . . . the large safari pockets. He looked as if he had just come from a beauty parlor, nails manicured and hair freshly trimmed.

"Where are you from?" I asked curiously.

"I'm from Nome," he replied casually, "A Native Alaskan," he added.

This was a shock to me. He wore a long overcoat, which Alaskans seldom wear, furthermore he wore well-shined leather boots, rather than conventional Arctic wear. I put this into my little brain computer and it was still processing when I saw him eyeball the workshop behind heavy glass windows where customers could observe the native artist as they created mukluks (fur boots), parkas and fur caps.

"You have been so wonderful to take your time to help me," he complimented. "Would you mind telling me what that flat stone dish is for? I would also like to see that bone doll behind it, the one in the far corner."

"It's a seal oil lamp," I informed, wondering why he didn't know. "It's very rare, a museum piece."

As I reached to the far corner of the case he gave me a peck on the cheek as his left hand reached back for a $695 dollar piece of intricately carved ivory.

Bingo! my mental computer came up with the answer. In Kashmier, India, where members of our Gem and Mineral Society were staying in ornately carved teak-wood boats, while rock hounding near the border of Tibet, I learned the answer in advance. Tall, pale-faced young Indians were hanging around the end of our dock. Two of them approached a couple of our senior women as they left the fenced area. Those of us who were left behind saw the women shaking their heads "no." When refused, the male prostitutes gave the women a kiss on the cheek, probably to throw them off balance, as they grabbed their purses and disappeared into the underbrush.

As prearranged with Lenora, when I had worked there previously during such winter festivities, I tried to stall the shoplifter as I saw Lenora head for the telephone.

"I have one more item I would like to show you," I stalled. "It too is a museum piece. It's right over there on the wall. A walrus-gut raincoat."

"But I need to call my boss before making large purchases, especially two museum pieces," he said uneasily.

I was nervous too, because I had already seen the rest of the help and the last customer leave the shop.

"Fine," I answered, "But we do appreciate having distinguished guests sign our register. It's right here on the counter."

As he bent down to sign he glared toward Lenora who was giving the name and street address of the shop. He must have heard her and suspected that she was calling the police. Dropping the pen he turned to run. I don't know what possessed me then, anger or a throw-back to my girlhood when I played football with my brothers. I lunged and tackled him around the knees.

Lenora made it to the door, locked it and guarded it with her body, arms opened. The hobbled thief managed to drag me to the door. He grabbed Lenora by the shoulders and started beating her head into the heavy plate glass.

"Help!" she yelled as a man and woman approached the door. Probably thinking they were interrupting a family brawl, the pair lost no time leaving.

"Help!" she called again as more prospective customers came within ear shot. Releasing Lenora, he drug me toward the back door, upsetting racks of fur.

"Let him go!" Lenora yelled as he drug me toward the sewing room. In he dashed, locking the door behind him.

"Good!" Lenora commented as he went straight through the workshop towards the store rooms. "The back door is barred and locked, he can't get into the alley," she said as she headed back towards the phone.

We heard loud thumping noises as he tried to crash his way outside. Finding my arms and legs still worked, I got up and dashed for the front door. Luckily I saw the mall security guard about half a block away. I screamed for help and as he started running toward the shop, I made it back to near the sewing room door and hid in a rack of fur coats.

Out he popped and again I lunged as we knocked over more racks. Grabbing fur parkas he threw them over my head, blinding me. Again the dragging, this time over the previously upset mess.

"Hold it!" a stern voice called, "or I'll shoot. Put your hands above your head!"

Crawling from beneath the tangle of fur parkas I thanked the guard and walked back up to check on Lenora. We were both battered but seemed O.K. otherwise.

After what seemed an eternity the city police arrived. Of course it took them longer because so many of the streets were blocked. They made it in by driving the wrong way on a one-way street. An ambulance followed. Lenora and I didn't think we needed x-rays for broken bones but they insisted we should go to the hospital for a check. There could be other things wrong.

That ended the bad part of the story. Now for the fun spots.

The news story that followed was quite accurate, except for one word. But that one word brought more laughs than any story I have ever written. The reporter quoted me as saying, "I think the shoplifter was insulted that a couple of old ladies 'seduced' him until the police arrived." The word should have been "subdued" but I like the way it came out in print better.

The real punch line came over a week later. Johnson, who has his own radio and T.V. talk show in Houston, called my daughter from Vancouver Island where he was vacationing. It happened something like this. Another fisherman on the same boat asked Doug Johnson if he knew a writer from Texas, an elderly woman living in Alaska who tackled a shoplifter and held him until the police arrived. The last the informant heard was that she was in the hospital and he was of the opinion that she had died.

"I know Mary Carey and her daughter, Jean Richardson quite well. They both write and I try to put them on my show each time either of them come out with a new book."

When they reached shore, he called saying, "Jean, I'm so sorry to hear about your mother."

"Oh, it wasn't that bad," Jean laughed. Silence on the other end of the line, and Jean continued. "She's coming to Texas next week."

"Would the two of you like to come on my show after she gets in. I've something I want to tell you when I get you on the air.

That something brought several calls from friends who were glad no obituary was needed.

I like the way my name was mentioned in the *Anchorage Daily News* in August of 1996. Sadly enough, a very good friend, Jack Spake had died. He was the chief engineer along the stretch of the Parks Highway which finally reached my homestead near Mount McKinley in 1970. Near the end of the obituary my name jumped at me. It read, "Mary Carey wrote about him in one of her books." I also did a magazine article about him. He was a great man and a tribute to the state of Alaska. I love writing about those whose achievements make for a better world.

Last fall, my adventurous friend, Oro Stewart led the Chugach Gem and Mineral Society of Anchorage on it's thirtieth overseas rock hunt, a world record in so far as can be determined. Many rock club members from over Alaska, as well as rock hounds from other states, join Mrs. Stewart in these overseas safaris. Most of us have known each other for years and the event is more like a family reunion than a tour group.

Recently, Oro was giggling when she called me in Talkeetna. I knew something was up. "Mary, I was just thinking that both of us are getting older." I knew something was up when she started with, "You know how we both love Hong Kong. I've been planning," she giggled, "that since both of us are getting pretty old, we should double up and make two foreign trips a year instead of one. I want to see this area again before it goes back to China. I bet the 'buys' are still good."

"You're on! When do we start? I need to be back in early

May to open my Fiddlehead Fern Farm and my gift shop. I don't have to worry about the lodge since Jean and her husband are taking care of it for me. Your photo shop should be getting pretty busy about then too. I know, I'll call you back tomorrow with our schedule."

Oro and her now deceased husband, Ivan Stewart, have included me in so many exciting adventures that it would take a book to relate to them. We've had a few close calls, for sure, like the earthquake in 1964 when we were trapped by rising water near Portage where the ground sunk four feet. The Stewarts were always far-out when it came to adventure, especially when using their amphibious car, their swamp buggy and their hover-craft.

Alaska is the greatest state of all when it comes to adventure. And when I embark on that last great trip, it will just be another to where I have never been before. Yet I'm not planning on this trip for a long, long time. I want to live to be 100 years old . . . and still be writing.

I've lived three lives already, and each one keeps getting better. Aren't kids, grand kids and great-grand kids the greatest! This is what I call heaven on earth.

Part

1

Chapter 1

I'm a Dummy, But it Hurts to Know It

*I*t seems I have lived three lives, and in three different worlds. But the road wasn't paved and I lost my way. Twice in my younger years I chose death, but failed. What pushes one to the brink of no return? When does self-destruction begin? Why? I was born at a bad time. Europe was on the brink of World War I. My father had just lost his fortune. My mother was sick.

■   ■   ■

I do not remember when my father William Z. Latch was first cashier of a bank in the small town of Spring Place, Georgia, where he also served as mayor. Before becoming Mrs. Latch, my mother, Miss Amanda Peeples, was a teacher and had been elected the beauty of Murray County. She was a community leader who was greatly admired. Neither do I remember all the gracious things my parents did for others, like giving land for schools and churches. Our home was the home for many others, like old man Love, a teacher who retired with no home, no money and no kin. Of course our parents took him in, as well as three orphaned children whose mother and father had drowned. At the time there were already four children in the Latch family. That made seven, with the eldest, my brother Roy, only eight years old.

There's little doubt that our father's greatest weakness was trusting others too much. Although he studied law at Mercer University, he turned down a career as a lawyer because he said he couldn't misrepresent the truth. Trusting a New York company too much before and during World War I cost our father his fortune. For years this company had bought talc from the Latch mines on Old Fort Mountain, and they always paid. Then the company started missing payments, kept promising to pay, and then took bankruptcy. Our father sold the mines, our home and everything he owned to pay his bills, but the New York company took bankruptcy to keep from paying theirs.

Rather than face friends and kin as "pore folks," my blue-blooded parents moved to east Texas, where Father had secured a cashier's position in a Queen City bank. But the move was for my mother's health as well. Father, who had gone to Texas in advance to prepare for our coming, waited with open arms to escort us to our first rented home. All seven of the Latch children were soon in school. I was a first grader, having been born April 1, 1913.

Our palatial Georgia home, kin and friends were all left behind. Mother cried a lot. We begged her to sing and recite poetry as she had when we lived in Georgia, but she didn't sing much anymore. It was not like when we all gathered around the old family organ at night for vespers. Then Mother would play the old pump organ as we all sang. Father would read a few passages from the Bible, then he insisted that each sibling contribute, according to age and observation. Responses ranged from reciting a times-table to seeing the first flowering wild plum tree in the spring.

Our father had just started his second year with the bank in Queen City, Texas in 1919 when we all took the flu from "over there." We were all sick, very sick, but Mother did not fully recover. Finally the family doctor said he believed she had contracted T.B. and that Father should move us farther west, to a drier climate than in East Texas.

I was seven years old when we moved to Cisco in 1920. Cisco was an oil boom town near Abilene, Texas. Our father and two older brothers went to work in the "oil patch." Things went better for us financially. I was next to the youngest of the Latch

Author's parents, Mr. William Z. Latch and Miss Amanda Peeples on their wedding day, October 1, 1899, at Fort Mountain, Georgia.

children at the time. According to my report card I had been promoted to the second grade, but I didn't stay there. My teacher called my mother in for a conference. I remember hearing her explain that I seemed to have learned none of the basics in the first grade, and saying, "Mrs. Latch, Mary is simply not ready for second grade work."

"Perhaps it's my fault," my mother answered. "We all had the flu and I was very sick for a long time. No one had the time nor the energy to help her."

I cried and cried. All my older brothers and sisters were "A" students, but reading and writing just didn't make sense to me. As my mother pointed out to the teacher, "She memorizes faster than any of the rest of the children, but I realize she can't read. Perhaps it is wise to hold her back. I've tried, but I just don't understand her problem."

Neither did I. All I really understood was that I had disgraced the family. I was a real dummy and I knew it. Now the kids would laugh at me more than ever for printing my letters backward. I did not want to return to the school.

In 1920 people just didn't know about dyslexia. Now we know it is not a disease but a learning disability — a neurological dysfunction. It is estimated that five to ten million children in the U.S.A. suffer some kind of learning disability. Einstein, Churchill, and Edison are among the "great" who suffered with dyslexia. Closer to home, three of our stage and T.V. stars, Tom Cruise, Cher and Margo Hemingway, are among those who have conquered dyslexia. John Horner, the world's top authority on dinosaurs, finally finished high school with a "D-" average, but failed in college, so severe was his handicap. But he, too, overcame.

I still have trouble spelling, but I know I can cope with this demon with a dictionary at my side. Yet dyslexia always strikes fear into my heart when split-second decisions must be made. It's not so much the traffic on the freeway, but the fear that I cannot read the signs in time to make the desired turn. But back to my story.

Now I realize that my problem was no disgrace, but then I thought it was. It hurt to be a dummy and know it. Little words

Our Georgia home where six of the Latch children were born. Present owner Dr. Mickey McNeill, Superintendent Murray County Public Schools, stands near the door with two of the Latch daughters born here. Center, Lela Latch Lloyd of Cisco, Texas, and Mary Latch Carey of Talkeetna, Alaska, as the two sisters visited their birthplace in 1992.

— Photo courtesy Jan McNeill

like "are" and "was" and "saw" were confusing. The kids really laughed when I read: " I 'was' a bird."

Failing the first grade was not my only heartbreak that first year in school. Just before school was out I lost my playmate, Edith Lovelady, the only little girl who lived anywhere near us in the country. Edith and I walked the mile-and-a-half to school together every day. We were also allowed to play together on weekends and we attended Sunday School together. We were inseparable until Edith died of diphtheria. I was devastated. I had no one to play with now, except boys.

The following year, Christmas finally came. My brothers, all five of them (including Bill, who had been born in Texas), loved to play baseball. But all I ever got to play was "pigtail," behind the catcher, chasing down the balls he missed. If I only had a catcher's mitt! I could make hind catcher — I just knew I could!

6

As Christmas drew nearer, I prayed and prayed for a catcher's mitt.

Christmas morning I awakened early and ran to the tree, where I was sure I would find a catcher's mitt. Not so! I was the only little girl in the family, the only one of doll age, and there was a big baby doll, one that would open and shut its eyes. One with a sewing kit for making baby doll clothes. And NO catcher's mitt.

I was crying when Mother appeared on the scene. "I only wanted a catcher's mitt," I sobbed, knowing full well that we would receive only one expensive present each.

"And I only wanted a little girl in the house," my mother responded as we both cried. "With Edith gone I thought I could help replace your loss by working with you and teaching you to sew. You are good with your hands. We could make clothes for your doll. I so wanted you to become a little girl, but I guess all you will ever be is a Tomboy." Thus began the erosion of our mother-daughter relationship.

Another incident which broke my heart took place in church. I loved Sunday school and church. I always knew my Bible verses and memorized the hymns we heard so often. I really belted out the songs, probably trying to prove I could memorize even though I could not read, until the Sunday of my mother's terrible embarrassment.

We had visitors in our little town. They came and sat beside my mother. I was on the front pew, as always, drinking everything in with my neck thrust forward and my mouth wide open, a habit which my mother had tried to help me break.

That night I heard my mother and father talking, long after they thought I was asleep. We had only two bedrooms for the nine of us, not like our plantation home, which had bedrooms to spare. I, being the youngest, slept on a cot in my parents' bedroom. My older sisters slept in what we called our parlor, and the boys were in what we called the "bunk room."

"Will," I heard my mother whisper to my father, "I denied my own child in church today. I don't think I will ever go to sleep again without confessing."

"What did you ask me?" my father responded. "I was asleep and don't think I understood you, Amanda."

7

"It was in church today, Will. I just couldn't answer when a visitor punched me and asked who that little girl was on the front row, the one with her mouth wide open and eyes staring. It was Mary, of course. I noticed the woman watching her earlier, during the singing. You know how Mary belts the words right out."

"And is that such a disgrace? I'll bet half the people in church don't know as many songs and scriptures as Mary does, and all by heart."

"Tell me, Will, do you think she will ever learn to read?"

"Yes, Amanda, I do. I know she has a problem, but I'm not blaming you. Things have been pretty tough for all of us. I'm the fool. It's all my fault, trusting the "higher ups" and losing our money like I did."

"Now don't go blaming yourself again, Will. Maybe it's my fault. You know I nearly went crazy while I was carrying her, with those sharks cheating us out of our money and home. Then the war, and me nearly dying with the flu, and us having to move again."

"Give her time, 'Mandy," my father consoled. "I don't believe there's anything seriously wrong with her. Maybe she will come out of it and prove everybody wrong. She's not an idiot. Give her time."

Summer finally came. I tried in every way I could to make up for embarrassing my mother. With summer came a revival meeting. The preacher offered a new Bible to the boy or girl who memorized the most verses and the names of the books in both the Old and New Testament. This was for me, my name embossed in gold! Maybe, if I could only win this prize, my mother wouldn't be ashamed of me anymore. Maybe I could show everyone I wasn't a complete dunce, even if I did fail in school. Every time I caught any member of my family alone or with enough time to read to me, I memorized, trying hard to remember how the words looked on the page.

Mother would read a verse from our Bible with the big print, then have me read the easier words right back, patiently helping me with the harder ones. I tried like I had never tried before. I HAD to win that Bible. And I did! This was my first real victory. Soon I could read the easy words in books, even though I still wrote some of my letters backward.

8

I spent so much time with the Bible that summer that I failed to make our baseball team. Neither did I the next, but there was one game where I excelled. We called it "I Dare You." After saying those words, the leader would do something like climbing to the roof of the woodshed and jumping off. I soon learned I could beat most of the boys my age and some who were older. "I double dare you!" I would call gleefully as I climbed to the highest limb on a tree or shinnied up a telephone pole, knowing full well that I would get a spanking when Mother got word.

Again I heard my parents talking and listened closely when I heard my name.

"I'll swear Mary could climb to the moon," my mother spoke in vexation. "She's a bigger daredevil than any of the boys. I just don't know what to do. I guess her teachers are right. She's simply a slow learner."

"Now, Mama," my daddy replied, "it seems to me Mary has good sense. We know she can learn when she applies herself."

"Yes, like winning a Bible. But she shows little interest in her schoolwork."

"Give her time," my father advised. "There's more to learning than making straight A's."

I tried harder. I stumbled through grade school and was doing even better in grammar school, now called Middle School, when tragedy struck again. After losing Edith, I did not have a close friend for some time. Then my older brother, Roy, fell in love with Lois Thames. Their courtship was the grandest thing I had ever seen. Lois had a younger brother, Grady, who was just a little older than I was. Soon he became my best friend. Grady wasn't too strong physically, so we sometimes spent a lot of time daydreaming. He never called me dumb. He was kind and helped his mother, sometimes while the rest of us played. We often fished for crayfish in a little stock tank near the house. "Crawdads," we called them, and we fished for them with bent pins for hours. Then we would clean and cook them. But mostly we daydreamed. We planned to get married when we got old enough, and told the world about it.

Then, when we were in the fifth grade, Grady became deathly ill. His family rushed him to the doctor, but it was too

My older sisters, Lela and Annie, and my brother, Paul Latch, won many school honors, including Debate.

Above:
Leonard Latch lettered six years, two years in Cisco high and four years at Texas Technological in Lubbock.

Left:
Bill Latch a four-year letterman in Cis-co high school and a two-year letterman in Colorado State of Colorado Springs.

10

late. His appendix had ruptured. An emergency operation failed to save him.

We were told of his death at school. I cried and cried. The kids teased me, "Mary's lost her boyfriend, Mary's lost her boyfriend. Mary will never marry because she's too stupid."

My air castles toppled. I wouldn't talk with God about it. I was cheated, twice. All the other girls and boys in school lived. Why did I have to lose my two best friends? The only two who did not call me "dummy?" Not even God loves a dummy, otherwise he would not punish me so much. I didn't even want to go to church.

I dragged through middle school, then junior high. My work was passing, but never too good. Gradually I overcame my loss and no longer blamed God for taking my two best friends. Yet I failed to develop others.

Soon I would be entering high school. Maybe, just maybe, I would find friends there. My grades were better and there would be students from other schools who did not know me during my real "dummy" years. I could make passing grades. I would work harder. And I did. Even made my first "A" (other than in conduct). Then the Great Depression struck.

Mother was going through the change of life at the time and she just couldn't cope. There was no work anywhere. Men were taking out large insurance policies on themselves and then committing suicide, in hopes their families could live.

My brother Paul who had just finished high school knew he could not attend college, even though he had earned a scholarship by winning debate at the state competition. There was not enough food at home and he could not find any type of work anywhere. The Hoover Dam project had just started. He broke my mother's heart by hopping a freight train to Arizona, where things were reported to be better. Daddy was still away from home looking for work. There was none.

Mother just couldn't take it. One morning while I was getting ready for school, she started laughing hysterically and couldn't stop. Laughing and crying, laughing and crying.

I ran to a neighbor who called a doctor — we could not afford a telephone ourselves. Neither of my sisters was home. My older sister Lela was attending Scarritt College for Christian

11

Workers in Nashville. My sister Annie lived in Indiana and was expecting her first baby. The doctor diagnosed my mother's problem as a nervous breakdown.

Thus I inherited all the household responsibilities. Trying to cook with nothing fit to cook was exasperating and became a more fearful challenge every day as the larder diminished. Washing and ironing my brother's shirts was something else. During one of her more lucid moments, my mother saw how much time went into washing and ironing shirts, as we used to do, with flatirons. She called my brothers to her bedside.

"Mary has enough to do without so many shirts to iron," she began her ultimatum. "I know you like football practice after school, but Mary has to do all the cooking and cleaning and taking care of me as well as doing her homework too. You boys will just have to iron your own shirts."

My brother Leonard was very proud of earning a football sweater, one of those pullover jobs. A Texas "blue norther" hit and he deduced that he could eliminate much ironing time by pressing only the collar and cuffs, since the rest of the shirt did not show. This worked fine for a couple of days, but the norther passed almost as quickly as it hit and he had to wear the heavy wool sweater all day. He came home steaming, and ironed the rest of his shirts all the way. Evidently this experience did not hurt him too much. Later, while playing with the Texas Tech Red Raiders, he was chosen for All American tackle.

In those days, before wash and wear became the fashion, everything, including sheets and pillow cases, was starched and ironed. One wash day I made a pan of starch and set it on the table to cool while I hung out the clothes. My younger brother, Bill, came home and spied the cooling starch.

"Hey, Sis," he called as I appeared, "how come you forgot to put the sugar in the pudding?"

"Pudding?" I gasped.

"Yeah, but I fixed it. I put the sugar in myself."

"Sugar? In the cornstarch?" I sputtered as I ran for Mother's protection.

Thus my high school years were spent taking care of Mother and doing the housework. My brothers were very popular, but I was dumb. Homely too, with a very pimply face. Paul won

12

scholastic honors in debate and extemporaneous speaking. Leonard and Bill were football captains. I never won anything. In fact, I never had a new dress during my high school years, just hand-me-downs from my older sisters. My hair was straight and stringy. A perm was out of the question — we did well to eat.

Gradually Mother gained strength and was able to help with a few of the chores. But she wasn't her old self, mentally or physically. Sometimes she would look at me and cry.

"Your sisters are so pretty and smart. I don't see why you couldn't have followed in their footsteps. Your stringy hair and pimply face don't help a bit. I just don't understand why you couldn't be pretty and smart like Lela and Annie."

Then I would go off and pinch my pimply face and cry. I would never get to go off to college like my older sisters. I would be doing well to finish high school. I did, but my only victory came through writing poetry. I always had a poem in the school paper, but I never had a date.

I won no laurels at graduation, but I did have a new dress of soft pink silk for baccalaureate. My mother sewed beautifully and expended much time and strength making it. Father had finally gotten a job and we were living and eating better.

"You look very presentable with your new dress and a permanent, almost pretty," my mother complimented. "I do believe you have a better figure than Lela and Annie and your face is looking much better. I was talking with your older brother Roy when he and Lois visited last weekend. Would you like to visit with them a while this summer? I can take care of myself now. They are expecting a new baby and the oldest one is only a year old. Maybe you could sell candy and pop in their little refreshment shop while your brother makes his run with the Coca Cola delivery truck. The doctor says Lois might lose the baby if she's on her feet too much."

I thought I had died and gone to heaven. My first time away from home, and almost a hundred miles. Maybe I had improved enough that I would no longer be considered a dummy. At least I would not have to watch my classmates getting ready for college. Maybe I could forget that I pretended to be sick because I had no date for the senior prom. Maybe, living in a nice house, with decent clothes . . . my dreams soared . . .

Somehow my brother's customers did not seem to realize I was dumb. My pimples were hardly noticeable anymore. I bought a new dress and shoes with my first paycheck. Maybe I didn't look too bad after all!

Then BOOM! Romeo appeared. His name was Roy King, and was he handsome! I just couldn't believe it when he asked me for a date. I was ecstatic. Soon we were planning. He wanted to become a doctor and I a foreign missionary. Wouldn't it be great if we could go overseas and work in the mission field together? Roy had never traveled either.

My brother Roy became alarmed with my falling so madly in love . . . and soon I was home again. This was during W.P.A. (Works Progress Administration) days and our New Deal president, Franklin D. Roosevelt, was pushing plans to put people to work.

While in high school, I did take two years of Spanish. Roosevelt was starting programs to help people become self-supporting. We had lots of Mexicans in our little Texas town, many who could not speak English to earn a U.S. citizenship.

My sister Lela was back home from college with her first teaching job. She insisted I apply to teach English as a second language in the night school that was being started. I did, and got the job.

Another score. A big one! My class was very successful. We taught each other. Christmas was near and several of my group could sing and play guitars. They taught me our carols in Spanish and together we literally serenaded the town. But funds were cut from the program in the spring and I was left jobless.

Things were little better for Roy. His dream of becoming a doctor seemed as unattainable as mine for becoming a foreign missionary. Roy's father, Ralph King of nearby Stamford, held a good job with the West Texas Utility Company, but he was already supporting two families, his and an older daughter's, under the same roof. There were seven children. Ralph's wife, Ruby, must have been an angel, otherwise they would never have survived.

Fortunately, a very good friend of the King family who owned a drug store took a great interest in Roy, who grew up with his own children. Roy jumped at an opportunity to go to work in the local drug store where he was to become an understudy for the pharmacist. This would be a definite step toward his goal. Formal schooling could come later, after we were married and the Depression had loosened its grip.

Roy had worked at his new job only two months when he asked me to marry him. He didn't have much to offer except a dream, but that was more than what was left for me. Life had become more unbearable as my classmates were getting ready for college. I had no job, no future. Mother's health was a little better and I was rapidly becoming just one more mouth to feed. With no formal training, work seemed nonexistent.

I told my parents of Roy's proposal and they objected to my marrying someone I had known less than three months. There was no money for a wedding and they had seen Roy only a few times, when he could borrow the family car and head for Cisco.

"My world has ended," I told my lover the following week when he returned. "My parents think we are too young to marry and we would have no place to live."

"I'm ready," Roy replied undaunted. "We do have a place to live. My sister's husband found a job and they have moved out. Mother says you are very welcome and father says it would be nice to have a car again. I stopped in Baird on the way down and procured a license. We'll elope. All we'll need is a J.P."

I guess love knows no bounds, certainly not a beautiful love like ours. What did it matter that I was not yet nineteen and he was only twenty-one?

We slipped out. I left a note at home saying we had eloped. Our honeymoon was a one-night stay at a small tourist court in the little town of Baird, where we hoped to get the ceremony completed before my parents found my note and tried to stop us. Things progressed beautifully for several months. We were blissfully happy with each other and our dreams. Then, BOOM! The Depression swallowed the drug store and pharmacy. Thus ended another chapter. Roy could not find work and I was three months pregnant.

Finally, in desperation, Roy's father helped him lease a service station with living quarters. For the first time we would have a home of our own, and before too long, there would be three of us. A real family. It was a wonderful dream, but it didn't last.

Few people had the cash for buying gas, so Roy sold on credit. Most of the customers were good people who wanted to pay, but couldn't. Some tried to pay their bills with produce, but no one seemed to have money for meat. Dried black-eyed peas and water cornbread was our diet for so long that we were worried that our unborn would suffer from malnutrition. There was no money to refill our one gas tank and we had to close the station. Every day Roy pounded the pavement, but there was no work.

Count down had begun. Only two weeks to go, and we ran out of corn meal for making bread. Roy HAD to find work. I had to have clothes for the baby. We were too proud to tell our parents we were destitute. Roy's father was again supporting two families. I couldn't go home, not even if I had wanted to. No car, no gas and no money. Besides, I had run away and was too proud to admit we were having as much or more trouble surviving than they.

We were completely desperate. I had never seen a doctor during my pregnancy and there was no arrangement for its arrival. I didn't even have a receiving blanket, much less a diaper. Desperately, I was trying to make baby clothes out of an old sheet I had laundered. I didn't have a nickel for a skein of pink or blue embroidery thread. The dress was ugly, so ugly I broke down and cried.

Roy came home and caught me crying, took an old pistol that wouldn't shoot, and robbed a store. He never made it home. He was caught with a bag of groceries in his arms and was given a twenty-year sentence for a first offense. This was during the bank robbing era of the Depression and robbery with firearms had been made a capital offense.

We had no money for a lawyer. The public defender was visibly intoxicated, and I feel I could have done a better job myself. I was never allowed to take the stand to say my husband robbed for me and our unborn child, that I felt it was my fault because he caught me crying.

I had no place to go, no food and no one to turn to. I knew the news of Roy's robbery would bring disgrace to my family. I could never face them again, so I began hitch-hiking, trying to reach an unwed mother and child home in Fort Worth. I was

16

shocked when I was told I had to sign papers to put the baby up for adoption before being admitted. In those days, during the Depression, there was no place for the homeless to go.

"But I am not an unwed mother," I insisted. "I want to keep my baby. I'll pay as soon as I can, any way I can, but I won't give up my baby, even if it's born on the street. I have no place to go and it's time."

"We're sorry, but rules are rules. All you have to do is sign and we'll give you good care and pay all the expenses. But you must give up the baby."

"Never," I said as I left the room. Home was the last place I wanted to go, but I had no choice and no time to spare. Again I drifted toward the highway and hitch-hiked.

I thought I had hit bottom, but what happened when I faced my parents was almost beyond comprehension.

"You've brought nothing but disgrace to our family," my mother wailed. "I hope the baby will be born dead. I could never love a prisoner's child. I know now that I did wrong when you were a baby yourself. You were very, very sick and Dr. Bates did not think you would pull through. I prayed for you to live, not asking that God's will be done. Haven't you brought enough disgrace to this family? Did you ever stop to think that your child might be retarded? Why did you have to come back so everyone in Cisco will know?"

"Now, Mama," I heard my father trying to calm her down. "You know we could never turn our own flesh and blood out of our house. Mary needs help and she needs it now."

"Only if she promises never to see that convict again."

"That sounds like a reasonable request," my father added. "We've never experienced this type of crisis before. It hurts us all, but if you want to stay here and do right, Mary, you and your baby are welcome."

"Not a prisoner's child," my mother wailed.

I made no promises. I really believed I hated my wonderful mother because of her cruel tongue. Couldn't she understand that my husband was not a criminal? Does pride and conventionality condemn a man for robbery when his wife and unborn baby are starving? He made the sacrifice for us, not for person-

17

al gain. We were both concerned about the baby suffering from malnutrition. Would my baby be normal? Was I?

In high school my grades had gotten a little better every year, despite responsibilities at home which left me precious little time for study. My English teacher, who sponsored the school paper, said that I should attend college, that I had potential as a writer. I loved my literature class and even made an "A" in it. I despised Algebra, but made good grades in Spanish. Surely I had a little sense.

Our baby daughter, Roy Jean King, was born at my parent's home in Cisco, November 12, 1933. Ten days later Roy was to be transferred to prison. I had to see him! I loved him and wanted to show him our beautiful baby girl. I felt sure that if I left, I couldn't come back home. My mother felt so disgraced that she would not even show her face in church.

"Ten days . . . ten days . . . ten days." I had to see Roy. I had to help him. His sentence was all a mistake. It was my fault.

I began the count down. Nine days, eight days . . . only a week to go and I was stronger. Three days, two days, and I had already hidden a few absolutely necessary clothes, and I am ashamed to say, a little food which might help keep me from starving until I could earn my own keep. Was that stealing?

Chapter 2

Alone, Afraid, and a Fool

As that caged truck pulled slowly away from me, carrying my husband to prison, the last glimpse of Roy's face seemed to pull the remaining hope and strength from me like a magnet. I had never been so utterly alone before. I wanted to cry out, "Take me! Take me with you to prison! At least in prison there is shelter and some kind of food. That is more than I have on the outside."

The ten-day-old baby in my arms tugged at an empty breast. Dazedly I crushed my darling daughter to me, picked up the battered suitcase so crammed with diapers that there was room for only one change of clothes for myself. I drifted in the direction the truck had taken.

Before I realized what I was doing, a man pulled up in a car and offered me a lift to where I was going. I can never forget that astounded look on his face when I told him I was going to Huntsville. He thought I was to be walking only a few blocks and could hardly believe his eyes when he saw how young my baby was. The man looked at me like he thought I had lost my mind, and didn't hesitate to tell me that he would gladly take me and my fine young baby home if I would only tell him where I lived. But to let me out on the edge of the highway to thumb a ride? "That's unthinkable!" he said.

Unthinkable, perhaps, but not to one who was forced to such a choice. My own mother had said she could never love a convict's child. How could anyone keep from loving an innocent baby?

That's how the chain of events began. My heart would not listen to reason. I hated my own mother and I hated society. I hated my mother because she had said my child would be better off if it had been born dead. I hated society because the man I loved had been given an unjust sentence. I must free him. I must follow him to prison . . .

I was back at the edge of the highway. Texas is a big state, a very big state when you're afoot and broke. Let it suffice to say that my trip began in West Texas on Thursday, November 22, and by Saturday I had covered 400 miles and was in Huntsville waiting for the prison gates to open Sunday afternoon.

If there is any place on earth with a harder heart for a prisoner's wife than a prison town, I never found it. Huntsville was fairly small and everyone seemed instinctively to know why new women were always showing up on Saturdays and Sundays.

While en route to Huntsville, I managed to spend Thursday night in a depot, pretending to wait for a train. Friday night I spent in a bus depot, but it was different in Huntsville. I went to the union depot but was promptly informed that there were no trains out that night. I sneaked into the bus station, was looked at skeptically, then informed that after 11:20, when the last bus pulled out, the station would close for the night.

Sleeping on a bench in a depot hadn't been exactly restful, especially with Jean whimpering of hunger and in constant need of dry diapers. My art of drying diapers in a depot wasn't easy and I would scarcely recommend it now. The only lines I had were the partitions enclosing commodes. These had to be dusted and the jar of opening and closing was a constant hazard.

Feeling greatly in need of a good night's sleep for myself and my little one, I looked the downtown area over as I stepped into the chill dark outside the bus station. My baby was only seventeen days old and the trip had been a hard one. I had to find a bed. About a block away was a big, white colonial-looking place with a hotel sign hung out. I had heard of people making beds and scrubbing floors for a place to sleep, so I decided to ask for a room. I will never forget how small and scared I felt as I walked up to that desk.

No one was there, just a sign reading "Push the Button." I pushed and a middle aged woman with a frost-bitten face cracked open a door and demanded to know what I wanted without even bothering to enter the lobby. Surely a child could have detected the sincerity of my voice as I asked to work for a night's lodging, but it didn't faze her.

"We don't keep that kind of girl here!" she barked at me and slammed the door in my face before I had a chance to say more. Then she again opened the door a crack and yelled, "All you women with men here at the prison are just alike. I can spot one of you a mile off."

"What kind of girl?" I wondered. Tears coursed my cheeks as I left the hotel. I had never spent but one night in a hotel in my whole life. That was the night Roy and I were married, only fourteen months before this happened, but it seemed like centuries.

All I wanted to do was find a place to hide, a place to bury my empty and aching heart until tomorrow when I could see my husband. Surely this would make things right. I stumbled along, not realizing where I was going. I was just trying to get away from it all. Several times I had to put the battered suitcase down to shift Jean, who slept peacefully, cradled in one arm. She was so sweet, such a little darling.

The load was getting too much for me when I saw what looked like a college, and across from it there was a park. I crossed the street, actually the highway to Houston, to a stand of tall pines. The only pines I had ever seen in West Texas were very small ones at Christmas. Trees were wonderful and I loved them. A tree is always a friend in West Texas, but there you have to plant and nurture them. These were real, so tall, and there were so many of them that I seemed to be in a very strange world. I pushed my way into the pines, to where the moon scarcely peeked through the branches, and sank on a bench. Soon I realized I was cold and hungry. I got up and pushed deeper into the park, away from the highway.

I was frightened, afraid of the deep darkness underneath the pines, but I kept telling myself that just this one night and then I would be able to see the one I loved. He could tell me the way. Nothing else mattered but seeing him.

I came to a long table which must have been placed there for picnickers. The branches of the big pine it was under drooped so low that they formed a sort of curtain around it. I had found my bed — a concrete slab. I sat the suitcase on the bench beside the table and one by one I took out every diaper, except one, and wrapped it around Jean, like a cocoon. The last one I tied on my own head. I took out my only change of clothing, a suit which I hoped would look presentable tomorrow, held it and shivered a moment, then pulled it on over my much-too-lived-in skirt and blouse.

I took off my shoes and tried to wrap my feet and legs in the short coat I had brought along. Late November in East Texas is warm, but it can get mighty cool for sleeping out at night. I wished for a pillow, the stone was so hard, but I had little energy for wishful thinking. The only other thing I remember was giving Jeannie credit for being an optimist, for how else could she have gotten any satisfaction from tugging at an empty breast as she lay cuddled in my arms. I was so glad she was too young to remember.

I was cold and numb when I awakened. It was still gray-dark. A heavy dew had fallen and my hair felt damp through the diaper I had tied around my head. My hunger became acute, and among other daylight sounds I heard the rattle of bottles. On the other side of the park I saw a white truck pull up and stop in front of a huge, rich looking brick house. I stepped from beneath the sheltering pine. When the truck pulled away I saw what looked like several bottles of milk showing white from the shadows on a side porch. I had never stolen, but hunger does something to a person's conscience. You begin compromising with it, at least I did, asking how people living in such a fine home would miss so small a thing as a bottle of milk. How much it would mean to my baby and me. Why, they would even want us to have it if they only knew. I must forget it.

I unwound the wettest diapers from Jean, hung them over the back of the bench to dry and told myself everything would be O.K. But my mind was still on those milk bottles across the street. Before I knew what I was doing I found myself edging

22

toward that house, baby in arm. It was not yet good daylight. I slipped across the street, stepped quietly up to the porch, slipped one bottle between Jean's body and mine, then pushed another under my coat and pressed it to my body with my free arm.

I must have squeezed Jeannie a little too tightly, for she let out a little cry and my heart stood still. I pressed her closer to my breast to try to stifle any sound and dashed across the street to the shadow of the pines. No light flashed on in the house, so I relaxed a little . . .

Never had milk tasted so good. I gulped down the first quart. I wanted to share it with Jean, but she was so tiny. This was her birthday. "Just wait a little bit," I consoled her as she whimpered. "Mommy will have a surprise for you on your second birthday. You're two weeks old today."

My courage rose with the sun. I fancied my baby smiled at me as she nursed, but it didn't ease my conscience too much. When she had finished I took a wash cloth from the practically empty suitcase and wet it at a nearby hydrant. I held it close to my heart until I felt it was warm enough for her bath. She must be pretty and clean to see her father. Church bells rang. It was the Sabbath. I said a little prayer in my own heart, asking forgiveness for stealing the milk and for a way to gain Roy's freedom. Perhaps the prayer was a sacrilege, for I drank the rest of the stolen milk. I almost popped, but I just couldn't waste it.

I was first in line at the prison for a pass. I shall never forget how those dull, gray walls looked as I approached the prison for the first time. There were guards with mounted machine guns stationed in little guard houses atop the wall every few hundred feet. A cold shiver hit my spine. It was the most foreboding place I had ever seen.

What is a visit like inside prison walls? I hope you never know. En route to the prison there had been a million things I wanted to talk to my husband about, but now that I was there we just sat staring through the cage at each other, hardly able to speak at all.

Finally, when we did come out of it, Roy had a plan. I must go to Austin, to the Board of Pardons, explain the situation and see if I couldn't get a parole. The pardon could come later.

Surely, under the circumstances, a man would be given a parole to earn a living for his wife and baby. When they were shown what a farce his trial had been, with a state-appointed lawyer who was so intoxicated he was worse than no defense at all, when they found out Roy had been given the limit on a first offense, surely he would at least be granted another trial.

How could I go to Austin without money? Roy had it planned. I was to go to a hotel, tell them that part of my luggage got set off the bus in the wrong town, and I would have to wait for it to come through. This way I would not have to pay my hotel bill until my luggage arrived and I checked out. Without luggage I could walk out of the hotel whenever I got ready without paying my bill. It scared me to even think of such a daring plan, but I said I would try. I had to find a place to stay, and I couldn't forget what happened when I tried to earn a night's lodging honestly. I wasn't sure whether my eyes were watering and my nose was sniffly because I was with Roy or because I had caught a cold.

Our hour to visit was up before I had time to think. Then I was walking out the highway again with Jean in one arm and the suitcase in the other. At least I didn't have so far to go this time, just about 150 miles. With luck I might catch a ride all the way and make it before midnight. It was around three in the afternoon. I didn't know what I'd do if I got caught out on the highway after dark, and I certainly didn't feel like spending another night in a park or depot.

I was in Austin before ten o'clock that night. The fellow who gave me a ride said he was going by the Capitol building. I shall never forget how that big gold dome gleamed in the floodlights. That made it the most beautiful building in the world to me. A couple of blocks from the Capitol I saw a cheap looking hotel and asked the man to let me out. He had been very nice all the way, even asked me if I needed money. I refused.

I don't think the hotel clerk believed my little story. I was a poor liar, but he called the porter to take me to a room. It was barren, not too clean and very small, but it did have a bed with white sheets and any kind of bed was a luxury to me. The only window in the room seemed to hang over a streetcar line and the cars woke me up before dawn. I had never slept near a streetcar line before — in fact, I had never even ridden one.

Everything was strange to me except my hunger. Jean was still asleep as I gathered her into my arms, crept down the stairs and through the empty lobby. I walked toward the nearest residential section, found what I was looking for, slipped a couple of milk bottles under Jeannie's blanket and headed back to the hotel. Stealing was easier this time. Luckily the lobby was still empty.

After I had drunk my breakfast I started washing clothes. What a luxury! Hot water and soap at the wash bowl. The bath was down the hall, but it was the first real all-over bath I had had in almost four days and it was even more wonderful than the bed.

Jean and I were waiting when the Board of Pardons opened. We waited . . . and waited. There were many waiting. A secretary took my name, but I had no appointment so I had to wait my turn. Jim Ferguson, or rather "Ma" Ferguson, was governor of our state and many sought pardons. Jim had been impeached during his term as governor. One of the allegations was the selling of prison pardons. But his wife, Miriam, had run for the office and was elected.

As the day wore on Jean grew restless. There was a girl sitting across from me in the office whom I thought I had seen at the prison. She grinned and winked at me and I was sure. She had been there during visiting hour the day before. She didn't seem to have an appointment either, but she wore such fine clothes that I was sure she must be from a rich family and would have no trouble at all.

Neither of us got in to see the Board of Pardons that day. As we left the office at closing time she offered to help me carry the baby.

"What's your old man in for?" she asked as we walked down the long corridor.

I told her and finally worked up enough nerve to ask if it was her husband or brother she was visiting at Huntsville and what he was in for.

"My old man," she replied, "he's in for paper hanging."

"Paper hanging!" I repeated with astonishment. "Why would they put your husband in prison for hanging paper?"

She laughed and patted me on the back. "You got a long way to go, kitten," was her only explanation. "Where you stayin'?"

I told her and she gave a little whistle of surprise as she asked, "What room?"

This seemed even more of a surprise, because I was in the room next to hers. This gave me a little feeling of elation, but she did not look pleased at all. Maybe she thought I would let the baby cry.

"I guess I'll be seeing you tomorrow at the Board of Pardons," I suggested as we reached the hotel.

"Oh, I don't know," she remarked casually. "A person just can't sit and wait. Anyway, I can tell my old man I tried. Unless you got money, kid, you're just fluffin' your duff."

As we walked through the lobby the porter approached us and addressed my companion. "There you is, Miss Betty. Where you all been so long? I'se been lookin' all ober for you. They's a man here been gettin powerful impatient . . ."

"Break it off, Apple Blossom," Betty retorted. "How come this girl is given a room in the wing on second? I thought that was reserved."

"Yessum, but yo see, I wasn't for sho . . ."

"Wasn't for sure, you simpleton, now get her room changed, but quick," Betty commanded.

I blushed in shame. I thought I had found a friend, but now I was sure she thought Jeannie would bother her, or was she afraid I would hang around and embarrass her? I knew my clothes were quite modest, but I didn't think they looked that bad.

I was ready and anxious to move when Apple Blossom knocked at the door a few moments later, but he said there wasn't another room available and that I might as well stay in the same room another night since I would probably be leaving early in the morning when my baggage arrived, anyway.

What a fool I was! If I had only had sense enough to understand Betty's real meaning I would never have stopped until I reached home.

26

SUCKERED IN, ALMOST

The second day at the capitol building was worse than the first. I coughed so much and Jean fretted so constantly that I think the receptionist finally gave me an appointment for the next morning at ten to see the Board of Pardons to get rid of me. Betty was not among those waiting and I was glad because Jeannie had been so fretful. I dreaded going back to the hotel. Two blocks seemed like two miles.

Apple Blossom saw me and asked me to come to the lobby and I felt sure I was in for trouble. Sure enough, I soon heard his knock at my door. I was sure it was him because I had heard that same, quiet knock on Betty's door several time the night before.

I opened my door just a crack, leaving the safety chain on.

"I jes' come to see if you'all wanted me to check on yo' baggage?" Apple Blossom greeted with a grin.

"I've already checked and it isn't there," I lied, feeling sure he detected the fear in my mind.

"Yessum, I knows. But don't you'all worry too much. I done fixed it up fine. We understands how this kind of thing happens. Ain't no hill for the man at the desk. I done tole him you'all had me check on it and it would be here in the morning fo' sho'."

I did not understand his sudden generosity in defending me but felt it was backed with sinister meaning when he continued:

"Isn't you'all jes a little lonesome all by yo'self? I'm not tryin' to get personal, but if . . ."

I slammed the door closed in no uncertain terms.

Evidently Betty was coming down the hallway because I heard her pounce upon Apple Blossom before I got back to my bed.

"If you knock on that girl's door one more time," I heard her saying, "there won't be a hair left on that wooly noggin of yours. Now why wasn't her room changed?"

I didn't hear the rest because I heard Betty's door close. They spoke in subdued tones. In just a moment I heard the door open again and I knew Apple Blossom was leaving.

I couldn't help but wonder why Betty left her room so often. At first I thought it must have been telephone calls, but I didn't hear the telephone ring. She couldn't eat that often. Why did Apple Blossom always speak to her quietly before she left? I was too tired to reason. Another fit of coughing sapped my strength and I slept restlessly.

I don't know how long I slept, but it was dark in the room when I heard a knock at my door. I listened, then it sounded again. It was the same slow, low knock I had heard on Betty's door several times. I didn't move. Then it sounded again. Maybe I could pretend to be asleep.

Then Apple Blossom's voice sounded through the door as he said:

"I been hearin' yo' baby fret. I been wonderin' 'bout gettin' somethin' fo' yo' cough."

He sounded sincere and I opened the door. "Don't you'all go worrin' about th' money. You can give it to me when you feels better. I hopes you'all fo'give me for gettin a little confidential, but they's a man done been seein' you'all come thru the lobby that sho' done took a powerful likin' to you'all. You know, I hesitates to tell you'all this, little mother, but th' nice man done give me a good tip to do it and you'all knows how hard money come these days. Fo'give me fo' askin', but ain't you'all jes' a little bit lonesome? The man done got more money than he know what to do wid, and he powerful generous."

I sprang to the door and closed it in Apple Blossom's face again. Why should a man whom I didn't know want to give me money? Suddenly the soft knock I had heard on Betty's door made sense. I had read of women who took money from men for favors, but I had never seen one before that I knew of. Betty didn't look like I expected that kind of woman to look, I was thinking as I drifted back off to sleep.

It was hours later when that fatal knock came. I jumped up thinking it must be morning, but it was still dark.

"Pardon me, Miss, but I wants to speak to you'all for jes a minute," Apple Blossom's voice came again through the door. "I was wonderin', Miss Mary, iffen yo' would talk jes one minute?" I was wondering how he learned my name when he continued, "They'se a man here wants to see you."

"I don't know anyone here and I don't want to see anyone," I replied through the door.

"Yessum, but this man is different," he continued in a very confidential tone. "Open the door jes a crack and I'll tell you'all, he's from the Board of Pardons."

This opened my door and the porter told me that the man was a member of the board and wanted to see me before I went back tomorrow. I didn't know how Apple Blossom knew where I had been going or how the man knew I was staying here. On second thought, I had left my address at the desk. Maybe he had seen me, but why was he looking for me? Deep within me there was a warning, but how could it hurt just to find out what he wanted? Perhaps he had seen me sitting and waiting for the past two days and really did want to help. Was it possible?

"He might be able to help you'all a powerful lot," Apple Blossom said as if reading my thoughts. "He said you'all couldn't talk about such things in the lobby in front where anybody could hear, so he's waitin' in room 316."

"Tell him I'll be right up," I said bravely as Apple Blossom left with a big, white grin.

I looked at my baby, asleep, blessed little darling. Why should I disturb her? I would only be gone a minute. She was too small to roll off the bed. Her rest seemed peaceful now and there was no fire in the room. Trying to justify myself, I left her for the first time in her short life.

The door was ajar when I reached 316. I did not recognize the man inside, but I had paid little attention to the men I had seen go in and out at the board of pardons. He was dressed in a dark suit, middle aged, stout, and I fancied he looked the part. He handed me his card. It was from the board of pardons.

"I've come to help you," he said as he indicated a chair. "Noticed you in the office. A girl like you doesn't stand much chance without pull. Suppose you tell me all about it so I will have the case cut and dried when you get in."

I told my story and he seemed very sympathetic. Then he asked me about money, if I had it, as he edged closer and closer to me. He patted my hand in a fatherly manner.

"You know," he remarked thoughtfully, "it takes lots of

29

money to handle these things, but it could be managed. You really love that man of yours, don't you? Just how much would it be worth to you to have him back? You'd give the world if you had it right now, wouldn't you?"

I quickly replied that I would as I clutched his card. "I know you probably don't have the money right now," he remarked, "but maybe we could work it out."

"Do you really think so?" I asked with great hope. "It would not take too long, if my husband was out to help me. Tell me how it could be done. But first I've got to run and see if my baby is still asleep."

"Take your time," he smiled.

When I returned he seemed different. He came very near, too near, just to talk, so I just asked him to tell me how we could help Roy. If some kind of deal would let him wait for the money.

"You're a beautiful young mother," he said. "A man is lucky to have a wife like you waiting for him. I can help you."

"But how?" I asked as he drew me uncomfortably close. I wanted to run. I wanted to slap his face, but I listened.

"It's going to be a long, hard row without anyone helping you," he said, "and why shouldn't I help you. Why, I could get a parole for him so easy. He wasn't even given a dog's chance."

I tried to pull away from him but he drew me closer, and said, "Of course it would take money, but you've got something that's worth more than money to me."

His nearness nauseated me and all the world seemed in confusion. I was so alone. Perhaps Betty was right. You did have to have an ace in the hole. Everything seemed to be swimming around me and I pretended I didn't feel that ugly kiss.

"Your husband will be out in less than a week," he consoled. "I knew you were a smart girl. No one will ever know. I'll have everything ready when you get to the office tomorrow. Just give them the card I gave you and ask for me. I'll take care of all the investigation expense. No one will ever be the wiser."

Wiser about what, I wondered. Then came the dawning. I started trying to break from his clutch.

"No! No! I won't hurt you. I just want to help you. It's strictly up to you. Do you or do you not want your husband back? You don't have to do anything for me. But I realize times are hard and you need a little money too. See? I've laid a $10 bill on the dresser for you," he explained, releasing his clutch as he turned toward the dresser to pick it up.

I sprang for the door, slamming it behind me. I didn't hear him give chase. Reaching my room, I made sure both the lock and chain were secure before sinking to the bed beside my precious baby, who was still asleep. I cried and cried. I was too confused to think straight. I was hot, too, and coughing. Maybe in the morning I could think straight.

The sun was bright when I awakened. I ran to the window and looked at the clock hanging in front of the jewelry store across the street. It was 9:29 — within thirty-one minutes I was due at the parole board. I thought of the night before. It had been a horrible nightmare. Then I saw his card where I had dropped it on the floor.

Tears of rage came to my eyes, but this was no time for crying. Hurriedly I dressed myself, then turned to Jean. I hated to waken her, but this was what we had been waiting for. Quickly I sponged her off, promising her a good bath when we got back. I didn't know how I could face that horrible man again. But maybe, just maybe, I was wrong. Could he possibly have been sincere about wanting to help me? Maybe he would be ashamed of himself for making such lewd advances. It was too late to think. I had to run.

I was breathless when I reached the office, but I need not have hurried. When my appointment was thirty minutes overdue I timidly handed the card, which was given to me the night before, to the receptionist.

Within a few minutes I was told that the board could see me. I didn't know how I could face the man who gave me the card, but I had to have my husband back. Maybe the card had gotten me in.

I sank into the chair offered me. An elderly man with white hair looked at me and asked: "Who gave you this card, young lady?"

I looked about the room but none of the faces that swam be-

31

fore me resembled the face of the man who had given me the card the night before.

"I . . . I don't see him," I answered.

"There must be some mistake," the elderly gentleman said sympathetically. "You have my card, but I'm sure I have never seen you before. You look pale. Do you feel well?"

I said I was all right and he explained, "I don't know how you came by my card, but so long as you have gone to the trouble of getting here we may as well see what we can do for you. Better let me hold that baby while you tell us your problem."

I told my story and they all listened.

"How long has your husband been in the prison?" one of the board members asked.

"This is the tenth day," I answered feebly.

"Then you should have been told," the man with the white hair said with real sympathy in his voice. "We never consider a case of this kind for parole until at least six months of the sentence has been served. Come back to see us then. You'd better get this baby home," he said as he handed Jeannie back to me. "She's too young to be dragged around."

SOME CALL THEM WHORES

Just like that I was dismissed from the room. All my air castles came tumbling down. Tricked! Rooked! How could anyone pull such a dirty trick on me? I guess it was easy. Betty was right when she said I had a lot to learn.

But now I had no desire to learn. My baby was crying. My whole body felt like a ball of fire. I was sure I was running a high fever, but I couldn't tell whether Jeannie was hungry or sick or both. I made my way back to the hotel and the manager eyed me keenly as I went up the stairs. I felt sure he knew I couldn't pay the bill. I would be kicked out today.

I pushed my way into the room and fell across the bed. Once I had a home, a modest one but a good one. My family had tried to tell me. My mother had almost driven herself insane worrying over me. I had ruined her life and the family name.

Once when I was a baby I had been very, very ill. The doctor said I didn't have a chance. My mother said she prayed to God to let me live. She had asked that her will and not God's will be done. This was her punishment, I could hear her saying over and over again. She could never love the baby of a convict who had brought disgrace to the family.

No food. No job. No home. No future. How could I have been such a fool? My life was a mistake, all a mistake. Where could I go if I left the hotel? I don't think I could have carried Jean and the battered suitcase a block, even if I could get out of the hotel with them. My mother was right. I should have died when I was a baby.

Jean was crying. I thought I heard the porter knocking at the door. Maybe another man wanted to see me. I had seen one man. He had lied and tried to trick me. Perhaps he had worked this scam several times, yet he was on the outside while my husband must remain a prisoner. Which was the greater crime? Nothing in the whole world seemed fair. Why should my baby be crying of hunger? Why should the innocent pay? How much should we suffer?

My lungs burned and I ached all over when I coughed. I was no longer hungry. Jean wouldn't stop crying. I couldn't remember when I had eaten. Was my child to suffer like I had? God forbid! There was no one in the world to love her, my sweet, innocent baby. My own mother had said she wished she had been born dead. Perhaps she would be better off dead. She would not have to face the things I had to face. I would not leave her in a world where she was not wanted. Babies go to heaven, of this I felt sure. Here she would be branded "prisoner's daughter."

"Just a minute, Darling, just a minute," I tried to console her. "It won't take long now. Mommy wants to go with you. Help Mommy pray."

Then I heard a knocking at my door. They wouldn't put us out. No one could. The door was locked.

"Just one more minute, Darling, just a minute. Mommy's got to turn on the gas. We're going on a wonderful journey. We won't be hungry or sick any more. Hold tight to Mommy, now.

Don't let me go! I've got to go with you! Please, God, don't let me go without my baby. She's so small."

Jean stopped crying and we seemed to be floating up toward the ceiling. I was mad because it was holding us down. I heard bells . . . beautiful bells. The ceiling opened up and we were floating high in the clouds, soft and silver with dazzling light . . . . . .

I came to in a hospital. Betty was sitting beside my bed. She smiled and rang for the nurse.

"My baby! Where's my baby?" I cried in alarm.

"Wait," Betty said in a promising manner. "I'll ask the nurse to bring her to you."

Betty returned with Jean and the nurse. The nurse laid my darling in one of my arms and put a shot in the other. I drifted back to sleep.

When I came to again Jeannie was crying.

"This young lady resents being starved to death," the nurse rebuffed gently. I was surprised that I had milk for her.

"We've been feeding you glucose through the veins," replied the nurse in way of explanation. "You've been a mighty sick girl. Delirious when your sister got you to the hospital. Your sister has certainly given your daughter ever-loving care while you were out of it. You'd make a fine mother," she said to Betty, who was so quiet I did not realize she was still in the room.

Betty winked at me without saying a word.

I must have looked puzzled.

Betty approached the bed as the nurse admonished, "All our patient needs now is rest. The baby will be fine."

"I'll make my visit short," Betty said, "but I would like to be with her a few minutes since she has come to."

As the nurse left the room Betty put her finger to her lip. "Now let me explain," she began. "I told them I was your sister to get you into the hospital. You were out of your head with a fever. I could hear you raving. We had to break down the door."

"But the gas . . . ?" I whispered.

"All in your mind," Betty assured. "Get some rest and keep your mouth shut, Sis."

With that she was gone. Why would she go to the trouble of saying I was her sister? I looked at Jean safely cradled in my arm, and went back to sleep. When I woke up again it was dark. I rang for the nurse. My baby was gone and I had to be sure.

When Jean was brought back to me and I was sure I had not been dreaming, I asked what day it was.

"Two minutes from now it'll be Sunday," the nurse replied as she looked at her watch, "and I'll be off duty."

"But what day of the month," I persisted.

"Today is December 1st," the nurse replied as she left the room.

"Then I must have been in the hospital since Wednesday," I said to myself. "Sunday, December 1st. Why, this is our baby's third birthday! She's three weeks old today." I gave her a little squeeze and remember wondering if Roy would be looking for me at the prison.

The next morning Betty was beside me asking, "Are you ready to go home, Kitten?"

When I did get to her room it was December 5th and Christmas was already waiting for us. There was a little tree with all the trimmings and lovely presents for Jean and myself.

"Just like having a family of my own," Betty answered my unasked question. "I had a baby once, illegitimate, and they took her from me. This makes me feel like I am having Christmas for her. Take a lesson from me, Mary, you've got something to live for. I haven't. Don't ever be like me. You have a fine family. You've told me about it over and over while you were delirious. I'm from a broken home. My mother was an alcoholic. My stepfather raped me when I was thirteen. Soon they had me hustling on the street, to support their alcoholism."

I was stunned. I couldn't imagine such a thing. It was even harder for me to realize that Betty was a whore. She was a wonderful person to me and I will love and appreciate her so long as I shall live. She had never known a family life like mine. They loved me and had only wanted me to do right. She said I must get back to them and forget I had ever met her and never try to get in touch with her again. We lived in two different worlds. She refused to even come to see Jean and me. "It would just hurt.

35

You gave me a look at the world I have longed for, but will never live in. We will always live in different worlds. You're going home."

On Sunday Betty went with me to see her husband and for me to show Roy King his daughter, for the first and last time. But Betty didn't trust me to go home alone. I could change my mind. She had made arrangements to have my father waiting for me.

"Your mother is heart broken and she's been praying for you to come home. She says she could never forgive herself if something happened to you and our granddaughter. We love you, Mary, and want you and Jean to have a good home." These were my father's first words of greeting. He said that my mother was contrite and begged forgiveness. My sister, Lela, was back home and teaching in Cisco. She and Mother had all kinds of plans for me. They would help take care of Jean while I attended Randolph Junior College, in our own home town. The Great Depression had lost its grip, and with a better education I would soon be earning a living for myself and my daughter.

Chapter 3

Get Set!
Prison Break Ahead!

*M*y whole family joined forces in my behalf. It was good having my sister, Lela back in Texas. She had been given a teaching position in Cisco High School. My married sister Ann still lived in Indiana, but she told me that she and her husband Bob would help pay my tuition if I started to college. We all loved our little Jeannie including Mother.

The dream was almost too good to come true, but fall found me in Cisco Junior College. Mother loved keeping Jean during the day, and enjoyed sharing "our daughter" with Lela at night while I ushered at a local theater. It made me feel more like I was doing my share when I could buy a few groceries and some of the things I wanted so much for my daughter.

There was just one thing I couldn't overcome, my love for Roy King, even though two years had now passed. I had managed to keep in touch with him through a college mate and friend, Oletha Rush, to whom he sent my letters.

I did so well finishing junior college that my family wanted me to attend a senior college and become a teacher. This sounded great, and Lady Luck smiled. I did find employment in the old Grace Hotel Coffee Shop in Abilene, where I hoped to attend McMurry University. The country had not yet fully recovered from the Depression and jobs were not plentiful. But I did agree to work the first two weeks without salary, just for food and tips. If my work proved satisfactory, I would be paid an extra $10 a week salary. The boss Cliff Baldwin, was as good as his word. By the time the fall session started I had earned enough to rent a room and send $5 a week home to Mother for Jean's care. It made me feel better. My food came with my job and I managed for the extras I had to have with my tips. I did become an excellent waitress. I had to. It wasn't easy, working all night and attending school by day. But I did get to sleep the afternoons I didn't have lab. It wasn't too bad. I averaged about four hours sleep on week days and longer on weekends.

I was doing well. I was still in touch with Roy, more than ever since I was not getting my mail at home. Wouldn't it be great if I could get Roy out of prison. He had gotten a job in the prison hospital and was doing well. Surely I could get him out on parole.

I worked on it. Even through my poetry writing, I worked on it. 'Pappy' W. Lee O'Daniel, who later was elected governor of Texas, was emcee for the Lightcrust Doughboys program aired over station W.F.A.A. in Dallas. Pappy was a master at a "Wrong that needed a rightin'." His "country western" style had a tremendous impact. Now if I could just write a song about Roy, maybe, just maybe, they would sing it. They did, to the tune of "*Drifting off to Dreamland*." The response was overwhelming. Here is a portion of the ballad which told the story which Pappy seemed delighted to challenge:

FORGETTING PRISON BARS

I'm rocking the babe by the fireside
As those evening shadow fall,
And I think of you at Huntsville,
Behind that prison wall.

The baby has grown, oh so much, Dear;
Learning to walk and talk.
That picture, Dear, of Heaven
Has been blurred and drenched with tears.

But we love you, yes Daddy, we love you,
No one could take your place.
Your spirit hovers near me
And it seems I see your face.

So we'll rock and drift to dreamworld,
For I know I'll find you there,
With a kiss for every teardrop
And a smile for every care.

So we'll rock and drift to dreamworld,
Forgetting prison bars.

Pappy followed though with my story, just as I had written it. Great was the response. He assured me that he would work with me but it would take time. This was great! Through my schoolwork I had won several honors with my writing and some of the features were being published in the *Abilene Reporter News*.

As he told me earlier, O'Daniel threw his hat into the governor's race. He made it! Never could I have been happier. Within ten days I would be a graduate of McMurry University. And best of all, I already had a job working at the *Abilene Reporter News*. I gave them ten days notice at the coffee shop, and then went to work at the newspaper, where two of my classmates were already employed. Soon I would have enough money to go to Austin and see the governor, and the chances for getting Roy a parole looked good.

I was walking on air. Soon Roy would be out of prison and we would be a happy family. With me working and the Depression over, my family and the whole world would realize Roy was not a criminal, but a good and talented man. We would be so happy they would soon forgive.

I loved my new job, a dream come true, when BOOM!

I had been with the *Reporter News* only two weeks when I received that fatal call:

"Are you Mary King?" a man's voice came over the phone. "You are? Then you must be the wife of 'Spider King.' If you are, I have a message for you," came the 220 jolt over the wire.

39

"Who are you and where are you?" I fired back.

"I said I have a message for you," the informer repeated emphatically, ignoring my questions. "It's from Roy. He said that if I couldn't contact you by phone to send this message as a telegram, but he hoped it wouldn't go down in print. I suggest you use pencil and paper. Are you ready?"

"WE ARE HAVING AN R.B.C. REUNION," came the telegraphic message. "SAME GROUNDS. BRING A BIG PICNIC LUNCH. DATE UNDETERMINED. STAY PUT. DETAILS FOLLOW. YOU ARE TO TRANSPLANT MY AMERICAN BEAUTY ROSE THE NEXT GOOD RAIN AT THE 'HAM.' "

"At the 'Ham!' I've got to talk with you."

"I'm sorry the message is a little late," the voice continued, never bothering to answer my pleading, "but there were a few unavoidable delays."

The telephone receiver clicked in my ear. Message delivered.

Wildly I clicked the receiver for the telephone operator. I had been disconnected. "Hello! Operator," I pleaded, "are you there? I've been disconnected."

"What number were you calling, please? If you wish I'll try it for you."

"No. Not me. I mean it was an incoming call."

"Was it long distance?"

"I don't think so, Operator, but it was urgent. You see, I'm a reporter here at the *Abilene Reporter News* office and . . ."

"Then I suggest that you hang up and give your party an opportunity to replace the call," came the reply.

I was defeated. The party had left the line, intentionally. I heard the receiver click, but I couldn't believe it. This was not the type call to have traced.

At the HAM? I recognized the word *Ham*, but Roy was not at "Burnin' Eastham" unit, as the prisoners called the toughest farm in the vast prison system spread over southeast Texas. Roy was inside the walls, working in the prison hospital. He couldn't be at the 'Ham.' He was a model prisoner, and near parole. I was stunned. I looked around me in the news room. No one seemed to be watching. How long had I sat there in a stupor looking at the note with the strange message? I had to go where I could try to decipher the message.

The newspaper had a library that was seldom used at night. I could go there if my legs would carry me. I could pretend I was going there for reference.

I don't know how I made it, but I did. Going to the back of the room I pulled out a book, then sat facing the doorway. When I was sure I had not been followed I pulled out the note. Concealing it behind the open book, I tried once again to grasp the message.

The words: "PLANNING AN R.B.C. REUNION" struck at me like a rattlesnake. Since Roy had been in the prison for almost five years, the initials R.B.C. had always meant 'Raymond, Bonnie and Clyde', the most ruthless bank robbers who had ever terrorized the Southwest. He couldn't mean them — they were dead. "SAME GROUNDS." Now I got the message. My husband was planning a prison break in the same area where Clyde Barrow and Bonnie Parker had come for Raymond Hamilton and his buddies in that infamous prison break where so many were killed.

How well I remembered that break, and every break since Roy had been imprisoned. The whole nation followed these headlines, and those made by Baby Face Nelson and Pretty Boy Floyd. The Depression was so deep that nothing else was happening. Like a continuing story they flashed across the headlines.

"BRING TRANSPORTATION AND BIG PICNIC LUNCH." Just because Bonnie and Clyde brought guns and a getaway car, Spider King needn't think I would. I hated that name for Roy and I didn't understand it until later, much later. "DATE UNDETERMINED. STAY PUT. DETAILS FOLLOW." This was not code, but the next sentence stumped me for the next few minutes.

"BE READY TO TRANSPLANT MY AMERICAN BEAUTY ROSE THE NEXT GOOD RAIN AT HAM."

We had no rose, but my hair was red. Suddenly the book was laid wide open. I was to bring the guns and a getaway car to the Eastham Prison Farm the next good rain. I was to transplant myself, whenever he directed.

41

I knew what he needed. Enough rain to start little streams to flowing. Enough rain to make water stand in long, shallow pools. Enough water to help an escaping convict throw bloodhounds off scent.

Yes, Roy knew all the tricks, like doubling back on his own trail and then jumping as far to one side as possible. Walking fences. Wrapping shoes in rags soaked with oil of mustard. But these were old tricks, tricks good enough to give an escaping convict a little start, to baffle the bloodhounds a few minutes.

But for me to bring a getaway car?

Secretly I prayed that the convicts had not managed to get hold of a gun. How could the man I loved ask me to bring guns and a getaway car? He must be out of his mind. Could he have forgotten our child? It was unthinkable.

Gradually the library came back into focus. I would have to warn Roy. I would have to send a telegram letting him know that I would have nothing to do with such a plan. What could I say? Could I code it so that the guards would not understand? When could I send it? Tonight? Tonight when I got off work so he would have it in the morning. What could I say that wouldn't be a dead give-away? I might say:

SORRY. CANNOT ATTEND REUNION. ROY JEAN VERY SICK.

How could I tell such a lie? Especially about our own precious daughter? God forgive me, I prayed. I could use a little strength and guidance. I simply could not conceive of taking part in such bloodshed, not even for my husband, despite my great love for him. We had a child to think of.

For five years I had worked hard to better myself. Mother had kept Jean. Of course she did it for less that anyone else would have done, and gave her infinitely better care. But I had paid for this tender, loving care to the best of my ability. I owed no one anything. It had to be that way. I wanted my little girl back, but I hadn't planned it this way. Not with a prison break!

True, the world had wronged my husband and me. But we would prove its mistake. This would take time. A prison break was the worst thing he could possibly do. That would ruin everything. I had to get moving.

"Wait, Roy, wait," was my silent prayer as I returned to my

desk. "Give me more time. What's happened? You were doing so well I just can't figure it out. Why are you on the worst farm where they keep the incorrigibles? What happened to your good prison job in the hospital?" I asked in dismay, knowing there would be no answer.

Again I was at my desk. It was midsummer and a heavy, unrelenting heat wave made it difficult to breathe. The windows were open, but the night air was too still to ruffle the litter of unweighted sheets of yellow copy paper in front of me. I couldn't think. I drifted toward the teletype machine, hoping it would bring me back to reality.

It was August 16, 1938, and the machine chattered of the proposed Munich Conference between Hitler and Prime Minister Chamberlain of England. Japanese troops were on the march again in China. President Roosevelt was asking Congress for more arms money for America. But the machine carried no news from East Texas. No news from the Eastham Prison farm.

No news was good news. The *Abilene Reporter-News* would go to press on time . . . if the world would stay asleep.

But I knew that at the prison farm the convicts would be gotten up before daylight and the hoe squads run out on the mile-long turn-tows at the crack of dawn. I had to send that telegram! Would I be caught if I tried sending a personal message from the news office? To the prison? Get fired before I got my first check?

I watched the teletype so closely that one might have thought I had placed my last nickel on the nose-diving stock market.

"Hey, Mary," one of the the reporters called to me. "Let's take a coffee break."

I must have looked reluctant because Charley called to Ted Randel, another reporter on the night shift. "Take a look at the way Mary's glued to that teletype. You'd think it was going to write her a check for a million bucks."

I must have been a little hard to bring down to earth for he continued:

"Don't you know the world's too dead for a story? The Depression's so tough that even the gangsters have given it up since Clyde and Bonnie got theirs."

43

I grinned and tore myself loose from the machine to join Charley and Ted in our regular midnight coffee session. They were my friends, these reporters, real pals. Especially Ted. He had broken me in on the job. Since then he had shown me in a dozen little ways that he was fond of me. Our midnight coffee session in the all-night cafe across the street had become a sort of ritual. After all, I was the only girl on the night shift and I guess a touch of femininity does add a little to a cup of coffee. They were so nice to me that I couldn't refuse. We had met our deadline.

If coffee drinking hadn't been second nature with me on that night drag, I couldn't ever have done that. I picked up my cup before that cooling off period respected by black coffee drinkers, and burned my tongue.

"Well, look at that," chided Charley. "A guy on either side of her and here she goes thinking about somebody else and burns her tongue. Come on, Kid, give! What's happened to you? You're out of the world if I ever saw it. Always did figure some guy would come along and melt that ice some day."

I tried desperately to pull myself back to normal. I resorted to a little wisecracking, but it fell flat. I kept wondering what I would say in that telegram, and whether it would reach Roy in time.

We finished our coffee and started back to see if there was any last minute news to be done before the presses began to roll. Lightning flashed! I stopped dead in my tracks, electrified. Did this mean rain?

Ted's arm locked in mine and I heard him say, "Hey, what's the matter? Didn't you ever see lightning before?"

No. Not this kind of lightning, the kind that meant a prison break. But was it really going to rain, or was this merely summer heat lightning? And if it did rain in Abilene, how could I tell whether it was raining in East Texas?

I had to send that telegram before daylight. It had to reach him. I was caught in a centrifigul force. Something I couldn't fight whirled me as in a vacuum, shutting out reality. It was like riding in the eye of a death-dealing tornado, ripping above the unsuspecting world and threatening to strike at any minute.

Please, God, don't let it rain before I can get that message to Roy.

Maybe I should change the telegram. Would I dare say, "YOUR PAROLE IS COMING THROUGH, POSSIBLY WITH-IN THE NEXT TEN DAYS."

What if it didn't, or he failed to believe me? Perhaps I could pretend I had never received the message at all and say: "AM ON MY WAY TO STATE CAPITOL. THE GOVERNOR AS-SURES A PAROLE, AND POSSIBLY A PARDON."

Dazzling streaks of lightning seemed to bolt me.

The three of us ran across the street and up the back stair-way. The night editor was bending tensely over the teletype, which was clicking wildly. He looked up and began barking or-ders.

"Stop the presses! Stop the presses! Tell them to stand by for an extra. Fine bunch of reporters you are! All gone for cof-fee while a young war is erupting down on the Eastham Prison Farm. Man! They're killing them off like flies!"

Eastham Prison Farm! A break! My legs went limp like a ripped parachute and I would have crashed except for my eyes holding to the swaying lines of the teletype.

"Pull the lead story, Charles. Get to work on the new make-up, Ted." The night editor was giving orders rapid-fire.

"No names coming through yet," came his commentary. "That hole must be way back in the piney woods. That break was made this morning and there's been shootin' enough for a bat-tle before we ever got wind of it. One of the cons nabbed a guard and rammed a knife through him with five hundred men look-ing on!"

"Let's get her moving," Ted cut in. "They'll get them all killed before we can get out an extra line. Fine thing, wait for a paper to go to press then come through with a banner spread."

If everyone on the staff hadn't been in such an uproar, I know that someone would have noticed I was petrified. Time stopped. Eternity began.

"Some names coming through," yelled Charley.

Afraid to watch, yet knowing it inevitable, my eyes devoured the tape as it clicked off telegraph like:

Two of the convicts killed in the break have been tenta-tively identified as John Kennon and Arthur Boswell. Guard

45

John Greer, who was stabbed by an escaping convict, remains in critical condition. Exact number and names of escaping convicts are not yet available. The break took place early this morning as the hoe squads were being run to the cotton fields.

Among those believed to be yet at large are Roy King, Leonard Brown, Frank Jackson, John Clay and Raymond Marlowe. Bloodhounds are on the trail of the fugitives and the Texas Rangers have joined the search. O. J. S. Ellington, general manager of the prison, has expressed confidence that the remaining convicts will be rounded up before midnight.

ROY KING! Was I imagining it? Was I reading it with my eyes or dreaming it with my heart? The long roll of yellow paper still ground out of the machine.

"Wake up, Mary," I heard Ted say teasingly. "A big story breaks and you stand there like a zombie. Go rewrite the old lead story and I'll handle this prison break. It's a real 'he man' story with blood and guts. Fems can't handle stories like this. How come you escaped the 'Pink Tea' division? Women belong in the society section. How come you're a regular reporter, and on the night drag, too? Some dames get all the breaks, but there's not enough iron in you for this story. Hey, Charles, how many inches for Mary on the old lead? And how much copy do you want on the prison break?"

Ted's orders seemed to be coming from another world. I made my way back to my desk and sat down, but I have no idea what I wrote. My mind was in East Texas with Roy, pushing through tangled underbrush, sloshing down small streams, gasping for breath, listening to the bay of the bloodhounds, ever nearer and nearer . . . ready to swim the swollen Trinity River.

Could he do it? He had been a good swimmer once. Five years of prison might have changed that. Was he wounded? Did he have a gun? I hoped not.

I don't know how I lived through the next two hours. A sort of breathless prayer filled my heart . . . "Don't let him die, God, don't let him die! He's not a real convict. He's different from most of them. He only robbed because I was expecting a baby and was hungry. He didn't hurt anyone. He wouldn't hurt anyone, ever. He just didn't stop to think. He was desperate. He had

46

to have money for the doctor . . . for food and baby clothes. He didn't do it for himself. He did it for us."

The next thing I knew the newsboys were on the street yelling, "Extra! Extra! Read all about it! Big prison break! Read all about it!"

Then Ted was tapping me on the shoulder. "Come on, Honey," he said. "I'll give you a lift home."

It was very unusual for Ted to call me "Honey." He only did it when I got a tough break or failed to get a story.

"The extra's out," he gloated, "and we've got our continuing story. This will really sell newspapers. It's kind of like reading about a race and wanting the underdog to win. Well, nobody's been killed in the last two hours, anyway. Big price they're paying."

I reached for my purse and Ted held my arm as we descended the stairs. Suddenly I was glad to have such a man for a friend. I needed a little steadying.

Neither of us said a word as we drove through the silent streets of Abilene toward my rooming house. Finally Ted pulled up to the curb under the branches of the mesquite tree that wove lacy patterns outside my window. He put his hands on my shoulders and turned me around to face himself.

"What is it, Mary? What's troubling you? And don't tell me there isn't anything."

I shook my head. "There's nothing wrong, Ted," I lied, hoping I was keeping my voice calm.

"Out with it," he coaxed. "Everybody has to have some one to confide in. You've pulled that widow stuff on me long enough. It may work with some of the other boys, but I always knew there was someone holding your heartstrings."

Eyeing me sharply he continued, "Remember that night when it was two below zero and I came by for you? You didn't have the heart to leave me out in that storm while you were getting on your hat and coat, so I sneaked a look at a little book of poems I found on your table. They were written by you and dedicated to a prisoner. How come you don't let people know about your achievements? You know I like your poetry. And those poems you always wrote for your college paper, wasn't I always the one who prophesied you would be poet laureate of Texas some day?"

"But how did you know about the poems," I asked.

"Remember the landlady calling you and asking if you wanted your fire lit in the morning? I spied the book and took a quick peek. Always did want to get up enough courage to ask you to let me read it. I'd love an autographed copy."

I fumbled for words but he cut in. "Remember this morning when the name Roy King came over the wire? You went and sat down, then. You worked too mechanically. The names 'Roy King' and 'Mary King' kept circling in my mind."

"King's not an uncommon name," I retorted.

"But a curvaceous young widow dedicating a book of poetry to a prisoner is. Seems he came to life."

I knew I was defeated. The dam broke and the tears flooded like a West Texas arroyo in a cloudburst.

"Always did want to let you cry on my shoulder," Ted chided. "You haven't fooled me much with your front."

He spoke again and his voice was very low. "I love you, Mary, you must know it by now. I want to marry you. I know that pretty little girl of yours is living with her grandmother. She deserves parents. Don't you see. I want to be your little girl's father, help her grow up. I want to love her, too."

"Sympathy certainly does deal a vulnerable hand," I finally managed to reply. "There's no need making love to me just because you feel sorry for me. I'm a big girl."

"But how big, Darling? Things like this don't go unnoticed. You know the old saying, 'To find a fugitive, watch his gal.' You've got too much at stake. Sooner or later the cops will wise up and track you down. The prison officials know where his letters go. They may have a tail on you now."

I looked out into the fading darkness and the coming day seemed to cast moving shadows beneath my friendly trees.

"You can't hide it, Mary. It's too big a story. I don't like to ask it, but why don't you let me do a feature story on you before the truth leaks out. It's inevitable. If the whole town is to know, let's make it good. I'll make a heroine of you, denouncing all evil. Why shouldn't the world know you have worked all night for four years and attended college days to better yourself and make a decent living for your child. You really are a heroine and the world should know it. Don't let them give you a black eye, Darling. You don't deserve it. You can't let them drag you down. You can't let a fugitive ruin your life. You've just finished college. You're just beginning your career. You can write, stories as well as poetry. Don't throw it all over!"

I didn't seem to be hearing him and he shook me ever so slightly.

"Don't you see," he continued. "That pretty little girl of yours doesn't deserve a fugitive for a daddy. You've got to think of more than yourself, or your husband. She needs parents. You can't take a chance on throwing away everything you've worked so hard for. You've always been so ambitious, yet so distant. Surely you realize I love you. I know this is no time to tell you, but I have no choice. We could wait."

How could I answer him? My lips parted, but no words came. I loved Roy, not Ted. Roy King was the father of my child. That love was the strongest thing in my life. I couldn't fight it; I didn't want to.

It was daylight now and the milkman looked toward the car as if he thought I was just getting in from an all-night party. I hoped he couldn't see my tears. I didn't want to cause a scandal in the neighborhood. I had to get into the house. I had to turn on the radio.

"You don't have to answer my question now," Ted said with compassion. "I know you are in no position to answer. I didn't mean to push. Just had to let you know how I feel. Especially since you are in trouble. I know I don't have any business offering advice, but I wouldn't leave the house today if I were you. You need sleep. Don't worry about the boss. I'll tell him you called and said you didn't feel like working."

He was just trying to be nice. I knew I wouldn't have a job if the boss learned the truth. I knew people would stare at me, like some sort of strange animal.

"Thanks for everything," I said, fumbling for the handle of the car door.

"You might at least let me try to be a gentleman," he teased as he walked me to the door. There was no parting embrace. Ted understood, but I knew I had hurt him deeply.

49

Chapter 4

Eight Try,
Seven Die

W hen I reached my room I locked the door, pulled down the shades and turned on the radio. A Bob Wills tune for early risers was playing when an announcer broke in:

"We interrupt this broadcast for a bulletin just received from Huntsville. Two of the convicts from the Eastham Prison Farm have been shot while resisting arrest. The slain fugitives were identified as John Clay and Raymond Marlowe. Three of the escaped convicts remain at large. They are Roy King, believed instigator of the break, Leonard Brown and Frank Jackson. The condition of John Greer, the guard who was stabbed through the abdomen, remains critical. Stay tuned for later developments."

Roy King was still alive! That was all that mattered. All day the radio provided fragmentary news, but not one word of Roy King. I was hungry but didn't dare leave my room for fear of missing some news. I was thankful for the few pieces of fruit I kept in a bowl on the table to supplement my cafe diet.

Day dragged into night. Three convicts were still at large. The dogs had lost the trail but the area was being combed by guards, Rangers and patrolmen. Highways were blocked.

Real torture ensued as one by one the radio stations left the air. A late dance band clung on here and there. Maybe they would interrupt the broadcast for a new bulletin. I prayed they would.

In the small hours of the morning my thoughts were with Roy. Would five years in prison change him? I wondered.

I remembered when we had first met . . . how handsome he was, and how sweet he had been to me. It was love at first sight for both of us. We could not live without each other. That was just three months after I graduated from high school. He was from a fine, religious family. We were both young, and so in love. We were a promising young couple, people said.

Promising? The word stuck in my throat. Promising? Strange this should be happening just after I had finished college. Fate took and twisted the encouraging word into a futile question, promising what?

Frantically I twisted the dial as the radio broadcasting stations began leaving the air. I had to have someone to talk to, but I was left in silence. I turned to the only friend I could talk to, my typewriter. The keys assembled a little prayer:

> Somewhere, God, somewhere,
> Somewhere in those lonely pines
> A hunted man with a haunted soul . . .

I could talk to my typewriter. It continued setting down the prayer in my heart. It always recorded my inmost thoughts.

News was sure to come with day, and it did. As the day broke sharp and clear came the first bulletin:

> "Early this morning," the radio blared forth, "bodies of two of the escaping convicts involved in yesterday's spectacular prison break were found in the Trinity River. Only one fugitive, Roy King, remains at large. Hope is expressed that he, too, will soon be apprehended. The Texas Rangers who have joined the search are leaving no stone unturned."

Hope dared breathe in my heart, but it differed from that of the announcer. I never realized the odds against stolen freedom were so great.

How had these men died? Their bodies were found in the

51

Trinity. Drowned men's bodies sink for several days before they float, don't they? If they had drowned, would Roy also have drowned? My womanly intuition would not have it so. The drownings I questioned. I learned about them later.

Except for reporting the condition of the guard, John Greer, who had been given a blood transfusion and remained in critical condition, no news of importance came through. The same gruesome details were reported over and over. There were a few interviews with guards who had witnessed the break. "Lifers and incorrigibles." That's how they referred to the convicts at the Eastham prison farm. "Most dangerous men in the whole system."

I wanted to scream my defiance as they pictured my husband a hardened criminal and put a price on his head. He was dangerous, probably armed, to be shot down like a dog. How wrong can the public be? My husband had never hurt anyone. How could they picture him like this?

In my mind's eye I saw his perpetual grin, punctuated with provocative dimples, his high forehead with blond waves spilling over. His wide, gray eyes so capable of holding me in their spell, even with prison walls between. Could this be the man they were describing?

Strange, the indelible picture the one word "convict" can stamp on the public mind. Never once was he spoken of as a young father, a husband . . . Maybe God had let him live for a reason. He wasn't a criminal, not in the real sense of the word.

I braved the daylight long enough to run outside and grab the newspaper as I heard it thud against the house. Screaming headlines proclaimed the break. Gruesome, horrible photos of the bodies of Leonard Brown and Frank Jackson on the bank of the Trinity River, partially submerged, made me sick. A mass burial was planned, but hope was still held that Roy King's body would be added to the pyre.

I tried to fight back, but my strength was sapped with emotional strain. Two days I had stayed holed up like a caged animal, fighting with my own conscience. Why had Roy been the only one to live? Would I help him, even if I could? Was he still caged in the river bottom? Could he escape the iron ring they had thrown around the area? Was he even alive? Again his message came to me:

Intense Search For Stamford Felon Ended

Roy King Only One In Escape Still At Large

CROCKETT, Aug. 17—(AP) —Six of eight convicts who engineered a break from Eastham prison farm lay dead tonight, the slaying of one leading to murder charges against a prison guard and the promise of a prison board member to investigate circumstances of his death.

FIND TWO DROWNED

Posse's bullets slew John Hendrix Frazier, 21, of Dallas, and Raymond Wilkerson, 24, of Fort Worth, in the Trinity river bottoms early today. Two convicts were found drowned in the Trinity river, and two were shot yesterday.

Dog Sergeant Bob Parker said Frazier and Wilkerson were shot when searchers caught up with them as the convicts were attempting to kill bloodhounds employed in the chase. He said the fugitives resisted arrest.

Roy King of Stamford, serving time for robbery, was the only one of the eight who stabbed a prison guard as they fled, to remain at large, and Capt. J. P. Hamilton of the prison farm said the intense search for him had been abandoned. Another, W. E. Garner, of Beaumont, alleged leader of the break, was captured yesterday.

At Crockett, County Attorney Leon Lusk of Houston county said Sheriff Arch Maples had filed a charge of murder in Justice of the Peace D. D. Long's court against Dog Sergeant Parker of the Eastham farm in connection with the death of Frazier.

Lusk said a warrant had been issued for the arrest of Parker.

Dr. C. W. Butler of Crockett, member of the prison board, said he was conducting a thorough investigation into the slayings.

The bodies of Leonard Smith and Frank Johnson, two of the fugitives, were found in the Trinity river between Ferguson prison camp and camp No. 2 today. Capt. John Baston, head of No. 2 camp, said he thought Smith, who could not swim, was being helped by Johnson when the two drowned. They were hard pressed by the posse at the time.

DIRK DISCOVERED

Prison officials said a three inch dirk which they surmised was the one used in stabbing Guard John Greer when the group fled, was found on Johnson's body. It was made from a kitchen caseknife.

Convicts Jack Kinsley and Elmer ·Buck· Aaron were shot yesterday, hours after the break, when Garner was captured.

Prison officials told today how

See MANHUNT, Pg. 16, Col. 6

53

STAY PUT. DETAILS TO FOLLOW.

I had little choice. A getaway car and guns were not needed for dead men. Getting to Roy was impossible too. Why should I even think of such a thing?

This reminded me of something. Was I being watched? Darkness had fallen. I turned out my light and raised the shade a little bit. I gazed into the darkness across the street. There was a park bench there at a bus stop. I had a strange feeling that eyes were glued to my window. Two or three times a match flared in cupped hands. I strained to see the partially lighted face. I remember wondering if the man wasn't smoking a pipe. It didn't glow like a cigarette. Was it the same man every time? Why did he sit in the deepest shadow? I promised myself I would strain for a closer look the next time a match flared, but consciousness slipped away from me.

It was daylight when I sprang to my feet, still fully dressed. This was the third day. Could it be the third day, really? My radio was still tuned in. It had been on all night. I twisted the dial. No news came. Surely Roy must have made a clean break by now. How far could he have gotten? It was less than three hundred miles from the prison farm to Abilene. Three hundred miles . . . three days . . . maybe even now. Strange how he was the only one who managed to stay alive. Now it was hope rather than fear that I seemed to feel.

My body was stiff and I was still groggy. A cold shower would help; then I could think. I turned the radio up a little to make sure I didn't miss the news.

The shower helped considerably. No news was the best news in the world. I felt more serene. The problem of meeting escaping convicts with a getaway car and guns was solved. If Roy lived, we would try it my way, on the legit.

I had been saving for the time when I could be with my husband and child. One hundred seventy-six dollars wasn't much of a showing, but it was hard enough to squeeze out of my small cafe wages while paying for my schooling and taking care of my daughter at the same time. It was a fortune during the Depression.

I couldn't have saved even this much without my mother's help. I paid her, to be sure, but the amount was pitifully small.

She, my father, and my sister, who taught school, gave Jean far greater care than I could ever have done. She had, not a rich, but a fine home. This was another thing to think about. They had become too attached to her, especially my mother. This worried me greatly.

First my family had wanted to keep Jean until I finished college. This I appreciated. In fact, it was a necessity with my going to school days and working nights. Then they wanted to keep her until my job was well established. Now they seemed to believe that, since I was working a night shift, they should continue keeping her. Recently our friendly feud had reached a semifinalized agreement. To my family, teaching seemed the most fitting profession for a woman. Now that I had a degree, I should apply for a teaching position. When I became a teacher and would have the same school hours as Jean, then, they felt, I could take proper care of her.

I knew Jean was safe, but my heart ached for her. If I helped an escaping convict, how would I ever get her back? I wouldn't! If I had the opportunity I would send Roy the money I had saved.

Although early morning, the sun was flexing its summer strength when I peeped through the glass in the door of my little room, which had become my prison cell. My heart hammered.

Coming up the sidewalk was my girl friend, Oletha. She and I had grown up together. We had always shared our innermost secrets and emotions. After Roy and I married and moved away from the old home town, she had spent weeks at a time with us. We helped her find work. When one ate, we all ate. In fact, we had even been rich enough at times to take in a movie. Maybe Roy had gone to her. She was the only one he could have trusted under the circumstances. I wanted to rush to meet her, but I thought of the man across the street and waited, straining for a reassuring smile from Oletha.

"He's waiting for you," were Oletha's soft words when I opened the door. To me she looked like an angel, standing in the doorway with the early morning sun haloing her golden blond hair. My fingers flew to my lips as I motioned her in and closed the door.

"Don't even trust the walls," I whispered, "they may have a dictaphone planted."

"I've come to see if you want to go shopping with me," she said loudly and cheerily as she gave me a wink. "Always did hate to go shopping by myself."

"I'll powder my nose and be ready in a jiffy."

"I'll help you pack," she whispered.

"No, that would be a dead giveaway. I'll have to leave everything just as it is, and walk out just as I am. I've saved some money that I've got to get to him."

At the moment I wasn't thinking of my trusty typewriter nor the little prayer I had finished and never taken from the cylinder. Little did I realize then that the next morning that prayer, a poem, 'A Prayer for a Fleeing Convict,' would be headlined in the *Abilene Reporter-News* and elevated to lead story position. In fact, I had never seen a poem in first story position, before nor since. Strange how quickly the world jumps to conclusions.

I felt sure I would be followed, but the fact that I would be branded 'fugitive' when I failed to return to my room by nightfall never entered my mind.

I snatched my purse as we walked into the hallway of the public rooming house. Then I did something I just couldn't help doing, any more than I could help going to Roy. Maybe this was my second big mistake. I don't know.

I called my mother's house. Luckily Jeannie answered.

"Mommy . . . Mommy!" her sweet voice reached me over the wire. I tried to talk happily.

"Hello, Darling," I tried to sound cheerful. "How's Mommy's girl?"

"I have a new doll, Mommy. I named it Jeannie after me. It's beautiful, Mommy. When are you coming home to see me and my doll, huh, Mommy?"

"Soon, Darling," I breathed into the phone. Oh, how I wanted to hold her in my arms and kiss her again and again. Why should I be so sentimental about it? I would see her again, soon.

"I'm a big girl now, Mommy. Pretty soon I'll be five. Can I have a birthday party?"

"Sure Darling," I tried to answer reassuringly, never once

56

thinking I would not be able to attend. "Where's your grand-mother?"

"She's out in the garden picking beans. Do you want me to call her?"

"No, Darling, no. Mommy just wanted to call and tell you she loves you. Be sure to be a good girl and help your grand-mother with the dishes."

"Will you come to see me before my birthday, Mommy? Grandma and Grandpa said that if you didn't come home by to-morrow we were coming to see you. That will be nice, won't it Mommy?"

"Yes, Darling, yes," I choked, afraid the wires had been tapped. "That would be wonderful. Then we could plan your birthday party. But why don't you ask Grandma and Grandpa to wait until Sunday, when I'll be off work." I stalled for time. "Goodbye, Darling."

"Wait! I think I see Grandma coming back to the house now," Jean called cheerily as I heard her drop the receiver and run to the window.

"Goodbye, Darling," I half screamed, not sure whether she had yet gotten back to the line.

I was blinded by tears as Oletha grabbed my arm and hung up the receiver.

"Isn't it a beautiful day for August?" she chortled as we hit the sidewalk.

"I hope it doesn't get too hot before we finish our shopping," I said loudly enough for the fox ears across the street to hear.

"That's a pretty salty smile," Oletha winked. "But keep up the good work. And dry up before someone gets a look at you. Keep smiling. Say something loud and happy like."

"I know just the place for a cup of coffee," I complied. "I doubt that the stores are open yet."

Oletha started to turn her head. Instinct told her that we were being followed.

"Don't look around," I cautioned quietly. "I know he's there — been outside my window two days and nights now. Sits across the street under the little willow tree in the park. He's about worn that bench out. Never got a good look at him, but I know he smokes a pipe."

"He's too far back to hear what we're saying, isn't he?" she asked in a breathless sort of manner.

"Yes, so tell me what I want to know. Is Roy O.K.? Was he hurt? Keep talking and don't look so serious. Take your own advice, keep smiling, laugh, clown, laugh. He could have someone stationed on some of these corners. Look casual!"

"He came to my door last night," she began. "He was afraid to come in. My family had gone visiting, but I told them I didn't feel like going. I was afraid to leave the house. I had a feeling he'd had time to get this far."

"Was he hurt?" I urged.

"He wasn't shot, but his left foot was an awful mess. Could hardly walk on it. Said the guard he was supposed to take had a black devil of a horse. He said that when he grabbed for the guard's gun that rodeo bronc reared and came down doing a tap dance on his left foot. The guard managed to get his finger on the trigger of his shotgun and it exploded, right over the horse's ear, while they were wrestling for it. He said that dancing devil took off like greased lightning. He didn't get the guard's gun, but at least the guard had to spend his time holding on."

Thank God, I said to myself.

"You know Roy," she continued with that whimsical grin. "He said he would like to have stayed and seen the show, but when he looked around he was the only spectator. All the cons who were not running fell flat on their faces in the cotton patch when it started raining buckshot. He said a scared jackrabbit started cuttin' through that patch with him, but he left it so far behind it just sat down and cried."

"Same old Roy," I chuckled for the first time in days. "No one else but Roy could have seen anything humorous in a rain of buckshot."

"I tried to get him to let me doctor his foot," Oletha continued, "but he said just start at his head with a chunk of beefsteak. There was some cold roast in the icebox. I grabbed it and a loaf of bread. He carried it out under the grape arbor and while he was eating that I tried to pack him a little lunch. When I got back, all the meat and most of the bread was gone. He grinned and asked me for the main course."

58

We were nearing downtown. Our shadow lurked a block back.

"We'll get our coffee at the corner drug," I suggested. "There's a booth where we can see the street. I'd like a look at our shadow."

About the time the girl brought coffee, I saw him. He hesitated near the door, and on second thought walked across the street and started browsing in a news stand. He always managed to face the drug store while fingering magazines. He finally bought some tobacco and fumbled with his pipe. I could have enjoyed making him hunt excuses to hang around all day just to see how versatile he really was, but there was more exciting business on hand. I had what I wanted, a good look at him.

"When we've finished with our coffee, we'll go to the Citizen's National Bank and I'll check out what money I have."

I started laying out our plans. "Then we'll walk into a dry goods store just to make sure our shadow doesn't think I've been to the bank with something other than a sale in mind. After that we'll go to the Union Depot. You buy two tickets home while I make phone calls."

We went through with our plans. Our tail, with the pipe, stuck close behind. When we got to the railroad station Oletha went to the passenger window and bought two tickets.

I went to the phone booth and called taxis from two different companies. From the first company I ordered a cab sent to the loading zone just south of the depot. At the other I asked for George. Luckily he was there. George had known me for a long time and had often driven me to school, and recently for hot news stories. I could trust him, I thought. I had to trust him.

I ordered George to go to the college and wait for me at the bookstore. He didn't ask questions. He knew that I meant McMurry, although there were two other colleges in Abilene at the time.

I joined Oletha and we started for the train. Good old *Sunshine Special,* always on schedule. As we boarded I looked back and saw our shadow at the ticket window, undoubtedly checking to find our destination.

We walked toward the front of the train. There was no one on the platforms between cars. This was just the set-up. I grabbed

59

Oletha's arm and whispered, "Now listen carefully because everything depends on this. I'm going to duck into the washroom in the next car, but you go right on and stand by the door at the front end. Just as our shadow enters the rear door, you go out the front as if I'm leading you to a forward car. He'll think he's following us both, I hope. Now, let's go!"

I made the washroom on the double, waited a few seconds and then peeked out to see the detective come through the car and follow Oletha to the next one. Then I ducked back toward the rear of the train and swung off just as the conductor was yelling "Board," and the train began to move.

A few feet south of me was an underground walkway for the safety of pedestrians who wished to cross the tracks. I shot through it and came up near the far loading zone. A cab was waiting. I jumped into it and told the driver to take me to McMurry College. "I'm late for class," I urged to try to speed him up a bit.

To me he seemed to drive much too slowly for comfort, yet I still didn't see anything suspicious as I a stole a few furtive glances to the rear.

"Just drop me at the ad building," I directed as I handed him the fare before we came to a complete stop. Straight through the building, out the back door and the bookstore I scampered. George was waiting. I could have hugged him.

"Set sail," I commanded. "When the cab gets to Avenue A, double back on Sayles Boulevard and head south."

"Hey, what's all this doubling back stuff, Mary?"

"George, I'm counting on you. Please don't ask any questions. Keep driving fast, but not too fast. Remember the old highway that parallels Highway 80 (later to become Interstate 10), a mile or so south of it? Well, head for that."

He nodded and ground the cab into gear, but I could see that he was brimming over with curiosity.

"It's a big story," I told him. "I can't tell what it is, but if you'll stay with me until dark and ask no questions I'll give you fifty dollars."

"For fifty bucks, Baby, I'll stay with you a lifetime. To hell with my job. That's a fortune."

I kept my eye out for anyone following us. No one seemed to be. I slumped down in the seat and drew a long breath. This was an all important step. Time was more precious now than money. Money, saved so slowly, spent so rashly.

George drove quickly and skillfully. We were soon on the old road which paralleled the highway. I was turning over in my mind the fact that before the day was over two people would know something of our secret, Oletha and George. I could only pray that George would not get suspicious.

How many people would have to know something about Roy and me before this night was over? Who might want the reward money? Would the fifty bucks look very big to George, compared to the reward for Roy's capture?

As the cab sped forward I thought back to the night . . . over five years before . . . when I had watched and waited in vain for Roy to come home, the night he had committed the crime that sent him to prison. We had been married fourteen months then, and I was eight months pregnant.

Roy had tried to make a living out of the small filling station, but the Depression was still holding on and no one had any money. He used to fix flats free, so he could pick up new customers. But there wasn't any business, no money at least.

That had been five long, agonizing years ago. Suddenly I came out of my reverie. "Do you know how to get to Cisco from the next crossroad?" I asked George.

He nodded and I continued, "I want to stop just short of there at an old wooden bridge that spans a fishing stream."

"All this to go fishing?" George asked with a questioning grin.

"I made a date with a guy I used to go fishing with in my younger days," I joked back.

"And he had a hell of a time keeping it," was George's leading remark. I knew he suspected.

"Now don't go knocking yourself out with any heavy thinking," I put in. "I'm here for a story. Just sit tight in the boat until I get back. You should know by now that a reporter doesn't start hollering 'EXTRA' before he gets a scoop. You've helped me chase down leads before. Just raise your hood, like you are tinkering with the motor, and keep your shirt on. I'll be back. Let's stop by that old wooden bridge."

IMPETUOUS RENDEZVOUS

It was almost dark as George eased up to the old wooden bridge that seemed to beckon to me with crossed arms, like an old friend.

I was out of the taxi, almost before it stopped. I slid down the embankment, climbed over the fence and headed downstream, my feet flying to keep pace with my pounding heart. Ahead was a grove of pecan trees, their branches hanging low over the water.

This was the spot! This was where Roy and I used to lie on our backs during long, lazy afternoons, gazing at the sky cut into delicate blue patterns by the branches overhead. This was the spot where we used to have picnics, and fry fish, if we were lucky enough to catch them. This was the spot which had lain hidden deep in our hearts for five years. Our secret spot, far enough from the road and civilization. Our secret rendezvous of love. And now, at long last, we were to meet here again.

I stepped beneath the pecan trees. The branches enfolded me, concealing me from everything but the sliver of moon just peeping as it, too, started its new venture across the sky.

"Going some place, Sweetheart?" came a voice from behind me. With a little cry I whirled around and threw myself into his arms.

For a moment we clung together in silent desperation, suspended in space, suspended in time, nothing real but the ache of our arms, the fierceness of Roy's lips against mine. We were together under the sky with the pale moonlight washing over us. I can still see Roy's eyes, deep and burning with the hunger of five years. I can still feel his caresses and still hear his words, which were always different from the conventional forms of love-making.

"Five years is a long time to wait for a kiss. Every time one of those bloodhounds let out a yap I jumped twenty yards closer to your arms. Make this kiss as hot as the bullets that singed the seat of my pants."

His banter ended in a provocative grin as his lips found mine. An agonizing thrill shook me as I clung to him. This moment was worth any cost. Hundreds of dreams melted into one.

"Together again," he murmured as he kissed me back to

consciousness. The moonlight etched his features, as he raised his face to look at me, showing his hollow cheeks in dark shadows. Around his mouth were deep lines of pain and bitterness which I had failed to notice during his banter. He had been through five years of hell. It was written there for me to see.

It was all a mistake, a cruel, stupid, unfair mistake. Roy was not the incorrigible the papers pictured. He wasn't even a criminal. All the world had made a mistake and we must prove it, yet I felt every confidence Roy could do it. With a feeling of uneasiness I remembered George at the bridge, and wondered how long we had kept him waiting.

"Our taxi is waiting at the bridge," I said, forcing us back to hard reality.

"TAXI? You can't mean you have a cabbie waiting for us? You don't expect me to ride a taxi?" Roy's voice was explosive. He raised himself on one elbow to stare at me. "I told you a getaway car!"

"I know, but . . . Well, since what happened to the others." I stammered, "I just thought things would be different."

"What do you mean, different?"

"Just you and me, so I told the taxi driver I was on a newspaper assignment. I don't think he'll recognize you. That newspaper photo didn't look like you at all. Besides, we need a quick ride to Sweetwater. That way you could get a head start. I'd go along, and then double back to Abilene with George, the cabbie, just to make sure. Then I could say I was real hungry. Since I am paying him well he would have to stop, and this would kill more time. I promise I won't let him out of my sight for hours. That would give you a real start."

"How long, Baby?"

"Maybe long enough for you to get to the border, if he doesn't stool. I don't believe he will, honestly."

"There'll be no cab for us. Understand? Did you bring the 'PICNIC'? He'll walk. We'll borrow his cab."

"No, Roy, no. I just can't let you take that route. Either you go on the legit or I'm through. I'll bring Jean to you as soon as you feel it's safe. You can trust George, honest. He's helped me lots of times when I was trying to get a story, like he thinks I'm trying to do now."

63

"We've got no friends. Get that into your head. It's you and me against the world. Our own mothers would turn us in to the cops. You go up there and get that hackie rollin'."

Ashamed of my mistake, I climbed to my feet to obey. I could at least stick with Roy a little longer. Seven men had died for this freedom. I couldn't desert him, not yet.

I found George waiting, as I knew he would be. I told him that the story had fallen through but that I was going to stick around awhile and see what broke. He offered to wait, but I said I had no idea how long it might be. I thought it best for him to go back to Abilene and wait at the taxi office until I called.

I handed him the $50 which I'd hoped would take us an extra hundred miles. I felt it pinch, but tried not to look too concerned as I remarked, "Hang by the cab stand as closely as possible. This way you won't be gone long enough to lose your job, I hope. If the story does break, I'll beat it to the nearest telephone and get you back here on the double."

"How could a guy refuse service to such a generous and charming young lady? Mysterious, too," he added. "Never a dull moment when a red-headed reporter gets on a rampage. I'll stick around. You can count on me." With a fond wave of the fifty bucks he was off.

Would he stick around the cab stand, without cops, I wondered as I walked back along the stream? He had been my friend, but Roy said we had no friends now. Anyway, I had tried a little stalling. Maybe it would work. Even if he did suspect I was to meet Roy there, maybe he would believe what I had said about waiting, and take his time about calling the cops. He hadn't seen anyone. I had never lied to him before. It was a chance I had to take. I felt sure Roy's judgment was better than mine, but how could he get away from here, in a hurry.

"How will you get out of here before George gets back to Abilene?" I asked with a dismal note in my voice as I again reached Roy. "With your foot like it is you can't do much walking, and our dough is short. I had that ride paid for, $50. Now we have only $126, but we could . . ."

"What you mean, Baby, is how do WE get into Abilene before they start looking for us here."

"Me! Abilene! I can't go there. I'm too well known."

"So you're chicken! You don't have to come along unless you have the guts. We're just a short way from Cisco. We've walked it many times to go fishing."

"What do you mean?" I cried in desperation.

"That's what I wonder. Does a guy live through hell, just for this? Go on home. Blabber to your parents. Keep your precious baby and your money. I went to prison for her, didn't I? Before she was even born. You were blubbering then too."

I was beyond speaking.

"Make it easy on yourself. Let your parents turn me in. Nice reward, Baby."

"Roy! You're out of your mind! I'll go with you, at least until you are safe. But I can't go through Abilene."

"Yes, Abilene. That's the shortest cut to Sweetwater. We don't have time to go around. That's another thing I've learned. Go where you least want to go. Unless you are far enough ahead of the searching party, get right in with them. They'll do the looking ahead. Maybe we can get through Abilene while they are still looking for just one person. We've got to make tracks."

"But what about Jean?" I asked under my breath.

"We're not going to a Sunday School party. We're riding a freight. If you had brought a rod we could go in style."

"A freight? You must be teasing. I have money. Not much, but enough."

"As I remember," Roy began with no apparent attention to my plea, "quite a number of freights come through here every night on the T&P. It's less that two miles from here to the tracks. With luck we won't have to wait long."

I insisted on examining Roy's foot before we started. It was well mangled, quite swollen and blue. There was little I could do except for bathing it in the stream and binding it up again, in the same dirty rags.

"Don't worry about it, Darling," Roy remarked as we cut through the fields. "Got wings in my feet now. Nothing matters, now that I'm with you.

"Those clothes you're wearing, Honey, nice and clean, but someone forgot to press them.

"You know, that colored gal wasn't home when I borrowed

65

this suit off her clothes line or I would have asked her to press it for me."

This sounded like the real Roy I knew. A big grin sank all the way into his dimples as he continued. "Did have a striped suit, but the stripes went around instead of up and down and it didn't make me look tall enough. A guy's always got to look his best, you know. Some day I'll put a new suit on that line in place of this one."

I was thinking of the pride Roy had always taken in his clothing and was glad he hadn't changed there. He broke into my chain of thought.

"I think I'll drop a sack of groceries there, too. That gal could really cook. Did a bang-up job with what few groceries she had in her kitchen. Couldn't you dream up a hamburger now?" Roy joked. "I've dreamed of such things by the hour."

"I was foolish not to bring food," I repented.

"Don't worry too much about it, baby, I know a patch between here and the railroad that has the best watermelons in the world. You should have seen them last night, dancing in the moonlight. Just one fence away if I remember correctly. Now they might be a little cooler, after the dew falls, if you care to wait."

I never realized how much fun a watermelon patch in the moonlight could be. For a few minutes we were like kids again, pretending our greatest fear was of a farmer's dog.

The spell was broken by four distinct whistles from a train in the distance.

"That's our chariot, Baby," Roy said as he dropped the half-eaten melon. We'll have to hurry, but we can make it. Stops several minutes for water. I watched it last night."

We reached the siding just as the pipe to the water tank came back up with a clang.

"Wait a minute," Roy cautioned as the engine let off steam. "She hasn't highballed yet. I'll find our pullman."

With that he made a quick dash and looked in the third boxcar before he seemed satisfied. Without realizing it I had started following him down the track.

"Here I am!" I yelled as the train whistled twice and started to move.

Roy picked me up and tossed me bodily aboard, then swung himself into the big empty boxcar.

"Most of the hobos are on top to catch a breath of air," he explained. "If we keep rolling we ought to have a private car into Sweetwater."

The moonlight was beautiful outside, but he pulled the door almost closed, or rather slid it almost closed. It seemed stuffy already.

"We can open her a little when we get rolling," he said by way of explanation. "Don't want to take a chance on any visitors swinging in."

"Say, what's 'highball'?" I asked as we settled down.

"You've been to college, baby. Didn't they teach you what highball is?" Roy never missed a chance to twist any question I asked him.

"I mean on a freight, you dope," I said in a very determined manner. "I very distinctly heard you say to wait until she 'high-balled'."

Roy laughed. "I see I'm going to have to finish your schooling, little girl. We may as well take the first lesson now. Don't you know trains can talk?"

I waited, for I knew he was fixing to answer his own question.

"Suppose we start with three easy words, forward, backward, and crossing. If forward's too big a word for you we can just say 'go'. That's when she highballs. Two short whistles, not snorts, mean a highball. A highball and you're off to the races."

"Sweet of you to put it so even a college graduate can understand," I said with irony. "Now if you'll just be as explicit with the other two, I'll do my best."

"Now, sometimes a train has to back up, then she blows three times."

"And a crossing," I yelled with delight, "that's four." I was surprised that I had never thought of the meaning before. Having heard the whistles all my life didn't make as much an impression as the four, long distinct blasts I had heard from the freight as it approached the crossing a few minutes earlier.

"Darling!" Roy applauded. "You can go to the head of the class now."

Chapter 5

Fugitives

$\mathcal{T}$here was something about Roy's wholesome fun that made even a freight train ride glorious, despite the fact that the whole world was looking for me. Perhaps this is what I had waited for during those long five years.

When they took Roy away they took the sparkle from my life. He had been given a dirty deal, but he hadn't changed. Sure, he had made a mistake, breaking out, but the world had made a mistake putting him into prison. It was now up to Roy to prove that mistake. All he needed was a little time. Surely the world would forgive him when it saw how much he wanted to go straight.

For ninety miles we feasted on hugs and kisses as telephone poles slid dizzily by. The setting doesn't matter. When fulfillment comes to the soul that has long been deprived, there is no time nor place. I scarcely realized we slid through Abilene, so recently my friend, so quickly my enemy.

"We'll quit her as she slows," Roy was instructing. "I'll jump out and lift you down."

Before I knew what was happening, Roy slid from the boxcar and was running alongside. He pulled me out into his arms and had taken several steps before I realized he was running with the train.

"Oh, let me down," I cried as I thought of his sore foot.

"Through this coupling," was Roy's only reply as he climbed between two cars on the siding and held his hand for me. "We're in the yards in Sweetwater."

Taking a quick look around, Roy picked our route across the maze of tracks. "It's almost daylight," he commented, "and a dress might be a little conspicuous in a railroad yard."

Breathless, I did not say another word until we were clear of the yards and had crawled a fence into a lonely looking pasture. We kept going until we came to a clump of juniper cedars which grew profusely around Sweetwater and the rolling plains of West Texas.

"We'll wait here until daylight," Roy said as he dropped to the ground. "Try to get a little rest. I wouldn't mind just a little more time with my sweetheart, and another picnic. Did you notice that grocery store, not two blocks from the tracks? Good girl! When it opens, you do the honors. We're rich. Be sure to get bologna and cheese and milk and candy bars and fruit."

"Seems we haven't eaten for a year," I admitted. "Let's try to get a little sleep and forget about it until morning."

When we awoke Roy asked, "See that long grade, where a freight will have to slow? I could grab it there, then you could walk back into Sweetwater, take in a couple of double features at the movie, and then catch a bus home. They still come through real often, don't they?"

I assured him this was true.

"The later the better. You could catch a bus back to Abilene after dark. Just before you get into town, tell the driver you want off. Don't tell him beforehand. Just pick a spot fairly close to home, where there is a car or service station, call a cab and don't stop until your back in your room. Maybe you will get back, even before you are missed, since this is Sunday."

My heart did a cartwheel, but I said nothing. I only hoped my family had not gone to Abilene. Too late to worry about it now.

When we judged it was about time for the grocery store to open I headed for town. Maybe I didn't look too bad. We had found a little water in a creek and had washed up. I applied a little make-up. Roy promised to soak his foot until I could get back with some first aid equipment.

69

Everything seemed more or less right with the world as I bought groceries. It was fun picking out goodies for my husband. Just like real people, almost. I also picked up some things which would not spoil so that Roy could have them after I left.

I checked out, unnoticed, and headed for the door. I eyed a news rack — an *Abilene Reporter News* rack — and gasped. Headlines: "WIFE OF FUGITIVE DISAPPEARS" jumped at me. Furtively I glanced about me, dropped a nickel into the slot and shot from the store. I had to read that paper. All the way back to Roy, after leaving the main part of town, I stole glances. There was my poem, and the feature. Thank heaven I had refused to give Ted permission to use my photo when he proposed making me a heroine. What could he or anyone else make of me now? Evidently the private detective, who had trailed me, reported that I had headed east on the train — probably to try a rendezvous with my husband — accompanied by an unidentified woman.

I was in tears by the time I reached Roy. The paper was more important than our hunger.

We read and reread. Neither of us said a word for a long time.

"Nice poem," said Roy, "but a dead giveaway."

How could I have been such a fool as to have left it in my typewriter? The police had searched my room, there was little doubt about it.

This is the poem which made them think I had become a fugitive.

August 18, 1939 *Abilene Reporter News*

PRAYER FOR A FLEEING CONVICT

Somewhere, God, somewhere!
Somewhere in those moaning pines
A hunted man with a haunted soul
Quivers when a bloodhound whines;
Jumps when a leaf is stirred by the air.
Cowers as those thirsty bullets tear
That have gotten the rest.
Or does he know?

70

Know that his blood-steeped pals are dead?
Of eight, he's the one
And the only one.
As closely he's pursued and pressed;
      His life their goal.
      They demand their toll.
Somewhere, God, somewhere
Condemned by law and man
He's starving while he's hiding.
Bruised and bleeding,
And justly so,
For other blood was shed.
But God, Dear God,
Before he's dead
Let him feel this tenderness:
One baby's smile
One mother's love,
One heart still held within his hand.
These things no law could reprimand.

Roy finally spoke. "I hate to tell you this, Baby, but if they catch you now you'll get five years for harboring a criminal."

"And if they catch you?"

"As you noticed, the guard who was stabbed is in very critical condition. If he dies, I'll be wanted as an accomplice for murder. They're sure to pin it on me, as sole survivor."

For a long while neither of us spoke. Then we ate, in silence. I did what I could for his foot. Sterile bandages and disinfectants would help, if it wasn't already too late. It looked terrible.

At last I broke the silence. "At least they think I am headed the other way, and with another woman."

"And they probably think I'm still holed up somewhere in East Texas," Roy concluded. "Maybe you could sneak back. How could they prove you have been with me. No one has recognized us . . . I hope."

"I'm not going back," I said decisively. "I know what I'll face. No job. No child. Cops and a prison sentence. Together we might make it. I'll go home when the heat is off. No one can prove I was with you, not yet, anyway. Sooner or later I'll think

up a good story and go back, when you are in Mexico or South America."

"Darling," Roy said as he bombarded me with kisses, "together we could make it to the moon."

"I'll catch that freight with you," I offered.

"Impossible! I would be taking a long chance by trying to catch it on that grade myself. Even if we could both grab it, a woman on the freight in broad daylight would be just the answer . . . the one the cops are looking for."

"Today we stay put, a little deeper into the woods," Roy commented. "Got to think this one out."

"Your move," I tried to say lightly. "Looks as though the 'King' has trapped the 'Queen'."

"Unless our next move is the right one, it looks as if both the King and Queen are trapped, but we'll outsmart them yet. We'll go to the moon, on a freight."

"Are you sure, my dear King, that a freight is the conventional way of reaching the moon?"

"Now you have it! It's not likely they'll be looking for a woman on a freight, but they don't know what a pal my gal is. Got it figured. Two freight lines, the Orient and the T&P, have junctions here. We came in on the Texas and Pacific, but since it runs east-west, through Cisco and Abilene, I suggest we leave on the Northwest Orient . . . heading south."

"I get you," I cried almost delightedly, "it heads to the border, too, but to the Texas-Mexican border, at Brownsville, where it picks up citrus fruit from the valley."

"You're cookin'. As well as I remember, we're less that two miles from the junction of the two railroads, but we'll have to skip town. If we could just make that Orient siding where the T&P sets off the empty refrigerator cars to be picked up by the Orient."

"We're on our way," I answered as I started gathering up the extra food and bandages, for which I was now very thankful.

We circled, rather than head straight for town along the railroad track. We must stay out of sight. Daylight might prove itself our greatest enemy. We skirted out-lying houses. There was no hurry. Before mid-afternoon Roy was limping painfully.

As we topped the long drag up a mesa the view was perfect.

"Look!" Roy exclaimed as he gazed into the distance, beyond the foot of the mesa where I was eyeing a windmill. "Our chariot is waiting."

As he pointed I shared the view of the waiting cars on a rail siding, at least half a mile away.

"We're in luck," he added with closer scrutiny. "They're empties, 'reefers,' refrigerator cars to you, Madam."

"How can you tell from this distance?"

"I can see the reefers, which are doors to the ice compartments at each end of the refrigerated car. They are open. That means the boxcar is empty."

I agreed, even though I wasn't sure. My attention was fixed on the windmill. Beside it was a round, galvanized water tank which appeared to be about waist high — the kind most commonly used in West Texas for watering livestock.

We made our way down the mesa to the windmill. First we drank, then washed up a bit. I suggested Roy soak his foot.

"Why not?" he agreed. "We have plenty of time before dark. Glad you brought our picnic along, what's left of it." Later I disinfected and re-bandaged that swollen foot as best I could. Roy insisted this wasn't necessary, but picked up the old wrapping and twisted it around the new to keep it from getting dirty before we "got to our train," as he said.

After a few minutes more of his painful walking, we finally came upon a dark row of empty refrigerator cars standing on the deserted siding. Roy squeezed my hand in congratulations. We climbed up the iron rungs to the roof of one of the cars. There we found two trap doors propped open, one on either end of the car. Those doors led down into the empty ice compartments.

Following Roy's directions, I eased through the trap, hung by one hand and with the other searched for a hold on the inside wall of the reefer. The walls were made of steel, but perforated with holes about the size of an egg. I found a hole and gripped it hard. Slowly I swung my weight against the steel wall and climbed down to the floor. Roy followed me. Our compartment was about five feet long, three feet wide and eight feet deep. The floor we sat on was made of small iron rods, which might not have been so bad . . . for ice. For a while Roy left one of the little trap doors at the top — used for chunking in hundred pound cakes of ice — open for air. As the gray light of day began to appear he climbed up and closed it.

It must have been about eight A.M. when we heard a train pull up, felt a bump as our cars were coupled to it, then began the rocking, switching and shifting back and forth. We were rolling at last! Roaring down the rails! Rolling to Mexico!

Roy must have felt my sentiment. He slipped an arm underneath my head to pillow it from the iron rods, kissed me as

74

gently as a mother promising her child a wonderful new tomorrow, and we both slept.

That afternoon as Roy and I lay gasping on the floor of the car, there came the hiss and screech of brakes. The train lumbered to a stop, and hurried steps crunched on the gravel just outside our car. There was the clanging of iron against iron. My heart pounded with sudden fear, for I was sure that we had somehow been discovered and the police were breaking into the car to drag us out. I think I started to scream, but Roy gripped my arm.

"Take it easy," he whispered. "We've got a hot box on this car and they're working on it."

There was a lot of pounding, and after a while we began to move, first forward, then back, then forward again. Finally our car was still. Roy was quite disturbed when he felt us cut loose from the rest of the train. We heard the engine highball and take off without us. We had been left behind.

We didn't dare climb up and open the hatch, for fear we might look right into the face of a railroad officer. But after an hour the heat and our curiosity got the upper hand and we pushed open the trap door for a peek out. It was sizzling hot. We were on another siding. Our car had apparently been left behind because of the hot box. But what brought a sob to my throat was a sign I saw beside the tracks. It simply read, "Van Horn." That was the name of a junction on the stretch between Abilene and El Paso! Our train had been going in the wrong direction. It was headed west for California, instead of south for the border.

El Paso was a border town, true enough, but it was internationally known and well guarded for underworld characters. Besides that, it was the wrong way and we were fighting for time. We were farther away from freedom now than ever. I felt sure they were looking for me, too, by now. We were caught like animals in a trap. One look from our stifling hole and we knew we were goners.

Roy must have been reading my mind, for he changed the subject.

"Know what a hot box is?" he asked.

I had been quite enthusiastic in learning how trains talked, but the spark had died.

"We're a cripple," he continued. "Our wheels have boxes at the hubs which are filled with oil-soaked string. If they get too hot, the oil-soaked string catches fire."

It didn't make sense to me at all, but Roy still talked with a cheerful strain, "You know, hobos sure give train crews a fit in winter by robbing the boxes to build fires. You ought to see how that oil-soaked stuff flares up."

I still showed little enthusiasm. I'm not sure whether I finally dozed off or passed out from the heat. I came to gasping.

"We'll be out of here in less than an hour," Roy consoled. "It won't be long until dark now. The nap did you good."

I wondered what good smothering to death could do, but quickly became ashamed of myself. Roy had suffered much more than I. Why should I be bitter when he tried so hard to be cheerful? How could moaning help? I thought of the prison break. I still had no idea how he managed to live when all the others were killed.

"Tell me about the prison break," I begged in an effort to get our minds off the horrible thought of another hour of waiting. Cotton filled my mouth and I thought I couldn't possible wait another hour without water.

You won't like it, Mary, not unless you have a good imagination. Fate can sure twist you around. I wanted out of the water that day, even more than I would like to get into it now. That was the day I turned into a fish. Are you sure you want to hear this? I can still feel the water running into my ears and strangling me as it forced it's way through my closed nostrils. I almost drown just thinking about it.

"Go on, Darling," I begged, beginning to feel the water myself.

Our farewell party was a hot one. When we hit that river it was raining buckshot. It splattered the water and thudded the bank on the other side as we scampered out like scared jackrabbits. When I hit the first clump of bushes I realized John Kennon wasn't with us and paused for a quick look.

76

'Go on, you fool!' I heard him yell. 'They got me, go on! I'll keep the yellow-bellied S.O.B.'s at bay.'

I heard him cry out as another round of buckshot riddled him. He had Greer's shotgun, the guard who was knifed. It was too late to help John now. I saw him drag himself to his elbow for a last stand as I took off.

I was shuddering and Roy looked as if he had opened the wrong box of memories. Quickly he put the lid back on and tried another.

"Oh, yes," he started off quickly, trying hard to shut out the last memory. "I was going to tell you how I made like a fish."

He seemed more like himself again as he began to joke about his short legs.

"You know, I just wasn't built long enough to outdistance guards with bloodhounds, especially with them bringing hounds in from the other side of the river from the Ferguson Farm."

I remembered the Ferguson Farm well. Only the Trinity separated it from Eastham No. 2. I had crossed the river on an old ferry, hand drawn by trusties. I remembered well how it capered when the river was up, and I shuddered at the very thought of trying to swim it after a hard rain. You could see from one farm to the other, if you looked straight down those mile-long turn-rows. The buildings were squat and foreboding. Usually people went though Weldon when they visited the No. 2 farm, but I had to reach the farms any way I could. This wasn't at all easy without your own mode of transportation. Sometimes I could catch a ride from Huntsville with relatives of inmates of the Ferguson or Eastham No. 1 farms, but no one frequented the No. 2 farm.

Eastham No. 2 wasn't put there for a sentimental public. That was where the prison system put lifers and incorrigibles. The Eastham No. 1 farm was just two miles from Weldon, which was little more than a clearing in the pines, which was hard enough to get to itself. From the Ferguson No. 1 farm I usually walked. I was thinking back to the disastrous event that landed Roy on the No. 2 farm when he continued with his story.

"Being built as close to the ground as I am kept me thinking how little trouble one of those lanky bloodhounds was going

77

to have to stretch to get at my throat. Those rascals are all the name implies around that prison system, and I didn't have any red corpuscles to spare at the moment. We'd all planned to split and get together at a certain meeting place later, anyway. Makes it more interesting for the hounds that way. A new batch of quick yelps from the hounds let us know they had picked up our trail again, and it was good and hot. They were a little too close for comfort. We headed for the river again. We had to shake them."

Again my sympathy was with my husband in East Texas as he battled the bloodhounds. Indeed, my own miserable state slid into the background and I could almost hear the baying of the bloodhounds.

"By the time we hit that river I was wonderin' just how far we'd get down that side before we'd be jumped by the guards from the Eastham Farm again. By now they'd know at Eastham No. 1 that there had been a break. They would join the guards from the Eastham No. 2, or what would be worse, they'd probably get ahead of them. Prospects weren't good. Guards and bloodhounds from the Ferguson Farm on one side of the river, guards from No. 2 back of us, guards from No. 1 in front of us."

I could picture the guards closing in from all directions as he talked.

"'Let's all jump in the river at different places, that'll make it more fun for the hounds. Spread out and come out in different spots,'" I yelled.

"As we fanned out," Roy continued, "I ran upstream looking for a good crossing. The river was pretty swift so I kept watching ahead for a nice clump of brush or overhanging branches on the other side to grab on to. I skidded my wheels enough getting up the slippery bank when the guards were shooting at us the other time. I didn't care for a repeat performance.

"Finally, I spotted it," he said. "It had to be there; the hounds were breathing down my neck. Four of my pals had climbed out on the other side before I entered the water. I dived in and made for the overhanging branches down stream. I wasn't quite across the river when I heard the dogs hit the spot where the first man had hit the river. They ran back and forth yapping. Then they picked up the spot where the next man hit the river.

"The guards rode up on horseback and started yelling 'Halt!' and shooting across the river. I didn't know whether they had someone spotted or were just bluffing. The hounds weren't bluffing, I knew, and they kept edging on down the river. I was across and under the branches I had headed for, but I was afraid to come out. A few yards on down the bank I saw an old log extending out into the water. There were reeds growing behind it. I eased toward it. I ducked underneath it and bobbed up like a cork on the other side.

"'Let's get the horses and dogs across the river,' I heard the dog sergeant yell.

"They weren't two hundred feet from me. Another few steps and the dogs would have known where I jumped in too. Neither the horses nor the dogs liked the river when it was swollen, but they urged them across. It was just a matter of minutes now until they'd be on me.

"I started 'crawdadding' down that tree trunk," I heard him say as I felt his body reliving the motion. "I just edged my way down until there wasn't nothing but one eye and a nose in the angle where the water lapped the underside of the log. One guard and a dog was driftin' mighty close my way. Looked like they were goin' to land right under the branch I first hit, or what was worse, right on top of me."

I heard him draw a long gulp of air.

"They were close enough I thought the dog might smell me when I gulped in all the air I could and crawdadded on down to the base of the old log. Sure was glad to feel an old root I could hook my foot under. If one of those dogs got hold of me he was going to have to pull me out. I tried to open my eyes but the water was so muddy it didn't do any good, just made them sting. I was thankful, for if I couldn't see out, maybe they couldn't see in. I heard the guard trying to get his horse out on the bank. I didn't hear the dog. This made it worse. They always get right quiet when they are right on you. A little more swearin' and the guard made it out of the water. Must have hit one of the branches, judgin' from the way he let it out. My lungs were bustin'."

"I heard muffled sounds under the water," Roy continued, "as if the dogs picked up the other trails. They really let it out. I was hanging on to the bottom of that log like a cork about to pop

79

from a bottle. I knew I was going to shoot right out into that hound's jaws.

"'Come on!' the other guards yelled from upstream. 'We've got a red-hot trail.'

"'But this here dog's actin' funny,' the guard yelled back.

"I could just feel that hound hopping out on the log.

"'Bring 'er on in,' the others called. 'We're right on 'em.'

"I was still hanging to the under side of the log but was sucking water into my bursting lungs when I heard the sergeant finally call that dog. My foot gave way and it seemed like I was clawing my way through a long, black tunnel. When I came to I was hanging just above water with one arm wrapped around that log. I don't remember, or will never know, how long I just hung there."

I felt him relax a little as he continued.

"I heard shooting, but the guards and dogs were too far away for me to understand why they were yelling. I edged a few feet from the bank, staying close to the log, and caught hold of the bottom of a reed and lodged myself in a sitting position. I was too beat to think or even move for a spell. When I did come to my senses I knew that those guards and dogs or other guards and dogs would be back along the river when they found some of the men missing. I wondered who had been caught. If the bloodhounds had chewed them up or if they had been shot. Maybe I'd best think a little about myself. There just wasn't any place to go. I looked around and saw a dead reed I could reach without touching the bank to give the dogs a scent. I reached out and cut it off with my shiv, which was the only weapon I had along, and finished hollowing it out. I tried breathing through it and it worked. I could lay under water and suck air through it into my mouth."

Roy moved restlessly and looked toward the hatch of our prison. It didn't seem quite so light around the edges.

"Well, I guess that's about all there is to it. I was afraid to crawl out on the bank, afraid the bloodhounds would pick up my scent, so I just stayed. Every time I heard anyone near the river I edged back under the log and used the old Indian trick. Holding myself down I could stay under a long time. The river was like Grand Central Station all day. By nightfall the dogs must have lost the trail of the ones who weren't caught, for I heard them being brought back to the kennels. Good thing it was warm. I stayed under water nearly all day."

"Water," I gasped. "I believe I could drink a barrel of it right out of that muddy river."

Roy climbed to the top of our trap and pushed open the hatch. He motioned for me to follow. The air was cool and I took deep, grateful gulps of it. But now as I walked I found myself trembling. I was weak from hunger and thirst. My blouse and skirt looked as if they had been wadded into a ball. I wanted to look pretty for Roy. I certainly didn't now, but nothing really mattered except our thirst.

There was a big, black water tank down the line where trains took on water. We headed for it, thankful for the benevolent, cool encasement of nightfall after our day's inferno.

Water never was so good before. After we had drunk gallons, it seemed, and washed our faces and hands, we slid off into the desert on the right hand side of the track.

A few hundred yards down the tracks were the lights of the village. The lights were pretty, but towns were not for us. I was beginning to wonder if they ever would be, if anything would. Roy had insisted that I throw away the paper, the one with my poem, which I wanted so much to keep. This was a different world.

"Doesn't the *Sunshine Special* still come through Abilene about six in the morning?" Roy asked.

I nodded assent.

"Then it should put in here about 1:00 A.M.," he calculated. "It looks like our best bet."

"But that's headed for California," I cried. "It doesn't even go down into Mexico."

"O.K., then, if you're so set on striking out south, why don't you take off. There's only about fifty miles of rattlesnakes between here and the river, but there's a thousand miles of trackless desert on the other side of it. If the *Sunshine Special* goes out of Texas," he said grimly, "it's good enough for me."

"But it's a passenger train," I said in dismay. "We don't have enough money for that kind of trip."

81

"I don't mean on the inside," Roy answered. "We'll ride the blinds. Now lie down and try to get some rest."

I was afraid to ask what 'riding the blinds' meant. I felt I would find out soon enough.

We lay down side by side. The moon hung low on the rim of the desert off to the north. I reached for Roy's hand in the darkness. I was tired and hungry and scared. My husband had spoken crossly to me for the first time. I wanted him to take me in his arms and comfort me and tell me how much he loved me. But Roy seemed far away. He just lay there on his back without moving his eyes and staring into the darkness.

I was doing a little thinking of my own, and a little lamenting. How cruel that 'Old Mexico' should be only fifty miles away, and yet so inaccessible. I knew Roy's foot was hurting him more all the time, and he couldn't have walked five miles. A thousand miles of trackless desert on the other side. I knew he was right, but El Paso? Of all the places I'd rather not be, that was it.

Roy's hand felt hot. I was afraid he had fever. He began talking, but he didn't seem to be talking to me. He talked slowly, haltingly, almost to himself.

"We worked in the cotton fields all day, with only two cups of water for each man. We were run out on the turn-rows before daylight and picked until dark. I planned the break a long time before the rain came. Every guy there knew just what to do. I was head of one hoe squad and Steve Clancey was head of another. When I decided the time was right, I slowed down my squad and Steve speeded up his so the two squads got jammed together. Then when the guards rode their horses over to break up the jam, we had all of them in one place and jumped them. We did it right, only that wild devil of a horse reared and came down on my foot." Roy's voice trailed off and he almost fell asleep, but a sharp pain brought him back with a loud moan.

I crept closer to him and put my hand on his shoulder. "Darling, try not to think about it," I begged. "That's all over. Forget it."

"Forget it!" he hissed. "I'll never forget it so long as I live. I didn't tell you about the next day, when I caught up with the

82

rest of the gang. 'Marlowe and Clay shot to death while resisting arrest.' That's how the papers put it, wasn't it?"

He let out a sob and continued. "I saw them resisting, with their hands over their heads, begging for their lives," he cried as sobs racked his body.

"Please, Darling, forget it," I begged.

"Forget it? What did the papers say about Leonard Brown and Frank Johnson? The papers said they drowned, didn't they?" Then he spoke lower. "Yes, that's what the papers said! They both drowned. But I saw them drown!" his voice broke forth in a high crescendo. "But it wasn't like the papers said." He broke into a fit of hysterical laughter and I was afraid that the strain had been too much for him.

"Roy! Roy! Roy, Darling, it's all over. We're together! Let's forget about it."

"Forget it! Men who have lived in prison don't forget. I'll never forget it! I'll get even. Somebody's going to pay. They'll pay!"

"No, Roy, we've got to mark it off. There's you and me and Roy Jean, that's all that matters now."

"Aren't you the Pollyanna?" he sneered. His tone was filled with contempt, almost as if he hated me. "There's only two kinds of people in the world, guards and prisoners. If you don't fight, you're ground down until you live on your belly like a snake. None of that for me. From now on I'm looking after Number One, and I'll beat the life out of anyone who stands in my way."

This man I loved was suddenly a stranger to me. I shrank from him. He was eaten by hatred for the whole world and everybody it it. He seemed disinterested in the future . . . the future happiness that I had wanted for us.

I shuddered, and he must have sensed the stark fear I felt at what he had said.

Abruptly he softened. "Sorry, Baby," he whispered. "I'm sort of shaken. Those five years were hell without you."

His arms reached for me and I went into them. But his love-making was rough, savage. I felt as if he were finding some kind of release through me, as if he were still hating instead of loving.

I remember thinking, "This isn't Roy. Not the man I loved.

Not the man who was taken from my arms five years ago. What has prison done to him?"

From far across the desert came the melancholy wail of a train whistle. That was the train we were waiting for, the next step in our flight. But now I wondered where we were fleeing to, what we were fleeing from. The train whistled again, closer this time, and I fought down the doubt and fear that had begun to swell within me.

"That's our train, Roy," I said gently. He looked up, startled, then climbed to his feet. He staggered as he tried to put his weight on his injured foot, and I sprang up to help him. With his arm over my shoulder, he hobbled up and down with clenched teeth, forcing the injured foot to bear his weight. After a few turns he thrust me aside and walked alone, flexing his muscles for the ordeal that lay ahead.

Five minutes passed and then we saw the train's headlight, its ghostly white finger probing the tracks in front of it. Roy pulled me down behind the water tank as the engine whistled four times to signal that it was slowing for the Van Horn junction.

"We don't board the train until after it has stopped and started up again," he said. "That way the crew is all inside the train and won't see us."

"Now!" Roy shouted. We both jumped up and ran along beside the moving train. As a coupling came abreast Roy grabbed the air hoses and swung himself up between two cars. Planting his feet firmly and leaning back against the heaving, accordion-pleated material that coupled the two coaches, he grabbed me and lifted me up so that my feet cleared the ground but dangled just above the flashing, grinding wheels.

"Grab those bars and pull yourself up."

With my last ounce of strength I pulled. I don't believe I could have made it without the stimulation given by those menacing wheels. Slowly I hoisted myself up until I could plant a foot on the narrow ledge extending from each car.

"Hold tight," Roy gasped. "Stay with your feet spread, one on each car, and don't move. There's only room for our feet. One misstep and you're off into space."

The train gathered speed. My feet grew numb and the cin-

84

ders cut my face. As we approached Guadalupe Pass the night wind became bitter cold and lashed at us, buffeting us back and forth.

We roared through the pass and began the long, winding decent to El Paso. The train gathered fearful speed, and the cars shook and lurched beneath us, threatening at any moment to hurl us under the wheels. It was like being on the end in a nightmarish game of snap-the-whip.

Hours — and centuries — later I felt the speed of the train slackening. Roy started shouting instructions into my ear.

"Get as close to the edge as possible," he instructed. "Then jump out as far as you can. Keep your legs in a running motion. Remember, you have to jump while the train is still going. If you don't pump your legs and lean back when you land, the ground will come up and smack you."

I was frightened beyond words. I clung desperately to those lurching cars.

"Let me edge myself in front of you," Roy said. "When the train slows a little more, I'll jump. You follow."

He peeked around the edge of the car toward the front, then jerked back. "Flashlights up ahead on the siding! That means yard dicks! They're looking for us. Gotta jump, now! Remember, keep your legs running and lean back."

He threw himself from between the cars and out into the night. I leaned out to watch him, and in the little slices of light thrown by the car windows I could see him running.

It was my turn. I felt as if I couldn't move. But I had to. Cops were up front. Closing my eyes, I threw myself forward with all the strength I had. I tried to pump my legs into a running motion as I flew through the air, but something pulled my body forward faster than my legs could move. The ground came shooting up to meet me. My last sensation was rolling over, head first, down the embankment.

Chapter 6

Now It's Murder

I was crying when I came to, and Roy was bending over me and stroking my head. He wiped a few spatterings of blood from my face and arms.

"I carried you across the highway from the tracks," he said. "We can't go any closer to town now. There's a tourist camp down the road a bit. We'll tell them we had an accident with our car and want to stay there till morning."

We made our way to the tourist cabins. The attendant growled at being awakened before daylight, but Roy's story seemed to soften him. The last thing I remember was sinking into bed between wonderfully white sheets.

When I opened my eyes again it was daylight. Roy was sitting on the bed with his foot in a pan of hot water. On the rickety table there was bread, bologna, milk, and cookies. I fell upon them with a ravenous appetite.

After I had eaten I examined Roy's foot. "That's blood poisoning! Look at those streaks. I'll get a doctor."

"That's what you think. Take a look at this!"

Roy tossed me a paper he had bought while I was asleep. His picture was on the front page. The guard who had been stabbed was now dead, the paper read. Roy was the only one of the original seven fugitives who was alive.

"It's a murder rap if they get me now," he said grimly. "I didn't kill the guard, Len Brown did, but they'll hang it on me."

In spite of Roy's protests, I knew something had to be done about his foot. I walked over to the little general store run by the attendant of the cabins. He had a dusty box of Epson salts on the back shelf and a roll of bandages, too, though they had been around so long that they hardly looked sterile. I bought this meager equipment and returned to the cabin to heat some water on a small gas plate that stood in a corner.

All night I kept salt water as hot as he could stand it on his foot. Some black-looking clots finally began appearing where the skin was broken on top of his foot. Later some thick, discolored pus came out. The red streaks climbed no higher. For this I was thankful.

By daylight I had hope that we had won the battle, though the foot would be terribly painful for a long time yet. I fell upon the bed and immediately drifted off into blessed sleep. Hours later it was dark again, and I felt myself being roughly shaken. Opening my eyes, I dimly saw Roy's face close to mine, his fingers pressed to his lips in a warning gesture. He took my hand and led me silently from the cabin into a waiting car, whose motor was left running.

Roy again motioned me not to speak as we pulled away from the tourist court.

"But Roy!" I cried as soon as we were on the highway, "where did you get it?"

"Isn't she a beaut," Roy teased. "You don't think a guy could stay in prison five years and not be a good poker player, do you? I knew we'd need a little money when we hit the outside."

"Stop teasing," I begged. "This is no time for such foolishness. I know you didn't have that much money. Now where did you get this car?"

"Well, I could have rented it, couldn't I?"

"You could have, but you didn't. If this car is stolen we're getting out of it right this minute. I didn't come with you for this sort of thing. We're staying on the legit."

"But, Darling," he cut in, "you forget circumstances alter all cases. You saw my picture. What chance do you think we'd have getting out of this town on the legit? Every exit will be watched. Do you want me to burn?"

It's hard to fight when you know you face the stark truth. I swallowed hard when I thought of what the courts had done before, giving Roy the maximum for a first offense. Many hardened criminals have received shorter sentences for greater crimes. Roy belonged to no syndicate, and we had no money to hire a lawyer. I blinked back the tears.

"Don't take it so hard, Mary," he softened. "I promise it won't happen again. There's no other way out. Seven cons and a guard died for my freedom! Remember? You're fleeing with the most wanted man in the Southwest. You can't play the game according to your Sunday School book."

"But it's the worst thing we could do." I fought back desperately. "Besides all that, they'll catch us before we can get out of town. They're probably looking for this license number right now."

"Give me credit for a little more judgment than that, baby. I borrowed this sweet little buggy from a couple who had just climbed out and entered a theater. I watched them buy tickets, to make sure. It's not likely they'll be out of the show before two hours have passed."

"But even at that," I continued in desperation, "as soon as they do come out and turn it in we're goners. You know we can't get across the border in a stolen car, and there's just one good highway from here to California. We won't have a dog's chance. As soon as this license number is turned in to the cops, we're done for."

"Maybe not quite that soon. The license plates have been changed. I picked up a pair off a wrecked car in the junk yard. We ought to be able to get out of here, anyway. Now you just sit up right straight and proud, like we owned this shiny little toy. Now slip over here close and put your arm around me while we head out the Las Cruces highway. No one ever looks twice at turtle doves."

My heart turned to lead, but I did as he said. Nothing exciting happened before we got to Las Cruces, but Roy skirted town carefully and hit highway 80 again at the outskirts and we headed west toward Deming and Lordsburg, New Mexico, and Tucson, Arizona.

We traveled for three hours, stopping once at a lonely station for gas and oil. We drove several extra miles feeling our way around Deming and Lordsburg. We had to stick with the one highway. I became more nervous by the minute. Surely they were looking for the car by now. I urged we abandon it, but there was no way through here but by car, or rail. I'd had enough of freights and blinds to last me for a lifetime. Roy said the quicker we could get through this "one way chute" the better. It was the first time he had driven a car or even ridden in one in five years, and this was so pleasant in comparison with the other modes of locomotion we had tried. We stuck with the car a little too long.

A few miles from Tucson, we turned one of the infrequent curves along this route and spotted a highway patrol car parked just on the other side of one of those too frequent drainage dips along the lower route to California. It was too late to turn around when our lights hit the car. There were five men in it.

"Guess this is it," Roy remarked in what seemed a casual tone in comparison to my jumping heart. "May fool them with the changed license plates, but they may be wise by now. Nothing to do but pass them. Hang tight. If they follow we'll give them a run for the money."

We had hardly passed the car when it eased out onto the highway behind us, lights off. Roy speeded up gradually and got a little start. When they realized Roy had speeded up, they too, stepped on the gas, lights on.

When they turned on that siren I nearly jumped out of the car. Roy told me to get on the floor board.

"They might start shooting," he cautioned.

A few seconds more and I felt the brakes screech and the car veer wildly. I was slung against the door as we turned off the highway. Roy had found a side road and was tearing down it at break-neck speed, lights off.

The cops realized we had turned, however, and were still in hot pursuit, lights on.

"They're gaining," Roy reported. "Get ready to quit the car when you feel me hit the next corner."

A shot rang out. A second and then a third. The car began careening wildly. I'm not sure how Roy managed to keep it upright. Before I realized we had stopped, Roy pushed me from the car and catapulted me across a fence into a clump of bushes. Grabbing my hand he started dragging me out of range, in case there was more gunfire.

By this time the police car had slid to a stop back of ours. We looked back. Nothing except a cloud of dust was visible. As we looked back we ran head-on into an irrigation ditch and plunged into waist-deep water.

"Come out! Come out or we'll shoot!" came the menacing command from the police car. I was ready to come out but a restraining hand held me back.

SURROUNDED

"Come out of that car with your hands up!" was the next command of our pursuers.

"They think we're still in the car," Roy whispered. "The dust fooled them. They're afraid we're armed. Follow me, but stay bent over so they can't skylight you."

With that we crawled out of the ditch and headed down a row of tall, irrigated cotton, crouched over.

"They're not in here," we heard one of the officers yell as we covered another hundred feet. "Get the spotlight to work!"

"Flatten out," Roy commanded, "and lie still."

"Let's go after them," one patrolman suggested.

"They're probably armed," cautioned another. "We'd make good clay pigeons."

"Call Tucson for more cars," the first voice was commanding. "Two of you go on up the road to the other end of the field. No, wait. Let's make it hot for them."

A shot rang out, then a fusillade. Bullets started raining in the field. They zinged over our heads and spatted into the ground in front of us and behind us. Rifle shots whistled over and into the far corners of the field. I was as flat as a sheet of paper.

"O.K.," a voice finally broke in. "That's enough. You two go on up to the other end of the field. Bob and I'll stay here. Redding, you stay here with the radio."

As the car started, we did. I learned what Roy meant when he said his pace down a cotton row made a jackrabbit sit down and cry. He dragged me along in that crouched position until my legs ached and my lungs burned and I grew dizzy and sick at my stomach. Just when I thought I could go no further, Roy stopped short. Both of us dropped to the ground and lay there gasping like animals brought to bay by hunters.

"We're cornered," I whispered hoarsely. "They've surrounded the field. They'll find us at daylight."

"We won't be here at daylight," Roy said. "We've been running parallel with the road, about a hundred and fifty yards to the side. I figure we're out of hearing and seeing distance in the dark, so we can start cutting across. Try not to hit the stalks too hard. Stand up and run, now!" he gasped.

Run we did. Fortunately for us there was a road on only two sides of the field. We were out of the field, had slowed to a fast walk, had crossed the second field and were ready to cross the third when we saw several headlights coming at a distance.

"They're getting help," I said with dismay.

"All we can do is put as much distance as possible between us and the road," Roy said between gasps for breath, "and pray for daylight not to come. They'll surround the whole area."

We were running again. My heart seemed about to burst each time before we stopped for breath. My lungs were on fire.

"I can't go another step," I gasped.

"They'll have bloodhounds here within an hour," Roy said, "so let's keep on moving."

"Bloodhounds!" I needed no more urging. We walked quietly, careful not to shake any cotton plants and reveal our position, for we knew cops could be anywhere by now.

Suddenly Roy pulled me down beside him. "Someone's coming."

We lay crouched for what seemed hours, holding our breath, fearing that any minute a cop would stumble upon us. Finally Roy whispered, "Edge over toward that irrigation ditch at the end of the field. We'll have to get across the highway before daylight and that isn't too far off. We'll have to follow the irrigation ditch until it does cross the highway. They do ever so often, I notice. We'll crawl through the culvert it flows through to the other side of the highway, otherwise they'll skylight us."

91

We slithered into the ditch and inched down it. Finally we found a place where a ditch flowing from the other side of the highway joined the one we were following at a right angle. One of the patrol cars was approaching. I wanted to stop but Roy kept leading me on, close enough for the flashing searchlight to hit us, I thought. Then he motioned me to get low in the water as the car moved slowly across the culvert.

We edged into the main ditch and were almost swimming as we headed straight for the culvert. As we started under it we could see the next patrol car coming.

"We'd best wait under the culvert until it passes," Roy advised. "Might pick us up with the spotlight on the other side."

But the car didn't pass over the culvert. It just rolled up and stopped. Roy put a finger to my lips as we edged back toward the center of our rounded bridge, where it was completely dark.

"I told them last night this radiator needed checking," one of the cops spoke up. "They can issue me a new cap for this."

We heard him walking toward the edge of the culvert and remained breathless, with just our noses above the water. We saw him dip his cap into the water and heard him return to the car.

"It won't be long now," one of the men in the car remarked. "A rat couldn't crawl through this blockade. At daylight we'll twist them out."

The cop with the cap growled as he returned to the ditch a second and third time. We could have touched him with a long fishing pole.

Apparently satisfied, he slammed down the hood and closed the car door. As he shifted gears we started wading.

The car still seemed fairly close when we emerged on the other side. Scurrying out of the ditch we lost no time in getting out of range before the next patrol car arrived. A few hundred yards away from the road we left the ditch and started climbing a little bald mountain.

On reaching the top we sat down to rest and watched what looked like about a two-mile area surrounded by slowly moving lights. Intermittently a spot of light shot here and there over the fields. We were out of the surrounded territory, but not far enough away for comfort. We had to make tracks.

Daylight was beginning to streak the sky as we lost sight of the lights. A few houses appeared here and there. A train whistled in the distance.

"That may be our way out," Roy said. "If we could just hop that train while they think they have us surrounded in the cotton patch . . . if we could just make it."

We quickened our pace and headed straight for town. We knew that Tucson was a big town and we also knew we were still several miles away.

"We're going to have to take a chance one way or another," I put in. "Why don't we just try to get to a telephone and call a taxi?"

Roy thought it a good idea.

Before long we came to a dairy on the outskirts of town. The lights were on and men were working away inside. Being less afraid of a cow than we were of the highway, Roy decided to walk up to one of the fellows loading his milk truck and ask if there was a telephone he could use.

"Say, fellow," Roy asked, "is there a telephone here we could use to call a cab? Had a little car trouble and it's a long walk into town."

"Especially with a sore foot," the milkman remarked, noticing Roy's now shredded bandage. "Looks like you've had too much already.

"If you don't mind riding in a milk truck," he continued, "this is my last case and my route is on the other side of town."

We were crawling in. It was my first milk truck ride. The milkman seemed in a talkative mood.

"Now if you'd been on Highway 80 you wouldn't need a ride into town," he teased. "They got some escaped convicts from Texas rounded up out there in some of those cotton patches. I saw the bloodhounds they brought in from the state prison on my way to work, about forty minutes ago. Brother, I'd hate for those rascals to get after me."

I was glad it wasn't too light yet because I'm sure I turned whiter than his milk, but it didn't seem to bother Roy.

"They must be tough hombres," Roy put in. "Maybe if you'd wait around awhile we'd get to see what a real desperado looks like. I hear they grow 'em tough in Texas."

"It doesn't matter how tough they are, those bloodhounds will flush them like quail. Those cops will use them for target practice."

I couldn't stand any more. "You can let us out anywhere downtown," I said in an effort to change the subject. "We can take a cab."

"Well, I go across the tracks, holler when."

I was afraid Roy was going to hunt himself another laugh, but the words about crossing the tracks struck home.

"Since we live in that direction, we'll ride a little further," Roy said simply, much to my relief.

We were within sight of the tracks when Roy asked him to let us out. I had nothing to say, although I certainly wished for another means of locomotion. There was no train waiting, that we could see, so we headed up the tracks, west, we thought. As we cut through someone's yard, Roy jerked some jeans and a blue denim shirt from a clothes line.

"First cover we find, you slip these on over your dress. A woman is too easy to spot in a freight yard. You need a hat."

It seemed good daylight to me now, but I huddled behind the next hedge, at Roy's suggestion, and drew on the pants. I had to hold them up around the waist, so he gave me his belt. Down the line we saw many tracks and many cars.

"Looks like a freight is being made up," Roy remarked. "I could wish for something faster, but when they find out we've made it to town, they'll turn this place inside out and everything leading from it. They'll probably expect us to try to pick up another auto. They don't know our deluxe mode of traveling," he grinned. "The sooner we're out, the better."

"That's the caboose," Roy continued. "It must be almost made up. We'll go down the track a way so we can catch it when it pulls out. We'll have to catch it on the fly. Can't mount it with everyone looking."

"Catch it on the fly?" I sheepishly asked, remembering my recent train experiences.

"Yes, the train will be between us and the men working in the yard. Now listen while I tell you how. See those boxcars near the front of the train? As it passes we will catch one of those. There are iron rungs, ladders to you, on the outside of each car, one at the front and one at the back. If you catch the one on the front of the car, the most it can do is slap you against the side of the car. If it jerks you loose, you at least fall clear of the wheels.

"You will have to catch on first. The lowest rungs are a little over waist high from the ground and I may need to help you get your feet up to them. Whatever you do, swing onto those bars with both hands for all you're worth."

Sounded like a simple way to commit suicide, but it had come to a point where it didn't matter much.

"It's headin' this way," he said with real cheer in his voice. "Now just remember what I have told you. Be running as fast as the train when you grab those bars and it won't slap you back against the side of the car."

We stayed off the siding until the engine passed us. Then Roy started heading for the tracks. I was a step behind him.

"The first two cars are oilers," he yelled. "It's that first boxcar we want. Do exactly as I told you. Been lots of hobos never grown old who flunked this lesson."

It was rushing toward us. Roy grabbed my hand and we started running along the roughly graveled siding.

"Here it comes," he yelled. "See those iron bars. If you miss 'em, grab the ones at the front of the next car. Don't try for those at the back." He was beside me and yelled, "Grab!"

I grabbed, almost as high as my head. My feet swung wildly, hitting back against the side of the car, but not hard enough to hurt me in my state of excitement.

"I've got your feet," Roy yelled. "Grab a rung higher with one hand."

This I did and then moved the other hand up as I felt my foot placed on something solid, more or less.

Roy, who was running alongside, yelled, "If you don't mind, would you step up a rung off my hand so I can get my feet up, too."

This brought me to my senses and I climbed on up the iron ladder as the train picked up speed. When we got to the top he instructed me to keep hold of the iron rungs until we got to the cat-walk running down the top of the car lengthwise.

Cat-walk! It didn't look to me like a mouse could walk down the board with comfort with the train in motion.

"Just crawl up there and sit down," he coached. "I know you can be seen, but don't worry about it. Just look at the 'Soldiers of the Depression' sitting on top of those cars near the back."

It was a very long train. I could see the "Soldiers of Fortune," or should we correct that statement to keep in tone with the time and say "Soldiers of Misfortune," victims of circumstance, sitting in twos and threes on top of the cars all the way back. Fortunately the nearest ones were three cars back of us.

"You didn't see this," my acrobatic husband yelled above the roar of the train as he produced a crumpled felt hat from his pocket. "I scooped it up off the siding as you watched the rungs. Better get those curly locks tucked under it before somebody decides to try to take my gal away from me. I'm not looking for a fight. I've had it."

The hat looked surprisingly clean. It was rather tight for my full head of hair, but that just helped hold it on. Our clothes were perfectly dry now. I'd held my breath while we rode with that milkman for fear he would notice we were a little damp, but darkness is a most welcome companion during moments of embarrassment.

"A person would never know your hair is red, in the dark," Roy continued, "because it is always black in shadow, even in daylight, but sunlight sets it afire. I don't need anyone to help put out the flame," he teased.

Things went smoothly for awhile. I was even beginning to think the desert lovely, with its tall, slender organ pipes and its giant saguaros. Here and there prickly pear matted its white floor, while in the distance blue and violet mountains made a perfect backdrop.

The sun was hardly an hour high, but it was already bearing down. We thought we were headed for the west coast when we started, but now that the sun was with us, we could tell that we were headed north, toward Phoenix. But as far as the direction was concerned, it really didn't matter much, so long as we were putting distance between us and Texas. Our problem was to keep moving. I was trying to remember when we had eaten when Roy disturbed my thoughts by stretching his neck.

"Why are we stopping out here in the middle of the desert?"

he asked. "There isn't even a siding here to pull on to for a passenger to pass. Something's wrong!"

SHOT OFF A FREIGHT

Alarmed, Roy stood up for a better look toward the back of the train.

"Holy Smoke! Look at those hobos scram!" he exclaimed. "There's two special dicks heading up each side of the track. They're holding a gun on some 'bos now. Wonder if any of them noticed a girl on the train? Let's get moving."

Two hobos headed for the desert but stopped right quicklike when the detectives fired in their direction.

"Let's head for the tender," Roy called as he started crawling down the rungs between our boxcar and the first oiler. I followed suit and stepped across the coupling as he did and we started scooting around the fat sides of the big, black oilers. An iron rung running parallel to the sides of the tank and about waist high helped us to hold on.

I thought Roy had lost his reason entirely when I saw him climb right up on the water tank, tender, as he called it, which was back of the engine. He opened a little round iron door, motioned me to follow, and jumped in. The water, up to my chin, was warm, but not hot.

We had ducked the fireman as he walked back down the track while we were on the far side of one of the oil tanks. Roy peeped out the door of the tender. He described the show:

"One of the dicks is holding the hobos they have rounded up at the point of a gun while the others shake down the train. They're about ten cars back. If they climb up and look in this tender we're done for."

A steam bath with a hat on wasn't my custom, but I was living in a different world now, a warm one. We heard them come on up the track. They were close enough now that we could hear them talking.

When they seemed even with us one of them was saying, "Looks like we've missed them, but they're here all right. A

97

snake couldn't have crawled off this track into the desert without us seeing it. They must be in the rods under one of the cars."

"Check underneath the cars. Check the reefers of every car on the way back," one of them was directing. "We'll flush them out. Keep your guns ready."

We heard them start back down the train, working it systematically.

"What are we going to do?" I whispered.

"They'll find us sooner or later," Roy whispered back. "If they're fool enough to all work back toward the rear of the train at the same time, we could crawl out and make a run for the desert when they're out of good range. They can't shoot straight with those pistols. We'll put a shotgun out of range and we'll zigzag until they can't draw a bead on us with a rifle before we get to the big tree cactus. Your being a girl, they'll probably try to talk us out without shooting. If we have to run for it, don't stop."

They must have been twenty or more cars back when we heard someone walking toward the tender from the rear of the train. The steps drew nearer and we heard someone swing up to the side of the tender, climbing toward us. It sounded like just one person. Roy motioned me back with his hand.

The second the iron door opened, Roy was ready. He grabbed what must have been the train's fireman, head and shoulders, and pulled him in with us. As Roy grappled with him he hollered for me to climb out. The water was so deep that all they could do was go into a clinch. Just as I got to the top, Roy did manage to get in one good punch at the fireman and he went under, spluttering.

Roy was right behind me now. As he emerged the fireman made a lunge for his legs. My heart was in my throat. What if he was knocked out? He could drown.

"Think you'd better see if he comes up?" I asked.

Roy laughed. "Quit your thinking and scramble down."

Evidently the engineer had heard nothing of the commotion, for just then he let off steam.

"Run in front of the steam," Roy yelled. "It's a blind."

We were hardly out of the steam when the fireman hit the top of the tender hollering bloody murder. Evidently he was slightly irritated, for he hit the ground and started running after us.

98

By that time we were well noticed. One of the special detectives fired a few shots into the air and yelled "Halt!" We kept running and so did the fireman. He was really gaining and I believe he would have caught us, especially me, if the engineer and everyone else hadn't been yelling for him to stop.

"Stop, you fool, so they can shoot!" the engineer's voice boomed from the cab.

But before the engineer could stop him we were across the right of way and headed for the first tall saguaros. There were no fences. They're not needed for rattlesnakes.

By not thinking to flatten out, the fireman shielded us from the rear. A few rifle shots whizzed around us, and some whistled over our heads. How I zigzagged! We worked in and out like a shuttle among the tree cactus, never slowing down.

By the time the cops had reached the vicinity where we had entered the desert we were well out of range, thanks to the saguaros.

Stocky, middle-aged men with heavy guns don't last very long in a desert, even in pursuit of fugitives. I don't believe even the best of them followed us a good half-mile before they stopped for consultation.

We stopped to catch our breath, too. We were well into the deep cactus country and it was doubtful whether they could even catch a glimpse of us any longer, but we could see them well enough to know what they were doing. They went into a little huddle, scattered and then started firing at random into the desert.

"Come out!" their spokesman commanded. "Come out! We've got you covered!"

Roy put a restraining hand on my back.

"Come out while you can get out alive!" he yelled.

Roy laughed aloud. Their little barrage didn't last long. We just lay on the desert floor and called their bluff. None of the bullets came very close, although they did have some high powered rifles that sung out of hearing into the desert.

We lay still as we saw all the officers, the crew and the hobos crawl back on the train. Evidently they made all the soldiers of fortune crawl into an empty boxcar. There must have been over thirty of them. The detectives climbed into the caboose with the brakemen.

We wondered if they would drop some of the officers, when they got out of sight, to try to fool us.

"Will they get bloodhounds?" I asked.

"Maybe so," my husband answered, "but it might not do them a whole lot of good. The dogs won't like this desert any more than the cops did. The trail will be hours old before they can get dogs out to this godforsaken place. With the sun like this, a scent won't last too long. Being too hot and dry makes it as hard for dogs to trail as being too wet.

"Step on rocks whenever you can and don't let your clothes brush against anything green," Roy admonished as we again headed into the desert. "Green stuff holds the scent longer."

The glue holding the straps to the soles of my sandals had given away and they slapped with each step. Roy's injured foot was bare, but it looked much better. Most of the discoloration had vanished. Only the little toe, which was evidently broken, remained puffed. We had only been on the desert a few minutes, but our well-soaked clothes seemed almost dry.

We had to stop for repairs before we could go farther. Roy tore strips from one trouser leg and tied the sandals to my feet. He then tore the other trouser leg off at the knee and wrapped and tied the cloth around his injured foot, more as insulation against the hot sand and rock than for any other purpose. I was thankful for the tight hat, which was still with me. My husband remained bareheaded.

Undaunted, my fugitive companion extracted his damp but well made prison billfold from his pocket and remarked, "Where do we eat?"

I was in no mood for jokes. I tried to remember when I had last seen my purse, but it didn't matter much. I had given the lone ten spot left in it to Roy. The make-up I didn't need, to mix with sand, although I could have used a comb.

"Well, navigator," Roy broke the silence, "have you any idea where we are?"

Having passed through this part of the country before, I expounded, "I think that mountain in the distance, in front of us and slightly to the right, is Superstition Mountain. It's about

100

thirty miles east of Phoenix. If we keep heading for that mountain we are bound to come to that highway."

"Highways are what we don't want," Roy teased, "but I'm glad to know we are about to strike it rich. Isn't Superstition Mountain where the Lost Dutchman's mine is?"

His banter didn't help much so he continued, "We know that the railroad track we just left parallels the highway running into Phoenix, and it is to our left, while Superstition is in front of us. As long as we head for that mountain, we're not lost. They'll guard every inch of the highway and railroad we just left. If there's any civilization on that highway coming down from those mountains, maybe we can get close enough to borrow a drink from a windmill."

I remembered a memorial at the base of Superstition Mountain and a tourist camp. I thought I could find them.

We walked . . . and we walked . . .

The sun climbed the heavens like a ball of fire. Everything fled from the heat until there was no sign of life except a few lizards and here and there a rattlesnake curled in the shade of a cactus. Perspiration ran down our arms and dripped from the ends of our fingers. I trudged ahead without thinking, conscious only of the pain that racked my body. Around mid-afternoon we fell into a thin slice of shade made by a tall saguaro.

As soon as we could catch our breath Roy took his knife and cut a branch from the saguaro. It was porous on the inside, but the woody, chewy pulp was not damp enough to cool our parched lips.

Then Roy cut some kind of cactus that we had always heard harbored water. We found none. He pulled up some yucca and peeled the spoonlike roots. They were beautiful, a golden color and smooth like satin, but we gnawed on them in vain.

Thirst drove us on. We staggered to our feet again and headed for Superstition Mountain. Hour after hour we pushed forward, losing all track of time, but the mountain never seemed to come any closer.

We heard no sound of pursuit. Many beautiful lakes appeared in the distance, but we knew they were mirages. The desert seemed nothing but tortured space. Earlier I had been thankful for the hat and borrowed trousers I wore over my dress, but now I was too numb to feel anything but thirst.

I felt as if I were drying up, like a mummy crumbling to dust. There was no moisture at all in my mouth, none in my eyes. No perspiration came now. I burned all over. Visions of my five-year-old daughter kept coming to me, and in the visions she was crying and begging me to come home to her. I reached for her outstretched fingers but could not touch them.

I don't know when I blacked out, but when I came to again it was night and freezing cold. I shivered uncontrollably and even wished for the agonizing sun. Roy lay beside me, his gaunt face lit by the desert moon. He looked gentle in sleep and I thought I saw in him some of the tenderness I had known five years before. Lonely, I touched my parched lips to his, and he stirred, murmuring something.

"Darling . . . darling . . . ," I whispered.

"Water," he moaned, then sat up. He looked about dully for a moment, then climbed to his feet.

"Come on, Mary. We gotta cover ground before the sun comes up."

I thought I couldn't move, but I did. I stood up and staggered after him through the desert, under one of the most beautiful star-dusted skies that God ever made.

We walked the rest of the night, and Superstition remained in the distance. The first streaks of dawn filled me with horror of the mounting sun. Soon there was no shade, no escape.

We plodded another hour, maybe two. There was nothing left. All strength seemed drained and my legs no longer held me up. I had gone as far as I could. My numbed mind was beyond hope, or fear or love.

Chapter 7

The Desert Deals a Deathly Hand

I don't know how long I lay blacked out, but the sun was still fierce when I came to a numbed consciousness which was most unwelcome in my tortured state. I closed my eyes and tried to black out again, but remained conscious. Roy lay prone at my side. Why should I disturb him? Perhaps he would never awaken.

Jeannie was with me every conscious moment now. She kept begging and begging me to come home. What had I done to my own little girl? Would she grow up thinking her mother never loved her? Would she and her grandmother ever know how we tried, how we died?

I wished I could just write a note telling how much her mother loved her, how I died with visions of my beautiful little daughter beckoning to me, but there was nothing to write with. A mute prayer stuck in my heart, begging God not to let my baby hate her own mother for deserting her. This must be about her birthday; I wasn't sure. Day or hours no longer mattered. I only wished to die, and that, quickly.

Roy groaned. The sun beat mercilessly on his upturned face. He had no hat. He hardly looked like a human being, and I was sure I didn't. I had worn the hat all along. At least I could pull him to me and we could both die with our faces in the shade if I placed the hat across them.

Jeannie was with me every conscious moment now. She kept begging and begging me to come home. What had I done to my own little girl? Would she or anyone ever know how I died? If I could only tell her she was the only thing I had to live for . . . But it was too late now, I was dying of thirst.

I reached out to try to drag him to me. I lay under the thin jointed fingers of some sort of cactus that afforded no real shade at all, but it seemed better to lie beneath something. Roy's eye opened and he pulled himself to a sitting position when he felt my tugging. He scooted as far underneath the cactus as possible and leaned back into its thorny arms, seemingly feeling no pain. I was sorry I had wakened him. I crawled to his side and he propped the hat to shade my face. Neither of us spoke.

After what seemed a long while, Roy began speaking, or rather rasping out words between parched lips.

"I'm sorry I got you into this, Sweetheart. Let's don't let nine people die for no freedom. That doesn't come out even, eight tried and nine died. You don't figure in on this deal, Darling. It's not right for you to die. The score's perfect without it."

I tried to follow him but numbers didn't make sense to me any more. There was just one word that had meaning to me and I was trying so hard to shut 'water' from my mind.

"I did a lot of reading," I heard Roy saying, but he seemed very distant. "I did a lot of reading during the five years I was in prison. There was a tribe of Aboriginals in Australia who raised sheep and lived off nothing but blood and milk. They would bleed their sheep."

I thought his mind was wandering and tried to pay no attention to his gruesome story until I saw him bring his knife from his pocket.

"I'm going to slash my wrist," he said. "When I do you drink the blood. It will give you strength to get to help. Maybe you can get back to me. I don't have much to look forward to anyway."

The very suggestion hurtled me to my feet in horror and I almost ran toward the mountain. He followed.

After a great length of silence he raised his arm and pointed to a low line of trees. "There's our chance," he rasped in a half prayer.

We headed for the trees. They seemed nearer. Twice I fell to my knees, but Roy dragged me up again. We were near enough that we could tell they were Joshua trees, but even Joshuas require some water. I envisioned a cool pool under the tallest one, which we were heading for.

Our struggle brought us to the brink of a dry gully, cursed

with some scattered rocks. Completely defeated, I sank in the shade of the tree.

A sharp rattle attracted my attention. At the base of the tree lay the largest rattler I had ever seen, unwilling to even share the shade. It raised its ugly diamond head above its singing rattles.

I almost laughed at the irony of what we had found. This wouldn't take long, and it would be easier, I thought, as I saw it tense to strike.

It sprung, but its forward lunge was intercepted by the impact of a heavy rock. Another rock thudded into the midst of that writhing mass before I realized what had happened.

I was wondering whether my life was worth thanking Roy for saving when I took note of his actions. Before the snake was fully still, he was cutting its head off with that knife and skinning its thick body.

"Steak, rattlesnake steak," he remarked as he sunk his swollen mouth into the white flesh, shoving me a hunk.

I watched a moment horrified, but nature took its course and I too began gnawing like a cannibal. After we had gorged we both fell asleep.

When we awoke or at least when consciousness returned, nature seemed trying to compensate with one of these lavish desert sunsets. I was wondering if it could possibly be the same day, the day that had dragged into an eternity?

At first I thought I had been dreaming, because nothing seemed real, not until thirst came as a grim reminder. I wanted to believe it was a dream, all a dream, especially what we had just eaten, but it was a big snake and I saw no flesh remaining. I remember closing my syes and telling myself that I was eating raw shrimp. The very thought of the cannibalistic instincts we had just exhibited made me shudder.

Mental bars had not affected the meat's nutritional value however, and we both felt stronger. I was even beginning to feel a little hopeful.

"Superstition looks a lot closer," I remarked as I gazed at its splendid dark blues and violet. "And look," I cried as I pointed at a ten o'clock angle, "that must be Camel Back Mountain on the other side of Phoenix."

"We'll get to water tonight," Roy encouraged. "Why, we could walk from Tucson to Phoenix in two days and a night."

We kept a good pace in the cool of the desert night, but things look much clearer than they really are when viewed over a vast expanse of sand. We had walked well into the night when we sat down for a brief rest. We said little because any movement of our parched lips or swollen throats brought sudden added pain. Although both of us were in our early twenties, lack of food and water and nervous exhaustion had taken their toll, leaving us feeling about as young and talkative as the Sphinx. The light of the moon, added to the white of the sand, was soft and quite beautiful after the dazzling light of day. Roy had no bandage on his foot now but said the cool sand felt good to it.

We walked all night with hardly a word passing between us. Even words took energy which we did not have, so we plodded on. Superstition Mountain seemed only a stone's throw away. Camel Back was outlined in the distance. We dared not rest because of the coming of the dawn.

With the first bright streaks came those agonizing fears of the sun. Strength seemed to leave my body as if extracted by the sun's rays. I couldn't stand a repetition of the last two days. The first rays touching my dehydrated frame seem to make me a flaming ball of desire . . . WATER. WATER. WATER. There was no other word or thought in the world except WATER!

"Come on, " Roy coaxed as he sensed my feelings. "Water can't be far now, if the highway is between us and Superstition. We've got to travel before it gets too hot."

He took my hand and pulled me along. We plodded another hour, maybe two, before I stumbled. Although quite young the sun was showing its desert strength. I felt as if it were clubbing me to the ground with its rays. I buried my head in my arms as I sank to my knees on the sand. Roy remained standing. Looking! Looking! Looking!

SAFE WITH THE STRANGEST SORT OF JESUS

Roy's voice seemed to come to me from a great distance, as if through a long, black tunnel. He was saying something over and over again, but I couldn't understand what it was. Suddenly the earth seemed to drop from under me. I cried out. It was only Roy pulling me to my feet. He held me with one arm and pointed with the other.

"Look!" he cried. "Smoke! Smoke from a campfire."

I looked where he pointed. It was true. A thin spiral of blue smoke was climbing the cloudless sky.

"Someone built that fire, and they have water," Roy commented.

We rushed forward, stumbling, falling, climbing to our feet again, mumbling to ourselves all the while. We were afraid to guess at the distance of that smoke. We must have walked an hour when our hopes started fading with the vanishing smoke. The last wisp vanished as we climbed a little rise, but at the spot where we had seen the smoke rose a tall cottonwood tree.

"Bound to be water," was the almost unrecognizable voice that forced its ray of hope through Roy's sandpapered esophagus.

As we pushed our way forward we saw lower trees. Willows, I fancied, willows by a river bank. I felt sure I could hear flowing water as we half ran and half crawled the last lap.

Babbling like lunatics we lunged toward the bank of a river. God was merciful.

We plunged our faces into the sparkling, clear water. We sucked up great mouthfuls and tried gulping it down, but our throats were too swollen. Swallowing was difficult. When we were able to slow down we held mouthfuls of the precious water and let it trickle down our sandpapered throats.

When we had drunk until we could drink no more we crawled into the river and sat down, waist deep, to absorb what we could through the pores of our dehydrated skin. The river flowed gently over a bottom of whitest sand. A million diamonds, I thought, as we splashed in laughing luxury.

Suddenly we became aware of the fact that we were being watched from the bank. My eyes followed Roy's and rested on a white-headed, brown-skinned old man.

"Madre de Dios," he commented as he approached, making the sign of the cross over his chest as he smiled broadly. *"No es goot, no es goot?"* he spoke in a jumble of English and Spanish. I

wasn't sure I understood him, but thanked God that he wore a smile instead of a gun.

"*Cafe y frijoles,*" he said in Spanish as he pointed over to a dead campfire and some pots in the shade of the huge cottonwood tree.

"Coffee and beans," I yelled as I climbed out of the water. I think I beat him back to the campsite and filled a tin plate with beans as he poured coffee into tin cups. I was sharing my beans with Roy. We both ate from the same pewter spoon. The old Mexican scurried over to a dug-out in the side of the bank and returned with another tin plate and pewter spoon, grinning broadly all the while.

Never was food better. The coffee was cold and the only seasoning in the beans was salt and chile peppers, but it was heavenly. The peppers burned our raw throats, but we didn't care.

I thought I could have eaten a barrel of beans, but when I was half finished with that first generous helping there seemed to be no more space. I was so sleepy. The last thing I remembered was the old Mexican man pointing to himself and repeating, "Jesús, me Jesús."

"He's Jesus," I interpreted, and I halfway believed he was, as I fell asleep.

I awakened with strange bleating sounds in my ears. As my eyes popped open I saw Roy and Jesús, with the white flowing beard, on the other side to the stream skinning a sheep. Roy and Jesús . . . what a strange combination. A sheep herder and an escaped convict . . . Jesús and the criminal! But Jesús liked us and seemed happy with our companionship. Could it be that lonely here?

"We're going to have mutton," Roy called to me as I sat up. "Jesús has killed the fatted calf."

It sounded strange to hear Roy talk that way. I didn't mind his muffing the story of the prodigal so long as the fatted calf was a reality.

Jesús smiled broadly when I told him my name was María, the Spanish for Mary. He seemed to like me all the more because I could halfway speak his own language and was named María.

Jesús and Roy could not understand each other and most of their conversation was carried on by a series of motions. Perhaps it was better that way. There couldn't be but one story.

Trying to think of a logical way to explain our presence I thought of the lost mines of Superstition. I could think of the Spanish word *'montaña,'* for mountain, but could not remember the Spanish word for lost.

"En la montaña," (in the mountain) I explained as I pointed and made a circle with my hand, shaking my head in a negative, puzzled manner.

"La montaña," Jesus repeated, *"la montaña es del diablo. Hay muchos hombres que se matan por el oro."*

"The mountain is possessed of the devil," I interpreted. "Many men are killed for gold."

"Es verdad," (It is true.) I agreed in one of the few Spanish expressions I remembered.

"Los muertos no hablan," (The dead don't talk.) he said with a plaintive smile.

I was quick to agree with him, thinking how nearly we had come to fitting his expression. Many stories I had heard of people who never returned from the mountain. I thought of the lives lost in the search for the Lost Dutchman's Mine. I felt the old Mexican could have told more, could we have understood each other better. I wondered if he had saved others.

We slept outside the crude dug-out on sheep skins and covered with the tattered blanket offered us. In the morning we discovered that Jesús' food supply was very menial, consisting of corn meal, with only a few weevils, a poor grade of coarsely ground coffee, salt and chili peppers, garlic gloves and one No. 2 can of tomatoes.

Having only two plates and cups, Roy used the empty tomato can to drink from. Jesús ate from the frying pan. What a rare delicacy, our first hot meal in many days.

To earn our keep I cleaned Jesús' simple dug-out and washed everything I could find and tried to make my skirt and blouse halfway presentable once more. Roy found a few fish hooks and managed to catch some beautiful golden sunfish and a few channel cats. A shave with an old straight razor made Roy look years younger. I cleaned an old comb I found in the dug-out and used it to good advantage.

There was no road to our new heaven, only a burro trail. We felt fairly safe. On the third night I ventured asking how far it was to the highway that lead into Phoenix. Jesús informed us that it was six miles.

It was good not to have to run nor hurry. Jesús never hur-ried. We loved our beautiful stream, which our sheepherder told us was a dry river bed used as an irrigation canal, with its waters flowing from the Roosevelt dam high in the ore-laden mountains.

It was a simple life. Looking back on it now, I think that in all the months we were pursued by the law, those were the only peaceful days we knew. Food and rest brought back our strength and cleared our minds. But the future still stretched grimly ahead of us. Where to run? How to hide? Mexico seemed too far away, too difficult to reach. The prospect of a wonderful new life with my husband and daughter dimmed. But we'd make the dream come true.

Doubt of the wisdom of our flight lay within me, but I throt-tled it. My decision had been made long ago. What the world thought made no difference. Roy was good and noble once, and he would be again. Nothing would ever force us apart.

We had been in the desert for a week when Jesús an-nounced that his boss man was due to arrive soon with new sup-plies. There was no need of our walking to the highway. We could go a half mile down the burro trail with him to meet the boss man and ride back to town with him in his truck.

That night Roy and I talked things over as we lay under the stars. The boss man coming threw a new light on the subject. He might not be as trusting as Jesús, especially since he could prob-ably read and write and was likely capable of deductive reason-ing, if he found us harbored in Jesús' heaven. The news made us restless.

The heat would be off in the search for us now, Roy rea-soned. Maybe the cops would have given us up for dead. At least there would be no highway blocks after all this time. We decid-ed to leave early in the morning. Three hours of walking should bring us to the highway before the sun got too hot.

Chapter 8

Back to Civilization

We had plenty of time to cook up a little story in case we needed it, as we walked toward the highway. We decided that the most feasible one, considering our well-worn look, was that: out of curiosity and a desire for unusual shapshots we had driven to Superstition Mountain and gotten lost. Many a poor soul had been lost there and looking at its jagged, bald upheavals, it didn't take much imagination to see how hard it would be to keep from getting lost if foolish enough to enter its vast, rugged expanse without a guide. Even those who knew the mountain or a portion of it, sometimes disappeared and searching parties were sent out from Phoenix.

We must have made a strange looking pair, standing on the edge of the highway. Roy's foot was again bandaged, this time more to hide the fact that he had but one shoe. He had tried to tack the straps back to the soles of my completely frayed sandals, but they looked and felt very crude and uncomfortable. Roy was wearing the blue jeans I had worn because he had torn the legs from his trousers for bandages for his foot from time to time. The jeans were as much too small for Roy as they had been too large for me.

The sun was getting pretty hot as we crossed the streak of asphalt that led into the mountains to the east and Phoenix to the west. We kept the water bag after pouring out a portion of its precious contents to keep it from looking suspiciously heavy.

We saw no sign of civilization and took our stance at the edge of the highway. A car came from the wrong direction. We left the highway and crouched behind some cactus until it passed. We heard another coming from the mountains. This would probably be going into Phoenix. Again we stood at the edge of the highway.

There was a lone man in the car and he screeched to a stop a few feet ahead of us. If for no other reason I suppose the man would have stopped out of curiosity. His questioning look demanded an explanation.

Roy presented our little story and he seemed satisfied with it. When we told him we had been lost for two days the salesman raised an eyebrow and asked if we were not quite hungry and thirsty.

I explained that we had carried a generous picnic lunch and a couple of water bags with us. Roy shook the little bit of water left in the bag to substantiate our story, explaining how we had drunk sparingly, not knowing when we would find civilization.

Our benefactor was a salesman from the east. This made us feel better. Perhaps he had seen nothing in the papers where he had been in the last few days to make him suspicious.

He insisted on stopping at the first outpost and buying cold drinks, some fresh oranges, dates and candy. We ate with great zest, much to his pleasure.

Roy made our story so interesting that before we reached Phoenix the salesman wanted to drive us back to Superstition to pick up our car.

I quickly assured him that we could get the family car. This was another mistake, for he began wondering if our folks wouldn't be worried about us.

"We live in an apartment across town from her folks," Roy came to my rescue, "and the people in the apartment house are used to our being gone over the weekend. They probably haven't even missed us yet. If the folks called they would just have thought we were out fishing or hunting good snapshots. We're great shutter-bugs."

Before there was time for another mistake to be made I

said, "You can just let us out at the next red light. We live just around the corner."

The salesman offered to let us out at our door but I already had the car door open and was crawling out of the car as it stopped for the light. He waved a reluctant goodbye. In fact if he could have had things his way he would have carried us right down to the newspaper office and had a feature story done on our being lost in the mountain. I think he fancied himself an unsung hero. Little did he suspect that our appearance in a newspaper office would have changed the tune.

When we crawled out of the car we found ourselves in a small shopping center. Roy did have a little change so he bought a newspaper. He held it well in front of us as we sat on a bench at a bus stop trying to figure our next move.

Handing me our last ten spot he instructed, "Go to the resale shop across the street and get us some shoes. I can't go with my foot wrapped in a rag. It will attract attention. Besides, the foot's okay now for a soft shoe."

While he sat with the paper before his face I went across the street to buy the things we had to have. I got a pretty good pair of secondhand shoes for myself for a dollar and bought Roy a pair of soft leather house shoes. Then I went to a dime store and bought a ten-cent lipstick, a pocket comb and a small box of powder. Being a woman, I couldn't resist these, even though I had been forced to buy secondhand clothes.

I returned to Roy and we cut over to another street. In the rest rooms of a service station we put on our shoes. I fixed up my face with the first make-up I'd had in ages. Funny what a little lipstick will do for a woman's morale. I felt almost light-hearted as I faced my lover once more. We emerged looking less strange, but were eyed curiously by the attendant. We headed down a side street.

"We had best get away from this side of town," Roy advised. "We might have attracted a little attention."

A city bus with "Five Points" printed on its placard emerged from somewhere. We had no idea where we were going, but we stayed with the bus until it had passed through town.

The bus left the business district and seemed to be heading out a highway. Finally we came to a spot where five roads

114

seemed to merge and traffic was controlled by one of those many sided lights.

Probably thinking that we had ridden long enough, or that we did not know the town, the driver glanced in the mirror and called, "Five Points."

We crawled off the bus. The sun was sweltering hot, but there were trees. I feasted my eyes on the palm trees and the green grass. We were hardly noticed.

"This is our happy home," Roy remarked as we emerged from the air conditioned coolness of a drug store into the blinding sun once more. "Let's look for a room."

As we left the shopping district built around Five Points we found a modest residential section. Everything seemed air conditioned, but we knew we could not afford such luxury. Just a room must suffice, and a very modest one at that, until I could get work.

The Depression still clung tenaciously on and there were plenty of 'For Rent' signs anywhere we looked. With our last few dollars we rented a room for a week on a quiet side street. We climbed to the second floor, opened the last door in a long hall, and we were home. It was a small room, barely big enough for the two pieces of furniture in it. An old brass bed stood against one wall, and opposite it was a scarred dresser with drawers that rested crookedly on their runners. In one corner of the room a closet had been formed by nailing curtains on a high shelf. Above the dresser was a mirror whose wavy surface threw back a warped reflection. But it was a room with walls and a ceiling to keep us from the eyes of the world. We were safe here.

"Roy," I said softly, turning to put my arms around his neck as he closed the door behind us, "We're people now."

"So far so good, Mary," he said, walking over to the window and looking out. "Except we're broke."

"It won't matter too much," I comforted. "We're safe and I can find work. I'll have to. I managed all during the worst of the Depression and I can manage now. I'm glad I learned to be a waitress while I was going through college. A waitress can always find work. Of course I'll have to start where they furnish uniforms because . . ."

"Forget it now, Baby," he said, pulling me to him, "we've got to celebrate. This is our happy home."

"Sure, Darling," I said, holding him close and kissing him. "Tomorrow can take care of itself."

Later, as I lay on the bed with Roy beside me, I stared at the ceiling and wondered what was wrong. I had gone through hell for this, turned my back on the world just to be with my husband, but now it seemed that I was left with something strangely empty. The wonder and beauty I had once known in being with Roy was gone. His caresses had been mechanical without any deep feeling, without love or so it seemed to me. Surely it was my imagination. It had to be.

All that I knew was that I felt terribly alone. Suddenly my arms ached for my little girl. Roy had done very little talking about her. I knew that there had been no time for such reminiscence, but she was our child, our responsibility.

What kind of mother had I been to Jeannie, leaving her with her grandmother, while I fled with Roy? I couldn't keep back the tears when I thought of her fifth birthday, with not even a word from her mother. If I only had the money to call her by phone, or if I could only drop a birthday card, they would know I was alive. I knew Roy would never agree to my taking such a chance. To whom should I be loyal, my child or my husband? Fine time now to ask myself such a question. The choice was made but was it the right one?

I searched for the answer, tortured by doubts. I remembered Ted Randel's offer to marry me when I was working in Abilene on the newspaper, his offer of safety and comfort and a respectable life for my baby. Should I have said yes to him? Should my love for Jean have outweighed my love for Roy? I closed my eyes tightly; I had to face this problem and come up with a solution.

I would talk it over with my husband. That was the way problems should be worked out.

With a sigh of relief I turned on my side and rested my head on Roy's shoulder. "Pretty soon now we'll all be together, you and me and Jean. Won't it be wonderful having a family? You never really had a chance to know what it is like," I murmured.

"As soon as I get a couple of weeks wages we'll take a bus to the border. You can disguise yourself."

"Huh?" he grunted.

"After we find work in Mexico we can send for Jean. You'll never know her, she's a young lady now, almost ready to enter school . . . well, in another year at least."

"You crazy?" Roy asked harshly. "What are you talking about?"

"Jean," I said. "We could get her before we cross the border, now that the heat's off. I don't mind working a little longer. We'll save every penny. Three of us could travel as cheaply as two. With Jeannie along we'd look even more like a family and avoid suspicion. I miss her, Roy, it's killing me."

"Forget it," Roy snapped. "We are not getting saddled with any kid, so get it out of your mind. Just because they're not shooting at us, don't think they've forgotten. Take a look at the post office bulletin board tomorrow when you go to town. They don't put those pictures up and post rewards to encourage people to forget."

I felt as if I had been slapped in the face. It was his tone that did it, so cold, so distant.

"Roy, you talk as if Jean were a stranger."

"Well, I haven't seen her since she was a tiny baby," he mumbled.

"But she's your daughter, Roy! Your own flesh and blood!"

"We're traveling light," he snapped. "Now let's shut up about it."

Everything seemed to go to pieces inside me. All during our flight from the police, on the trains, through the cotton fields with bullets flying around me, across the blistering desert . . . in all that time something inside me, a faith in Roy, kept me going. If that faith vanished I knew my strength would be gone. I would be beaten not by bullets or starvation, but by Roy.

I was just tired out, and so was he. The strain had been too much for both of us. Tomorrow would be another day. Tonight was just a bad dream. Everything would be right tomorrow.

I was downtown when the stores opened the next morning with the want ads in my hand. My clothes were so shabby that it gave me a false sense of timidity. I was beginning to think that I was going to fail in finding work, for the first time, as I was turned down in place after place. Maybe I just looked too terrible. Maybe they thought I was a Latin American my skin was so brown. Fear was closing in on me. I no longer felt sure of myself.

The shoes I had bought the day before were white, and they didn't look too bad, but my skirt and blouse were faded and I felt sure they looked like I had been picking cotton in them. Perhaps that's where they thought I belonged, in the cotton field with the Mexican labor.

I walked in front of a linen place that had out a sign advertising all kinds of uniforms for rent. I didn't have the money to buy one, but maybe I could rent one. We had less than half a dollar in change left. If I rented it and failed to find work there would be no food today nor tomorrow. I walked on.

In the next block there was a "Waitress Wanted" card in the window of what looked like a working man's cafe. I hesitated in front of the cafe long enough to get a glance through the glassed-in front. The waitresses were wearing different kinds of uniforms. That meant they weren't furnished like they were in classier places. I had to take the chance. I walked back to the linen place and rented a uniform and put it on. They wanted a deposit. I asked if it was all right for me to leave my clothes there. I would give them the thirty-five cent laundry fee and pick up my clothes tomorrow when I came by for another clean uniform. They agreed. I didn't tell them I didn't even have a job.

I walked back to the cafe that had out the sign, drew a deep breath, lifted my chin and walked in like I belonged. "I'm ready to go to work," I told the manager as he eyed me with evident surprise. "I saw your sign, so I just came ready to start."

Evidently he doubted my ability even as a waitress, but since I was ready he said he would let me finish the day. If my work proved satisfactory I could return tomorrow. It was almost lunch time and I wasted no time in showing him that I knew what I was doing. I stacked the dishes high on my trembling arm and tried harder than I ever tried in my life to remember every order perfectly. I let no small service slip by me and received some show of gratitude from customers in form of tips. If they only knew how badly I needed them. After luncheon was served and the tables and counters cleaned, I sat down to lunch with another waitress. I was ashamed to eat all I really wanted, but what I did eat gave me strength for the dinner run.

I was extremely happy when the dinner run was over and the manager asked me to return the next morning at six. I had enough tips in my pocket to rent another uniform and to buy food for Roy. He could at least have a good evening meal and food tomorrow while I worked. Soon we would have clothes and money for a little apartment. We could begin saving money for our trip to Mexico.

When I had worked in the little cafe for two weeks the manager threatened not to pay me again if I kept forgetting to bring my social security card. I knew I could not go on working in the same place, for I could not use the card with the name Mary King and I had no other. I would just have to fail to show up for work after I got my pay and look for another job. I didn't like doing things this way, but life was different now.

With pay I got decent looking clothes for myself and some slacks and a sport shirt for Roy. I also bought some dye and used it on both mine and Roy's hair. He was no longer a sandy blond, and there was no red left in my hair. Being a brunette did change Roy's appearance. I cut my own hair with a razor blade. My once shoulder-length locks were now short cropped and very black. It looked fairly natural with our highly suntanned skins.

On each new job I made up a new lie about no social security card and worked until they refused me further pay without it. It was always the same story in many cities in several states. Roy was afraid to show himself during the day, often moving without notice at night if we thought we were being observed too closely by anyone.

Twice I became so desperately lonely for my little girl that I sneaked in long distance phone calls just before we left a state to hear her voice. On other occasions I slipped out a letter or two or sent presents to Jeannie, just before we changed addresses. I never posted any return nor signed a letter. I was always afraid the mail would be watched or my own family would turn Roy in if they found out where we were.

As the months passed my lies grew smoother and easier, but

119

my mind was never at ease. I now tried to work at only the best coffee shops because my apron pocket grew heavier there. But as my pocket grew heavier, I grew thinner.

Trouble had set in hard and fast. Roy was rapidly becoming an introvert and he seemed to grow more afraid of the outside world. He had too much to think about, too little to do. We could never get money together to go to Mexico as I had planned. Work was hard to find and Roy was afraid to try for it without a social security card.

At first we were hopeful to say the least, at first. But if an idle mind is the devil's workshop, he certainly had a free range and the tools of hatred to work with were in Roy's head. I tried every kind of hobby our finances would afford, but he took little or no interest in any of them.

Once when we were moving to San Francisco, I asked if he didn't think it would be safe for me to return home and try to get my mother to let us have Jean. We had been away for five months now and the ache in my heart for her was almost unbearable. I could not control my tears. Tears always seemed near the surface now.

"Stop crying!" Roy shouted as he sprang from the bed. "I can't stand a blubbering, bawling dame."

He dressed and stalked out of the room slamming the door after him. I was utterly and completely alone.

The next morning I awoke early. I slipped out of bed without disturbing Roy and went downtown to look for work. I was elated over finding work in one of the best restaurants in San Francisco with little trouble. I started at once. The tips were good. By the end of the day I had seven dollars.

When I got back home and entered our room Roy whirled around and asked me where I had been.

"Why, I — I got a job, Roy. I made seven dollars."

He relaxed at the sight of the money and a half-apologetic smile spread over his face as he took it and put it in his pocket. When I realized that he thought I had run away because of our quarrel over our daughter I felt a little sorry for him. I tried to tell myself that he was just afraid, tortured and all mixed up.

His apology seemed sincere. He said he would try to make things more pleasant.

In the days that followed he seemed to be trying. He was usually more cheerful. True he was very moody, but I thought his being alone too much while I was away at work was the cause for this. I urged him to get outside more. Surely the heat was off by now, and he was looking sallow and hollow cheeked.

Sometimes when Roy was in a good mood, he would go out with me. Often we walked through Golden Gate Memorial Park. He loved the Golden Gate and Oakland bridges. We would watch cars crossing the bay on them by the hour. When a fog hung over the harbor, Golden Gate seemed to rise right out of the clouds. Somehow we liked it better when there was fog, for then we couldn't see 'The Rock.' Always our dream ships would carry us out toward Alcatraz, and then they would hit 'The Rock.' Roy wouldn't even look across the bay on a clear day because of this grim reminder.

Often we spent hours in the Golden Gate Art Galleries, browsing through the old masterpieces which were always so realistic and restful, especially the pastoral scenes. Sometimes we would look at the grotesque modern art, much of which gave us nothing but a sense of undefinable blotches of undetermined unrest. When we really sought amusement we would watch the facial expressions of persons leaving the halls where masterpieces were exhibited as they entered the realms of the moderns. Brazen blotches of color would jump at them, or an obese nude distorted with exaggerations or inexplicable nothings caused some surprising facial contortions in the viewers. Some looked puzzled, others would become disgusted or amused, whichever way it seemed to strike them. Others pretended to understand modern art and would remain to discuss the boldness of line, the individuality of expression or its abstraction.

Being a recently graduated art major kindled my interest in such observations. My values were so mixed that I am sure any criticism I could have made would have been of no note, but I finally drew a parallel in my own mind which satisfied my own questioning.

Modern art was like the King's "invisible robe," nothing there!

Roy could not appreciate the modern art either, but when he was in a good mood he really got a bang out of watching

121

other people look at it. But I was worried about Roy. Sometimes he took no interest in anything and at other times everything amused him. He was growing thinner by the day and showed no interest in my plans for the future. He seemed to have no thought of Jean or of security.

Then there was always the money problem. I made pretty good wages, enough to support the two of us in a small room, but Roy was always demanding more money. For a time I thought he might be drinking it up, but I never smelled whiskey on his breath. Then I wondered whether he might be playing the horses, but at least he would win sometimes if that were the case.

I must find some way to jar Roy back to reality. He was living in the past, a tortured world of memories. He talked to himself so much now that I became quite worried about how the other people in the rooming house looked at us.

One day Roy was gone when I got back home. I walked down the hall to the bathroom to bathe and get off my uniform while I tried to decide what to do. The walls were the kind that are anything but soundproof. As I walked toward the bath I heard what sounded like confidential voices behind closed doors. I eased into the bathroom and closed the door, almost. I listened.

"He was raving today like a maniac," I heard what sounded like the agitated voice of the landlady. "I tell you, Mable, I don't blame you for being afraid of him. Of course he's never bothered anybody, but I tell you there's something wrong. Why does he stay holed up in that room all day while his wife works?"

Mable kept trying to get her say in and finally cut in with, "I tell you he just raves about shootings and getting even until it curdles my blood. Do you reckon he has killed someone and is hiding out?"

"I don't know," the landlady answered. "But I can tell you this, when my husband comes home from work tonight, if he doesn't call the cops I'm going to. I'm going to turn him in for disturbing the public peace."

I slithered out of the bathroom. It was growing dusk outside and I knew that both the landlady's husband and Roy might show up any minute. I reached our door and closed it ever so quietly. I started grabbing our scanty wardrobes from the hangers.

"And he's always raving about a prison break," I heard Mable call as an afterthought as the landlady was leaving her room.

"That settles it," the landlady said decisively. "He could be an ex-convict, or even an escaped convict. I'll not wait for my husband to get home. I'll call the cops this very minute and have them waiting when he gets back. It's about time for his wife to get in from work and I don't want her to know what's going on. That's just the thing to do," I heard her say as she clomped down the hallway. "I'll give him a warm reception."

There was very little to pack, and I always kept things ready for flight at a moment's notice. My hand was on the doorknob by the time the landlady reached the bottom of the stairs. I was peeping to make sure that Mable's door was closed when I realized I still had on my cafe uniform. I ripped it off and pulled a dress over my head.

As I tiptoed for the back stairs I could hear the dial clicking from the open door of the living room. I held my breath as I reached the bottom of the stairs and opened the back door. I had used the telephone in the living room several times and knew that if she heard a noise at the back all she would have to do to see me was lean back in her chair and peep into the hallway. I was gone by the time she finished dialing.

I didn't have time to wonder where I was going to find Roy for I ran smack into him as I rounded the corner of the house at full speed. He started to speak but I didn't give him a chance. A packed suitcase and full speed ahead made it unnecessary for him to ask questions.

FLIGHT TO L.A.

I was thankful it was so nearly dark as we rushed down the sidewalk. Perhaps even now the landlady had heard us and was opening the door. What was worse, there might be a cop's car just around the corner that could have been alerted. I hoped she had trouble in getting them to believe at the police station that her call was important. There was a drug store nearby and I wasted no time getting to it and calling a cab. We waited outside in the semidarkness for it to arrive.

123

"The landlady's turned you in to the cops," was about all I had time to whisper. "We'll have to make tracks."

"Hotel Mark," I ordered as we crawled into the cab. I knew there would be other cabs at the hotel waiting, for we couldn't take a cab directly to any destination for fear we would be traced. Roy and I had always planned to go to the "Top of the Mark" for an evening of entertainment if our ship ever came in. At the rate our money had disappeared recently we couldn't afford one such extravagance, however much Roy had dreamed of it during his imprisonment.

I was thinking how pretty the lights would look from the top of the hotel as the cab started up the hill behind the old trolley that always fascinated me. Once we had ventured to the "Top of the Mark," as spectators. The city stretching below us and the bridges spanning the bay were breathtaking. I wondered how it would look tonight?

"Let's grab another cab," I said to Roy as the first one pulled off. We walked a few steps and Roy motioned another cab alongside as the first one turned the corner.

"The Oakland Bus Terminal," I directed the new driver. As we crossed the bridge I drew a slight breath of relief. Getting across a span of water, however short the distance, made me feel further away from our immediate danger. Maybe the landlady hadn't ventured out to our room. Maybe she had told the cops to lay low until Roy arrived. I hoped so.

We hesitated for brief planning before we entered the terminal. "We'd better take the first bus out," Roy said, "regardless of where it's headed."

There was a bus scheduled to leave for Phoenix within the next seven minutes. We looked queerly at one another. Life there had been better than what I had faced recently. We couldn't go too far because of our financial status, but Phoenix was within reach. Maybe if Roy saw Superstition Mountain again it would bring back old memories. When he remembered how dearly we had paid for the freedom he was now squandering . . .

We were at the ticket window. I raised my eyebrow and Roy nodded yes as we bought two tickets to Phoenix one way. As we climbed aboard the bus I was remembering the old Ford Grill, one of the first places I had worked. I was wondering if they would take me back. I didn't think it wise to go back to the same place, but I was remembering Ham the bartender, and Arkey, a waitress who was from Arkansas. They had been real friends and I was so desperately lonely. I was remembering the boss, Peter Marcon, too, and how he sympathized with me when I told him my husband was ill and unable to work. I remember how patient he had been in teaching me the different kinds of Italian foods that were served there.

I had never worked where Italian food and wine were served and sometimes got my orders mixed. I didn't know the difference between a martini and an old fashioned when I started there. The good-natured bartender would point out my cocktails for me in the least conspicuous manner. I could never have made it without Ham.

I thought again of Arkey and Peter and how they had helped me, each trying to hide the fact from the others. Nothing but beer had ever been legal in Texas and I was exceedingly ignorant about intoxicants coming from a family of total abstainers. Once I ordered ravioli from the bartender and muscatel from the cook.

All these things ran through my mind as we again crossed the desert, this time on a bus. I was wondering if Death Valley could be any worse than the part of the desert we went through when I thought of Jesús.

"Maybe we could visit Jesús sometime," I mused aloud, but Roy was asleep. Nothing seemed to bother him any more. He didn't even bother to ask why the landlady turned him in. I was beginning to think that maybe I should do the asking. Why was he taking so many chances recently. I was beginning to think his mind was affected with too much thinking.

What else could make him so moody that I was even afraid to approach the subject. Not that I expected him to go out and get a job and dress me in furs, but I did want him to be interested in what I was doing and help me plan for the future. He seemed to have lost all interest in me and Jean.

Surely when he saw Phoenix and remembered how hard we had struggled for life and this freedom so insecurely won, surely he would straighten up.

I couldn't help but return to the old Ford Grill. I felt a desperate need of friendship. If there had been anyone in the world I could have talked to it would have helped, but I had to bear it alone. Just the sight of old friends made me feel better. I didn't even have to ask for a job. Peter just asked me if I had come back to work and I said "yes" with all my heart.

When I got home that first night from work I found Roy had either hocked or sold our radio I had bought especially to keep him company while I was away. He wouldn't talk about it. Before payday came Roy was waiting for me to get off work. Once he even came into the cafe and asked me for my tips. I was quite alarmed. Maybe they would be looking for Roy out in this part of the country if they made the association in Frisco when the landlady turned him in.

One day I saw the police talking with Peter a little while before time for me to get off work. They hung around the front of the cafe or loitered near the courthouse across the street.

I had a feeling they wanted a look at Roy. Maybe they were suspicious. I held my breath for fear Roy would show up. My boss had been so lenient in dealing with me, but he had told me in no uncertain terms to bring my social security card, or else he would have to hold up my pay.

When I left the place I didn't head for home, for I had a feeling I was being followed. I was always careful to give the wrong address when I went to work any place. I didn't want to do anything that would alert my shadow, if I was being followed, to the fact that I was alarmed.

Wondering what to do, I walked into a grocery store. I bought an armload of the biggest, bulkiest groceries I could find for the least money. This would give me good reason for taking a cab. I called one and gave an address a couple of blocks from home. When the cab was out of sight I chucked my bulky sack and fairly ran. Fortunately Roy was in the room asleep.

"We're going to take our first plane ride," I said as I shook him. "We've always wanted to ride on a plane and I think I was being followed on the way home. I gave them the slip. I don't think they suspected I knew I was being watched. Maybe they'll wait for me to show up to work in the morning.

"I saw plainclothesmen talking with the boss and sneaking looks at me. I know they were dicks because I saw them pull

126

open their coats. There were two of them, but only one followed. I had a feeling the other one was waiting for you to show up."

"Your imagination's sort of getting the best of you here lately, isn't it, Mary? I didn't see any cops the last time we ran. Are you sure you aren't seein' things?"

"I don't know, Roy," I confessed, "but I am sure I was being tailed. Besides the boss acted so funny and looked at me so strangely that I am almost positive they were talking about us in the cafe."

"Couldn't they have been there for a thousand other reasons?" Roy asked nonchalantly.

"I don't know," I replied. "but I do know I can't get paid again. I was lucky to get it today. I had a feeling he wasn't going to let me have it this time until I produced my card. He won't take any more excuses."

"Where to this time?" he asked with a sigh as we began throwing things in the bag.

"Let's make it Los Angeles," I suggested. "We can make it our first plane trip. We will be there in no time."

"Take all our money, won't it?" Roy asked with an alarmed look on his face.

"Yes honey, but you could go to work too. Honestly I don't think they'd think as much of your working as hanging around where I work. We could both work a couple of weeks without cards. Maybe we could save enough to go to Mexico."

"Work!" Roy exploded. "And get caught again? You think I'm crazy? Look honey someday I'll give you the things you deserve. Someday the big breaks will come my way. Don't think I'm not planning for it. I am but it won't be for small change. It'll be in the big 'G's' and you'll be loaded with rocks."

I didn't follow him. Maybe I didn't want to understand. All I knew was that we must get to another place and in a hurry. I had a feeling we were doomed. In a way I was afraid I would find out the truth. I was not the type person to admit defeat but somehow I felt it inevitable.

Chapter 9

The Inevitable

*I*n a new town and with a new job I tried to make myself believe things would be different. I tried to shut my eyes to the truth, but Roy had been in the cafe where I was working that very day, asking for my tips. It was like trying to fight an unknown foe. I couldn't remember my orders and was making a terrible botch of my work. I had tried so hard to ignore all the little signs that pointed in one direction, silently praying that I was wrong, but that night I couldn't duck the evidence any longer because it was right before my eyes.

My strength and courage had left me and I was dog-tired after the long day at the restaurant, so I took a taxi home instead of enduring the hour's trolley ride across Los Angeles. When the cab rolled to a stop in front of our rooming house I looked up to see that the window of our room was dark. That was strange. With a growing sense of uneasiness, I paid the cabbie ran into the house and up the stairs to our room.

I fumbled with the lock for a moment, then stepped into total darkness and felt along the wall for a light switch. At the flick of the switch the room flooded with light and I saw Roy. He was sprawled on the bed fully dressed, his head propped up by two pillows. His eyes were staring ahead with a strange glassy expression, and his lips were parted with a loose grin.

"How ya, Sweetheart," he muttered. "How's everything?"

"Roy, what's the matter with you?"

"Huh? Matter with me? I'm fine, Baby, just fine!"

Running to the bed, I grabbed him by the shoulders and pulled him to a sitting position. The grin never left his face, and his eyes continued to look past me at something only he could see.

My eyes swept the room for some clue and finding none, I ran to the dresser and began to pull out the drawers, one by one. In the bottom drawer underneath Roy's shirts, I found it. There in a little box were half a dozen "decks" of white powder and a hypodermic needle. Now I knew beyond a doubt that Roy's trouble was dope, although I had never seen it before. How could I have been so blind?

Despair washed over me as I swung around to face him. For a moment I felt sick, deathly sick. "Roy . . . Roy . . . Roy . . . ," I moaned. "Why? Why did you have to do this?"

"Because I like it," he said gaily.

Nothing seemed to bother him. He was completely befuddled by dope. I knew now that this wasn't the first time, but he had never been this "high" before.

This explained his moodiness, his restlessness at times and his complete abandon of caution at others. This was my unseen foe, and I had been a fool not to recognize any of the symptoms. But how can you recognize a thing you have never seen before?

"But how . . . where did you get the dope?"

"I got connections, Baby. I know a few boys here in town. Five years in prison is a lot of schooling. I could make connections in any big town in America. You learn a lot in prison, Baby."

So this was what he had been doing while I was at work. I felt sure he must have been on it some while we were in Phoenix, but it was worse now. When had it started? Where? How long had he been hiding it from me? What a cruel and senseless waste of man! What a bitter end for my dreams!

"I never knew," I sobbed, "I never knew you took dope. When did you start? Where?"

"Remember when I used to work in the prison hospital, Baby, when I had the good job in the walls? You'd be surprised how much this stuff can make you forget. Lifts you right out of this world. That was the only way I had of getting out of prison while I was in."

"Oh, Roy," I moaned, "how can a man do such a thing to forget his misery."

"It's easy, Baby, it's easy."

"But when you broke out of prison," I insisted, "you seemed all right then. You were more like the sweetheart I used to know. Surely you couldn't have been taking it then? You couldn't have while you were in the desert!"

"Yeah, that's it, Baby, I was broke of the habit, and I can do it now, anytime I want to."

I wondered about that, but now that his talk was making sense I had to push to get what information I could while he was still in a talkative mood.

"But how did you get it, while you were in prison I mean?"

"Some of the boys in prison used to have it smuggled in, I'd sniff it from time to time. Makes you feel real good. Then when I landed that hospital job, I didn't have much trouble. Even made a little money on the side."

"But you said you were broken of the habit," I insisted. "How?"

"Remember when I got ranked, Baby, ranked and sent to the farm? That was when Clyde Barrow made his break. Bonnie was waiting for him at the time, Baby, just like you were waiting for me."

I shuddered at the comparison. How well I remembered their ruthless flight, the bloodshed and coldblooded murder.

"She wrote poetry, Baby, like you except not so good. Remember, they even found a poem on her when she and Clyde were ambushed. How many hundred bullet holes did they say they found in that car?"

"Please, darling," I cried in desperation, "how did they break you of the habit?"

"Clyde wasn't so bad," he continued, determined to tell the story his way. "I was in the same cell block with him for a long time. He wasn't so bad, just a little tough. It's the cops and guards that make people bad. Bonnie might not have been any worse that you, she just loved her man."

"Stop!" I cried. "I don't want to hear any more. I'm not like Bonnie and you're not like Clyde."

"That's just what I am trying to tell you Baby. People are

130

never bad until the world starts to pushing them around. They aren't even desperate until they are cornered like animals."

I couldn't stand any more. I got up from the bed where I had been sitting and started to leave the room.

"Hold on, Baby," he called. "You asked for it and now you're going to get it. Pull up a chair and make yourself comfortable."

I sank into the only chair exhausted. There wasn't any use trying to fight his talking spell and I knew it. If I left he would probably talk loudly enough for other people staying in the house to hear. This must be what happened before while I was working. He must have had so much he was talking to himself.

"I'm right by you, Roy, and you don't have to talk so the neighbors can hear."

"Like I was telling you, Baby," he continued in a somewhat modified tone. "I've been broke of the habit and I could quit it myself just like that," he said with a snap of his fingers. "I'm not an addict."

"But how?" I tried again.

"I never will forget that day Clyde broke out of prison. I was working in the prison hospital then. Whitey was in the death cell. Whitey and Clyde were buddies. I could have been in on that break myself, but you remember how close I was to getting a parole then. I felt sorry for Whitey. He was going to burn. There ain't nothin' that hurts so much as a guy gettin' burned. The lights flicker and then get dim as they throw on the current . . ."

"Please don't," I cried.

"But you wanted to hear how I got broke, Baby. I'm telling you. Whitey's hand was shot up in his last bank robbery, that's why I had been dressing it, that's why I got to him. I was the hospital attendant. That's why I had you send me ten bucks a month, to keep a good job," he added.

I was silent and he continued.

"I had been dressing Whitey's hand for a long time. Then Clyde told me about the break and told me he had a pistol he wanted bandaged in Whitey's hand. He even told me where they had buried the loot from their last bank robbery. I could have been one of their gang, but you had been working for my parole so long I hated to muff it."

I squirmed restlessly in my uncomfortable chair.

131

"There ain't much to it," he said. "You read in the papers how Whitey was shot from the wall just as he got to the top. It was a tough break but if they had all been killed I was to go dig up the loot when I got out on the legit. Pretty good set-up, huh Baby. If Clyde hadn't left that place alive we could have dug up sixty grand for me wrapping that bandage. If he did come out alive he was going to stake us when I did get out. How could I lose? I could have gone to medical school."

"Except for the fact that Clyde was killed after he dug up the loot. The bills were marked and part of them were found in the car."

"Yeah I know, but what if Whitey hadn't been shot off that wall? We had it made. I couldn't stand to see a guy burn. You know that would have been something him escaping."

"Is that why you lost your good prison job?" I asked. "They kept telling me how well you were doing. You were filling prescriptions and everything. Remember when you told me about the math professor who visited you from Sam Houston State College? You had worked out a remarkable formula for breaking dope addicts whereby you didn't have to mix every shot separately. Is that how you mean? You mixed it with water didn't you, a little more and a little more water each time? Didn't they find your formula mathematically perfect?"

"Yeah," Roy grinned. "At first they thought I was going to kill some of those dopies, but I got a way of working out formulas."

He laughed until I had to shush him up.

"They took away all my overtime when they found that pistol bandaged in Whitey's hand. That's why I had to break out. I couldn't stand it on the farm. I had a soft job and they threw me out to chop cotton right when the sun was getting hottest. That's when I got sick. I would have died. They cut off my snow and I felt sure I was going to die. That's when I saw the big black widow spider on the cotton leaf just before I passed out. I knew what they did to guys who fell out. They put the whip to them and told them to die and prove it. They said I still had that black widow in my hand when I got to the hospital. I had to coax her to bite. That's where I got my name, Spider King. That's what they called me after that."

132

He rambled on with his story as I tried to think of other things.

"It was nice in the hospital, while the others were in the fields, but I got out too soon. I wasn't ready for those hot fields so I ate a little cotton soaked in soap. That gives you a high fever for a while, but it doesn't keep you in the hospital long. A lot of guys were mutilating. I could have severed my heel string or chopped off a few toes, but I wanted to break. Clyde Barrow chopped off two of his toes once. That's how he got back into the walls."

I couldn't stand any more about Barrow so I got up from my chair indicating I had had enough.

"You're right, Baby," he concluded. "I didn't have any snow while we were in the desert. I'd been broke for over two months. Down there you have to die to prove it. I'm not an addict."

I looked at him lying there drugged, and I knew what an empty boast that was. He was caught, he was addicted, he could never lay off without the worst sort of agony. But maybe . . . maybe with my help! Even in my deepest despair I wanted to believe there was still hope for Roy, hope for us.

At what stage does one give up marriage? When does one stop loving, stop hoping? I suppose it depends upon the woman, but for my part I couldn't stop loving Roy, not even then.

The next day after the dope had worn off, Roy and I had a long talk. He cried in my arms and promised he'd never touch the stuff again. He made such wonderful promises. But as the days passed my heart began to shrink within me. Roy didn't change a bit. In fact now that I shared his secret, he seemed to get worse. I lost several jobs because he'd hang around the kitchen door to take my tips as fast as I made them. The one night when I came home from work he grabbed me and tried to shove the needle into my arm so I'd feel the way he did.

"I'LL QUIT — I PROMISE"

"I'm leaving you, Roy," I said the next day after the dope had worn off. "It's been bad enough with you taking the stuff, but trying to shove it into my arm, that's different."

133

Roy's mouth fell open in disbelief. "Honestly Mary, I didn't do it? Did I?"

"Just as sure as you're alive. You won't quit it and I'll have nothing to do with it. I'm sick and tired. Six months I've tried to make a man of you. What's happened to you, Roy? How can a man with your nerve give in to a habit? You fought the whole world for this freedom, now you're trying to throw it away. Well you can throw it away by yourself. I'm going home to Jeannie."

"Oh, no, Baby. You can't leave me! I can't live without you. I couldn't get snow. They'd pick me up. I'd burn for murder."

"Then you'll have to burn. I'm through I tell you. I'm tired of paying for dope with sweat and blood. You're not the man I married! He was sweet and good and tender. You're a demon of hell fired with poisonous venom. You're not fit to be the father of your own child."

Sobs were racking his body as he pleaded, "I'll quit, Darling, I'll quit. I'll do anything if you just won't leave me. I'll never take another jolt."

"That's getting to be a broken record, isn't it?"

"Here's all I got, honest. I won't ever touch it. I'll lay it here on the dresser and it'll be here when you come home from work. I've got nothing to live for without you. We'll get Roy Jean just as soon as I get straightened out. Will you forgive me if I prove to you I can? I know I'm an addict. I'm not fooling myself, but I'll quit or die trying."

I wondered if he could lay off it just one day. He had been taking two or more jolts every day recently. It was time for me to go to work. I felt like I should just keep going, but I couldn't help but wonder if he could leave the deck on the dresser for eight hours while I was gone. One day more wouldn't matter and I needed it for my fare home. I was almost happy in my own heart during the day. I was giving him one more opportunity and I knew he couldn't resist. I felt I was going the extra mile. Tomorrow I would be on my way to Jean.

The room was dark when I returned. I was remembering what had happened once before when I had entered and switched on the light. I hesitated with my hand on the knob, then I heard him. Heard him moan and then heard something thudding against the wall.

134

What I had seen before when I switched on the light was nothing compared with the writhing mass I now saw on the bed. He didn't even realize the light had been turned on. He was deathly white. Blood oozed from his skin in a dozen places where he had dug his flesh with his fingernails. All this was glossed with sweat. Every muscle in his body seemed in torment. He rolled on his stomach and gripped the head of the bed until his knuckles were white, then he shook it like an animal in a cage.

I ran to him crying, "Roy! Roy!"

The deck lay on the dresser, untouched. "Roy," I cried, pulling him over, "can you hear me?" He looked at me with glassy eyes that saw nothing as he cried out in pain. I threw my arms around him and his fingers dug into my flesh, bringing blood.

"You've got to do something," I cried, jumping from the bed. "I'll get a doctor."

"The doctor's on the dresser," he moaned, "but I'll die before I'll touch it. You can't leave me. I'll die!"

I had never known there could be torment like this before. I watched in horror as he shook and writhed and then lay still and exhausted, only to repeat the performance a few minutes later. Once he was still so long I was afraid he would die. His eyes stared without seeing and his mouth hung half open. He was pale as death and I was wondering if he was still breathing when he went into another spasm. I couldn't stand any more.

"Roy, Roy darling can you hear me? I won't leave you I promise I won't I've never lied to you Roy. Take it. You've got to have it. I'll stay with you, Roy. We'll break it off slow, like you broke the dopies in prison,"

He reached for it like a dying man. I fell on the bed he left and hid my face in the wet pillow. I couldn't see him take it. We couldn't talk. I had built my own little dream world and it had toppled.

When he had finished I changed the sheets on the bed and bathed his wounds. He looked at me like a sick dog one had befriended. He didn't get wild nor talkative. I said he must have food and went to prepare it. Before I returned he was asleep. I lay beside him far into the night . . . thinking . . . thinking . . . thinking.

The next morning we had a good talk. We made plans. All the long summer and fall we had looked at and longed for the beautiful mountains which lay just out of our reach. Now that the tourist trade was over I had been watching advertisements in the papers. Cabins could be rented for almost half price. Maybe we could. Although it was early December, mineral baths were still being advertised in the Box Mountains near Los Angeles. Maybe it would even snow. I could count the snowfalls I had seen in my lifetime on my fingers. "Oh, if we only could."

"If we only could what?" Roy asked with real tenderness.

"If we could only get a lonely little cabin in the mountains by one of those mineral springs," I said. "Why, you could take hot baths in a walled off part of a pool and fish for Rainbows in the clear, cold water downstream. That's what the paper says. Some of them are only an hour's drive from downtown Los Angeles."

"Yeah, that would be heaven," Roy answered, "but how could we get the money. Waitresses don't make that kind of money. Maybe I could go to work."

My heart leaped with joy at the very thought of his mentioning work. "No, darling, no. You have your part to do. First you must help yourself. After that I intend for you to take care of your daughter and me. How does that sound, honey? I worked nights and went to school four years while you were in prison. Why couldn't I do it a few days now? I could get a job in a night spot. I know my drinks now," I said, thinking of the short time ago when I had ordered a martini from the kitchen and ravioli from the bar. "My family never drank, not even at Christmas, and nothing but beer was ever legal in Texas, so I was really as dumb as they come."

"But how? How could I help?" Roy asked with enthusiasm.

"Yours would be the hardest part," I continued. "We can do it if you cut yourself off dope entirely. Do you think you could work out a little formula for yourself like you did for the dopies in Huntsville and cut yourself off in ten days? If you could I believe I could scrape up enough money for a week in Box Mountains. Would a week without dope make you sure of yourself again? Could you do it? I'd be with you every minute."

"Sure I can do it," he assured me. "It won't be easy but having you with me all the time when I have to do without it, I could make it. My formula will be easy to work out with ten for a denominator. Ten more days and I'll never take another jolt. But how do you think you can manage the trip?"

"I'll keep working days, and I'll get a night job. I've never worked in a night club but it won't be for long. Just ten days and then my husband can start taking care of me."

It was with real hope and enthusiasm that I set out to find work in a night spot. I was really scared at first, but I caught the hang of it before the first night was finished.

Roy bought five decks of snow which he had all figured out so he could cut himself down to nothing in ten days. He stuck by his guns and I could tell he was doing his part. On the third day after we made our little pact I put down a $10 deposit to get the cabin reserved, the rest to be paid in advance when the wonderful day came for us to take possession of a little corner of heaven for a week. I was already picturing fresh, crisp vegetables cached in a crystal, cold stream flowing back of the cabin and rainbow trout freshly caught. How wonderful and extraordinary to bathe in a hot spa bubbling from the heart of the earth, and then becoming a part of the cold stream. The spring was walled off from the rest of the stream, the advertising agent had told me. It was nature's own bathtub with miraculous curative powers. I could close my eyes and vision the hot spring cleansing Roy's pores of the last vestige of dope. He would feel so good and clean he would never want to touch the horrible stuff again.

I never worked so hard, and by the time seven days of working day and night were past, I felt like I could use a little rest at the cabin myself. Every day we were living on one of my salaries and putting away what I made at night. I was trusting Roy with the money and our pot grew. It was easier now that it didn't go for dope.

Eight days passed and I was jubilant. Roy was sticking to his part of the bargain. I had wanted to surprise him with a fly rod or an automatic reel, but it looked as if I wouldn't be able to make it. It would be the most wonderful surprise in the world, but many fish are caught without fancy equipment.

One day to go finally, and then came the tenth day. I was so nervous and high strung that I couldn't be still a minute. If I could just make enough for the rod and reel, but chances looked slim. I hadn't made too much during the day and I was never sure what I would make at night. I had to keep doing something. I had to keep moving.

While I was filling the sugar bowls during the slack time in the cafe, I spilled some sugar down in back of one of the leatherette cushions of a booth. I tried to wipe it out but it was too deep in the crack for my cloth to reach. I removed the cushion and found it badly in need of cleaning where it fitted against the back rest. Then I decided I would clean all the cushions on my station while I wasn't busy. Then it happened. I found, beneath one of the cushions, a $20 bill. That was a fortune to me at the time. It meant I could buy the rod and reel I wanted so badly for Roy. I know I should have turned it in, but it may have been lying there for weeks and I felt sure no one would ever know to whom it belonged. My desire for the rod and reel won out so I stuck it into my pocket.

I hadn't been going home between jobs because I didn't have time to make it on the street cars and I couldn't afford taxi fares, so I had just been eating luxuriously in order to catch a few moments of rest before catching a car for my evening job.

This afternoon I didn't stop to eat. I dashed out of the cafe the minute my time was up to get that wonderful rod and reel to make our stay in the mountains complete. I just couldn't keep the secret. If I hurried I could buy it and catch a taxi home and show Roy. This would make the last night much easier, because this was the night he was to do without dope. Just the thought of it made me nervous. I had to surprise him. I had to help. What a wonderful thrill I had for him. This would be his Christmas in advance. I could just see him trying to practice with it in that small room while I spent my last night at work. Maybe I would be lucky my last night too.

I told the taxi to wait for I hardly had time to make it from one job to the other, but I had to surprise Roy. I hit the door with a joyous cry of "Surprise! Surprise!" But it was I who received the surprise.

How quickly can one's heart fall from the peak of expectancy to the darkest depths of doom. One look at Roy's glossy eyes and that half crooked grin did it for me. I had flown from the taxi to the house but my feet were like lead as I dragged back to dismiss the cab driver.

Roy didn't even know I was in the room. He kept saying over and over, "I'll die without it! I'll die without it!"

I ran to where I kept our savings hid for the week at the cabin. He had bought more than one deck, but a major portion of the money was left. I opened his suitcase which was already packed. I couldn't find anything suspicious.

"She'll never know I have it. She won't be home before two in the morning," he continued. "I won't take any of the deck I got hid, but I got to have it along, so far away from everything in a cabin for a week."

So near and yet so far, my heart cried out. I knew if he had it hid in his things there was nothing I could do. My defeat was final. Somehow I had known it all along but I couldn't make myself give it up. I couldn't stop loving the father of my *own child*.

Suddenly I was crying. My own child needed me too of this I was sure. Tears streamed down my face and splattered to the floor as I sat the prized rod and reel in the corner.

I went to my suitcase which was partially packed. It all seemed so much like a dream which I knew was too good to come true, but it made such a bright spot in a drab life that I couldn't turn it loose. I knew what I must do. I was in no condition to work that night and I no longer had the heart for it. There was enough money left for my ticket home. Sobs shook my thin tired frame and I seemed very cold. The face I saw in the mirror when I tried to apply a little make up looked old, very old for a young mother.

I would leave enough money for Roy to eat on a day or two. I wondered what he would do with the rod and reel. Like the few other nice things I had been able to buy him, it too would be hocked for dope. Somehow the thought didn't bother me. I had gone the last mile. All dreams were dead. There was no future. Roy slept, or had passed out.

Chapter 10

Together We Die

*M*y heart was numb as I packed my suitcase, just as I had done so often before. But this time it was final. This was the last trip. The last bond was broken.

I dared not think what would become of Roy. There was nothing to say in a note. When he came to he would see the rod and reel and the receipt for holding the cabin for us. Dope meant more than these. When he came to it would probably be time for us to be on our way to heaven in the mountains, but I wouldn't be there.

If it hadn't been for the ache in my heart for Christmas with Jeannie I don't think I could have stood leaving him so hopeless, but staying would be throwing my life away with my eyes open. Six years now I had devoted to a lost cause. It wasn't so bad as long as there was hope. I was completely defeated but I had to face my family to see my daughter. I felt I couldn't go on living without her.

I tiptoed from the room, leaving Roy just as he lay. At the bus station I bought a ticket for my hometown and found there would be two layovers on the way, three hours in El Paso and one hour in Abilene.

Abilene! How different things might have been if I had stayed there. I had my college degree and could have been teaching school. Jean would have been with me if I had only had sense enough not to try the impossible.

But all this was over now. I must put it out of mind and start a new life with Jeannie. I had plenty of time for thinking things over while en route.

Finally two day later, the bus pulled into Abilene. It was during the early morning hours, but I couldn't resist taking a walk during my layover past the *Reporter-News,* where I used to work.

"Where do you think you're going, sister?" a rough voice asked. My scream was choked off. I was trapped, terrified. Then I looked up . . . into the bloodshot eyes of Roy King! My lips fell open with amazement. Roy, here? How could he have found me? He must have wakened to find me gone, guessed where I would head and somehow beaten me here. How could he dare do such a thing? It was the worst thing he could do. After working all night in the town for four years the first cop who saw me would probably sound the alarm.

"Left me!" he hissed. "So you left me! Well it isn't as easy as that. Don't you know that when the cops pick you up they'll try to pin every unsolved robbery and murder on you? You gonna tell them you tagged along with me to try to make a Boy Scout out of me? They'll give you a medal for that!"

He turned me around and marched me ahead of him through the streets to the edge of town. We came to a tourist court. Keeping the gun on me from his coat pocket, Roy rented the last cabin in the row. Once inside he locked the door, tilted a chair against it and sat down.

"Make yourself comfortable, Baby," he said. "We're gonna be here for awhile. We got lots to talk over."

I walked over to the bed and sat on it, not caring much what happened. Roy began to talk in a rambling manner about the prison, about his childhood, about anything that crossed his mind, but mostly about his plans for the future.

"I got big things in mind, Baby. I got plans to bust that prison wide open and set my buddies free. Then I'll have a gang that nothing can stop. We'll be riding on top of the world . . . you and me."

Delusions of grandeur I thought. I wondered if taking dope did that to the brain.

141

"I know I've never done much for you," he was saying, "but from now on it'll be different because we're going to live my way. A couple of good jobs and we're on easy street. There's no turning back for us, Baby. Our names are on the same marker. We go out and make history together or we die here together." He pulled the gun from his pocket and aimed it straight at my heart. "Make up your mind."

I thought of Jean and of what Roy had just said. Maybe he was right. I had nothing to look forward to but a prison sentence. Maybe our names were on the same marker and there was no turning back . . . only death. Could death be so bad?

But face to face with death, I was desperately frightened. My sins seemed so small for so great a retaliation . . . all committed to help the man I thought the world had wronged.

Six years I had wasted for a lost cause. Now it was to cost me my life. Strange but now that I was to pay in full it was difficult for me to see what I had set out to accomplish. My intentions were good and my purpose had looked noble in my own eyes, but how could I have been snared in such a web? My strength was sapped. I no longer felt a desire to fight. My former weight, one twenty-six, had dwindled to ninety-seven. I was a skeleton with just nerves hanging on. I cried without provocation and uttered a mute scream at the slightest sound.

Yes, I was sure my child would be better off without a mother than with one in the pen or crazy house. Perhaps her memories would be pleasant if she never saw me again. Certainly I had no intention of bringing more suffering into the world, more crime and bloodshed. No one but an inexperienced fool dreams of glamour in connection with crime. What did it matter which way I died? If I could only embrace my daughter once more. She was mine but I was the one who had made the choice, I was the one who must pay.

"I'm ready," I whispered, looking long and hard at Roy. "Go ahead and pull the trigger if you want to. I don't care."

I closed my eyes and braced myself for the bullet as he leveled the pistol at my head. If it would only be over quickly. "Please, God," I prayed. "Make it quick."

Four seconds, five, six . . . then a long sob filled the room.

"I can't do it," Roy said brokenly. "My aim's not very steady. You do the honors. I'll go first."

I hid my face in the pillow. After a long silence I opened my eyes to see Roy fumble in his pocket and bring out a hypodermic needle. He prepared himself a shot. The needle sank into the tender flesh, then slowly he pushed the plunger. In a matter of minutes his face began to relax.

"A little shot of this won't hurt you any," he remarked. "Makes it a lot easier."

"It's robbed me of every dream I lived for," I bitterly remarked. "I don't see why I should embrace it in death. I'll die hating it."

"But you won't look very pretty," he remarked as I burst into a new flow of tears. "Go wash your face and put on some make-up. You wouldn't think I was doing you a favor. Comb your hair real pretty and spread it out on the pillow."

How could he carry on such banter in the face of death? Dazedly I followed his instructions, knowing morphine would give him courage to finish the job where he had faltered a few minutes before.

Dope is the very soul of the devil, I was thinking as I applied a little lipstick. Not being able to find my comb, I pulled open the dresser drawer through habit I suppose. There lay a Bible. I picked it up and fumbled it curiously. "Gideons" was stamped on it.

I heard Roy laughing. The dope had taken effect and he was laughing at the irony of the situation. The joke seemed too good to end abruptly.

"It won't hurt you none," he was laughing. "Read it!"

I hesitated, but could think of nothing to say.

"Read it. It won't hurt you none," he repeated. "Maybe it will carry you to heaven in a chariot of fire. This is your last chance kid. Better catch up on your readin'. Read all you want. I can wait. Our rent's paid up for a week. You're not going any place. You're going to die. Death's pretty permanent they tell me. You still got time to change your mind."

Mentally I recalled some of the passages I knew as a child. Once when I had dreamed of becoming a foreign missionary, I was very familiar with its passages. How well I knew the laws of God and the Ten Commandments, many of which I had broken.

I thought of the First Commandment, "Thou shalt have no other Gods before Me."

I had forgotten God. In my struggle I had depended upon love as an indestructable force. I had wanted to do right, but with my own motivation, which stemmed from the love of a man, not God. I had wanted to prove to the world that it had made a big mistake, that the man I loved was not a criminal.

Roy seemed engrossed in his own thoughts so I climbed back into bed with the Bible. I had little desire to read. How well I knew the old passage, "As a man soweth, so shall he also reap." Yes, I had sown destruction. Now I was faced with the harvest of my errors. I laid the Bible aside.

"Go on and read," Roy was saying. "It's your last chance. Better be sure you're finished."

I don't know why but I picked up the Bible and opened it to the New Testament as he again leveled the gun at my head. I came to that verse in the eleventh chaper of Matthew: "Give not that which is holy unto the dogs, neither cast your pearls before swine, lest they trample them under their feet, and turn again and rend you."

As I dropped the Bible beside me on the bed it fell open and my eyes were drawn to a strange passage:

"Fear not them which kill the body, but are not able to kill the soul; but rather fear him which is able to destroy both soul and body in hell." (Matthew 10:28)

"I'd like to think it over a little longer," I said as Roy again lowered the pistol.

"I thought you would see it my way," he gloated. "It's not easy to say no in the face of a gun. Take all the time you want. Think it over good. I learned a lot in prison, Baby. I'd rather see you wearin' rocks than have them shoveled into your face, six foot under."

In celebration of his supposedly gained victory, Roy again fumbled for the needle. I looked toward the windows. Light filtered around the edges of the drawn blinds. Our vigil with death had lasted all night.

"Whatsoever you ask in prayer," I was reading. Then I began praying, praying like I had never prayed before. Praying for a chance to be a real Christian mother to the little girl who needed me. Praying for a chance to build upon a rock.

I don't know how long I prayed for forgiveness and a chance to live for my daughter, but when I looked at Roy his eyes were glazed and unseeing. Then the gun slipped from his fingers and landed on the floor with a metallic thud. Roy seemed beyond hearing.

The chair which Roy had tilted against the door teetered on one leg for an instant as his body slumped, then toppled over carrying Roy with it. This never fazed him. He lay sprawled on the floor limp. Removing the key from his pocket, I opened the door and ran into the budding light of day.

ONE DAY IN HEAVEN, ALMOST

I was running . . . running . . . running. Now I was not only running from the law, I was running from Roy too. The law and the lawless. I was not sure which I feared more. If the law caught me, I would be held for harboring a fugitive, tried for my part in the prison break. But if Roy found me, he might kill me, no questions asked. He was a desperate man, a sick man . . . I knew that.

There are only two sides. I belonged to neither. I knew Roy couldn't live without me. Turning him in to the law would have been the last thing I would have thought of then, but now I can see it would have been doing him a great favor, saved him time, prison time. But how could I have turned to the law to protect my own life, even if I had wanted to?

My run slowed to a walk. People were appearing on the street . . . going to work. Inadvertently, I walked to the little park across the street from where I lived when Roy escaped from prison. I had to think. I sank on a bench.

Oh, how I ached to get back to my daughter. It had been an eternity since I had heard her voice and felt her arms around my neck. But could I go? Roy might follow.

Crisp on the morning air, church bells chimed. "Joy to the World, the Lord is Come." A Christmas carol I loved. But there was no joy within me.

145

Christmas! Would my darling have to spend it without her mother? I thought of her fifth birthday, the one I spent on the desert thinking I would never see her again. There had been no present, no word from me.

How long could a child love a mother, one so young as she, when that mother had disappeared from the face of the earth? Perhaps she had forgotten me already. Maybe my mother had tried to let her forget me. There was nothing her little heart could understand about my life.

The ache, the longing, the yearning were unbearable. I knew that going to see her was the wrong thing to do, but nothing short of death could stop me now. There was nothing in the world except my longing for her.

Tears streamed down my face as I got up from the little bench and walked down the familiar street toward the bus station. What if someone who knew me saw me now? What if Roy came to quicker that I thought. It was a chance I would have to take.

I called the bus station. I was lucky. In only a few minutes I could catch one for home and my darling . . . but I didn't dare just go in the station and wait. I window shopped . . . for a Christmas present for Jeannie. I hesitated in front of a bookstore window, thinking how she had always loved poetry. I went in and found a wonderful book of illustrated poems. There were some of her favorites in it so I bought it. I would have given her the whole world if I could have bought it with my heart, but the few cents I had left were slightly inadequate as a down payment.

I saw no sign of Roy when I ventured back to the bus station. He would probably be knocked out for hours I hoped, as I climbed aboard. I thumbed through the little book in my hands, but my mind was reading only the past . . . the last time I had heard my daughter's voice.

"Mommie, Mommie, I have a new doll. When are you coming home, huh? Can I have a birthday party, please Mommie?"

When at last I was in my own home town again, my heart pounded messages like a jungle drum. Outside my parent's house it seemed to stop. I was afraid to go in.

Then I saw Jeannie through the window putting tinsel on the tree. Looking out the window suddenly, she saw me. She screamed, "Mommie! Mommie! Mommie!" and raced for the door.

She looked like a Christmas angel as she flew toward me with outstretched arms, her long golden curls streaming behind her.

I crushed her to me and she kept crying, "Mommie . . . Mommie."

Then she broke from me suddenly and raced for the kitchen. "Grandma! Grandma! I told you my Mommie would come for Christmas."

My mother walked into the hall with a plate of goodies in her hand. At sight of me she dropped the plate. "Oh, for the faith of a child," she breathed.

I whispered, "Mother, maybe I shouldn't be here . . . but I had to come . . ."

Mother went on as if she hadn't heard me. "When I thought you were dead, Jean kept saying over and over you'd be sure to come for Christmas because you missed her birthday party. We wouldn't believe her and tried to discourage her in the thought."

My father came in then. "I've left Roy for good," I said simply, answering his silent question. "Once he had the makings of a good man in him, but prison ruined him. He's not the same man I married."

"Get some food on the table, Mama," was my father's only reply.

I must have looked pretty shabby, as well as hungry, for my mother replied, "The clothes you left are still in your closet. I'll have food on the table by the time you get bathed and changed. Looks like the kind of life you chose wasn't so glamorous after all. I've always told you . . ."

"Let's not talk about it Mama, let's just be thankful she's home alive. There's only one thing I want to know," Father said as he turned to me. "Where's Roy? Will he follow you and cause trouble?"

How could I tell him? What if I told my family Roy was only fifty miles away and on my trail? Why should I ruin Christmas? I had so dreamed of this day of happiness. Surely he would be afraid to come to my father's home. Why should the police be looking for us . . . any more than they had been since our trail grew cold, unless . . . ?

"I've left him for good," was my truthful reply. "I hope I never see him again."

"I want to take a bath with my mommie," Jean cut in. "I want to get dressed pretty for Santa too. Did you know Santa is coming tomorrow, Mommie, did you?"

"Yes, Darling, yes," were the only words I could manage. Lifting her from the floor drained every ounce of strength from me.

"Santa is coming tomorrow, Santa is coming tomorrow . . ." she chimed over and over as I drew our bath. Somehow in my muddled brain it always came out, "Roy is coming tomorrow, Roy is coming tomorrow."

It was time for the evening meal before our baths were finished. I was reluctant in giving up our private session, for I had had only half my fill of kisses.

When the evening meal was finished my father turned on the radio as the women folk headed for the dishpan. Christmas carols peeled from the living room, "Peace on Earth, Good Will toward Men."

This is what home should be, I thought as Jean pulled up a stool to stand on and told me she was her grandmother's little helper when it came to drying dishes.

"We interrupt this program to bring a flash from the news room," a voice burst suddenly. "A laughing bandit has just held up a filling station on Sycamore Street in Abilene. An undetermined amount of cash has been taken. Stay tuned for details."

I know I must have turned pale, but mother didn't seem to catch the announcement.

"A laughing bandit," the flash had said, and in Abilene. That one adjective, "laughing," struck fear into my heart. Roy had always laughed and joked when he had robbed, even the first time.

"In Abilene." Those words, too, struck home. He had had time enough to come out from under the influence of the heroin and probably needed more . . . or was he getting money to come after me?

Jean had finished drying the dishes and was again in the living room, dreaming around the Christmas tree. Father had turned off the radio but something in his face told me he knew.

"Didn't we used to have the tree on Christmas Eve?" I asked. I wasn't sure whether I was speaking for myself or Jeannie. The

148

childish yearning in her eyes was a factor I'm sure, yet my fear of tomorrow was overpowering.

"Yes," Mother answered, "but I thought we'd wait until the other children come in tomorrow with the rest of the grandchildren. I love to watch them open the presents."

"Please Grandmother, couldn't I just open one little package tonight?" Jeannie begged.

"Well, maybe," Grandmother hesitated.

"Oh, goody," Jean cried for joy, for she knew her grandmother's weakness. "I did want to open the big one Santa brought me most of all, but now I want to open the one from my very own mother."

With squeals of delight she extracted the Nursery Rhymes from the wrapping. "Oh, goody, goody. Read to me, Mommie, read to me."

"But we haven't had a chance to talk," my mother admonished. "I spend half my time reading to you. Couldn't you let it go until tomorrow? I want to talk with your mother."

"Let's sing," my father suggested in an effort to change the subject. "Come to the organ, Mother. This is Christmas Eve."

The organ had always meant so much to my daddy. He wasn't willing to see it go when pianos became the fad. He liked the organ so much more. Since I was Jean's age I remembered the family gathering around the organ at night. Sometimes we put on little programs.

We sang all the Christmas carols we knew. Daddy told us a story about the first Christmas tree he ever cut, when he was very young. Mother didn't feel like reciting poetry, so her granddaughter filled in with "The Night Before Christmas."

"Surely Grandpa's gal rates another package for that performance," my father urged. "The one Santa brought for her."

A white, cuddly teddy bear brought stars to her eyes.

"Could I sleep with it?" she begged as Father reached for the Bible.

After the scripture I retired with Jean to her room. She begged me to read from her new book, which I did until she drowsed, with teddy bear cradled in her arms.

As I lay staring into the night I heard my father turn on the radio for the ten o'clock newscast. This was his custom. I was glad Jean was asleep as I strained to hear.

149

Panic gripped my heart as I heard them start off on a story about "The laughing bandit strikes again. Must be stocking up for a Merry Christmas," the commentator ad-libbed. "A good description of the bandit is now available, since both victims got a good look at the hold-up man. The bandit is described as fairly short, about twenty-five or twenty-six years of age, blond wavy hair and a perpetual grin. Fingerprints have been sent to Austin. Local authorities now have a lead. Witnesses say pictures shown them of an escaped convict, Roy King, matched the . . ."

I heard father curse as he turned off the radio. He rarely used profanity.

Stark terror struck my heart. Jeannie slept. I had to talk with father. Pulling on my clothes I re-entered the living room to face him.

"Looks like this will be his next stop," father commented. "I'll kill him if he comes here, so help me."

"That's a job for the police," Mother cried hysterically as she burst in, pulling a robe about her nightgown without bothering to put her arms in the sleeves. "They'll watch the house. We'll be disgraced again, and on Christmas."

"And if they find out you're home, daughter, they'll come for you," Father commented. "There's a law against harboring criminals."

"He might try to kill us, or take Mary and Jean as hostages," Mother wailed in horror.

"Now, Mama," Daddy cut in, "there's enough to face without that. We can get police protection for Jean if we have to, but we've got to get Mary out of here until this blows over. Get packed!" he commanded.

While mother cried I threw a few of the dresses left in my closet into a much battered hand bag. Jeannie slept, peacefully. A smile tugged at the corner of her lips. Would I ever see her again? Would I ever possess my own baby? I had to steal just one kiss . . . one kiss to last an eternity.

"Now the police don't know for sure," I heard Father reassure Mother. "They won't know until the fingerprints have been checked. No one should bother tonight. I won't be gone long, but I think I should drive Mary to Ranger. She can catch the *Sunshine Special* out. They would notice her here . . . might even

150

try to hold her. I never thought I would work against the law," I heard him break into a dry sob, "but my own daughter . . ."

Mother was white with fear. "What if he comes tonight," she moaned, "while I'm alone with Jean."

"Call the police, and use this," Father admonished as he strode to the closet and dug out the twelve-guage. "You know how."

I saw mother head for Jean's room with the shotgun as I heard my father start the motor of the old family car.

For a man who would never lie nor misrepresent anything, my father was making the supreme sacrifice.

"Now you stay away until he's dead or back in prison," my father advised as he handed me what money he had. "Stay on the train as long as you can, at least to Texarkana. God bless you and take care of you," he added in a broken voice.

The world went numb again as the train pulled away from the station, leaving all I loved behind in disgrace and sorrow. I hid my face and pretended to sleep.

Perhaps I should have died. Why didn't I let Roy kill both of us in that tourist cabin? Why did a prostitute save my life five years ago? My mother was right. My baby would never have a chance in life. People wouldn't let her live. If it wasn't for Jean I could die in peace. When I prayed in the tourist cabin I asked to live for my daughter. When I prayed out on the desert it was Jeannie I wanted to live for. Now I realized that she was better off without a mother at all . . . yet she loved me and I couldn't hurt her . . . not on Christmas.

I tried to pray, but I couldn't find anything to pray for. I couldn't pray for Roy to live, I couldn't pray for him to die. Should I pray for him to be caught? To be tried for murder? To burn?

The answer finally came. Just pray that no one gets hurt. Just pray to God there is no violence.

It was morning when we pulled into Texarkana. Christmas morning. I wondered how Jeannie would feel when she bolted upright in bed, remembering it was Christmas. Christmas morning, and her mommie not with her. I felt a traitor even to myself. How long does a child trust? For most persons it was Christmas I hoped, but for me it was crucifixion.

I wondered what was going on at home? Would Roy dare go to my father's home? I had to find out. I needed a newspaper.

All I could find was a local paper. It told nothing of Roy. That was good. Everything was quiet I hoped.

"Merry Christmas, Jeannie," I said over and over to myself, as if she could hear. "Merry Christmas! Merry Christmas to everybody!" I repeated as I broke into tears.

Chapter 11

Capture

$\mathcal{T}$ ime . . . time . . . I thought desperately. If I could only get far enough away fast enough, before Roy was positively identified . . . before he was caught . . . before I was caught . . . before he caught me, or before the police caught me or him. Everything spun around in my mind.

I moved from city to city from paper to paper as I read of six more armed robberies by the Laughing Bandit. These robberies would be added to the murder rap which Roy would have to face when caught. He knew he faced a death sentence because of the death of prison guard John Greer.

Roy was the only convict participating in the break to escape with his life. What could it matter to him now? He said he would never be taken alive.

"Please God, don't let him hurt my family. Don't let him kill anybody." I should have killed him myself, but I always took the hard way out.

When apprehended I knew I would be sent to prison. Roy was right. I could expect no mercy. They would never believe I had fled with Roy because I thought I could make a good man of him, a reformed man, maybe even a doctor.

What a fool! I would have no defense. What Roy was doing would make things immeasurably worse.

Then the most horrible thought of all struck. They would

think I was still with Roy living off blood money as he had wanted me to do.

Robberies and more armed robberies by the Laughing Bandit. Why couldn't the police catch him? Now there were seventeen. He was in Dallas. Why didn't he leave Texas? He was still looking for me! He still hung near my hometown thinking I would be back. He might snatch Jean.

There's only one thing I can do, I thought. I'll go to Dallas and turn myself in to the police. When they smear my photograph on the front page of the newspaper Roy will know I'm in Big "D," in jail. He'll have no reason to go to my hometown.

I was in St. Louis. If I tried to turn myself in so far away from Texas they might not know the story. I might not hit the front page here, or Roy might not see the paper. I had to get back to Dallas. My money was all but gone. I'd thumb a ride, but what if I were recognized en route?

Keeping up with Roy's whereabouts was no trouble. He was a continuing headline. He jumped from Dallas to Fort Worth, from Fort Worth to Abilene . . . closer home. THE LAUGHING BANDIT! THE LAUGHING BANDIT! He was bound to be mainlining heavier and heavier. I had to get to Texas. If I could just get as close as Dallas, then turn myself in as the Laughing Bandit's wife, surely the story would hit every Texas newspaper.

I wasn't covering ground fast enough. I would hitchhike at night too. Most of my rides were with truck drivers, and they were nice. They fed me and did not try to force themselves upon me. But trucks were slow. I would have to try a car.

I was lucky, I thought. I caught a salesman going into Oklahoma City. He said he planned to travel all night. But it was his hands that did the traveling. I had a fight that would have lasted all night if I hadn't been able to break away. I lost time. He was fat and easy to out-run, but I had to hide in the woods until he gave up the search and drove back to the highway. I was deathly afraid to try for another ride . . . in the middle of the night, but a truck driver picked me up and he was nice.

My progress was too slow. I would never make it back to Texas in time. I would have to turn myself in here. It was close enough. They would know.

"Just drop me off at the police station," I told the truck driver in a casual voice.

"So someone did rape you," the truck driver commented. "I thought that was your trouble, judging from your clothes and the scratches on your arms. I wish you luck, kid."

"But no one raped me, just tried," I said.

"Then maybe you are making a mistake turning him in. You'll just be hurting yourself more, ruining your name in your own hometown. Why don't you take my advice and keep it quiet."

"But I wasn't going to the police because of the attempted rape. I'm going to turn myself in. I'm a criminal."

"You a criminal! Come on, kid!" he laughed. "Tell me about it while we eat breakfast. They tell me the food's pretty bad in the jail here," he said as he pulled up at a truck stop.

"But I'd rather go on," I said meekly, having my mind made up and impatient with the delay.

"Then just five minutes for a cup of coffee," he said with firmness. "I don't care what you've done. I need a cup of coffee, and you look like you could use one. You won't lose any time. I'll drop you off within a block of the police station . . . but durned if I want to get involved."

"It won't involve you," I promised. "No one except myself."

We walked in.

"See the headlines," a waitress commented as she handed the truck driver the morning paper. "They've finally caught the Laughing Bandit."

I drank my coffee, too weak to say a word. And the truck driver ordered breakfast . . . breakfast for two.

"It's a shame such a good-looking guy as him could turn out so bad," the waitress commented as she brought our bacon and eggs. "They say he's wanted for murder."

"Yeah!" the truck driver grunted. "Too bad he didn't get killed. Would have saved the state the trouble and expense."

I couldn't say a word. I was afraid to reach for the paper; it might be a dead giveaway. Maybe the truck driver would put two and two together.

"Feel better?" he asked as we again headed for the truck. "The world's never so bad . . . on a full stomach. Do you still want to turn yourself in? You just don't look like a criminal to

155

me. If I thought you had done something bad . . . like that Laughing Bandit's wife . . . helping him in a prison break and probably living it up now . . . I'd turn you in myself."

"She must be a tough one," I commented, adopting Roy's tactics in an effort to throw him off trail. "Maybe as tough as Bonnie Parker," I tried in an effort to change the conversation.

"Never could figure a woman," he muttered. "How one could love a man like that Clyde Barrow or that Laughing Bandit is beyond me."

"They're bound to be as bad as the men," I said hatefully. "Maybe I'm not so bad after all."

"I knew it was nothing," he smiled. "Always was a good judge of character. Now if you'll just tell me where you want out . . ."

"The next red light will be fine," I said as I wondered how near the police station was. "I can catch a street car home."

"I don't mind taking you, no trouble at all."

"Maybe not to you," I added (delighted that I had learned to resort to Roy King's light banter, or just plain lies, when in trouble), "but I spent the night with a girl friend. I'd have a little trouble explaining a truck driver to my father."

"Or to your husband?" the truck driver added as he raised a knowing brow. "Good luck, you'll probably need it," he concluded as he applied the brakes for the light.

Then I hit the sidewalk I felt like I had just escaped the noose. But when I got my own copy of the paper and locked myself in a restroom to read, I wondered.

I read the fine print. Roy had been taken in his sleep in a hotel room in Dallas, a doped up wreck of a man.

"Where's your wife?" an officer had asked.

"I must have been out," they quoted Roy, "if there was a dame in my room without me knowing it!"

They found no evidence, but felt certain the dragnet set for Mary King would finish the story.

If I was caught now with heat on Roy, I might never get to be with Jean again. The police would never believe my story. I could never prove I was going to turn myself in. I had even lied to the truck driver.

I didn't want to go to prison. I didn't want to implicate my family. I knew I would get five years . . . plus . . . plus whatever they could hang on me.

Suddenly I was cheating, cheating strictly for myself. I didn't want to pay for my crime. If I did I may never get my daughter back. I'd rather be dead than go through life without her.

I'd hide. I'd kidnap my own child when the heat was off, if I had to. Nobody could keep my child from me, neither the police nor my parents. I'd been a fugitive before.

I knew I couldn't hit the road without money. It was a sure way of getting caught. Maybe I could try my old trick. It worked in Phoenix. I'd rent a uniform and look for work as a waitress. Just as soon as I had the fare I'd go far away to New York City where there would be plenty of cafes for me to work in a week or two at a time until they demanded my social security card.

Before the trial started I was in New York. I frequented big news stands where they sold out-of-state papers. Roy was finally brought to trial.

They grilled him and cross questioned him, asked him over and over about my part in his flight. He denied that he had ever seen me.

They could produce no evidence. In all those fugitive months no one had been close enough to identify me positively. No one who could have identified me got close enough to us during our flight.

I wondered if they would be unmerciful enough to put my parents on the stand . . . my child.

"But you were seen with a woman while you were an escaped convict," the prosecutor accused. "What has become of your wife? Where is Mary King? If she is innocent let her prove where she has been the past nine months. Why couldn't she be reached with a subpoena? Is it because she knows there is a warrant out for her arrest? Where is Mrs. Mary King?"

It was here that Roy showed his magnanimous heart and clear thinking. Whether he did it for me or for his daughter, or for whatever reason, the fact remains that this was his reply:

"Where is Mary King?" Roy echoed. "That's what I'd like to know," he threw at the court with a spark of his old banter. "I've been looking for my wife ever since I escaped, but I've never found her."

"What?" roared the prosecutor. "Are you trying to tell the court that you have never seen, nor been with your wife, who disappeared from this very town with you after the break? Do you expect this jury to swallow that?"

Witness after witness was called to the stand. No one who knew me had seen me since I had disappeared. Several officers thought they had seen Roy and me at a distance, but none of them had been closer than shooting distance. None of those who were even that close knew me. There was only one officer who could have identified me, and that was Ray Hilton, the officer to first pick Roy up. He knew both Roy and me, but he had not seen us during the time we were fugitives.

He was put on our trail because he knew us both, had seen us both before and after my baby was born and had a better chance of recognizing us than anyone else . . . Yet he had never been close to us during our flight.

"But you were seen with a woman while you were an escaped convict," the prosecutor accused. "Twice when you were shot at a woman was with you. You were with your wife when you were seen in a stolen car near Tucson. She was still with you when you were shot and jumped from a freight train near Phoenix. There are at least half a dozen officers who can testify to the fact that you were with a woman on both occasions. Do you deny that fact to the court?" the prosecutor roared.

"Does being shot at while with a woman necessarily make that woman your wife?" Roy countered.

This brought the house down. The judge pounded with an unheeded staccato. When the court finally did settle down he suggested they get to the business at hand.

Roy was given 99 years . . . in addition to the 20 year sentence he was already serving. He was tried in other counties. The total rolled to 173 years. He was returned to prison.

My name vanished from the papers. Perhaps there was not enough evidence to bring me to trial . . . even if brought into custody. The court had its man. Maybe it was appeased.

Gradually I worked my way back toward Texas and home. I had to see my daughter. Because of Roy's magnificent lie I felt fairly safe. I wished I could have thanked him for it. I felt sure he must have done it as a benediction to our love.

In a strange way Roy's statement was true. We had never found each other at all.

A great burden was lifted and my heart was almost light as I neared home. I told myself that I would find work in my own town and make a home for my daughter. God had been good to me. I would humble myself if need be in seeking another chance at a new life.

Chapter 12

The Letter

erhaps my story would have ended here if society would
have let it. If this were fiction, my daughter and I could
have lived happily ever after. But this is not fiction.

I should have known better. Six years earlier when I first returned to bear a prisoner's child, there were those who felt compassion and would have forgiven my mistake. Now I was a 'gun
moll.' I had helped a man escape prison. I had deserted my own
daughter!

People looked at me as if I were some kind of animal.
Heads bent and tongues wagged until I was out of sight on the
street. I was stared right out of church. I was no longer the
hometown girl who had wanted to become a missionary. My
church work seemed forgotten.

Detective writers came to town and asked for me. Rumor
had it that I had helped with the bloody prison break. That I was
waiting with guns. That I staged the break. That I was at least
partially responsible for the death of eight men. I couldn't stand
the pressure.

I seemed to be a criminal and child deserter to almost everyone except my own daughter. To Jeannie I was an angel
mother who came to visit on special occasions. Since I never
lived with her as most mothers live with their children, I guess

her childish heart never demanded that which she had never known.

Jobs opened in my hometown, but not for me. I had to leave home to find work. My parents wouldn't let me take Jean with me. This could never be, not until I had a good job and a good home for her.

I found a good job, several of them, but I still had a lot to learn. The cops who had been on our trail couldn't quite give up the fact that I was on the outside and the courts had seemingly forgotten I had harboured an escaped convict.

Every time I got a fairly decent job close enough to home that I could see Jean often, the cops caught up with me or someone recognized me. Tongues wagged, and I was out of work again. I was even accused of instigating crimes that took place after Roy was returned to prison. What had happened before was my fault, but so help me the public won't let a person with a record live.

For once, I confided in my parents. I wanted a good job and I wanted my daughter, but there was no future, not for Mary King. Together we planned. My older sister was a teacher and believed in higher education. She wanted me to go back to college. Bless her, I'll always feel she taught away from home because of my troubles, but she never failed to come up with helpful suggestions. She thought I could get my credits transferred from McMurry College in Abilene to Texas Tech in Lubbock in my maiden name. My whole family would help if I divorced Roy King immediately. By the time spring semester started, it would be no lie. I could take the family name back.

The transferring of my credits in my maiden name was a false pretense, because I did not have it back yet. It hurt because I had compromised the family integrity so many times with my escapades. But just one small white lie which I would make come true, then I could get on the straight and narrow again.

My mother and father loved Jean so much now that there was no doubt as to who would keep her. In fact, it bothered me. They loved her too much.

I wrote to McMurry and had my credits transferred to Texas Tech in my maiden name, pretending my divorce was already final.

I still had a few days I could spend with my daughter before the spring semester opened. Going back to school as a decoy to change my name in hopes of securing a teaching position hardly seemed fair, but I was driven to it. Tech had a good journalism department. A little graduate work in writing would be easy enough.

Of course I would have to hold down a job, one in a cafe, but Lubbock was a big town and perhaps no one would know. Meantime I would look for a teaching position. Even if I couldn't find work by fall as a teacher, my journalism experience should enable me to hold down a good newspaper job.

Joyfully, I told Jean that by the time school started in the fall she would get to live with her mother. Tearfully I told her that Mother would have to leave again, but only for a while. I explained that Mother would have to work and go to college again so she could become a teacher, like her sister. Then when she was seven (seven was the school age then) she could come and live with me. Maybe she would go to the same school where I would teach. Wouldn't that be fun?

My heart was light as I raced with Jean to meet the postman. Only one more day with my precious child before I left for Lubbock to start back to school. True, it was a week early, but I had to find work and get settled before the spring semester opened. I not only had to find work, I would have to fit my working hours to my school hours. This would probably mean night work again, but it didn't matter. It would only be for a few months.

Meeting the postman was an old habit of ours. Mother had managed, while I was away from home, to get a subscription to *Jack and Jill,* a child's magazine, for Jean. She loved it . . . even if Mother did have to barter four old hens and two dozen eggs for it when food was hard to come by, it seemed worth the sacrifice.

Jeannie squealed with delight when she saw a small magazine in the postman's hand. I no longer expected any mail, but strangely enough there was a letter addressed to Mrs. Roy King. It was in a plain white envelope, postmarked "Huntsville."

"Any mail?" I heard my mother call.

Quickly I concealed the letter. No sense hurting my family

again, or start them fretting. Maybe he had a lawyer. It wasn't his writing. I'd read it later.

"My *Jack and Jill*, my *Jack and Jill*," Jean announced with delight, having no interest in the other letter.

"I'm glad you're still here to read it to her," my mother stated as we entered and she returned to her work in the kitchen. "It takes half my day when her magazine arrives. Sure will be glad when next fall comes and she learns to read for herself."

"Read this one to me first, Mommie, read this one first," she urged as she pulled me to an armed chair where we could both sit.

I read words, never knowing what they said.

"But Mommie . . . you skipped a page," Jean complained.

Inpatiently I read the little stories.

"Tell you what," I finally suggested, "you work the puzzle, then Mommie will come back and read the magazine all the way through."

Who could the letter be from, I wondered as I locked myself in the bathroom. It wasn't Roy's handwriting . . . yet it had no legal return, either. Should have, if it was from a lawyer. I hadn't heard from Roy since the trials, but I didn't expect to, either. Hastily I tore it open:

Dear Mrs. King,

I don't like to tell you this, and Roy didn't ask me to, but he's in trouble and he can't live much longer without your help. There's other boys here, too, needin' help on the Eastham No. 2 farm.

Don't come here, but go to Dr. Jason. He's on the prison board. Don't tell him who sent you, but tell him there's some boys out here needing medical attention bad.

I know you don't see Roy anymore, but if he ever needed you, he needs you now. I know you once loved him. I know you'll remember me, too. I'm Capt. Owen, the one who let you talk overtime and mailed extra letters from Roy to you when I could. That's how I know your address.

The letter was signed, "Capt. A. N. Owen."

How well I remember the guard who had been good to us. My hands crushed the letter desperately.

I cried in anguish. I can't go! I have no husband! He's my husband in name only. In my heart he's dead. I have his baby. She needs me. I owe Roy nothing. Nothing!

All through the day it was hard to hide the turmoil in my soul. I tried desperately to be cheerful with Jean as she chattered away. Soon she would be in school and learn to read for herself she told me over and over. And she would have lots and lots of books. She was going to live with Mommie when she started to school. I had promised her.

Finally she lay asleep beside me. Deep into the night I fought with myself. I just had to make good! I couldn't change my plans now. I had promised my daughter . . .

Why did the letter have to come? Why now? Why must something always have to happen in my life just the opposite to what I expected or wanted. Perhaps if I had not been at home my parents would have opened it and torn it up. I had promised that nothing from the prison should ever touch me again.

Then I thought of Roy and how he had lied to save me from a prison sentence. "I never saw Mary King," I could almost hear him saying. "In all the months that I was a fugitive I kept looking for her but I never found her."

In my own heart and mind I had never committed a real crime, at least no crime for personal gain. My only crimes were committed for the man I loved, the man I thought the world had wronged. Now he might die without my help. This would be murder in my own heart. And the others . . . could I let men die if I could help?

Maybe it was all exaggeration but I had to know. I could not refuse just one trip to be sure. I doubted that Captain Owen, a man on the side of the law, would have any reason to lie.

Just one trip and no more. I wouldn't even see Roy, just the prison doctor. Then I'd go to Lubbock as planned with time to enroll for the spring term of college.

"Mommie will be back for Easter," I had promised as Jeannie's arms tightly encircled my neck the next morning. "Don't forget the Easter bunnies are better to little girls who help their grandmothers. Just a few months now until school starts next fall . . . and we'll go together. Won't it be wonderful? Mommie will start teaching the day her darling starts to school."

164

I bade my parents goodbye. I left saying nothing of the six-hundred mile detour I must make to go to the prison.

When I arrived in Huntsville on that gloomy Saturday afternoon, little did I know that before I was through I would play a part in the smashing and cleansing of one of the rottenest, most bestial and corrupt prison systems in the United States.

I tried to call Dr. C. W. Jason, Jr., as he was listed in the telephone directory as soon as I arrived, but received no answer.

I would have to wait. I walked toward the park across from the college, the park where I had slept on the concrete table with Jean in my arms when Roy was first sent to prison six years before.

Six years, and it was not enough that I should be left in peace. Now they wouldn't even let Roy live.

I dug out the letter, thinking of Captain Owen as a rare guard, one with a heart. A guard who treated prisoners as if they were human beings. He always gave Roy and me a little break when he could. Many times after Roy was sent to Eastham No. 1 Farm, he let me talk with my husband almost two hours rather than the allotted one. He never seemed to hang on every word of conversation.

EASTHAM NO. 2! For the first time the words jumped at me from the letter. Eastham No 2? That's where the incorrigibles were kept. Roy had been on Eastham No. 1 when I had visited him . . . so had Captain Owen. I knew that the No. 2 farm was somewhere back of the No. 1 farm, but I had never been there. I had heard it was a tomb for the living.

It wasn't fair. Roy had never killed anyone. Why had he been put with the perverts, the criminally insane, incorrigibles and murderers?

And why was Captain Owen there? Did Roy's prison break from the No. 1 farm have anything to do with it? Was Captain Owen demoted too? Certainly no one would ask to go to the No. 2 farm. Roy had repeatedly said it was worse that No. 1. Could the captain be demoted for letting prisoners write too many letters or talking overtime with their visitors?

The clouds grew as dark as the questions on my mind. I must try again. I had to reach Dr. Jason.

By the time I got to a phone, it was raining. Dr. Jason was

out of town I was told by someone whom I assumed to be his wife. She said he wouldn't be back until tomorrow.

Impatient with the delay, I rented a little hotel room. From it I could see the gray prison walls. My mind flew back to the time Roy had described Raymond Hamilton's break from the death cell. Clyde and Bonnie were already dead. Why, oh why did Roy always try to help someone else?

If it hadn't been for that break, Roy would never have been ranked and sent to Eastham No. 2. He would have left the prison a free man. His parole was so near. Call it circumstance . . . call it fate . . . but that's the way it had to happen for Roy and me.

If there was ever a trap, one of us always managed to get into it. I closed my eyes and covered my head to cut out all conscious sights and sounds. Tomorrow I would see the doctor and he would surely investigate. There were other sick men who couldn't be overlooked. The doctor would take care of this, then I would be on my way back to Lubbock, my conscience at rest. I would never see the prison again.

The next morning I waited for what I thought was a decent hour to call. It was still raining. A sleepy voice informed me that the doctor had not yet returned. Would I leave my number?

It was early afternoon before Dr. Jason reached home and returned my call. I told him my story and asked him if he would go to the prison farm to see about these men. When he asked my name and I had to tell him Mary King, Roy King's wife, I think he was quite skeptical. Where had this information come from? The doctor seemed to appreciate me even less when I told him I couldn't reveal the source of my information.

He reminded me that it had been raining hard and that it was useless to try to visit the Eastham No. 2 Farm when it was muddy. In fact it was practically a physical impossibility. Yet, if it would make me feel any better, he would go just as soon as he thought he could get there.

Why of all times, did it have to be raining, I thought in desperation as the telephone receiver clicked in my ear. It might be too late when the doctor arrived at the farm. Maybe he didn't believe me at all. Maybe he would just let it slide. How many prisoner's wives called to gripe?I wondered. I could see his side of the question. If I only had more proof, then I could get the doctor to make it. I must have conclusive proof — but how?

I walked through the rain to the prison walls to ask Warden Bailey for a pass to the Eastham Prison Farm No. 2 to see Roy King. He refused it. Sunday had always been visitor's day, so I asked why the pass was refused.

In the first place, I was informed, Roy was in solitaire and allowed no visitors. In the second place, I couldn't get to the prison farm even if I had a pass. The road was too muddy.

(to get a good start they wont a Man or two killed to scare the rest - They Made a statement to that affect

On Feb. 15, 1940, nearly 38 days ago, the Eastham Prison farm under went another change of Management and a radical change in policy. After fifteen under an administration that handled the affairs of the convicts and Guards alike, with a tolerant Broadmindof efficiency, It is once more under the management of a group of Men who have time and again been fired, Blackballed and hand around over the vast prison system, for practicing brutality in all of its hideousforms amoung an unfortunate Class of human being who are hepless; with out recourse to Violence

Some fifteen months ago these same Guards were transfered from the Eastham Prison farm for Acts of Violence that startled the Whole Nation and focused the spot light of public Disapproval upon the System. Instead of a complete Dismisial they were only transfered to Another unit of the system, to Continue their sadistic outrages with immunity This arrangements were Made through the efforts of An influential Politician, who is paid a monthly salary as a Legal adviser — and Bondsman to Systems Executive personell, including the Gourds and their families, This salary is paid from a Over)

This is #1 in a series of eight letters telling of the all but unbelievable brutality, corruption and graft practiced in the Texas State Prison System in the thirties and forties.

168

Chapter 13

Hell Hole of Texas

$\mathcal{I}$t was then I told the warden that I wanted to see my husband because I had heard he was very sick. I was asked how I had received such information. Men in solitaire are not allowed to write. I refused to answer his question and Warden Bailey stuck with his refusal to give me a pass.

I went back to town and started calling members of the prison board. I didn't have much luck getting in touch with them. Most of them lived in other cities and I didn't have the money for long distance calls. Finally I did get Mrs. C. A. Leonard, secretary of the board. She promised to call the warden and call me back in a few minutes. When she did call back I was told I would be granted a pass if I returned to the prison walls.

It was mid-afternoon when Warden Bailey signed the pass. I had the feeling it was given to me because those concerned felt I would never make it to the farm. Visiting hours are over at five and I had more than forty miles to go. Much of the distance was mud . . . mucky, sticky gumbo.

My money was dangerously low for renting a car, but I could think of no other way of getting there. From Huntsville to Midway I had about thirty miles of poor pavement. From the one-station town of Midway I turned east on a sand road so corduroyed that I never knew whether to brace myself for the next encounter with the top of the car or to stiffen my neck in hope of avoiding another bruise with the black mire I hit nearing the river bottom.

Twice I crawled from the car into the mud and walked through the slime in search of someone to pull me out. Each time I found a shanty inhabited by blacks. No one seemed to own more than one mule and I was informed that it would take more than one mule to pull me out. I had to sit and wait for one man to go off in search of another with a mule.

I didn't know what to expect. I was afraid to think. Roy had told me of the difficulty in reaching the Eastham Farm where the incorrigibles were housed. It was never meant for a sentimental public to see.

It had stopped raining but the dark pine bottoms were gruesome. It was impossible to see over twenty-five or thirty feet on either side of the road. I had a feeling that the world had closed in on me, leaving me in a hole where the sun never shone.

I must have broken the speed record of a snail because a wagon caught up with me, and was traveling behind me when I got stuck the third time. Two young men clad in dingy white ducking climbed from the wagon and approached the car.

"We're trustees from the Ferguson Prison Farm," one of the men informed me as they both removed their hats and held them politely as they offered their services.

"Isn't the Ferguson Farm just across the river from the East-han No. 2 Farm?" I asked, remembering Roy's description from his stories of the prison break. "Are you going there?"

"Yes'um," one of the trustees answered. "We're goin' there and it is across the Trinity from the Eastham No. 2 Farm. But to get to the Eastham you have to take the ferry, and I ain't sure the ferry's crossin'. The river's high. Out of banks in places. We'll pull you to the Ferguson Farm if that'll help you any. We're in the mail wagon and it's the only vehicle running along here now that the road's so bad."

"I don't see the Ferguson Farm," I said. "How far are we from it now?"

"Why, it's just about a quarter-mile down the road. Don't you see that clearin'?"

A guard met us at the gate. I felt a little absurd, in a car

170

pulled by mules, but I was at the farm and that was good enough for me.

The trustees unhitched the car. They refused pay for their services. I was thankful considering the status of my pocketbook. The guard looked at me as though I was crazy when I told him I wanted to go to the Eastham Farm.

"Ye can't git no further in a car. Who air ye and who air ye goin' ter see?" he demanded.

I produced the slip from Warden Bailey, but the guard looked at it with a blank face. He passed it to another guard who was now at his side. The newcomer gave a "no thank you" look and carried it into a squat gray house which must have been the office. Evidently there was someone inside who could read because the guard came back and said that I had the proper permission from Warden Bailey.

"This here ain't no time to go acrost. The river's up and the ferry's dangerous," the guard warned. "Even ifen you do get acrost, you got nearly two miles to go afore you git to the Eastham Farm. You can see it from here."

The guard pointed his finger. In the gray distance I could barely distinguish a group of low, gray buildings.

I asked how they got to the Eastham Farm in this kind of weather and was informed in no uncertain terms that they were not allowed to permit such going's on. I said I would walk.

The guards and trustees hauled me as far as the river in the wagon. When I looked at the river they asked me if I was ready to return.

So this was why Warden Bailey had given me permission! Even if I got to the river, he probably thought I would never have the nerve to cross.

The river was muddy and swollen. It was laden with occasional logs. The ferry was an old wooden affair, dependent upon a wire cable. The convicts pulled it across by hand.

I knew they would think I would be afraid but by now in my life, I had forgotten what being afraid meant.

"This here girl wants to git acrost th' river," one of the guards addressed the two convicts who were puttering around the ferry. "Think you can get 'er acrost?"

All the while I was watching a nanny goat that was standing

near the edge of the ferry. She was watching the logs in the swirling current as they were carried down stream.

The trustees agreed to take me across the river and wait for me on the other side. They would wait and bring me back for a dollar each crossing. Ordinarily they would have charged twenty-five cents each crossing, but today it would be dangerous and unusually hard work getting across.

The guards warned me again against crossing and seemed quite angry at my being fool enough to disregard the elements. I think they were wishing I were a convict, then they could handle me.

"We're not responsible for anything that happens if'en ye cross the' river agin' our advice," the guard cautioned. "Warden Bailey wouldn't 'ave give ye the slip if'en he had seen th' river."

I didn't tell them that Warden Bailey regretted my being here as much as they.

"The only way to git to Eastham camp after ye leave th' river is to walk up one o' them turn-rows," the guard warned as the trustees started pulling the ferry across.

Miraculous how far that cable would give without breaking. The old raft, it would come closer qualifying as a raft than a ferry, capered like a game fish on the end of a line. The nanny goat stood perilously near the edge of the bobbing raft, wholly unconcerned except for an owl-like turning of her head as she watched the logs rush downstream.

Being a woman, my curiosity finally made me ask, "Isn't it dangerous for that goat to ride so near the edge of the ferry?"

"She rides every time the ferry crosses and ain't never happened to a mishap yet," one of the trustees informed me.

An abrupt yank on the cable brought me to an undignified sitting position on the wet boards which topped the logs. The goat maintained perfect balance and remained wholly undisturbed. I kept my mouth shut.

The guards were still watching when the trustees unloaded me on the other side of the river and helped me up the slippery bank.

"Keep right up that turn-row Miss, till you get to the end of the field. Then take the one to your right and it will lead you right to the prison yards," one of the ferrymen instructed.

I could not see the end of the turn-row, but I knew it was a mile long. The field looked five miles long to me, but I had no intention of turning back now that I was within reach of my destination.

A few steps from the river bank my right shoe was sucked off by the black mud. I dug it out, draining the water to make room for my foot again. I clenched my toes so tightly against the soles of my shoes in an effort to keep them on that my toes soon became cramped. I relaxed them and lost another shoe. This time I took both shoes and hose off as I felt the mud ooze between my toes. I debated whether I should keep these now oddly shaped balls of mud that had once been footwear, or throw them away. I might look a little queer on my way back to civilization barefoot.

I wondered what time it was as I made my way down the long turn-row barefoot. Maybe it was already past visiting hours. Would I get to see either Roy or Captain Owen?

The so called 'turn-row' was a sort of wagon trail at the side of the field. To my left was a field, to my right trees and brush, back of me the river and Ferguson Farm, and in front of me I could see the low gray buildings which would have to be the Burnin' Eastham, as Roy often spoke of it. From Roy's descriptions I could picture the convicts being run out on these turn-rows before daylight to work in the cotton or corn fields.

Long before I reached the right angle to turn toward the squat buildings, I could feel eyes peeled my way. At the turn, I wiped my feet with my muddy, tattered hose, and threw them away. Shoes, however muddy, were a comfort.

As I drew near, I could see little towers on top of some of the buildings, where I knew machine guns were housed. I felt one angle in my direction.

One building was not barred. The porch on it was occupied by several men who wore scabbards and gun belts fastened around pudgy bellies.

"I've come to visit Roy King," I ventured to the guards eyeing me. "I'm his wife Mary King. I have a pass."

"It's way past visitin' time, Ma'am. Besides that Spider's not allowed visitors. They should've told you."

"But I've come a long way," I refuted, still grasping desperately for some fragment worth the sacrifice I had made. "Who is in charge? May I speak with him?"

"Captain Owen is in charge. I'll call him, Ma'am, but it won't do no good. That's orders from the warden."

Nervously I waited for Captain Owen to appear. What could a man do under such circumstances? What could I say to him? He had written in his letter that I was NOT to come to the farm. One wrong word . . .

"I hear say you're Mrs. Roy King," the captain clued me in with no sign of recognition as we reached the guard's quarters. "Visiting hours are past. Anyway, your husband is in solitary confinement. Didn't they tell you that at the Walls?"

My heart sank. Captain Owen had always been so good to me. I had no business coming to the farm. It was the doctor I was supposed to get. I was helpless, insofar as explaining the circumstances. Maybe the same was true with him. There were plenty of eyes and ears around.

"Isn't there any way?" I pleaded as I stalled for time, hoping some of our gun-studded audience would move along.

"Those are the warden's orders," Captain Owen said with finality.

I had no words. I couldn't have spoken then for fear of betraying him. There was nothing to do but leave. All this trip for nothing.

"By the way," Captain Owen said as a sort of second thought when I turned to leave, "would you mind postin' a mail order for me in town? Been no mail out of this place for several days and things don't look any better. My wife's afraid this birthday present won't get here in time if it keeps rainin'."

I took the Sears Roebuck envelope he handed me. As I did his eyes held mine for a brief instant, speaking to me. They conveyed the message. The envelope was loosely sealed. I could hardly wait to get out of sight to confirm the unspoken message.

It was from Roy, written in the semi-darkness of solitaire. It was hard to read, but harder yet to believe. I had to get help, he pleaded. There had been many self-mutilations. George Barton and Irvin Darden were in the morgue at the Walls and they needed medical attention quick. Clark Thomas had been in the morgue for sixteen months.

In the morgue? I shuddered. The morgue is for the dead. Sixteen months? Impossible . . . or so the public would think.

Note that this letter does not have the prisoner's name and number on the prison heading, as you will see on the opposite page. This means that it was "kited" from the prison and uncensored, as regular mail was.

Next page:
This letter does carry the regular prison heading, meaning it was censored. The author has preserved Roy's letters for over fifty years. Without them this story is unbelievable. The author won the national True Story *award in 1955 with a fictionized version of her flight with escaped convict husband, but the name was Roy "Gregg." This is the first publication revealing the true name, Roy King.*

Name **Ray King**   No. **91551**   Unit **Huntsville**

Huntsville Texas
April 18, 1940

Dearest Mary -

I am about as full of new
as a monkey, first I'll comment
on the weather, then the crops
the political situation and last
but not least, the high price
and quality of Milk. Lets leave
the war out of this because
my opinion and expression cant
stand the competition and too
I think that maybe I have
mentioned too many Topics to
elaborate upon within the limit
space of one page, but lets take
the weather first, as I have it
listed in that order. It cant be
called typical April weather, seem
sort of a misfit and about four
months too late, not to change
the subject but I should have
told you Sunday, I really intended
to, about how much I want to
spend another First Night at
feuders. Please tell me something
about Jeanne in your next letter
she is such a sweet little rascal
she haunts me, maybe that is
one of the Prices I have to
pray.

You must forgive me for
this short letter and you can
expect more next time - I wrote
you Monday.

Love
Ray -

176

The Brutality is condemned by society, still
these men have recoursed to violence as a
last resort, and then only after there plight has
been minimized by the sceptical eye of
their own free fellow man and ~~is cruel~~
by peculiar ~~nepo~~ easily by their opinion
also censure adjust such a situation.
Since Col. O.J.S. Ellingston transfered Capt
Joe Oliver Back here, there has been an
average of two mutilations, and self
inflicted wounds a day. The proof of
this statement remains to be seen. A
timely investigation would ~~appear~~ the
riddle some ~~agen~~. Two of the men who
cut their ~~legs~~ legs off were shipped
immediately to the Wynne farm and
a half dozen or more with broken arm
are in the walls, also some of these ha
Burned themselves severly with lye
on their Buttock's to evade the walls
one cut his heal complettly off - he is in
the walls. Most of these here on the farm
have broken legs - Broken arms and
lye Burns and from all indications there
will be more mutilations should Joe
Oliver, John Eastman, Gordon E. Bruis
W.W. Waid and O.J.S. Ellingston have their
way - To these convicts the ~~two~~ capsions

I knew Clark Thomas. He had been sentenced from my home county. I had no sympathy for him because he was a murderer. Yet he was a human being. How could they put a man in the morgue before he was dead? I didn't understand. It didn't make sense.

I read on, "There is much mutilation, conspiracy and graft going on at the prison. The mutilations are staged in an effort to draw the public's attention to our hopeless state. We are be-

The Houston Press

April 8, 1940

Mr. Harry McCormick,
Dallas News,
Dallas, Texas.

Dear Harry:

I have been without a city editor for a week which accounts for my delay in answering your last letter. I certainly would appreciate it if you would make every effort to get the original of that Burns letter for me, or let me have your suggestion for getting it myself. Thanks for your help.

Sincerely,

Royal H. Roussel

Note that this letter is on Houston Press letterhead and is dated. In April of 1940 your author was leading a dual life, working toward a master's degree in Journalism at Texas Tech in Lubbock. At night I was Mary King. My mail was sent general delivery while I beat a path from Lubbock to Huntsville in South Texas while working as an undercover reporter.

178

yond helping ourselves, but if I can stay alive long enough and can get help, I can break this place wide open with the evidence I have. For God's sake get us some publicity.

"Go to the newspapers," he wrote. "Keep on until you find someone who will listen. If you can't find anyone any closer go to Dallas. Harry McCormick is with the *Dallas Morning News* now. Since you've gone to him before surely he will listen again. Tell him things are just like they used to be except worse. I don't know whether his newspaper will go along, but I believe he will help. Get someone out here in a hurry. Our lives depend on it."

McCormick was a police reporter, well-known for his exclusive stories and exposès. He had previously been with the *Houston Press.*

Vainly I sought help from newspaper to newspaper. The story sounded too fantastic. The prison had been rehabilitated. The story was dead, and so was the *Houston Press* editor who had fought with Harry McCormick once before for prison rehabilitation.

War had broken out in Europe. That was the story the public wanted to see.

I went to Dallas to see Harry McCormick. He had believed the information I had funneled him from Roy in the past, but would he want to face the fact that his hard fought crusade might not be won? Would he go?

The first crusade had all but cost McCormick's life. Roy was on Eastham No. 1 and smuggling out stories to "Mack," as the convicts called him, when Clyde Barrow chopped off a little toe for publicity's sake. He was still there when Clyde and his brother, Buck, were released as well as when Raymond Hamilton, early running mate of Clyde and Bonnie, was imprisoned. Ray bragged that Bonnie and Clyde would come for him. They did. A guard was killed during the break.

Many bank robberies later, Raymond Hamilton was recaptured and sentenced to the chair for the murder of the guard killed during his break, despite the fact that another of the convicts, Joe Palmer, admitted killing the guard himself. Ray contended he had never killed anyone and was sentenced to die because no jail nor prison could hold him. He had seventeen escapes to substantiate his claim.

179

When Hamilton's death sentence was read, he bragged openly to McCormick, who was near him in the courtroom, that he would escape the death house in the Walls at Huntsville. Ray did.

While every cop in the nation was ordered to 'shoot on sight,' the nation's most wanted managed to get a message to McCormick. Mack met him at the designated spot on a lonely road. Ralph Fults, also an early teammate of Clyde and Bonnie, was with Ray. He was one of the convicts in the break in which Clyde and Bonnie were featured. But Ralph, like Joe Palmer and Raymond Hamilton, had split with Clyde and Bonnie.

During this "impossible interview," when Raymond picked up McCormick, Ralph sat watching in the back seat of the car, machine gun ready, in case the cops should show. After driving most of the night, while Ray related his story, they returned Mack to his own car. They laughed as they tied and gagged him. Raymond plastered Mack's windshield with fingerprints to prove who did the "kidnapping."

Harry screamed that he had been kidnapped by Raymond Hamilton, who had escaped from the death cell. He failed to mention Ralph Fults, of course, who was still a fugitive. But Mack did tell Hamilton's side of the story, and well. Unfortunately, he was unable to prove it until after Ray's electrocution. Raymond Hamilton never killed anyone.

It was on the night of Ray's electrocution that prison officials tried to trap Harry McCormick. They made promises and offered bribes to both Ray and Ralph if they would say that Harry came to them of his own free will, rather than being kidnapped by them. Neither squealed.

Did McCormick know the old vanguard was again in power at the prison? He had been told once that there was a slab in the prison morgue with his name on it. Would he go? Why should he become involved again? The public thought his crusade was won.

Chapter 14

Never Underestimate Harry McCormick

I never felt so small as when I entered the big city room of the *Dallas Morning News*. Everyone was so busy no one seemed to realize I was alive. I just stood there until I spotted Harry McCormick in a far corner. His desk was among dozens in the room. He looked up.

"What th' hell are you doing here, Mary," he blurted out as I approached his desk. Unwinding his gangling thin legs and stubbing his ever-present cigarette, he stuck out his hand. "Did you want to see me? Here, take my chair while I hunt another."

He took off his horn-rimmed glasses which had been added since I last saw him and retrieved a chair. Tall, gaunt and ruggedly handsome, Harry was the friend of the guy who needed him always.

"What's on your mind?" he asked, realizing perhaps that no one ever came to him except when in trouble.

"Roy," came my expected answer. "He's at the Ham, in 'sol.'"

I handed him the letter. He read it through quickly, all eight pages, then turned back and reread a portion of it before he said a word.

Soon he was firing questions, fast and to the point. Many of them I couldn't answer, especially those concerning prison personnel and the transfer of guards.

"I don't think my newspaper will handle this," he said as my heart sank. "You see, besides being almost two hundred miles away from the prison, and there being plenty of war news to hit the front page, the *Dallas Morning News* has always been a conservative paper. I'm not sure I could talk my editor into it. But Royal Roussel of the *Houston Press* might," he added as I breathed again.

"Can it be soon?"

"It will have to be," he replied understandingly. "I wanted an excuse to go to Houston anyway. Maybe Royal will carry the torch. Could you help us, Mary?"

While I was in mental debate with myself Harry explained.

"Although I am no longer barred from the prison, I am not the guest of honor, especially since Dave Nelson died. (Nelson was the new prison manager who did so much toward rehabilitation then suffered a heart attack.) But Roussel might go along since he did some work with 'Mefo' and me (Mefo Foster was former editor-in-chief of the *Houston Press*) on our crusade to clean up the joint. I'm not in close contact with the prison anymore, otherwise I would not ask you to help."

There was a sinking feeling within me, but it was too late to turn back. Harry did not know, of course, that it was over with Roy and me. Neither did he know that this move would jeopardize my getting my own daughter back.

"You mean you'll go to Houston? It may be too late already."

"I'll go," he assured. "Meantime, I'll have to depend upon you to get this information from Roy King and whatever contacts there are now. I'm no longer on the grapevine. I'll let you know what Royal thinks. He's editor now. I'll need this letter, of course. We'll have to check it out. What is your address?"

"Just write me general delivery," I stammered, "Mary King, General Delivery, Lubbock, Texas."

The truth would have taken too much explaining.

When I finally got back to Lubbock I started collecting mail under two names. At the college I was Mary Latch, but at the downtown office I was Mary King.

By day I was a coed, at night I was a waitress. Whenever I managed for a weekend I was mother for a day as I visited Jean and my family, never telling them of course, that I was en route to the prison. Thus, I started smuggling information from the rottenest prison in the nation, unless Louisiana or Georgia tied for the honors during this time.

Letters came. As prearranged with Roy King and Harry Mc-Cormick, I made copies of the letters and sent them not to Harry McCormick, but to McCormick's wife at their home address. *The Dallas News* did use a portion of the material, but it was Royal Roussel who really took up the battle. Later, I carried some of my material directly to Roussel. I attended classes at Texas Tech spasmodically.

I made a visit home to see my daughter, but only en route to Huntsville. I lied again, spending only a brief time with my family. Although it was spring vacation at the college, I was also a waitress. I told my parents I had to work, even though I had managed to get the time off from the cafe. You can bet I took every precaution not to mention the kind of work which would occupy most of my time during Easter holidays.

This part of the story may be difficult to understand. Certainly the conditions mentioned do not prevail at the Texas prison today. Later, the rehabilitation program was resumed under the directorship of J. R. Everett. Yet, few persons know the story behind the headlines.

It is hard to comprehend the vastness of the Texas Prison System, chiefly because it is spread over so vast a territory.

There is the main unit in Huntsville, usually referred to as "The Walls." During the 1940s there were fourteen farms spread over hundreds of miles in south and east Texas. The Walls and some of the farms were easily accessible. Those were the ones the public saw. But behind them were swampland farms of the Trinity River bottoms. Unless personally concerned, most were unaware of their existence.

Because of this it was easy to hide a convict who had mutilated himself. He could be shipped out to another farm before investigators arrived. In like manner, the prison system managed to keep brutal guards. If their sadistic action attracted too much public attention, those who regained power after the death of Dave Nelson would transfer rather than fire the guards.

Hands, feet, and even legs were chopped off, yet the convicts were fighting a losing battle. However hard the prisoners tried to stay in the public spotlight, prison officials managed to thwart their efforts.

As too much attention was called to one farm, the men mutilating themselves were shipped to other farms. Before reporters could arrive for evidence there was none, or just enough to make the story look highly exaggerated. This is where Roy King's camera and tip-offs as to when and where mutilations were to be staged helped win, or at least focus public attention and action when and where it was most needed.

There were many types of graft in the prison system. Most prisons had a good behavior plan worked out. This plan could knock years off a man's prison sentence if he kept his nose clean. Every prisoner leaving the institution was given mustering out pay. In the Texas prison it was $50. During the Depression this was a lot of money, especially when it could be multiplied many times monthly throughout the vast prison system and over many years.

The deplorable condition at the prison was no secret. For many years many attempts had been made to get at the bottom of the mess. In the early 1930s Governor Dan Moody introduced a bill which was defeated. During the Raymond Hamilton, Bonnie and Clyde era, W. C. Windsor, then chairman of the State Prison Board, stated before the legislature that: "The Texas Prison System is the greatest University of Crime in the Nation."

During the earlier crusade McCormick and "Mefo" Foster had pointed out that the prison system, which had previously operated at a profit now robbed the taxpayer's pocket, although the prisoners themselves were half starved. Public attention had also been called to the existing brutality and 'slave labor,' yet no one knew enough nor seemed to care that these same practices were merely arrested not eradicated.

Roy had been able to tip me off several times as to when and where mutilations were to take place. I made sure the press was on hand for photos and stories yet this was not sufficient.

I honestly believe it was a guard's open rebellion which caused that seething volcano, which had been rumbling and hissing from the thirties to the early forties to explode.

It happened because Capt. A. N. Owen didn't like to see his

men robbed of their mustering out pay. When a prisoner who was supposed to be gaining his freedom failed to board a bus which carried such freed prisoners back to civilization, Captain Owen wanted to know why. The prisoner told Owen he had promised his $50 to get his overtime restored.

He had lost his overtime because of a fight in which he never "hit a lick." In other words he had been framed, as many prisoners were, and he lost his overtime for good behavior. He then had to promise his $50 mustering out pay to get the overtime restored. When he was freed before turning in this "legal fee," a collector was appointed.

Captain Owen was furious. He had seen many prisoners framed, robbed, and stranded. He demanded that the convict who was being freed be given his bus fare to Huntsville and that it be deducted from the "legal fee." You can be sure that Harry McCormick and the *Houston Press* got the story.

Without advance notice, Captain Owen was demoted and transferred to the Wayne Farm, where black prisoners were kept. To cover up, guards who had worked under Owen at Eastham No. 2 were made to sign statements that prisoners were served coffee in the fields, that beer had been found in the kitchen, and that prisoners were allowed to buy and eat candy.

Roy King wasted no time in getting the information to me. These are extracts from his next letter:

On Feb. 15, 1940, nearly 30 days ago, the Eastham Prison farm underwent another change of management and a radical change in policy. After fifteen months under an administration that handled the affairs of the convicts and guards alike, withtolerant, broad minded efficiency, it is once more under the management of a group of men who have time and again been fired, blackballed and transferred around over the vast prison system for practicing brutality in all its hideous forms upon an unfortunate class of human beings who are helpless, without recourse to violence.

Some fifteen months ago these same guards were transferred from the Eastham prison farm for acts of violence that startled the whole nation and focused the spotlight of public disapproval upon the whole system. Instead of complete dismissal they were only transferred to another unit of the system to continue their sadistic outrages with impunity. These arrangements were made through the efforts of an influential politician who is paid a monthly salary as a legal advisor and bondsman to the system's executive personnel, including the guards. This salary is paid from a fund accrued from each guard's monthly wage.

However stern the prison system's rules governing punishment, they are considered too lenient under these people's administration. The barrel, the sweat box and leather, including 20 lashes a month, isn't capable of attaining the intended goal when administered by men who find themselves unfortunate and foolish enough to be under their jurisdiction. To get a good start they want a man or two killed to scare the rest. They have made a statement to this effect.

For fifteen months these same convicts have worked and cooperated with the new management successfully, with minor infractions of the rules, therefore no brutality. In fact, they have proven beyond a reasonable doubt that they could be handled without even stern discipline, only to be rewarded with a shift in the farm management which has not one motive other that exploitation and sadistic cruelty. Let's take these convicts into consideration. As a whole, they are convicted felons who have been classified and segregated to the Eastham as incorrigibles. Individually they are only unfortunate men who have each found justice through incarceration. They are human, however foolish.

Sometimes I had to agree with Harry McCormick that Roy King should have been a lawyer, judging from the way he pleaded his own case and that of his fellow prisoners. I felt Roy would have made a good writer, and much of the material he sent me was published, word for word, yet Roy's one and only ambition in life was to become a doctor. I still believe he would have made a good one if he had not become a victim of circumstances during the Depression. His first mistake was made in an effort to help me. Perhaps that, and his sworn statement that he had never found me during the time he was a fugitive, kept me funneling this material to the press. He wrote:

Brutality is condemned by society. Still these men have recourse to violence as a last resort, and then only after their

186

plight has been minimized by the skeptical eye of their own free fellow man and ignored by executives who could by their opinion and censure, adjust such a situation.

Since the prison manager transferred Capt. Joe Baker back here there has been an average of two mutilations and self inflicted wounds a day. The proof of this statement remains to be seen.

A timely investigation would expose the whole sorry mess. Two of the men who cut their legs off were shipped immediately to the Wayne farm and a half dozen or more with broken arms are in The Walls, also some of these have burned themselves severely with lye on the buttocks to evade the twenty lashes. One cut his hand completely off. He is in The Walls. Most of these here on the farm have broken legs, broken arms and lye burns. From all indications there will be more mutilations should Joe Baker, John West, Gordon Burns, W. W. Bailey and O. B. Simpson have their way. To these convicts the two captains, warden, prison manager and the Right Honorable Senator Burns form a syndicate of terror, and rightfully so. But why?

Each and every man who has mutilated himself to escape punishment or to evade a few days work under these slave drivers found such measures unnecessary under Capt. Owen. Mad Maniaco spent fifteen months under Capt. Owen with a clear record. There had been only a few minor infractions of the rules and no brutality. But two days after Capt. Joe Baker returned to power every privilege had been forfeited without cause. A stern set of rules was put into effect.

The Captain let not one man of the thousand here on Eastham misunderstand his policy and immediate intentions. The convicts are at a loss to explain this sudden change in management, much less the unwarranted change in the policy of the Texas Prison Board who define the policy of the executive personnel. To me it is indeed a sad event because I have been elected by the manager to partly shoulder the blame for his failure to come into a complete slave-like submission. (If so), a majority of these men would really be on the spot, for sure. Today someone gave the man a list of names that they claimed were agitators. So I guess there will be more mutilations tomorrow. If so I will write and let you know with the names of those who have already been mutilated.

I have made a home made camera and got two rolls of

film. I will send you pictures of guys and their mutilations, stabbings and suicides since these captains were transferred back in charge here . . .

Both *The Dallas News* and *The Houston Press* published stories on the brutality and the mutilations at the prison, yet neither was ready to stick its neck out in accusing Senator Gordon Burns and prison officials without positive evidence. This would be asking for a libel suit.

When given tips from Roy, we did manage to get reporters to the prison. Roy was as good as his word about getting the film out, and for a homemade camera the shots were better than expected. If they had caught him, I am sure it would have meant his life.

His next letter really frightened me.

Today I was interviewed with ten other men for agitating so maybe I will be reclassified and punished. If so then I am going to mutilate myself and mutiny to stay out of the field. I hope not though. You should know from my letters that I wouldn't dare agitate anyone against Joe Baker and John West.

Baker is supposed to have a trusty chained out somewhere, trying to get out of him some details about smuggling. How true it is I can't say but for God's sake be careful.

Capt. Joe Baker's slogan is 'More lead and more lashes.' It has caused more hate, misery and sorrow than crime has for me.

The building tenders were given orders by Joe Baker to kill any man caught mutilating or agitating. Six hours later his No. 1 building tender Ray Gordon had been stabbed. He is in The Walls now. Baker has told every man that he would kill anyone caught helping get rid of Sen. Gordon Burns and the prison manager.

The feeling of these men is hard to describe. It is a cross between desperation and baffled resignation, because as convicts they have seen Burns win out time and time again with his little dictatorship.

Capt. Baker's pet killer is 'Machine Gun Kelly', a vicious maniac from hell. His mind seems to register only the blackest of expressions judging from his talk. He told me if he didn't kill me that he would 'suck my dick'. He must want to because that was several days ago and I am still alive.

188

Just reading this letter was embarrassing enough, but it describes the desperateness of the situation, thus I have quoted it verbatim.

Roy did manage to obtain a letter from Senator Burns, demanding the $50 mustering out pay from a short-timer for restoration of his overtime. But like similar letters from him, it was not on a Senate letterhead and did not bear his signature. Royal needed a letter with the Burns signature.

Time seemed suspended. Only the days on the calendar moved. My grades suffered. My journalism teacher cut me down to the lowest passing grade. He talked with me saying he didn't understand. My stories, when I got them in, were the best in the class. I should be making all "A's." Several times I had been absent without apparent reason.

How could I tell him that my news stories were making continued headlines? It hurt me to feel his concern. I have never had a journalism professor as good as Cecil Horne and I told him so. I told him how much passing the course meant to me, and that there was something which I couldn't tell him that required a great deal of my time. I even told him that I was working for a "cause." He believed me, of this I feel certain, for my grades came up.

A few days before school was out a letter came from Roy, saying that he could get that "all important" letter. After ten years of graft and virtual control of prison personnel, Senator Burns had finally become careless. In an unguarded moment he or his secretary had written a letter to George Watson demanding $50 for restoration of his overtime. Through some inexplicable error he had signed it. A letter on his Senate stationery and with his signature was what had been needed for months. Roy was hot to get it and wrote it had been promised.

I went to McCormick with the news.

"For God's sake, Mary, forget it," he pleaded. "I never thought you would go this far. Even if Roy managed to get this letter in your hands you'd never get out with it alive. They've turned the prison inside out. Everyone is watching for that letter. Stoolies are planted everywhere. Unless we can get Watson out before the letter is published he will be killed."

"He will be anyway if they don't find the letter, won't he?"

"Or maybe he will be kept alive until the letter is found . . . or published."

"Then how?" I asked.

"Only one way I guess," Mack said thoughtfully. "And that's have someone from the press waiting at the prison the day he is scheduled to come out, or maybe have some sort of outside protection arranged. The letter should be published simultaneously with his release. They'll demand it and the money or he won't come out not alive."

"If Roy has it, I'll get it."

"No! For God's sake, no! You've a baby to think about. She's a pretty big girl now isn't she?"

I exhibited the ever-present photo.

"It's a promise, you'll forget the letter? I don't know why I ever let you get mixed up in this deal. You have a fine family, Mary, and a real opportunity in life. Don't throw it over now. You've gone far enough. There is a point of no return."

"You've risked your life many times doing prison stories," I refuted, "and you have a good wife and fine young son who need you too."

"But I get paid for my stories. It's my job."

"Reporting is your work Harry and you do get paid for it, but you seem to have forgotten how 'Mefo' (Harry's crusading editor) begged you not to risk your neck on these prison stories. In fact, he told you NOT to go for that interview with Raymond Hamilton while he was an escapee from the death house. Every cop in the nation was ordered to shoot on sight. If either Raymond or Ralph had told the truth on the night of Raymond's execution, you probably wouldn't be here now. You didn't get that kind of money, not enough to risk your neck over and over."

"But this is a man's work, Mary. Look what happened to Bonnie."

"It's too late to scare me out, Harry. Your ten-year struggle, as well as many lives, will have been thrown away if we fail now. What would make you think they would ever suspect me anyway?"

"The very walls have eyes. You know this as well as I do."

"And if Roy King hadn't lied, saying he'd never found me

190

*This headline story tells what Harry McCormick suffered while
working toward prison clean-up in the thirties. Years later he
told the author that he was never kidnapped at all but went to
McCormick of his own accord. He would probably have been
given a five year prison sentence himself for helping a fugitive.
It took him thirty years to prove Hamilton never killed anyone.*

while he was on the outside I'd be on the inside. You know that,
Harry."

"Females!" Harry said in way of parting. "Never have any
sense when it comes to loving a man, not even a convict."

I didn't bother to tell him I was divorcing Roy. He thought
I was nuts enough as it was. I had to get back to school. This was
dead week, as the week before exams is called at college, when
all other activities are stopped for study. If a student ever needed to cram, I did.

Only one more week of school, and still no letter from Roy.
I was worried about that more than my grades.

On the night before I took my last exam I received a telephone call. I never saw the man who put in the call and he did
not identify himself. He merely stated that he was in stir with
Roy and had come out on clemency.

"Roy has a letter," he stated, " 'THE LETTER,' but no one

191

could come out of 'the joint' with it and stay alive. Roy says that if you have the nerve to walk into and out of the prison with it, the whole batch, from senator to prison manager, warden and guards would be fired. It's dynamite."

"But how can I get it?" I asked with alarm. "They know me! I would be watched."

"The only way is to walk in and out at night."

"At night?" I gasped.

"Roy says to wait in the bushes at the end of the turn-row, the one you walked up when he was in trouble, on the edge of the field between the Ham and the Ferguson Farm."

How well I remembered, and reminded my informant that the turn-rows were a mile long.

"Near the river," he said, "at the end of the row, where it does the right angle, there's a good covering of brush. Wait in that. Cross two sticks about ten yards ahead of the turn to signal you are there. They'll trot the hoe squad out and they'll be alongside that patch of brush before good daylight. Roy will throw the letter to you in an empty tobacco sack. Be sure to stay out of sight. Stoolies are planted. Walk all the way through the trees down by the river and only after dark."

What a sentence! I felt exiled.

"Oh, yes," he cautioned, "Roy will be looking for you Sunday. That way he will know that you will be waiting before daylight on the turn-row. Give no indication of any kind of communication. Leave the prison area all the way. Take the Greyhound bus out of Lovelady, get off near the Trinity River, and wait until after dark."

"But, who are you," I blurted as he seemed to be ready to hang up the phone. "How do I know this is not a . . ."

"Good girl! Spider said that if you doubted just say that you are to plant his American Beauty Rose — whatever that means," he said as the receiver clicked.

It meant a lot. It was the same code which Roy had used when he broke from the prison. It meant that it really was a message from Roy.

I don't know how I got through my exam the next morning. I knew I would have to quit my job at the cafe. I had missed too many shifts already. This would be my last night as a waitress. I

192

would hardly have time to make it to Huntsville via home. I had to see my daughter, our daughter, before this last venture. My family must think I had only taken a day off from the cafe.

Friday afternoon I was on the bus. One day at home with my family and Jean. Saturday I had to leave to go back to work, I lied.

I headed out of Cisco toward Lubbock, as far as Abilene. There I crawled off the bus and headed east instead of north.

Sunday afternoon found me back in the chicken-wire coop called visiting quarters. A guard sat in the aisle which separated the visitors and convicts, further than arm's reach. Other were visiting. This made it easier for Roy and myself. Our eyes did most of the talking. But there was one fellow in that coop who seemed to be waiting for a visitor who failed to show.

Roy talked about Jean and the weather. I had no idea what he was saying but his eyes kept talking. He pulled out a Bull Durham sack, rolled a cigarette, and sort of tapped the bag with his fingers as he pulled the string taut with his teeth. His eyes never left mine during this operation. This sack was what I was to look for.

"Did you plant my American Beauty Rose?" he asked as visiting hour closed.

"No, but I will just as soon as I get back," I promised, letting him know for sure that I had received the message.

"I know it will be a real beaut. The most beautiful," Roy grinned reassuringly as the convicts were marched from the coop.

Chapter 15

Too Scared to Die

The visiting hour was up. I crawled on the shuttle which would take me to Lovelady where I would wait for the bus, as instructed. My mind recorded every landmark. There was no way to get lost between the river and the road, but Eastham No.1 Farm must be given a wide berth as well as the community of Weldon and some Negro shanties. The Eastham No. 1 and 2 Farms were across the river from the Ferguson Farm. They formed a sort of triangle, with the mile-long turn-row in between serving as a base. Just the thought of penetrating this triangle gave me the creeps.

I had another hour to think about it while I waited in Lovelady for the bus. I hoped the driver would think me a native when I asked to be let off in the middle of nowhere about halfway between Lovelady and Trinity. I hid underneath a secluded pine near the river until almost dark. Spanish moss hanging from the cypress trees gave me the creeps, especially when there was air enough for animation. I waged war with the insects and later put on the dark slacks and jacket I had brought along in a little shopping bag.

After dark I emerged on the side of the little road, if you could call it that, which staggered toward Weldon and the prison farms. I would have to stick close to it or the river. The road seemed the lesser of two evils and less likely to be inhabited by cottonmouth moccasins. I would have to skirt the farm houses because of the dogs.

As the darkness deepened, I felt as if I was walking into a tomb — my own. I made a wide circle back of the first two shanties. Underbrush tore at my clothing. Mosquitoes were unmerciful. Hidden roots and berry brambles allied with the mosquitoes and my fear of snakes. My mind was paralyzed with fear. I just couldn't penetrate deeply enough between these houses and the river, to escape the trained noses of the dogs, which every squatter seemed to have. Fortunately they seemed to keep them tied up. There was a $100 bounty for the capture of an escaped convict, and I hoped neither dog nor man would mistake me for one. I had counted the houses on my way out. I had made it back of the first three. I saw no more between the third and the community of Weldon. I had to chance the road.

I walked in deep sand in breathless silence. It was dark, very dark, the air was sticky and damp. I could hear myself breathing and my heart pounded as if trying to escape my body. I was all but running.

Suddenly, the moon broke through the clouds and a host of shrouded ghosts were before me on the roadway. I thought I was losing my mind. Then I remembered the graveyard. It sprawled on a mound in a bend of the road near Weldon. It looked as if there were more people here than in town. I wondered if it was really peaceful. How would it feel to be dead?

At least I knew where I was. I didn't know how long I had been walking, but it was seven miles from the highway to Weldon and the graveyard was fairly close to town. From Weldon it was one mile to the No. 1 Farm and another mile further on to the No. 2 Farm — the Ham.

I didn't see a light in town. I didn't know whether this was good or bad. It must have been near midnight. I didn't have a watch — couldn't afford one. I skirted half a dozen houses in Weldon and started the long mile to the Eastham No. 1 Farm.

What if someone in the prison saw me? At least they couldn't get out, I surmised, not sure whether the thought was comforting. I would have to give it a wide berth. I didn't know whether there were any dogs at either of the Eastham farms. When Roy had told me the story of his escape, he said they got the bloodhounds from the Ferguson Farm across the river. I hoped they kept them all there.

Now to give the No. 1 Farm a wide berth. The going wasn't so bad as the brush. I stayed along a fence row near the creeping, crawling vegetation which reached inside the fence here and there for a little open space. I didn't dare walk through the field. I had to blend with the underbrush.

Finally I was back of the No. 1 Farm heading for Eastham No. 2. Again the moon broke through. This time I saw the real tomb, a tomb where men are interred for their misdeeds while yet alive. I was wet with cold sweat. What if this was a trap?

I knew there were some two thousand prisoners and guards near me, yet I was never more alone. There were more across the river and dogs. A bird flushed from the brush and I was just sure a stoolie was swinging an ax toward me. I fell to the ground trying to choke back the dry sobs. I don't know how long I lay there. Gradually my fear subsided, at least to a degree that would let me think.

This couldn't be a trap. Roy's words had told me that this very afternoon or was it a century ago? The worst part of the trip was behind me. I was less than a mile from my destination. Nothing had harmed me . . . unless I caught malaria from the mosquitoes. At least I wasn't snake bit, not yet. It would be after daylight when I started back, yet there wasn't too much comfort in this thought.

What if I were caught? I would be killed, no doubt, and no one would ever know what became of me. Again I thought of Jean. Why did I always have to be such a fool? I would turn back now before I got the letter.

"Coward," I accused myself. "Go through all this and then turn tail and run?"

"There is a point of no return," I seemed to hear McCormick saying.

The battle raged within me and I must admit I said a few prayers.

"This time, God," I promised over and over, "if you will stick by me I'll never turn from the straight and narrow again. If it is right for humanity, please help me to get this letter. This one letter, God, and I'll spend the rest of my life trying to make amends to my daughter and family. I'm so alone, God."

Strength and some courage returned. At least I had regained self control and some composure. I must follow Roy's instructions. Now, before daylight. I headed for the rendezvous — the turn-row between the ferry and the Eastham No. 2 Farm.

When I reached familiar ground the world seemed less strange and hostile. I couldn't go too near the building. I would cut through a patch of brush and hit it about a quarter-mile away. I stopped and looked at the prison building, a real tomb. In my heart I felt there was someone with me. Roy must be lying awake in his cell. I was not alone. Roy and God knew. I hoped no one else did. I didn't want to die.

Soon I broke through the brush to the turn-row. The other fields had cotton, but this one had corn, and it was high. I felt I could walk on the turn-row itself between the corn and the brush with comparative safety. As I kept walking I felt I was getting uncomfortably near the sensitive noses of the bloodhounds across the river.

Through the darkness I could see where the turn-row made a right angle. The brush nearby was quite thick. This had to be the spot. I looked the situation over. Yes, this is where Roy had mentioned the squad slowing as it turned the corner.

I must do as I was instructed now, and make the cross with branches. I thought of breaking fresh ones, but this would make noise. Rotten ones would have to do. Since the field was dry rather than muddy this time, I knew I must leave no tracks. I did break off a small branch with leaves to brush out my tracks.

Using the brush to eradicate my footprints, I walked back up the turn-row a distance I figured to be ten yards, stepped out to the edge of it, crossed two fair sized limbs, and brushed out my tracks as I again ducked into the woods. Now I must wait.

Because of my afternoon visit, Roy would assume I would be here, but he must know positively before parting with the all-important letter. My crossed branches were certainly large enough for him to see, even in moonlight. I felt sure this must be the right spot. From his instructions I could figure no other place. It had to be right.

197

The clouds grew heavier. What if it rained? The men might not come to the fields at all. Please God, no rain, not now.

My scant preparations finished, I hunted for the thickest part of the brush nearest the corner of the turn-row. I needed rest but I mustn't sleep. I took a mashed sandwich from my shopping bag. Maybe I could eat a bite. It helped me stay awake, but it stuck in my throat and felt like a rock in my knotted stomach. I wondered and wondered what time it was. It seemed the sky was a little lighter in the east or was it my imagination?

After an eternity of waiting in the damp chill of the pre-dawn hours, the prison lights came on. Now I could see both the Eastham Farms as well as the Ferguson Farm across the Trinity. Suddenly, I heard the baying of bloodhounds and tensed. The barking ceased. It was merely the dogs awakening too.

It wasn't good daylight yet when I heard the men leaving the buildings. Fog curtained the Ferguson Farm across the river. The rising fog seemed to be spreading. Carefully I glanced about me in the underbrush, making sure I had left no tell-tale prints.

Now I could hear voices and curt commands. The men were heading toward the fields, but I could not see them. The fog was thicker than I thought. The squad sounded closer, but I saw no one. Abruptly, the head and shoulders of one man appeared. He seemed floating along. It was eerie. Then I saw the head of his horse. It was a guard. Only the guards rode. The men trotted alongside. Miles didn't matter, not to the guards.

Then the heads of a file of convicts rose from the fog. I hadn't realized the fog was so thick, so near me. The coming light of day added to the distortion. The line of heads floated toward me. I was glad for a momentary break in the density which showed me there were bodies too.

Some of the men were in white. They made their own clothes from white ducking in the prison shop, this I knew. A few of the prisoners wore stripes. Those wearing stripes were the ones who needed closer watching because of infractions of prison regulations. I knew Roy would be in stripes. He had been in them when I had seen him on Sunday afternoon. He would be in the second squad. This I had been told. I strained my eyes.

I spotted him glide long before I could see his facial features. A sudden tautness in Roy's gait made me realize that he had seen the sticks. As he came closer I felt his eyes were directly upon me, even though I was praying I could not be seen.

Roy slowed down and I held my breath. He was rolling a cigarette. He emptied the tobacco sack and slung it in my direction, lighting the cigarette almost simultaneously. I could see the tenseness in his face as he cupped his hands and the match flared momentarily. Quickly, the guard rode alongside and reined in his mount.

I had moved! The brush shook! The guard had seen! This was it! The secret was out!

"Hurry it up, you God damned lazy bastard!" the guard shouted as he cracked a whip in Roy's direction.

I sighed with relief as the guard clucked to his horse and resumed his former position at a safe distance from the cons.

The fog was so heavy I could hardly see the sack. As the last guard turned his back to me making the right angle at the turn-row, I wanted to dash out. I forced myself to wait until I could barely hear their swearing.

The fog didn't feel as thick as it looked when I crawled from the brush to the turn-row. I dared not stand up. It was thicker near the ground, yet it seemed a thousand eyes were upon me. Snatching the sack, I scrambled back on all fours like a long-haired rabbit in a prairie fire. I had to get out of there. The fog would have to cover me. Clutching my treasure, I plunged for the brush.

I had the letter. The letter which would nail Senator Gordon Burns to the cross. The letter demanding $50 from convict Watson for the restoration of his overtime. The letter which finally caught Senator Burns during an unguarded moment. The letter which bore his signature. The letter which caused all the search.

With the coming of daylight my fear subsided to a degree that I could live with. The cargo which I carried was far too precious to lose through an unguarded moment. Carefully, I picked my way through the pine forest where wood chopping crews from Eastham No. 1 had left evidence of their logging. My breath came easier as I hit an old logging trail. All convicts on the farms were busy with crops at this time of the year and I reasoned rightfully, that they would not be in this area.

199

I made good time now because I could see the ground where I was walking and fell into fewer traps. The sun was my friend too, and I headed due east into it with no fear of getting lost. The river was on my right, the road to Weldon on my left, and the highway straight ahead. About an hour past the Eastham No. 1 Farm my logging trail ended. My pine forest without too much underbrush was studded with more and more of those moss-back cypress. This meant the swampland of the river bottom. I hate swamps, but I didn't dare use the road now that it was daylight and I had the letter. A few yards past the end of the logging trail I sat down beneath a magnolia tree for a breath, and to think. Finding this wild magnolia made me feel better. The blossoms were large and fragrant. Too bad their beauty was lost to the world. Clasping one of the creamy white blossoms in my hands, I bowed my head in a silent prayer of thanks. The worst of my ordeal was over.

While I rested I carefully loosened the draw strings of the tobacco sack and extracted the carefully folded letter. The letter itself didn't say much, insofar as I was concerned, just demanded that Watson leave his $50 mustering out pay with a clerk in the prison office on the day he was released. Other unsigned communications had carried a similar message. But this one was on the Senate letterhead and bore the signature which made it the most important document of my life. I must get it to Harry McCormick.

Folding the letter very carefully so as not to make more creases, I put the letter into the pocket of the light jacket which I was wearing to protect myself from the underbrush and mosquitoes, extracted a safety pin from my purse and pinned the pocket closed.

Nearing the highway I secluded myself underneath the protective curtain of an old moss-back, as the trees heavily draped with Spanish moss were called, and changed clothes. Carefully, I unpinned the pocket, extracted the letter and hid it deep within a zippered pocket of my purse. Again in a dress, I discarded the mutilated slacks and jacket in some thick brush. My muddy oxfords would have to stick with me a little longer until I was closer to the road. When I was within seeing distance of the highway I took my slippers and hose from the bag. These were its only contents now, save for my dirty blouse, which I had saved for this purpose. Dipping the blouse into a little stream which flowed into the river, I washed my face and applied a little make-up. After washing my feet I threw away the blouse and oddly shaped balls of mud which had once been fairly decent school oxfords. Wearing a dress, as well as hose and high heels, I felt sure no one would suspect that I had spent the night in the swampy bottomland. Clutching my purse as if it contained all the gold in the world, I cautiously crept out to the edge of the highway when no car was within seeing distance. I timed it just so, when I heard a big truck groaning in the distance.

I had to be lucky and was. When the truck driver stopped to pick me up I explained that I was walking into Lovelady to catch a bus to Dallas. My prayers were answered. He was driving a through truck on this run and insisted that I ride with him. Within an hour we stopped for breakfast. I was starved. I insisted on paying for my own meal but the truck driver would have none of it.

Once in Dallas I wasted no time in calling McCormick. He left the *News* office and almost immediately came to the Walgreen Drug store from which I had made the call. Never could a man have been more grateful or relieved. I told him that I felt fairly positive that I was not being followed. It would have been impossible. Besides, if they had known, I would have been killed in the woods rather than being allowed to escape with the letter.

Here, Harry agreed with me, but he cautioned, "This does not mean that they won't suspect, or put a tail on you later. Now promise me to get out and stay out of this mess. I'll take the letter to Royal myself."

"But do you think he will use the letter right away?"

"He will more than likely have it photocopied ready and waiting. The timing will have to be just right. First, we use the first letter you sent without the signature. Burns will deny it, naturally. Then, boom with the killing blow, when we're sure it won't cost Watson his neck. We'll be ready and waiting when he comes out of prison, or at least when he is supposed to emerge. No one will get his fifty bucks. We'll have a photostat of the letter just waiting for them to stop him. We've got the kingpin this time."

"Are you sure?"

"Absolutely! We've had an investigation committee on other types of grafts. This signature is all that is needed to clean house, from Senator Burns right down through the prison management to the guards. Just keep your nose clean."

Never was I happier to make such a promise.

In 1940 the author was still afraid to reveal her identity, fearing both the law and the lawless. There was no work for Mary King, tagged "Gun Moll" while fleeing with escaped convict husband.

Part

2

Chapter 16

LOVE,

Strange and Unpredictable

Thus my new life began. True to my word, I never saw Roy King again. My debt was paid my conscience clear. His life was spared. Perhaps he too felt proud of his part in exposing the sordid conditions at the prison. Hopefully he became a better man one free of dope. He had laid his own life on the line to help his fellow prisoners. We had won.

Seven years I had fought to help the man I loved. I lost the battle, but won the war. With the unwavering help of Harry McCormick and Roy King, we had won our war against a state senator and officials of the Texas Prison System. Rehabilitation was well under way. It was good to hear Roy was no longer a dope addict and doing well. Perhaps we had repaid our debt to each other and to society. This phase of my life was truly ended.

Life was wonderful. My daughter and I were together and I had two years teaching experience under my belt. In 1940 I taught at Roosevelt, a small rural community ten miles from Lubbock. My wages were $97.50 per month. The following year I got a better position teaching a fourth grade in Dupre Elementary of Lubbock. Both my sisters Lela and Annie were living in Cisco. Lela was teaching and Ann was raising a family. Her husband Robert Rendall found work in the oil field near Cisco and

204

we all loved having them home. Our brothers, Roy, Van, Paul, and Leonard all had good jobs and were raising families. Bill had finished college and joined the Marine Corps. I was back in Texas Tech, doing graduate work.

Things were rather serene for our family since the depression until World War II struck. Then my older brother, Roy Latch, developed lympahatic leukemia. His days were numbered. The doctor said he needed blood. I rushed to Odessa and gave. Bob drove Ann and the children to West Texas. Ann had the same type "A" blood as Roy and I; but Bob was type "O." Friends gave, but the situation became difficult.

The Red Cross got Bill an extended furlough and he gave. Lela, a true patriot, had resigned teaching and joined the W.A.C. She was based at Kingman Air Force Base in Arizona. She too managed to get to Odessa and give. But as the doctor predicted, Roy's leukemia accelerated and he needed to be in a larger hospital where there was a better blood supply and more adequate facilities.

Roy was transferred to the Lubbock General Hospital where specialists could study and treat his rare and hopeless malady. Lymphatic leukemia! Why would a man who had lived near the soil and closer to God fall victim of this rare disease? Where a battle is waged within the blood stream . . . a losing battle.

The doctors had pulled no punches in telling us that this was a fatal type anemia where the red corpuscles are destroyed by the white. For no apparent reason the white corpuscles suddenly go rampant, feed upon the red and multiply at a fantastic rate of speed. The life of a patient is prolonged by the transfusion of blood, but not saved. Both the cause and cure of this strangely slow but fatal disease of the blood-stream remain a challenge which science will surely conquer in the near future.

Driven by that sort of desperation which shortage of time can inflict upon mortals, I stood trembling a female alone at the doorway of a Service Man's Night Club on College Avenue past midnight, urging myself to enter. If I had suddenly been transplanted on a new continent my mission nor my surroundings could hardly have seemed less strange. Yet there was no time to think before casting myself upon humanity in quest of that which could sustain the flickering light of life, a borrowed moment.

This is Roy Latch, with his wife, Lois Thames Latch and their daughters, Roylene and Lois Marie, before Roy became critically ill with lymphatic leukemia.

W.A.C. Lela Latch and Marine Bill Latch, both received emergency leave to give blood to their brother, Roy Latch, who was slowly dying of lymphatic leukemia. Lela was serving as a Link trainer at Kingman Air Force Base in Arizona, and Bill was serving in the Southwest Pacific.

As I stood faltering under the blinking beer sign, my mind flicked back to the hallway outside my brother's hospital room where the specialist had told me less than an hour ago what must be done.

"A pint of blood," I could still hear him saying, "a pint of blood will be needed every day now to sustain life as long as possible."

Eyeing me keenly, the physician continued. "As you know, 'A' is not the rarest, nor a common type of blood. It will be hard to find, and with so many medics overseas, all hospitals are pushed to the limit."

I braced myself for the rest as that unfathomable look of sympathy which comes to a doctor's face when he knows he is combatting the inevitable, flicked momentarily across his strong and customarily reassuring countenance.

"We don't have time to type your friends or college students," he continued. "Perhaps one out of every twenty-five might do, but the labs are pushed to the limit too due to the war."

With unquestionable finality he resumed his speech.

"The best thing for you to do is try for soldiers at the Lubbock Air Force Base. Those boys are typed and have been very generous. We have no type 'A' on hand. Have three boys waiting in the morning at eight. Three will be needed every morning." Glancing at his watch and giving me a sympathetic pat on the back he concluded, "Sorry I couldn't have gotten to this sooner. All supervisory personnel at the base who I could contact have been off duty now as many hours as I should have been. You couldn't get into that place with dynamite. You're on your own now young lady."

I was too stunned to think. Few transfusions had been needed in the preceding months. Fortunately and by rare coincidence the doctors said all our family had the same type blood. But we were beyond the point where we could give. Our brother's life hung in the balance.

I was alone, yes, all alone. Back home our aging mother lay restless in her bed denied her last request to go to the bedside of her eldest son who was fighting a losing battle with time. With her heart like it was it could mean both of them, the doctor advised.

Mrs. Amanda Peeples Latch, mother of eight children, was too sick herself to go anywhere, while her son lay on his death bed.

Alone, I was all alone in a city among thousands of people. What to do? Even if I had the money where was I to find donors? Blood cost $35 a pint and I was assured that it would take many transfusions.

America has a heart, an especially big one in the military, I was sure. But was it big enough to donate blood to a man never seen before, one who had not even been in the service?

I tried the U.S.O. It was closed. Only the night spots were alive. I had no choice. Standing there in the doorway of that club, the music and laughter spilling out of it seemed to be piped from another world. Resolutely I pushed my way against the out-flowing tide of uniforms. Time was a precious moment. Perhaps even now opportunity had passed with arm's length and I had been a faltering coward. A life depended upon my courage.

As I hit the mellow crimson light from the inside some of the boys stepped back and started to give with that soft, musical wolf call, but the 'something' which must have shown in my eyes stopped them between syllables.

I walked straight to a large table well-laden with Oak Leaf Clusters and blurted out my mission without stopping for breath.

Uproarious laughter burst forth from a soldier with a much decorated uniform. Staggering to his feet he soliloquized, "I thought I had heard them all, but this baby's sure hit a new angle." Then he mushed, "A pint of blood she asks, and in a joint like this past midnight. What have you been drinking, Baby?

Come on! Let's dance! What are you waitin' for? A pint of blood? Sure, you can have a quart if you want it, but let's dance first."

Hot tears of anger and frustration stung my face but swimming through them a pair of eyes held mine like a vise as I turned to run.

I no longer heard the banter of my assailant, but was drawn to those eyes like an Arab to an oasis. They now hovered above me and the place seemed strangely quiet as a soft voice calmly drawled, "Join us at our table for a cup of coffee, Miss?"

He guided me like a canoe drifting downstream. I sank at his table and came out of the fog to hear him saying, "Our table is not as well decorated as theirs but give us time. You've got to understand those boys. They've just come back from overseas and flying fifty missions isn't exactly a picnic. Most of them have a few memories to drown. No harm meant."

Real sympathy registered in his roughly handsome face which now assumed other features than eyes. The rest of the boys at the table remained an audience as he continued. "Now, if it isn't too much trouble will you come with that little story again?"

Before I had finished I had quite an audience and half a dozen of the boys volunteered to give. My much decorated assailant, who had hung in the background, drew nearer and was still having a great deal of trouble with his "s's" as he attempted an apology and proudly exhibited his dog tags with an "A" plainly engraved upon it. My knight with the holding eyes, a staff sergeant, was directing.

"Now you be at gate No. 1 in the morning at seven, Miss. There will be three of us waiting. I don't know how we'll get out, but we'll jump the fence if necessary."

If I live to be a mummy I could never express my gratitude to those boys nor to Top Sergeant Tomlin who said, "If the boys aren't waiting, I'll round them up."

But the boys were always waiting and somewhere, always in the background, stood either a much decorated uniform or that pair of enchanting eyes sometimes both. Staff Sergeant Carey was the name that belonged to the uniform with "those eyes."

It wasn't easy entertaining three soldiers from seven in the morning until noon. They were typed at eight provided they had eaten no breakfast, and not allowed to eat nor drink anything except water until four or five hours later, when the technicians finally selected the most perfect cross-type from the blood specimens taken earlier.

I guarded my captives carefully to make sure they did not forget these instructions and did what little I could to help them pass away those long hours until the "winner" was selected.

If it had not been for the U.S.O. opening its doors earlier than usual for my convenience, I don't know what I would have done. I played ping-pong, bridge, rummy, danced, and even learned to play pool as the days dragged into weeks.

Twice my hero, Sgt. Richard C. Carey, had come to the hospital, but twice he had been turned down because he wasn't a perfect cross-type.

"Not cross-typing once doesn't necessarily mean that a person won't cross-type the next time," the technicians had assured me. "So long as they are the same type bring them back if they want to try again."

Hadn't I myself given three times and been turned down the fourth time because I didn't cross-type?

Not so much because I thought he might be selected to give, but more because of my strange fascination for him and his determination to give, I carried Dick Carey back with me the third time within less than five weeks.

Being a college student and at least average for looks, several of the boys asked me for a date but not Dick. I was not interested in going out considering the circumstances, but that certain percentage of invitations does something for a girl's ego, regardless of time and place.

That morning at the U.S.O. I was thinking of what the specialist had told me about not needing many more transfusions when Dick suggested a drink of water, since Cokes were out of order.

When alone he finally gave with, "I can't dance like some of the other fellows, but I'll tune up the old juke box if you'll try a round with me."

His dance was smooth not fancy.

"Mary," he addressed me, "I just wanted to get you away from the others long enough to tell you I feel like a heel. I've wanted to give just as badly as any of them, but as much as I have wanted to give I believe I've wanted to see you more."

210

"I've heard of more criminal aspirations," I smiled back at him.

As the music slowed he guided me to a half-secluded corner and breathed a kiss so softly upon my ear that I half-wondered if it had really happened. Without another word he guided me back to the table where the other two prospective donors were playing pool.

Dropping his cue Sergeant Bender fired, "Trying to play a game of monopoly, Buddy?"

A feminine voice broke in, "A call for Miss Latch from the hospital." I ran to answer the phone.

"We want Sergeant Carey this time," the technician's voice came over the wire. "We are ready for you now."

One would have thought Dick was making a triumphant march instead of a trip to surgery. Only two other transfusions were needed.

The morning after my brother's heroic struggle ended I found myself driving toward the Lubbock Air Force Base. I was not sure of the impulse. I was sure the boys would understand had I failed to show up, yet something drew me on.

As I neared the gate tears blurred my vision and I had to stop. As the waiting soldiers approached the car I tried desperately to tell them that no more blood was needed, but words would not come.

"We know," Dick started slowly, "but coming here has gotten to be sort of a habit and we wanted to pay our last respects to him."

"I'm really sorry I missed my turn," spoke up a young private with a slick chin.

"He was a grand guy to the very last," spoke up PFC Joe Austin, the last donor who was from the nation's capital.

"And when he thanked us he made a man feel like he had done something good and noble," added Waselski, a "Polock" from Minnesota.

"Couldn't lift the hand he asked us to shake," rejoined Dick, "but he could smile. Must have been a wonderful guy, this Roy Latch, a wonderful guy to take it on the chin like he did and all the time knowing . . ."

That was the last I saw or heard from Sergeant Carey, I thought . . .

211

Did he ever think of me?

After the funeral in West Texas I drove back to Texas Tech to try to pick up the pieces. Less than two weeks of summer session remained, and I had missed most of my classes. Making up this much work in so short a time while finishing the courses, too, was impossible. Knowing I would receive only "incompletes" rather than credits hurt. But when you are dealing with the inevitable you are not in the driver's seat.

As I was getting ready to drive to Cisco to get Jean and to start teaching again, I thought once more of Richard Carey. On my way out I just couldn't help looking in the Service Man's Club again. He was not there. Neither was anyone I recognized.

Things happen so suddenly in the military. Did Dick tell me he was scheduled for overseas? Would he write? He didn't even have my address. Maybe he didn't want it. It was all in my head. Perhaps he didn't even love me at all. Maybe he just felt sorry for me and wanted to boost my morale.

Ships that pass in the night that's all. It was over. He should be the aggressor and come looking for me if he really loved me. It was over.

Again I was teaching and things went well for us, but when I listened to the war news I always thought of Sergeant Carey. So much was happening and the time was so tense that there was no time to think of self.

Pearl Harbor was bombed, December 7, 1941. My brother Bill was on the U.S.S. *Helena*. She took a bomb down her stack and was severely damaged. Most of the crew survived. Fortunately, our brother was among the survivors. The cruiser was floated, repaired and again firing away in Kula Gulf when she was again attacked. This time she sank to the bottom in three pieces. Bill was reported missing and presumed lost in action.

"Bill is not dead," my mother reported the next morning. "He came to me last night. He said he was safe. I saw him."

We all wanted to believe her. I'll always believe that mothers have a God-given intuition when an offspring is in danger. Two weeks passed. No word but Mother refused to believe he was lost. "He keeps coming to me," she repeated several times. "His arms are outstretched."

What did happen is truly stranger than fiction. Most of the

212

While serving at Pearl Harbor, the U.S.S. Helena, *on which Bill Latch served as turret gunner, took a direct hit, down the stack. It was repaired, and later went down in three pieces in the Battle of Kula Gulf. Bill was reported missing in action. Our mother kept the faith, saying that Bill came to her, over and over.*

Helena's crew did go down with the ship, but Bill and several others made it to a life raft.

"The water was burning all around us," Bill later reported. "Many did not make it through the fire which was burning the oil slick. We were all coughing and gasping for breath. We managed to clear the fire. We took turns riding and hanging onto the raft. It helped but after two days some of the fellows just slipped under. We were too weak to help. On the third day we saw an island and tried to make it. We couldn't. The current was too swift and the coral was cutting our feet to ribbons. Suddenly there was an outrigger right by us. The biggest blackest native I ever saw held up a hatchet and asked, 'Amelican or Nipponese?' Our faces were so black and swollen that we did not look human. I did not know who held the island, but feared it was the Japs. We had no way of knowing which side the islanders were on.

"The question was too much to answer. Come through all this and our lives depended upon one word. None of the seven of us could speak, or at least were afraid to try. I passed out. When I came to the natives had me in a boat and were pouring water over me. Finally convinced that we were 'Amelicans,' they hid us and brought us food and water. We mostly lived on green bananas. They hid us deep in the jungle. We could always tell

213

when they were coming because they sang 'Onward Christian Soldiers' in English."

"So you owe your lives to American missionaries?" my mother gasped.

"The Lord works in mysterious ways," my father concluded. "But tell us son how were you rescued?"

"There was an Australian radio base hidden on the island. They finally contacted the Destroyer *Nicholas* and told them where to pick us up with P.T. boats. So many heroes are unsung and we can never thank them. We could not speak the language of the island and had no way of finding out, but hopefully some day, I will meet an English, American or Australian missionary who was on 'Vella la Vella' Island and taught these natives to sing 'Onward Christian Soldiers.' "

Jean wanted Uncle Bill to tell more and more stories, but we had to get back to Lubbock. The Christmas holidays were expended.

When school was over in the spring nothing could have kept us from Cisco. Bill had received many honors from the service and was being discharged. Jeannie and her cousins were all looking forward to that wonderful day when Bill again became the narrator at Grandma and Grandpa's house. Jean would stay there while I returned to Lubbock alone to finish the work in journalism I had started the previous summer. Loving arms kept me a little longer in Cisco than I had planned. It was almost midnight when I found myself near the Service Man's Club, which was just off campus on College Avenue in Lubbock. Thoughts of Dick Carey invaded my heart. It had been a long, hard drive and I could use a little refreshment. Everything on campus would be closed. Why not?

Again I found myself underneath that same blinking beer sign. This time I was not trembling, but still hesitating. I wanted to go in, to look around just for memory's sake, but no one would understand that. Nevertheless I eased inside the doorway, straining for a glimpse of those same soft eyes. Suddenly they floated toward me through the smoke haze. They seemed lighted with an expectant glow. Was it a dream? If so the vision spoke and with that same casual drawl.

"Been waiting for you Mary. Come inside. Been waiting almost a year for this. Remember this table?"

It was the same table where I had told my little story a thousand dreams ago. Yes he was the same Sergeant Carey, except now he wore many decorations and was several shades darker. I recognized the Distinguished Flying Cross, the Air Medal and three Oak Leaf Clusters, but he had some ribbons I didn't recognize. It was the soldier I loved not the decorations. To me he was the most wonderful soldier in the whole world. How else could a love born of tragedy reunite us? We just sat there sharing dreams with our eyes until he finally got up and slipped a nickel into the juke box, which broke out with a popular song of the day with words that said it all:

"You've got to accentuate the positive, eliminate the negative, latch on to the affirmative, and don't mess with Mr. Inbetween."

"Strange how much philosophy can be packed into a silly jitterbug number like that," Dick soliloquized. "Every time I hear it, the words 'Latch on' somehow jump at me. Your last name Latch, seemed strange to me at first, but somehow I just 'Latched on' to a memory and it turned into a dream, eliminating the war and everything we had to go through."

His eyes were misty and oceans away as he continued. "All the time I was in New Guinea, I visioned coming back here and meeting you again. You were with me on all my missions. It wouldn't have been fair to ask you for a date while you were so sad. Life is strange."

"And very unpredictable," I added as I felt a pair of strong arms drawing me closer to those ribbons.

"How about that date?" he asked as tantalizing lips drew near mine.

Strange I had never noticed his lips before but this time those eyes were closed and he went straight for the target.

We made up for those lost months by dating every night. I finally got up courage enough to tell him about Roy King and Jean. He wanted to meet Jeannie and my parents, so we drove to Cisco. Jeannie knew we were coming and as soon as the

215

unnecessary introductions were finished she asked, "Did you get hurt in the war like my Uncle Bill?" Her sharp eyes caught the ugly scar on Dick's right wrist. "Did you get the Purple Heart?"

"No, I cut my own wrist."

"You did? How?"

Then Dick shared the same story he told me earlier, when I asked the same question about the prominent scar which all but encircled his right wrist.

"Coming back from a bombing mission our plane was hit not bad enough to bring her down immediately, but she began losing altitude," Dick replied. "We were over the jungle, headed for our base in New Guinea. We thought we could make it, but the plane began losing altitude too fast. We had to jump. Our parachutes got caught in all sorts of trees and vines, but we all made it down. We knew we were not too far from the air strip, so we started hacking our way through the jungle. Getting hurt was my own fault. I hacked at a vine which was too big for my machete, and it bounced. The machete was thrown into the air and landed across my wrist, dern near cutting my hand off."

Jean gasped and Dick continued. "Fortunately they had seen our B-17 go down and another member of our squadron reported our location, saying we had jumped. My buddies managed to put enough pressure on my spurting arteries to slow the flow of blood. Within minutes the chopper had picked me up and I was in the base hospital. For three months they wanted to amputate. I had gotten jungle rot but I wouldn't agree. It finally got well but it isn't very strong yet."

Jean wanted more details, but Dick was very hesitant to talk about his war experiences.

Jean adored Sergeant Carey and I could see that my parents liked him too. I knew they would agree to marriage, if Dick ever asked me to marry him.

On our next date Dick announced, "I'm scheduled to be discharged soon from where I entered the service at Camp Atterbery, Indiana. I'm coming out on the point system since I have flown my fifty missions."

I was strangely quiet, so he continued, "Then I would like to drive on up to Marion, Ohio, to see my mother. My father died while I was overseas, but I do want to see my mother and

216

my two sisters too. Betty lives in Columbus and Glendora in West Virginia. Would you like to come along? You say you will be finished with the journalism courses you are taking next week."

"I would love to," I admitted, "but don't you think such a trip would be a little improper?"

"I don't think so. I want my mother and my sisters to meet my wife."

I was speechless as he continued. "I would like to take you to the 'Indy Five Hundred.' I haven't seen the races in years and thought we might enjoy them together on our honeymoon."

Again his lips sought mine . . . and you know the answer . . .

Chapter 17

At Last, A Real Family

Together we drove to Cisco to reveal our plans. There was only one hitch. Dick wanted to return to school on his G.I. Bill of Rights. He wanted to study electronics, but the school he hoped to attend was in New York City. Our finances were limited, but I insisted I could find work in a newspaper office. If not I could always resort to being a waitress until I found something better. War had escalated and jobs were plentiful. V.E. (Victory over Europe) Day had already been celebrated May 7, 1945. Now we awaited V.J. (Victory over Japan) Day, when all would be right with the world.

However much my parents liked Dick I could tell that taking Jean so far away for so long a time would be a very painful decision. But here our Jeannie came through. The trip sounded so exciting that her eyes glowed. Her happiness came first. After all, she was hardly a child anymore. She was ready for junior high and capable of making her own decisions.

Perhaps only those who have been deprived of the joy of a real family could understand our happiness. I resigned teaching to be with my husband. After our glorious honeymoon the three of us set off for New York City, leaving not one but two precious families behind.

Upon arrival Richard was all set to enter the electronics school, but we couldn't find a place to live. We beat out Manhat-

A happy mother and daughter, Jean Carey and Mary Carey, shortly after the author married Sgt. Richard C. Carey and just before they left Texas to live in Washington, DC, where Carey would study electronics, Jean would enter junior high and I would teach school.

tan, then Jersey shore. Finding living quarters in a decent place we could afford seemed impossible. After a ten-day search, we were beaten. Facing defeat we discussed what we should do. Our finances living in a hotel and eating out were dwindling at a rapid rate, and we had a family to consider. Perhaps not surrender but retreat would be the better alternative.

Thus we started driving back to Texas where we knew we could find employment and a place to live. Dick could enter school later. His ambition would just have to be put on hold a little longer. As we neared a turn to the west, a highway sign read, "Washington, D.C., next exit."

"My pilot lives in D.C.," Dick commented.

"Do you want to see him," I asked as I read his heart. "Then you better take the next exit."

"It's less than 200 miles," Dick noted as we exited for a turn to the east.

When we found Dick's pilot, he asked, "Why don't you enter a watchmaking school here in D.C.? They are advertising openings for G.I.'s. You may not want to become a watchmaker," Joe added, "but you could handle it even with a weak wrist. I never thought I would see you with a right hand again. I saw you the last time you were in the hospital in New Guinea. They were threatening amputation. How long were you there?"

"Three months," Dick replied, "but she's in pretty good shape now. Almost as strong as my left."

Again we were searching for an apartment this time with better luck. It was only a basement apartment, but it was clean and in a good part of town, Mt. Pleasant.

"I'm going to find a publications job here in Washington," I announced, "where I'll get to know potentates. I'm going to put my journalism training to work," I declared as we settled in our modest abode.

"Could we see the White House," Jeannie begged. "I can't start to school because there aren't enough teachers. Will you get to visit the president if you do newspaper work?"

This question shot a guilt dagger through my heart. We had all heard the announcements over the radio, not enough teachers to open the schools. Anyone holding a degree should come down and take a qualifying test for positions still open, otherwise schools may not open on time.

"Surely they will find enough teachers," I thought aloud. "Not even their appeal to patriotism will work. Both our families have paid their dues. Opportunity for such a position may never present itself again," I reasoned with myself, "and this could launch me into publications. Must I give up that for which I have been studying without even trying for such a position?"

We did take Jeannie to the White House, to the Smithsonian and to Rock Creek Park that first weekend. Monday Dick and Jean should start school and I would look for work.

"Schools will not be opened tomorrow," came the announcement over radio Sunday night. "They will remain closed all week if enough teachers are not found. Remember loyalty to your country is also served at home."

"I capitulate," I moaned to Dick when we retired. "My Texas certificate is not good here, but they said anyone who could pass the test would be provided with an emergency certificate and be placed."

"That's up to you, Darling," Dick replied thoughtfully. "Wish I could have flown more than two missions over Japan. We

220

could have watched the action if we had a television set. I might have recognized some of the planes bombing Japan. I sure hated to leave my buddies, but they've WON! It's all over now. I sure do wish we could have watched the action as it happened."

"Me too," I agreed, "but to watch a TV newscast takes lots of jostling in front of an electronics show window."

"I would soon be working on TVs if we had found a place to live in New York City. And if I hadn't been so careless with my machete I would have been with my crew in a B-17 helping win the war."

"Or maybe dead. Let's forget about it. Our new life begins tomorrow. I'll teach another year and another if it is necessary to help keep our schools in operation. Journalistic opportunities may not be as great. I know you had much rather study electronics but we will both cling to our dreams. They will come true and things will open for us. Good night sweetheart."

Early the next morning I went down to take that test. When I returned home I was very elated. "I flunked that test," I reported as Dick opened the door. "D.C. is the leader with that modern progressive junk and no textbooks. Each teacher must develop her own study unit around a central theme and everything must be oriented toward this theme. What does arithmetic have to do with geography? I can't teach without textbooks. I can't, despite what Benét advocates in his books. I didn't even finish his first book . . . and I didn't even try to answer the questions."

"At least you've cleared your conscience," Dick consoled.

"And when you go to school in the morning I'm going to scout a newspaper job," I replied happily.

I was in the process of getting dressed the next morning when the telephone rang. "It's for you," Dick called, "from the school board office."

"Are you Mrs. Carey?" came the voice over the wire. "Then we're delighted to report we have an opening for you in the sixth grade. If you will come down right away and sign a contract it will be one step more toward opening the schools Monday. So many teachers have responded to our plea that we are delighted."

"But I didn't pass that test," I stammered in disbelief. "I

221

didn't even answer a whole raft of questions. Do you really need teachers that badly?"

A short silence on the other end of the line gave me the answer. "Your name is on the list for me to call. You are to report to our central office to sign a contract as soon as possible."

When I got to the downtown office I was even more surprised. Along with my contract were paragraphs I had never seen before, such as, "I will not strike against the U.S. Government."

"You mean this is a Civil Service job?" I asked in surprise.

"You will be working for the District of Columbia. Everything is Civil Service here."

Thus our life in the nation's capitol began. Dick and Jean were both in school and I was teaching. Time passed quickly. There were so many things to see and do — many of them for free. We loved driving to Chain Creek bridge, renting a canoe and fishing or floating down to Watergate where there were free performances from military bands. Visiting the national cemetery and watching the changing of the guard at the "Tomb of the Unknown Soldier" held a strange attraction for Jean. We all loved riding to the top of Washington Monument and gazing out over the city. Dick was especially fond of fishing for carp in the Tidal Basin with mulberries. Jeannie and I loved the basin most during cherry blossom time, and we all liked the Lincoln Memorial.

Yes, there was always something delightful to do free of charge in Washington, D.C. If the weather was bad we could always visit one of the many museums, Congress, or one of the best libraries in the world. Sometimes we would drive across one of the many bridges and visit outlying areas. D.C. was never dull.

School was out for all three of us the following spring, and again we were headed for Texas for a glorious reunion. My parents were delighted to hear that Dick and I were both assured of positions in Wichita Falls, Texas, close enough to drive down on holidays, or even weekends. Jean was becoming quite a young lady. She played the flute and the piano beautifully and twirled a baton like a dream. Dick secured a job at Shepherd Air Force Base during the day and took night courses at Midwestern University. The first year back I taught at Holiday only ten miles

Top Honors: Jean Carey, left, twirler, and Jerry Massey, drum major, both members of the Wichita Falls High School Band, won top honors with their duet ensemble at the Waurika band festival Friday. Massey also placed first with his solo, and Miss Carey won second with her solo.

from Wichita Falls. The second year I taught at Travis Elementary in town.

When Jeannie was a junior in high school we had a little mother-daughter talk.

"Honey," I began, "you're a beautiful young lady and very accomplished for your age. But next year you'll be a senior and the following year you plan to attend college. I've just been wondering, shouldn't you drop some of your extracurricular activities and concentrate on earning a scholarship? I don't feel there's too much of a future in twirling and it takes so much of your time."

"But Mama, I have a straight 'A' average. But there are two in my class who have 'A+' averages and I don't think I could beat them. I've been thinking that I've won several honors in twirling and in band and that I will come closer to getting a full scholarship as a majorette."

"You may Darling, but I don't see too much future in being a majorette."

"Let's make a deal," she begged. "If I keep up my 'A' average, can I keep twirling? I do love it, and I do feel it will earn me a scholarship."

You know who won and she did win that scholarship and to Midwestern where we lived.

Only once while Jean was growing up did I see Richard Carey really apply a disciplinary action against her, and in a very surprising manner. Jeannie never liked milk. She was only 5'2" and weighed only ninety-eight pounds. She was so afraid of getting roly-poly that she was very picky about her food. On this particular occasion she was all dressed in a beautiful new red and white satin majorette uniform and ready to go. She didn't want to eat.

"Then take some time to drink your milk," I admonished.

She picked it up, took a sip and promptly set it back down saying, "It's blinky."

"It can't be," I said in disbelief. "I just bought it on the way home from school today."

"But it is," she sassed, "and I'm not going to drink it."

Picking up the milk Dick tasted it, said it was good and without another word threw the contents of the glass into her face. Milk and tears mixed as they streamed down her beautiful white satin uniform.

"Never sass your mother again," Richard Carey proclaimed with militant authority . . . and she never did.

During her senior year in high school Jean fell in love with Frank Richardson of Sweeny, Texas, who was a freshman at Midwestern. It was love at first sight and she never changed her mind. During her junior year in college they asked our blessing in marriage, saying they would both finish college, but they wanted to do it together.

We felt they were both pretty young but Dick had just gotten a good job in electronics with a new company, Texas Instruments in Dallas. This time we knew our daughter would not come with us. She and Frank wanted to study geology together. We liked Frank and his mother, who was superintendent of the Sweeny schools, invited us down for a visit. We liked Vadis and Joe very much, and parents on both sides gave their blessing.

Thus Dick and I moved to Dallas without our little girl. She told Frank and his family that she was a prisoner's daughter, but they did not seem to hold that against her. They fell in love with Jean, and what happened before she was born didn't seem to

224

shake their confidence. If the kids wanted to finish college together the family would help.

Dick became a charter employee of Texas Instruments and loved his work. For the first time I found work in my own field, teaching journalism in North Dallas High School. It took time to recover from the "empty nest" syndrome, but soon we were both busy with our own hobbies. Dick wanted to build a cabin cruiser, a thirty-two footer. I encouraged him even though we both knew it would take years of after-hours work.

My heart was set on writing about the time I spent with Roy King as a fugitive. I knew I could not write the story using real names because of fear that there might still be someone who would try to kill me, or that Roy might come out of prison looking for me. Besides it would hurt many families unnecessarily, naming everyone concerned, from a senator to prison officials and convicts. Thus I fictionized the story and entered it in the National *True Confession* contest in 1954.

I tried to forget about it while awaiting the results. Helping my husband was the best way to cure my anxiety. Faithfully I worked with him on the cabin cruiser. The hull was near completion. Dick bought a plug cutter and I dipped every plug in marine glue, tapped it into place, and matched it with the grain

Mary Carey sits on keel of unfinished boat hull which they built in their own back yard. While living in Dallas Mary taught Journalism at North Dallas High School and Dick became a charter employee of Texas Instruments.

of the mahogany. I helped with the sanding. Twice I was knocked from the sawhorse platform while using a four-inch belt sander. I helped with the interior while Dick installed the motors. She was ready for a virgin voyage before I heard from the *True Confessions* national contest.

The Dallas Morning News sent a photographer and reporter to do a story just before we moved our cruiser to Lake Texhoma on the Texas-Oklahoma border. It was the largest lake around and good fishing. We loved our new toy and were having so much fun that it was difficult to realize time passed so rapidly.

In 1955 two things happened that literally changed our lives. I won the $5,000 first place *True Confessions* award, and Texas Instruments put a plant in Houston. Our ultimate dream seemed to be coming closer to realization. Dick asked for a transfer to Houston where he could gain experience navigating in salt water. With the extra $5,000 in savings I could try full-time writing as I had always dreamed of doing.

Meanwhile Frank and Jean were doing quite well too. Since Midwestern University did not offer a degree in geology, they transferred to the University of Texas in Austin, the state capital. My pride skyrocketed when the prisoner's daughter finished in the upper one-and-a-half percent of her class. Since Frank needed another year for his degree in geology, Jean taught to

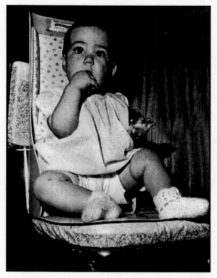

help him finish. Both the Richardsons and the Careys were very proud when Frank got his first job for which he had been trained. Soon they announced that they were starting a family. Their first baby would be due in March. We were all extremely happy.

Richard Carey was on his way up too. He made several

Linda Jane Richardson, first grandchild of author Mary Carey.

— Photo by Dick Carey

226

*This is the little "Gad About" which Dick and Mary towed behind
their cruiser. It served many purposes such as life boat, a duck blind,
and for beaching.*

*This is the mile-long causeway, forty-six-miles south of Houston, where the
pile-drivers caused Carey's sensitive instruments to shake while they were
driving piles when the bridge was under construction. To remedy this, Texas
Instruments dug a hole in their basement and floated Dick in a space-like
capsule on air. Dick thought this "living in space" eight hours daily could
have contributed to his heart problem.*

*The "Gad About" provided transportation to shallow beaches where one could
surf, beach comb or explore.*

minor inventions in his years with Texas Instruments for which he never received recognition. One which was not minor combined his watchmaking skills with a new instrument, a gravity meter which was being used in search of oil . . . it literally weighed the earth and could tell geologists whether there was sand, rock or cavities which might hold water or oil deep below the surface. Only one problem — the spring was metal and affected by the north pole and magnetic materials. Dick Carey became the first man to pull quartz springs from rock to replace the metal springs in gravity meters. Quartz is not affected by magnetism and remains constant in extremes of heat or cold. Naturally I wrote about it for "Roto Magazine" of the *Houston Chronicle*, in my weekly column, "My Job is Different."

If truth was not stranger than fiction, it would be ridiculous to even suggest that the building of a causeway almost fifty miles away in Galveston would help lead to Dick's demise.

Since moving to Houston we often drove down to our boat, which was berthed near the end of a mile-long causeway connecting Galveston Island to the mainland. Like in all growing areas, traffic increased and the two-way bridge became congested and a dangerous bottleneck. A new bridge alongside the old would eliminate this evil since each stretch would be made "one way."

When they started using pile drivers for pounding in supports for the bridge, Dick's instruments shook so badly that they were of no use. The gravity meter was too sensitive to be properly built and tested.

To remedy this Texas Instruments dug a deep hole in the basement of the plant and floated a space-like capsule on air. This would eliminate the vibrations. When Dick first went to work in the capsule, he teased about being the first man in space, but soon the job started getting to him.

Although the capsule was air-conditioned and Texas Instruments made every effort to keep him comfortable and in contact with those about him, he said he felt as if he were in prison. Always a lover of the great out-of-doors, he began complaining to me of claustrophobia. Working through a magnifying glass all day while seemingly floating in space got to him.

"It's worse than trying to read all day in a moving vehicle," he complained. "My arms get tired, my eyes water, and sometimes I feel pain shooting down my left arm and can't seem to get a good breath of air."

"That settles it," I asserted. "You're going to see a doctor."

He did go to a doctor, two of them. The company doctor sent him to a heart specialist, but he found no indication of his having a minor heart attack or any trouble at all.

"Why don't you resign?" I asked. "You've been working for T.I. a long time and have been buying stock from your paycheck from the time they first offered it. You have over ten years of "Cinderella Stock." It's grown, split, and split again. It's worth lots of money. We could take off for Alaska even sooner than we planned."

Finally I talked him into a target date. He would give the plant notice and on June, 1, 1962, we would board our cruiser for the long-awaited voyage. Alaska, a new world of excitement and adventure beckoned, and we were on the final countdown. Dick was still working, but he had less than a month to go on the six-week notice he had given Texas Instruments.

It would hurt to leave Jean and Frank and it broke our hearts to think of leaving Linda, our two-and-a-half year old granddaughter. Fortunately Frank was working closer to Houston now and they visited more often. Photographing Linda was Dick's pride and joy. He was prouder yet when I sold a photo story on her and her dog Rags to a magazine. His photos! A first photo sale! Now he knew that he could do the photos while I wrote the stories.

Chapter 18

Dick Carey Dies

We were on countdown. Only April and May to go. Soon we would board our cruiser for the long-awaited adventure. Our whole life seemed geared toward this trip. We both loved to hunt and fish. Big game hunting was not our forté. Our shooting was mostly done with a camera and ours was a beautiful world.

What we wanted most was adventure and to write about it. Dick had adopted my hobby, photography, and we had a small niche to develop film and do enlargements in the bathroom, or "head" as it is more properly called in nautical language. I had adopted Dick's hobbies of boating, fishing and rock hunting. I had been writing magazine articles for many years and felt I was ready for books. What more wonderful idea than doing a book on our upcoming adventure?

Although it was only April and we would not leave until summer, our preparations were nearing completion. We felt our boat could withstand the trip beautifully. Her keel was of the hardest white oak and her hull of three-quarter inch Philippine mahogany. For power we had twin-screw 135-horse power Gray Marine engines. Our cruiser was well equipped with such things as automatic pilot, depthometer, and many other navigational aids. On deck we could carry six 1000-pound cakes of ice in the transom. The lid of the transom was covered by cushioned life

Photo of Richard C. Carey,
made shortly before his death by E. C. Lloyd, my sister Lela's husband.

preservers, which served as an extra bunk or seats for fishing whenever needed.

Insofar as navigation was concerned I had no qualms. Dick Carey had been belly gunner and navigator with the Fifth Air Corps based in New Guinea during World War II. He had flown fifty-two missions over the Southwest Pacific and Japan and was well-decorated, including the Air Medal, with several Oak Leaf Clusters and a group Presidential Citation.

When Texas Instruments put a plant in Houston in 1956, Dick asked for a transfer in order that we might become more familiar with salt water navigation. Several times we had done

The United States of America
honors the memory of

RICHARD C CARY

This certificate is awarded by a grateful
nation in recognition of devoted and
selfless consecration to the service
of mankind in the Armed Forces of
the United States.

President of the United States

This certificate, signed by President John F. Kennedy, was sent to Mary Carey to honor her husband, Richard C. Carey. Dick Carey was recipient of the air medal, several oak leaf clusters and a group Presidential Citation. Carey flew fifty-two missions in the Southwest Pacific and over Japan.

pre-cruises up and down the Texas coast, usually following the Intercoastal Waterway to the Mexican border.

Our next trip coming June 1 would take us through the Panama Canal and on up the west coast to Canada and Alaska.

When Dick transferred to Houston I resigned teaching journalism in North Dallas High School and started freelancing and working the magazine section of the *Houston Chronicle*. In fact I was very proud of the title given me when I taught at writer's conferences, "The World's Most Versatile Female Writer." I had been published in practically every type of magazine except

232

women's. On the others I had run the gauntlet from men's to children's, from scientific to detectives and religious.

Then suddenly on April 8, 1962, our world ended. Dick died of a heart attack while we were rock hunting for an intriguing gem, a tektite, which probably comes from space. We were near Bedias in Montgomery County north of Houston, when he was stricken. There was no second chance, and he was only forty-six. Perhaps the doctors tried to make me feel better by saying the massive cardiac arrest would have meant death even if he had been in the hospital at the time it struck.

My world ended. I seemed very calm and mechanical while I called our families telling of the tragic event, which happened about five in the afternoon. My daughter Jean and her husband Frank were first to arrive, about two o'clock in the morning. Later they told me I was reliving the tragedy over and over like a broken record to the kindly R.N. and neighbors who sat with me until family arrived. The nurse suggested giving me another shot, but I refused saying the first one seemed to make my tongue thick. I did not realize that I was stuttering, saying the same thing over and over, seemingly unmindful of those about me.

My daughter put me to bed. The morning was well spent when I was gently awakened with a kiss from our greatly beloved grandchild, two-year-old Linda. I opened my mouth to speak, but no sound came out.

Although hugs and kisses speak an international language, neither she nor her mother understood why I could not speak. The doctor diagnosed it as a case of shock, perhaps a temporary paralysis of the vocal cords. More than likely my power of speech would return.

I went through the funeral like a Sphinx. My family made all arrangements for burial in my hometown of Cisco, Texas. About the only thing I remembered was the flag-draped coffin.

Gradually I began speaking — almost. I stuttered terribly. Now I know how a handicapped person must feel. I would go to a strange grocery store to shop because when friends saw me and I tried to speak with them I could see the shock on their faces. I was beginning to wish I had died too.

My greatest help came from my granddaughter Linda.

When Jean and Frank came to see me they would usually take us for a drive into the country. When Linda spotted an animal in the field she would say "cow" or "horsie," whatever her budding vocabulary spanned. I repeated stutteringly after her and she was completely delighted, sharing her newly acquired skill.

May and June passed and I still stuttered. In July I was to speak at the Southwest Writer's conference in Corpus Christi. Several of my favorite Texas writers were also speakers, including Fred Gipson of "Old Yeller" fame, and J. Frank Dobbie, writer of western lore, including *Coronado's Children*. I tried to resign, but they, Dee Woods and Fay Venable, Texas historian, would not let me. Strangely enough when I got up to speak my fear of stuttering vanished. I felt an unusual sort of calm. A good audience is always an inspiration to a speaker. My strength seemed to come from them and I spoke without a bobble. I received a standing ovation. This gave me courage. I would fly to Bloomington and teach at the Indiana University Writer's Conference, return home and head for Alaska.

"Alaska!" my daughter gasped when I revealed my plan. "But Mama, it's so far away . . . we really don't want you to go there! You mean you want to drive alone to Alaska?"

"And why not?" I asked. "You seemed perfectly willing after Dick died, when the doctor told me I should get away."

"Yes, but . . ." Jeannie stammered.

The silence was punctuated by my son-in-law's knowing grin.

"All right, Son, out with it," I countered.

"What she should have told you," Frank said haltingly, "was that the doctor said we must get you away from here, everything and everybody who brought back memories. That was when you had to write your communications. The doctor said you would probably change your mind a hundred times, so when you wrote 'Alaska' on your pad we naturally agreed. When you sold the cruiser, we felt you had changed your mind about going there."

"But I never changed my mind not ever once," I answered with conviction. "You agreed and I'm on my way!"

"Not alone! Not driving!" my daughter pleaded.

"Just following the doctor's order," I replied in way of finalizing the conversation. "I'll be leaving the first week in August. If

I like Alaska I'll try for a teaching job, or perhaps go to work for a newspaper. But probably teaching for I need the students, and I'll probably winter there."

"But why of all places?" my daughter again tried to change my mind. "You don't need a job. You have plenty of money to vacation anywhere you please. Then you would be ready to come back home and live where your family and friends are. Don't you want to see your second grandchild, who is to be born in September?"

"Of course I do but you said the baby is not due until late September or early October. I'm not selling our home. Maybe I won't like Alaska and will be back by then but it's sort of a covenant I made with Dick Carey. I'll see Alaska for both of us."

Within less than a week I started the long drive alone, from my going away party in Galveston to Alaska. I said my neighbors, fellow journalists and friends must be glad to get rid of me, as many parties as they dreamed up. Believe it or not my whole neighborhood went together and bought me a fingertip length mink coat, saying it was a partial payback for the boat rides, fish, shrimp and crab that Dick and I had furnished over the years. The Houston Writer's Club gave me a glowing introduction to Alaska and a sign to drive down among the many alongside the highway in Watson Lake, Canada.

And it was while I was driving down this sign that I met the person who would mean the most to me during my first years in Alaska, although I certainly did not know it at the time. In fact we didn't even speak.

As I was driving the sign, which I so carefully tendered from Houston to Watson Lake, Canada, I realized a Volkswagon with a woman driver pulled up alongside. Yet I was so busy pounding on the sign stake and making a self-photo, via delayed timing on my Rolliflex, that I hardly noticed. Then I realized that her hair was quite white, the whitest I had ever seen. Perhaps she thought I was taking the photo to bolster my ego. Maybe I was. Or maybe she thought a woman my age shouldn't be wearing shorts. But I still felt young and was quite trim, despite the fact that I was a grandmother. Why should I let it bother me? I forgot her but not for long.

The following day I could have sworn it was she who passed

me speeding like a long-haired rabbit in a prairie fire. It had to be her, that same red VW and the same white hair. "I hope she makes it to her grandchildren," I said under my breath, thinking she would stop at the next town. She did but she soon passed me again.

Would you believe that on the third day this sweet bit of arsenic passed me again and this time on a curve! "Persons her age shouldn't be allowed to drive," I said aloud, "and they should have strict law enforcement along this highway . . . if you could call this graveled pretzel such."

The farther we drove the greater seemed her joy in passing me. This wounded my pride as a driver. I'll admit I was afraid because most of my driving had been done on Texas plains and I was probably overly cautious in mountains. But she didn't have to make things worse by waving each time she zipped by, usually going up a mountain.

My fervent prayer was that if she was going as far as Tok Junction, she would head in an opposite direction. I was tired of her flying rocks and her cocky attitude. A real kibitzer, she.

Driving alone to Alaska was one of the greater adventures of my life to that date. The newspapers in Houston, Galveston and Cisco, had all published features about my making the drive alone, and I was to keep a travelogue.

Some of my nearest friends and kin feared for my life and swore I could never make it. And there I was steeled against starving, freezing, going over a cliff, and what have you, and this little old lady was making a fool of me. I had enough grub in my car to last a month, and so many spare tires and parts that I couldn't see back of the driver's seat. Although I had installed overload springs, my little red and white station wagon was as full as a tortoise shell and almost as graceful and speedy.

If you are planning a trip to Alaska in a reasonably dependable car forget the junk. If your car isn't dependable forget the trip. I didn't have a single flat tire en route. Neither did I have any trouble whatsoever, although I must admit that I got mighty sick of swallowing so much dust and fighting the mud. I hardly touched the ton of food I brought along, most of which spoiled. I did not have to sleep in the car but one night and this was my own fault. I could have called ahead or stopped earlier,

236

but the midnight sun just keeps one driving and driving. I had plenty of blankets, so I can't say I even got cold.

I didn't see the white-haired plague again after leaving Tok, but she had deflated my ego. I can still see that little red bug scooting along the gravel, taking the curves faster than I dared to drive. Her dust was still choking me even after I entered Alaska.

There hadn't been time for me to secure a teaching position through regular channels before leaving Texas, but I wasn't concerned. I had never had difficulty finding employment as a teacher. Not so in Alaska, where standards are quite high and salaries higher that anywhere else in the U.S.A. By the time I was turned down in Fairbanks and Anchorage, I was beginning to wonder if Alaska was really a land of promise. With degrees from two universities and glowing recommendations, I had no fear of obtaining a teaching position. One thing however I did not know. There is a state law, and it is a good one, that a teacher must go back to college at least once every five years and gain six additional credits to receive and hold a valid certificate in Alaska. This I had not done, and the only way I could possibly have been hired was as an emergency teacher.

School started the week I hit Alaska, and no emergencies cropped up in my field whereby those in authority could have issued an emergency certificate and hire me, so I was rejected.

Yet I was determined to teach. Not because I was broke, nor because I had no other means of earning a livelihood, but because I was so lonely I felt I had to have the companionship of children. I looked further. I went to the branch office of state schools in Anchorage. There were two openings both in very isolated areas where there were only natives — no telephones, no roads, and no regular mail service. I did not feel I was ready for such complete isolation, so I turned them down. I went to the Air Force base schools, with wholehearted cooperation from the heads of the Anchorage and state school system, but to no avail.

There was no opening at the military base for which I was qualified. Besides as the superintendent pointed out, I was grief-stricken. Conditions were different to those which I was accustomed and it could likely be assumed that I would soon be heading home. I would probably last one year at the most I was told. Teaching for so short a term insofar as the school was concerned would be a loss because a new and younger teacher could add this year to her experience—and she would probably remain in Alaska. The man seemed to want to hire me, yet years of experience had taught him a hard lesson and he was trying to build a school system second to none.

The door was closed. I would go back to Texas. Alaska neither wanted me nor needed me. I was spoiled even pampered. I had received recognition in my own state both as a teacher and as a writer, but here my reception was a skeptical one. I wanted no more of Alaska.

I was very tired and it was late, but I started driving. I left Anchorage and passed the Air Force base where I had just been rejected. I was headin' back to Texas.

But I was too tired to get very far. I spotted a bar and motel sign. Why not? Drinking was not a habit with me; in fact it was quite a rare thing, but I was too lonely and disconsolate to face my misery alone, so I sought a bit of bottled courage. I tried for a room. There were no vacancies. The young couple with whom I talked as I had a drink invited me to stay in their house, which was of all places on the base — if I didn't mind a houseful of children.

Children! Suddenly I realized that more than anything else in the world I missed children. That night with little arms around my neck, I made up my mind.

Over and over I kept thinking of what I was told in the state office about a one-teacher high school which they thought would materialize in Talkeetna, a historic little village near Mount McKinley where Alaska's most colorful bush pilot lived.

Thus far there were no books, no desks, and no teacher's quarters. It could be an expensive venture because I would have to stay in a hotel until the teacherage was finished, and this might be from four to six weeks. Besides there were only eight students of high school age in the village, the minimum number required for a pilot high school. If I lost one pupil I was warned, I would be out of a job.

That was the challenge I needed, but I haven't told you yet about the white-headed lady who passed me so often on the Alcan.

Since there was no road leading into Talkeetna, where I was

238

to become "the faculty" of a one-room school, I stored my car in Anchorage and took the train, the only transportation available without chartering a plane.

For five thousand and five hundred miles my hands had been on a steering wheel and my eyes on the road. I was going to enjoy this 114-mile trip from Anchorage to Talkeetna on the train. After dashing to a grocery store and buying enough groceries to make me look like a fool trying to lay in a winter's supply, I headed for the bush, the end of the world where there was no road in nor out.

I was lugging so much baggage that the freight agent in Anchorage knew that I was another "Damn Cheechako" (newcomer), but he helped me with repacking and reorganizing. My lonely little ticket fell far short of the poundage allotment, although the helpful agents rarely say a word about overweight along the Alaska Railroad.

Finally inside the train I was ready and set for adventure in a wild new world, interior Alaska. I dug for my guide book. In this setting I could read ahead and watch every milepost. I would be as well oriented on this wilderness village as possible before I reached it.

Talkeetna was on the map before Anchorage was born. During her gold mining days and while the railroad was being pushed through during World War I, Talkeetna was a roaring Alaska boom town. She again came to life during World War II, when a large landing strip and an F.A.A. station was put in, but now she slept — population 76.

I was so engrossed in my reading that I didn't look up until the train started moving, or something moving or entering from the other end of the car caught my eye . . . an apparition or something. Merciful heaven! It couldn't be! But it was!

Quickly I buried my head in my guide book. If I ignored it maybe . . .

"Excuse me, but aren't you the lady I passed on the highway?" came the understatement of a lifetime as the apparition closed in.

She just stood there smiling like a puppy wagging its tail and waiting for you to invite it into your lap. The seat beside me was vacant. What else?

239

"Where are you going?" she asked as I again buried my head in my book to indicate my preference.

"Talkeetna."

"Now isn't that delightful! I'm going to Talkeetna too."

"Grandchildren?"

"Mercy, no! I'm going there to teach."

"Teach?"

"Yes. I'm the new grade school teacher. I've never been there. I'm from Sparks, Nevada, and the whole thing is completely fascinating. I'll meet my roommate when I get there."

"Roommate?" I echoed in a sort of dazed way.

"Yes, she's to be the new high school teacher. This is the first year they've had a high school in Talkeetna," she babbled as I faced the firing squad.

Mary Carey, teacher-writer, about the time I came to Alaska.

240

Part

3

Chapter 19

My New World, Alaska

*P*erhaps there is no village in the world like Talkeetna, so small and yet so internationally known. Nestled in the foothills of Mount McKinley, the nation's tallest peak, and at the confluence of three rivers, it was little more than a quaint resort with log structures when I arrived in 1962. In winter you could shoot a shotgun down Main Street and never hit a soul. In summer I was soon to learn one might have difficulty in getting down the main drag, about a two-block long strip of pavement.

Although there were no roads leading into our village, we did have two airstrips, the village strip just outside our school window, and the F.A.A. strip just across the tracks. The federal strip was built for emergency landing for larger planes . . . just in case the Japanese decided to extend what is now known as the "Thousand Mile War" along the Aleutian Chain to our bases in Fairbanks and Anchorage.

In Talkeetna there were two great bi-weekly events — mail call on Tuesday and Saturday when the train made its pilgrimage along the Alaska railroad.

In my new home town there were two hotels, three bars, two liquor stores, two grocery stores, and a new motel under construction. This seemed odd to me at the time, since we had no road leading into our village, but I had a lot to learn. We had no church, at least insofar as a building is concerned. The Rev.

242

B&K Trading Post: Moved upriver log by log when Susitna Station was wiped out by an influenza epidemic in 1919. First it was located on the bank of the Susitna River, then moved to its present location during a flood.

— Photo by Harold Heinze

Kenneth Lobdell of the Arctic Mission held services in his quonset hut. He and his wife folded their children's cots each Sunday morning and then unfolded a few chairs which were seldom occupied by grownups.

Despite the fact that we had no highway connecting us with the outside world, there were eighteen cars in our village. These were brought in on the Alaska railroad. We had no telephones but emergency calls would go out over the railroad line.

Although I lived in the same village as Don Sheldon, one of Alaska's most famous bush pilots, I had never gotten any closer than a casual "hello" in the local post office, which was a niche in the corner of the B & K Trading Post. It was said that there were two types of people he hated: reporters and photographers, and only one thing in the world he was afraid of . . . a woman. The latter fact was evident. The other two I tried to keep secret but it was difficult.

243

Talkeetna slept. I wept. More and more I gazed out our up-stairs window from our apartment above the schoolhouse at the cold splendor of Mount McKinley, which had become an obsession. I came to the village in hopes of flying the mountain, as much for the adventure as to report for the news media.

Although I endured my roommate, I felt no love for her. I felt she was cruel and her tongue was very sharp. At night I would cry but Mrs. Campbell always seemed to hear me.

"Shut up! Quit your blubbering," Mildred Campbell would call. "Don't you know we have to teach school in the morning? Do you think you are the only person in the world who has ever had any trouble?"

Never again I swore to myself would I ever take on another roommate. There was no other place in the village to live, and I am not a quitter. I must admit that her students and most of the villagers seemed to like her but not I.

Finally I resigned myself to the inevitable and was doing pretty well I thought. I loved my students. They gave me life and challenge. My roommate was the worst part of it but I had said I would accept a roommate when I applied for the job. My fate was sealed. I would just have to live with the situation.

Mrs. Campbell liked to cook and clean. I dreamed and moaned of my misfortune. I was especially miserable on the eve of my wedding anniversary.

"What you need is to get out," Mrs. Campbell said. "You need to mix with folks, have a drink maybe and to dance. You don't die just because someone you love dies. The world goes on. I'm taking you out tomorrow night to dinner in the den of iniquity."

This was our name for the Fairview Inn where the drinking and dancing was quite as robust as during goldrush days in my way of thinking. There was always music and profanity and men stealing glances from the uncurtained windows as Mrs. Campbell and I went for our mail or to the grocery store. I never went anywhere alone, not anywhere at all unless it was a school function.

Curiosity is one thing which most women can't overcome, and I guess I am no different. The old saloon was particularly appealing to me, or would have been as a historical spot to write about if I were still writing. Yes I had been in Alaska almost three months and there was still a wall between me and my typewriter.

*Fairview Inn:
Built in 1920-21,
a favorite water-
ing hole during
the gold rush days.
President Warren
Harding and wife
visited here in
1923, when the
railroad was fin-
ished.*
—Photo by
Harold Heinze

*The Talkeetna Roadhouse: An overnight stop for early-day miners along the
way when there was only a foot path. It just grew. It was home for Millie
Campbell and Mary Carey until the first high school, one room, was made
ready.* — Photo by Harold Heinze

The dinner was good Alaskan cooking served family style.
Much to my surprise there were several familiar faces inside the
Fairview, and it didn't look so much like a den of iniquity as I
had thought.

245

"Come on we're going to have a drink," Mrs. Campbell said as the music sounded more inviting. "I like an afterdinner drink and I want to see inside this bar. They can't fire us, at least they could hardly run us off before the end of the school year. We have contracts."

I did have one afterdinner drink and then another. The people were all so friendly. They welcomed us, they didn't look down their noses at us because we were teachers in a bar. They seemed happy that we had finally come to the party.

I should have know better but one of the men on our school board asked me to dance. His wife insisted that I do so. In Alaska all teachers seem expected to dance, otherwise they're considered snobbish, having no desire to associate with the village folk. This was a revelation to me because Talkeetna is not a native village. Most of the people were white and worked for the railroad or the F.A.A. There were four pilots with two air services and a few homesteaders and prospectors. There were only two native families in the village.

Common sense told me not to accept that third drink but Frank Monnekies, proprietor of the inn, had just come in and seemed so happy we were there. He had done so much for the school that we couldn't refuse. I would just sort of let my drink sit while I danced. I had always loved to dance to. I was having a ball, the first good time I had in Alaska until someone played a record that my husband and I loved to dance. The record that I used to dance with Dick Carey I was now dancing with a stranger and on our wedding anniversary.

I started blubbering and Mrs. Campbell took me home.

"The very idea," she came down on me the next morning. "Can't you keep your bawling to yourself? You could at least maintain your dignity as a teacher."

Although I knew she was right I didn't love her any more for such criticism.

"You're young at least young in comparison to me, and not too ugly, not bad at all. The men still look at you I see. But you spend half your time bawling or mooning at the mountain."

"You love it too," I fought back.

"Of course I do Mary Carey, but you must be nuts to think you'll ever fly that mountain. Forget it. You know that bachelor is never going to fly you there. In the first place you're a woman and people would talk. In the second place you're a reporter, and you know he hates them."

Thus our little battle raged from September to December. I couldn't even cry under my breath without her seeming to know. How many times I swore to myself that if I ever got away from this sharp-tongued, stone-hearted, little old woman who looked and smelled like lilac but was arsenic to the core, I'd never commit myself to living with anyone I did not know again. She said little about herself or her family. In fact I guess I gave her little opportunity.

I told her all about how I had lost my mother and father recently. In fact I had lost six members of my family one by one, in the three years prior to my husband's heart attack. Then when he dropped dead at the age of forty-six while seemingly in good health, it was almost too much.

The school days were now a century long. I was just living for Christmas vacation when I would get to see my second granddaughter, who was born while I was teaching in Alaska. In fact I had my ticket and was doing a Texas countdown when Mrs. Campbell called me in for a talk. I wondered what I had done wrong this time.

"I see you are not crying as much as you were," was her first remark.

How could I, with her yelling at me every time she heard.

"Now that you are leaving for Christmas I thought we might have a little talk. I know I have been hard on you," she confessed, "but if I hadn't you would never have stopped feeling sorry for yourself. I apologize."

Was I hearing what she was saying correctly? I had stopped much of my crying and spoke little of my grief anymore.

"Thank you," I mumbled. "I guess I did go overboard. I'm sure I'm not the only one who has ever had trouble. In fact you seldom mention your family. Tell me about them. Is your husband dead?"

"No, he left me a long time ago for a younger woman. I worked very hard for many years taking care of our children until they were grown. Then on my youngest daughter's wedding day she was killed in a car wreck. My oldest daughter died of

247

Glacier pilot Donald E. Sheldon and Mildred Campbell. Millie became the author's roommate after arrival in Talkeetna.

cancer. You are not the only one who has run away from sorrow. I too wanted a new life."

"I'm so sorry, so terribly sorry," I said as we embraced. "How stupid could I be never thinking of anyone except myself. Please forgive me. Without your help I would never have stopped feeling sorry for myself and just to think . . ."

"Forget it. I just wanted to wish you a Merry Christmas. Give that new grandbaby a hug for me. From this day forward we count only our blessings."

Little did I realize at the time that our friendship would grow stronger and stronger . . . at least for the next twenty-six years. Millie, as she finally let me call her, is retired and much older now, but I'll always swear she has more psychology in her little finger than many doctors put in books.

Lena Morrison, **left,** *who taught the women folk of the village to hula, shares cup honors with Minnie Swanda, who coordinated the March of Dimes program 1963-1965, winning more per capita than any other town in the nation. Minnie is now a living legend and fourth generation grandmother. During the first year of Alaska's statehood, 1959, Minnie was elected by the Business & Professional Women's Club of Anchorage to represent them in Switzerland.*

This is the red schoolhouse in which the author and Millie Campbell, the grade school teacher, lived. The top window, where the ladder leans, gave a magnificent view of Mt. McKinley as we sat at our dining table. The side windows were directly across from Don Sheldon's hangar. His home and office were just across the street from the front of this building which now serves as the village museum.

249

By January of 1963 I had picked up two newspaper columns, "Talkeetna Ticky-Tac" in the *Palmer Frontiersman*, and "Talkeetna Topics" in the *Fairbanks News-Miner*. Suddenly there seemed much to write about and I was so engrossed in community activities that I was too busy to moan. I wrote about everything that happened. One thing I crowed a great deal about was the "March of Dimes."

Minnie Swanda, grandmother of one of my students, Dorothy Jones, planned three gala events: a bingo game at the Talkeetna Roadhouse, a spaghetti dinner at the Fairview Inn, and a floor show at the newly opened Rainbow Lodge. In way of advertisement, Minnie's posters read, "Go to Them All and Have a Ball!"

That we did and our little village raised more per capita than any other town in the nation. How proud we were! And I can say the same thing for the following two years, as we were first in the nation three years in succession for raising more money per capita than any town in the U.S.A.

Things were really beginning to pop, news-wise. Dr. Brad Washburn, director of the Boston Museum of Science, was in the village, flying Mount McKinley with Don Sheldon to map the 20,320-foot peak which was becoming more popular with climbers every year. That summer would be the fiftieth anniversary of the first climb of the nation's tallest peak. Don Sheldon, who would sometimes even talk briefly with me now, said he had more mountain climbing expeditions coming in the spring than there had been climbers since the first climb in 1913. In the summer there was to be a full eclipse of the sun and scientists were coming from throughout the world to study it from the most advantageous viewpoint, which happened to be Mount McKinley. I should stay and write about it.

How could I write about these things, so long as Don refused to let me fly the mountain. Then an unusually heavy spring snow in March of 1963 brought misfortune to Don but a most unusual break for me insofar as my writing about him was concerned.

It was late and I was listening to some droning country-western on the radio when a newscaster broke in with this report: "We interrupt this broadcast to report that Alaska's inter-

250

nationally renowned bush and glacier pilot, Don Sheldon of Talkeetna, is reportedly forced down somewhere in the foothills of the Alaska Range. Sheldon called in several hours ago saying he was low on fuel and forced to attempt a landing under white-out conditions in an uncharted area. This is an unconfirmed report. Stay tuned for further developments."

I froze, but not from the cold.

I thought of the spectacular rescues for which Sheldon was noted. The hunter was now the hunted. This seemed strange. Did he crack up? Was he hurt? If so, would he freeze to death?

Later, the reporter gave this commentary: "Veteran bush pilot Donald E Sheldon, who recently received the Exceptional Service Award, the highest peacetime award given to civilians by the Air Force, is now down somewhere in the foothills of the Alaska Range. Sheldon, who has been flying in Alaska since 1942, has distinguished himself many times in rescue missions throughout the area. In 1954 he landed one of his light planes on a mountainside near a downed Air Force C-113 and brought out three survivors. In 1958 Sheldon identified a plane which crashed into Mt. Iliamna, a 10,116-foot volcanic crater. To identify the plane, Sheldon risked his own life in flying through turbulent air currents which commonly sweep around this awesome crater. In 1960 Sheldon made two magnificent rescues on Mount McKinley one involving the John Day party, the most massive mountain rescue in U.S. history. The other involved the rescue of a woman, Helga Bading. To effect this rescue Sheldon made the highest fixed wing landing yet recorded, 14,000 feet. Both rescues were written up in the June 6 *Life* Magazine."

For six days the air was filled with stories about Sheldon. News reporters were thicker than huskies in our village. On the seventh day just before noon, Don's position was pinpointed by a sonic-grid pattern, the first time such a rescue method had been used successfully in Alaska. Don reported he and his plane were both O.K. — and that with more gas he would be able to fly his own plane home.

All afternoon newspeople and the naturally curious milled about the town talking with persons who knew Don and picking up fragments of information here and there. I must admit I was jealous.

HIGHEST AWARD — Don Sheldon, right, famed bush pilot of Talkeetna, Alaska, and an Air Force veteran of World War II, was recently honored by the Department of the Air Force for his heroic activity in identifying a downed C-54 aircraft on Mt. Iliamna. Sheldon received the Exceptional Service award at a formal review by the entire 10th Air Division (Defense) and one unit of the Alaskan Air Command, both at Elmendorf AFB. Maj. Gen. C. F. Necrason, Commander AAC, presented the award to Mr. Sheldon just before the troops passed in review.

Just before school was out I saw reporters grabbing cameras and rushing toward the Talkeetna Air Service office. A scoop was breaking outside my window and I was tied in a schoolroom. I was dead.

Suddenly there was a rush from the office to the air strip. This was it! Sheldon was coming in. It was four o'clock but I really didn't care whether school was out or not.

As the room emptied I stumbled upstairs and took my camera out of hibernation. Useless I knew but a long-time habit. I was cleaning the lenses when Mrs. Campbell rushed up the stairs and yelled, "Come on!"

"Is he here?" I asked dully.

"No silly don't you listen. He's coming in on the F.A.A. strip. Come on before we miss our ride."

We joined the multitude. Reporters with cameras ventured further and further out on the field, vying for position. It was almost five-thirty before Sheldon was reported nearing Talkeetna.

How could a plane be so slow? Soon there would be too little light to get a good shot, even if one could get within range. Why hadn't I grabbed my strobe light? Since there were so many reporters around maybe Don wouldn't notice me at all. It was worth a try. I was looking for a ride back to the schoolhouse to pick up my flash unit when a yell went up. His plane was spotted in the distance across the Susitna River. He would be in before I could reach the school.

I took off my yellow filter and opened up the stops on my camera as much as I could. Maybe there would be light enough as I saw Don's plane bank between the bluff downriver and the runway approach. Then — it happened!

The plane was just behind the trees of course it had to be. No it was too low! Would he crash? On the edge of the runway? My roommate and I looked at each other realization breaking on our faces. We both knew what had happened.

It was always difficult to tell which strip a plane was coming in on, since practically the same approach was used when coming from the west and south — skirt the bluff and skim in over the Susitna River.

Now Don was past the bluff over the river — but where? He wouldn't! He couldn't! Yes, he would — and he did.

A murmur then suddenly those familiar with the approach knew what had happened. Sheldon was coming in on the village strip. Photographers raced for their rides, but it did them no good. The nearest one reportedly got only close enough to see a lanky figure gallop across from a Cessna 180 which was pulled up between the schoolhouse and the hanger then disappear into the office of Talkeetna Air Service.

To the best of my knowledge no one has seen Sheldon when he was not clean-shaven and his teeth brushed as sparking white as ptarmigan feathers in winter. His heavy crop of sandy dark hair was always newly combed. His angular six feet of rawbone was nothing but hide and muscle, always parka-clad, probably over double layers of thermal underwear. His hip bones served as hangers for his loose trousers and shoulder bones for his shirts. He was never gaited for walking and always went at a lope.

Impatiently reporters waited . . . and waited.

Finally Don sent word to them. "I have no comment to make at this time except to thank everyone who helped with the search. I'll think it over while I sleep for a week. But no dice on a story right now. I appreciate your coming but we'll just have to make it later."

There was no doubt about Don needing the rest.

In a way I was glad it had happened. My thought completely ran away with any reasoning power that I might have had. What if I could get this interview? I must be crazy! I was the last person he would trust. I was completely miserable. Yet I was obsessed. There must be a way.

Chapter 20

Get Sheldon's Story

wo days I sweated it out. Not a sign of Don Sheldon. On the morning of the third day I saw him lope from the office to the hangar. Although I was at my desk in the schoolroom, my eyes never left the hangar not completely. Just before noon I saw him lope back to the office. Then I saw his secretary Mrs. Jones leave the office for lunch. This would leave Don there alone. Suddenly I just had to ask Mrs. Jones (of course I didn't see her leave), who was president of our P.T.A. a question.

Don's office was in front of the schoolhouse and the hangar across the street so the poor guy had little chance of my not knowing his whereabouts. I had not the faintest idea of what I would say to him or ask him but I had to give it a try.

I knocked at the office door. After a short hesitance Sheldon answered the knock himself.

"I saw it was you," he grinned. "Is there something wrong at the schoolhouse?"

"I just had a question I wanted to ask Mrs. Jones." I put up a weak front.

"Sit down," he gestured with a swing of his arm like a long loop. "Tell me about it. How about a glass of goat's milk? Good for you. Just push my scribbling aside," came the constant chit-chat as he went to the refrigerator and poured milk for me before I could answer.

255

"Thanks, it does sound good," I said grateful for a moment's reprieve and knowing how much it pleased Don for anyone to share his "good for you" goodies such as milk and goat cheese and ice cream. I was remembering what had happened to an advertising agent who wanted him to endorse a liquor ad. Don all but kicked him.

"My scribbling is sort of sad," Don apologized as he turned to the refrigerator and came back with his arms loaded, "but I sort of promised the newspapers . . ."

"Wonderful!" I encouraged. "Is this your own story of the time you were down?"

"Yeah. The newspapers write too much about me. But since they've put themselves out so — well, maybe this way it won't get all garbled. I didn't want to do it but this is the first time they've used a sonic grid pattern to locate someone lost and down in a white-out. It might save somebody's life."

"You've done a lot of work on it several pages."

"Yeah but I don't' know if they can read my scribbling."

"Could I type it for you?" I asked before I actually realized I had spoken. He hesitated. Maybe I had scared him out of it.

"Would you?" came his studied answer as he read my face. "I'll bring it over to you after school if you're not too busy."

I made it a point to get the kids out in a hurry. I dashed up the stairs for my typewriter, cleared my desk, pushed it near a plug-in socket, inserted a sheet of paper, and was ready to turn on the juice.

"Yoohoo!" Don called from the schoolhouse door as he dislodged the snow from his mukluks, gave a whistle, which I later found out was his calling trademark and entered without further announcement.

"I know you can't make this out," he was saying as he closed the door tightly against the breath of the arctic. "Maybe it will be better if I just sort of dictate?"

"My typewriter is ready. Shoot."

"You mean you can rattle that thing as fast as I ramble?"

"I'll try."

"Then you must be pretty good," he surmised as he began his story.

"As you know — but not for print," he pointed out, "I flew to

Point Barrow on a rescue mission when I heard the Paddocks were down. You remember them. They came through here on their way to hunt polar bear. Old friends of mine — but this is not for publication. When I heard they were down I started flying, but they were already rescued before I reached them."

I rattled the typewriter keys.

"Oh no," he said quickly, "this is just to fill you in. I knew just about where they would be, but fortunately someone else located them just before I got to Point Hope.

"Since the Paddocks were rescued and all was well, 39-Tango departed." (39-Tango is the identification of Sheldon's Cessna 180).

"A three-front angry weather system boiled in from the southwest of Bristol Bay, but with any luck at all I could make it Kotzebue-Talkeetna non-stop."

At least Sheldon seemed to be back to the story so I started clicking the keys thankful for the prologue which filled me in on unknown factors.

"About 150 miles southeast of Kotzebue weather enroute described as rapidly deteriorating encouraged an alternate stop at Moses Point, 90 degrees and 125 miles to the west of the original course. Accomplished."

Sheldon seldom took time to put in such time-consumers as understood subjects, verbs, or personal pronouns. To him they must have seemed unimportant and unnecessary as commas and periods which tended to slow down his train of thought.

Failing to bother with such cumbersome continuity as "take off after refueling and heading for Talkeetna," Sheldon began reliving the rugged portion of his flight his hands constantly gyrating.

"A curious shuddering-type turbulence is encountered. A series of solid bottom bumps — the horizon in all quadrants is instantly obscured by an endless sea of snowflakes as big as fifty dollar bills. 39-Tango peels off in a 180 degree turn . . . NO DICE!

"Air speed's got the hiccups . . . directional gyro is swapping lies with the compass. Whoops! Watch the white-out! Miss that rockpile! Smooth that turn! Now, full bore! Climb that mountain!

"Easy boy! Can this be the one-way payoff? After twenty years of near misses and questionable successes laced across the land from south of the border to the far north coasts, hundreds of high altitude glacier landing, polar bear and wolf hunting expeditions, lucky in rescue mission recovery, and now within an ace of being a statistic myself.

"Shut up! Cut the chit-chat! Shocking revelation! Just discovered that the sometime-exceeded red-line dive recoveries are not responsible for my near black-out condition. Simply not breathing . . . retract tongue . . . half-bit off."

Throughout this tense discourse as Don reconstructed the scene his eyes read the instruments, gauged the weather, and his hands constantly manipulated the gadgets. As he retracted his tongue I heard my roommate Mrs. Campbell come home from the grade school and go up the back stairs to our living quarters above my one-room schoolhouse. Don and I were so engrossed that it hardly registered with either of us.

"By the clock," he continued, "one hour and three minutes so far in this rat race and still in one piece. THERE SHE IS! A whited-out ridge. One fast look and I park this holy terror. NO GOOD! Rocks as big as houses! Anyway, the whole works floated off in the white-out," he explained as he reached for the two-way and pressed the button, speaking into the mike which seemed as real to him as it was while he held it in his hand during the turbulent flight.

"McGrath, McGrath, 39-Tango advises precautionary landing.

"Friendly voice of Bob Huff, N.C.L., McGrath comes back instantly. 'Copy, Roger! Please advise!'

"Fast glance out the side window, more ice build-up on windshield, leading edges of wings look like baseball bats. In luck! Some slipped off! Temperature 34 degrees.

"'N.C.L., McGrath calling 39-Tango. Are you down? What happened? REPLY!'

"Can't see well enough to crack this thing up gracefully, low on gas . . .

"Zero-zero . . . swirling garbage . . . sand-trapped by the weather the great deceiver, forced into a delicate compromise. Sizzle among these scattered rock piles . . . close enough to see them . . . just far enough away to miss them.

258

Best friends are lost this way. Some leverage in comparable position with a belligerent prisoner in a violent argument with the
executioner.

"There was a possibility! Don't lose it! PARK ON IT!"

I doubt if anyone tells a tale more enthusiastically, gets
more wound up, or puts in more detail and pantomime than
Don Sheldon — always laughing, usually at himself.

This was not what I had expected. Not at all. I was more
than pleased when he became so engrossed in his subject. I had
to have this story, my very first one about Don Sheldon. But
how? This was his story. I was only the typewriter.

Suddenly there came a knocking from the overhead apartment. "I think it's time for you two to take a break," came Mrs.
Campbell's commanding voice. "I have spiced tea and cookies
on the table."

Don made a sizable dent in the freshly baked oatmeal cookies and really went for the spiced tea, which was a great favorite
with Mrs. Campbell. I went along with the tea angle when it was
made but coffee was my standby.

Noticing that it was past 10:00 o'clock, Don said we had best
knock it off for the night, but wondered if I could make any
sense of what he had said since he had repeated some portions
of the story so many times, adding a word here and subtracting
a phrase when he thought it slowed the story down.

I said that I believed I could make it though, but it was the
longest sentence I had ever written in my life. We all laughed.

"I'll admit that I can hardly wait for my favorite pilot to get
rescued," said Mrs. Campbell, "but tomorrow is a school day. I
won't need to read the story. Every word comes through our
foot-warmer loud and clear."

It was pretty neat. With our table over the register we could
warm our feet as we gazed out the window at Mount McKinley.

"She never gets enough of the mountain," commented Mrs.
Campbell, "but I must say I love it too, especially in winter when
it is pastel pink."

Again Don noted the time. "I better go now," he said a little uneasily. Suddenly he seemed to realize that he was in an
apartment with two widows, even though Mrs. Campbell was
quite old enough to be his mother and I was nine years his

senior. "I hope you can make this rambling out," he again apologized as he got to his feet.

"Time for bed," Mrs. Campbell remarked as the front door to the schoolhouse clicked shut.

"Not tonight," I replied calmly to her commanding tone, wondering what her reaction would be. "Furthermore," I added, "it may take me most of the night. Maybe I can just hang a curtain to block out part of the light and noise from my typewriter."

"Never mind. I understand."

Dashing down the stairway I returned with my typewriter. Staying downstairs in the schoolroom and writing would have been more or less like working in the window of a department store since there were no blinds.

It was daylight before my typewriter stopped clicking. I worked and reworked every page, trying to orient the reader without changing Don's wording. Then as now I must confess that without the aid of his eyes and explicit hands, trying to reconstruct one of Don's yarns gives me the feeling of a stage without props.

Of course Mrs. Campbell reamed me out for staying up all night but somehow it seemed like a commendation rather than a reprimand.

The school day was a century long and I found myself dozing during book reports. The last parka-clad teen had hardly cleared the door when I heard Don's "Yoohoo" and whistle as he scraped and tapped the snow from his mukluks.

"Neat!" he exclaimed with a low whistle as I handed him the first part of the story and waited for his comment.

"Following day," he grinned as he plunged into it.

Thus we spent three nights from the time school was out to 10 P.M. After that I worked into the wee hours as one obsessed. I was never so glad to see Friday come. Maybe we could finish the story and I could sleep.

"For heaven's sake!" Mrs. Campbell called down through the register. "Did you get rescued? Come up and have a cup of tea and a bite to eat. Must we work right through mealtime again without food?"

Don took the pages I had just finished upstairs and half read and half ate.

"For heaven's sake!" Mrs. Campbell reprimanded. "Put down that paper and eat your dinner."

"I apologize," Don grinned, "but I sort of promised the *Anchorage Times* I would have this story ready by tomorrow noon. I have a charter into Anchorage at ten."

"It will be ready," I promised.

We worked and worked. It was past midnight when we got to the thank you part of the story.

"Do you think you can finish it, Kid? It'll be hard on you. You didn't sleep again last night I know. What can I do for you? Pay you for your time maybe? No I'll tell you, you've done this story. Why not put your name on it? You could change the 'I's, couldn't you?"

"And ruin your story? Never! But I'll tell you what I would like to do. Could I possible put, 'by Don Sheldon as told to Mary Carey?' "

"Sure Kid," he answered, and I knew I had him trapped.

But it wasn't as easy as I thought.

Despite the fact that both the Anchorage and Fairbanks newspapers came out with full-page banner spreads, not changing a word of his very lengthy story, Don had evidently not changed his mind about my flying the mountain despite the fact he was lavish in his praise about my story of Dr. Bradford Washburn mapping Mount McKinley.

That's the way things were rocking when the first group of mountain climbers hit Talkeetna. They came on the train as many do with all their gear. From Talkeetna Don flies them to the mountain. I saw Don's pick-up truck at the railroad station. The train came in on schedule at 12:30 P.M. How I wanted to get a picture. Surely it would be time for books before they ever got together at the hangar. I just had to get photos and learn their names and a little about them. But by the time they got their gear to the hangar, I had already begun my first lesson of the afternoon.

How long would they be at the hangar? Would Don fly them to the mountain one at a time? My eyes were across the narrow runway as much as on my books. I saw the student's eyes stray too. Although mountain climbers came every year they were always new and interesting.

We had physical education period at 2:00 P.M. Snow was still on the ground but that made little difference to my group. We played soccer and the snow cushioned the fall. I usually played with them. At first when I was knocked down the boys would stop, apologize, and help me up. I ended that right away. "I'm just one of the team on the playing field," I coached. "Please don't apologize or stop to help me up when you bowl me over. It slows the game."

As few of us as there were all players were needed. Since there were six boys and only two girls in the class the girls contented themselves with boy's sports. Clothes were no problem since the girls wore stretch pants rather than dresses, which is more practical in Alaska and much warmer.

Living in the schoolhouse made it easy for me to wear a dress. Each day I would make the next day's written assignment and give the students a short study period just before physical education. Near the close of the study period I would slip up the stairs and into slacks. On this day I failed to do so. As the hands of the clock neared two, one of my girls Susan Devore a precious helpful student, whispered and asked me if I had forgotten to change.

It was then I confessed that I was not going to play with them that day, but was going to try to get pictures of the mountain climbers. As yet I had still never gotten a single shot of Sheldon nor at the climbers.

When Don Sheldon saw me coming toward the hangar with camera and note pad, he asked why I wasn't with my "knuckle heads." When I told him what I wanted he said I should go back to my students. There would be enough time for this sort of thing after school was out.

The next hour was long and fraught with misgivings. The activity outside our window helped some. I never realized how much preparation there was to be made before flying anyone to the mountain. Stacks and stacks of gear had to be sorted and repacked for air drops. Only a small amount of survival gear could be taken with each man for the glacier landing. Yet each one had to carry in a sleeping bag, rations and emergency gear for himself. One could never tell how long he might be alone on a glacier. Don might land one climber there and it be perfectly

262

clear, but before he could get back with another one the mountain might be all clobbered in and stay that way for a week.

I became desperate when I saw Don tying snow shoes to the strut of the plane and the hands of the clock had not reached four. Gear was packed inside and it looked as if the first climber would be gone before school was out. He was crawling into the plane when Don said something pointing to a spruce tree. Don loped over to the tree, broke off a short bough, and indicated the climber should do likewise. I made it just as the climber was again crawling into the plane and Don was handing him the boughs.

"What are they for?" I asked.

"To mark touch-down," Don replied. "In a white world you cannot gauge touch-down."

It made no sense at all to me but I asked Don if he would hold still with the last of the boughs as he handed them inside the plane to the climber. He accommodated reluctantly, and they were off.

From the rest of the climbers I found out the name of the first climber Don had ferried in, Warren Blesser. He was stationed at Ft. Wainwright out of Fairbanks.

The remaining mountaineers explained that Don had said the spruce boughs were to be thrown from the plane to make a dark spot on the snow which he could see and use to help gauge touch-down. A series of these spruce boughs marked a landing field on a glacier in the vast whiteness, where it is sometimes impossible to tell where snow and sky meet.

"If the spruce just disappears," one of them quoted Sheldon, "no dice! Crevasse!"

Don airlifted all the climbers to the glacier with little difficulty and again all was quiet in Talkeetna.

Soon more climbers would be coming in. The first expedition had been on the mountain three weeks and was pinned down by weather. I had gotten that picture I made of Warren Blesser and the spruce boughs into the paper, as well as one of Don with the Alaskan-Teton group as they called themselves.

Can you feature trying to get a picture into a newspaper while it is still news, yet having to send the film away by train to have it developed, wait for it to come back by train — and the train running only twice weekly? I did have a problem, but I got my stories out as they happened.

For three seeks I worried Don for news each time he flew in from the mountain. His glacier flights were not hard to distinguish because when he flew to the mountain he took off in his yellow Super Cub with ski-wheels. He had planes for every occasion including a pontoon plane. The snow was gone from the village strip, but by lowering his retractable skis during flight, he could land on snow, then raise them before returning to the graveled strip.

Then after he came in from one particular flight, he seemed worried and gave in to my questioning.

"The expedition now on the mountain is fighting case-hardened ice and snow to their eyeballs," he explained, and I knew he was talking for publication. "This group of Teton guides has climbed little over 7,000 feet in three weeks, since I landed them on the 5,800-foot level," Don fretted. "Yet, considering the weather their progress is encouraging."

My progress was encouraging too. The story appeared May 20 in Anchorage and Fairbanks papers, and it was picked up on the wires.

I tried to help Don in every way I could with the climbers. He had many air drops to make. Soon my roommate and I were making cookies and buying fresh fruit to be put into boxes for air drops to the climbers. I was writing to girlfriends and mothers for the climbers.

"If I could ever help you with an air drop, I would be glad to," I reminded Don as I passed by the hangar. "Is there anything the boys especially like?"

"Ice cream," came his reply. "Nothing as good as ice cream for sun-scorched tonsils. You're doing some mighty fine writing Kid, but the mountain is no place for a woman. Might have to walk back."

"But I'm a grandmother," I refuted. "I've already lived a good life. If I can't keep living — then I'm not alive anyway."

"Don't tell your secrets Kid. You don't qualify as a grandmother and no one would believe you anyway, so keep quiet about it. One thing is certain though, no one doubts that Mary Carey is alive!"

"Shush with the mush!" I flung back as his eyes twinkled. "I just can't write a story unless I live it. I can't describe that mountain."

The Don Liska and Dick Barrymore groups came in. A Canadian group led by Hans Gmoser was expected in on May 26. A twelve-man expedition led by Dick McGowan of Seattle was scheduled for the last day of May. Thank heaven, school would be out. There were more stories than I could write, but I was no closer to the mountain.

Mildred Campbell, the grade school teacher who was my roommate, and I became experts at packing boxes for air drops. She made cookies and we bought fruit and vegetables, but she said that ice cream at $2.50 per quart was just too expensive for her Scotch blood—with so many on the mountain and each climber able to eat a gallon as an appetizer. All groceries had to be wrapped well. Mail was tied quite securely and tucked into the center of the box after it had been cached in a plastic bag and tied with a string so that if the box were to burst open when it was dropped, the mail wouldn't get wet, lost, or scattered. We were working together and enjoying it.

"The Sheldon 'shuttle' from Talkeetna to Mount McKinley is now on a 24-hour schedule," I wrote, telling of mountain climbing activity through news column and story.

Only one week of school left now, and it was a good thing because I never slighted teaching so much in my life. Everything was going at such a feverish rate that the students hardly seemed to notice, or else they were too engrossed in their own activity.

Chapter 21

Tricked on the First Flight

wo days before school was out Don appeared at the schoolhouse door just as we turned out for lunch. "Hurry," he called from the doorway. "We've gotta get movin'. Can you get a substitute this afternoon? Don't just stand there. You want to go to the mountain don't you? Grab your fluffies and cameras." (Don always called eider down and such things as Arctic wear "fluffy.")

I sent a lanky, six-foot ninth grader Ronald Robeson, whose mother had said she would substitute for me on a minute's notice, scrambling home. Vera Robeson, a homesteading widow from Texas, was as good as her word.

Mrs. Robeson arrived a breath ahead of Don. I pointed at my lesson plans on my desk as I saw him drive up and heard him call. "Hurry! Hop in the truck, got to keep movin'," sounded the familiar phrase. "We're leaving from the F.A.A. field," he explained as we drove past the hangar and headed for the larger strip just outside town.

Trying to keep "fluffy stuff," three cameras — color, black and white, and movie — plus film together, I hit the runway before Don could open the pick-up door for me at the strip. I headed for 39-Tango, paying no attention to any other plane. As usual there were six or eight planes parked around. Suddenly I realized 39-Tango was already occupied — a colonel with a lot of brass.

266

"You ride in that plane," Don pointed. "Colonel Bennett goes with me. Ft. Wainright wanting to check on their boy Warren Blesser. Might be a first in it. The East Face is still unscaled, insofar as we know."

I tried not to show my disappointment, and indeed I was not disappointed because I was headed for the mountain.

"You ride with Stu Ramstead. Stu's a good pilot," Don explained. "We have eighteen air drops to make, so you'll have plenty of action. Shoot away! I see you've brought your movie camera too."

A quick intro to Stu and we were on our way. Suddenly I was remembering what Don said about eighteen air drops and that it took him two weeks to clean his plane after he took another woman to the mountain. Tricked! I should have known it. But it didn't matter now. I was headed for Mount McKinley!

The grandeur of what we saw as we flew up glaciers and through walled canyons was something I could never describe. No one could. It was a different world. Don led the way and just the minute I was sure he would crash into a solid rock wall of the Great Gorge, he disappeared at a right angle. We made the same sharp turn and emerged into a huge basin. Lengthwise it extended farther than I could see into the whiteness. Crosswise it was a broad frozen river inching its way through unrelenting walls of granite throughout the centuries. "I've been in here several times to help Don with air drops," explained my pilot as we bored on and on through the whitest world I have ever seen. "I've helped him through peak mountain climbing and hunting seasons for several years."

"I trust you all the way," I said. "It's just that I've never seen anything like this and it leaves me sort of speechless."

"Look! Look below us! There they are! The climbers! Don is right over their camp."

I thought we were already low enough to grab a snowball, but Don's plane was below us and no bigger than a dragonfly. Those yellow and orange handkerchiefs, were they tents?

SWOOSH! Up we climbed a razor-edge while I was still looking backward trying to figure out whether those specks beside the tents were men.

Suddenly my camera was too heavy to lift. I felt as if I would

267

sink through the tail of the plane. My body was made of mercury. We couldn't climb any more! We would crash into this razor rim! We were stalling!

But we were not. We just leveled off and I almost caught my breath when . . . ZOOM! Down we bored. Only my seat belt held me down, otherwise I would have floated free, and my head would have hit a little harder against the top of the cockpit than it did.

"There's a good shot." Stu pointed as we leveled off again. "Don's going in low right over their camp."

"What's the matter with you guys?" Don chided over the intercom. "Thought you were coming in close enough for a picture. Bring her in a little closer Stu, if you have the feel of this basin."

If this was just the beginning — I thought, but there was no time for thinking. As Stu gave her full bore we again climbed that razor edge and it seemed as close as before. The only difference was that I thought, since we had made it once, maybe we could make it again without stalling or crashing. As we leveled off I tried to get ready with my cameras, but I had not caught them in my view finder until we were again down that elevator shaft.

Around and around time after time my stomach churned and my heart pounded and my breath failed to come. Thank heaven Stu was most helpful and always yelled, "There they are!" and pointed just before we zoomed over them. I really couldn't have sworn whether we were upside down or right side up.

"Did you see that?" Don chuckled over the intercom. "If that guy hadn't done a nose dive, that can of alcohol would have hit him on the head. How's that for dive bombing? Is Mary getting enough pictures? Can she see the air drops beneath my plane? Whoops! Trouble! Box caught on the fuselage. Ribbons holding her. Cut the ribbon, Colonel, cut it!"

"Wow! The Colonel didn't chuck that one far enough away from the plane," Stu observed. "There she goes! That one's lost, but it could have caused real trouble. We'll have to do better ourselves," he said as he readied his first drop.

I was so engrossed and overwhelmed by the icy wind rushing into the plane as Stu lowered the window to make a drop that I forgot to click my shutter.

"You're on target," Don complimented Stu. "But did Mary get a good shot of that drop?" he asked as if nothing had gone wrong.

I said I didn't think I had in the understatement of a lifetime. Don knew I hadn't.

"If you'll come down a little closer," Don coaxed, "she can get a better shot. There's still a lot of room between you and the snow. But watch! This stuff's tricky."

He never made one reference to his own close call as we shot up the roller-coaster and down again, even closer, but I felt I got a satisfactory shot. I had to.

"Did you get her?" came Don's voice into the cockpit again.

"Sure thing!" I replied loudly enough for the mike to pick me up from the back seat. I certainly hoped my voice sounded convincing enough this time. Each time around I was sure we would crash as closer and closer we came to those yawning, blue-green chasms beneath us on the floor of the glacier. Nearer touch-down they looked bigger and deeper, and as dangerous as the granite walls above.

"One more drop and we go check on the Blesser group," Don explained. "Are you ready for the other side of the mountain? Follow me to the East Face!"

After the next drop we did not head up the rim, but up the glacier. On and on winding in and out, dodging from on glacier to another. How many I can't remember. We headed down what seemed to be dead ends and through mile-high canyon walls. When we finally got to the north side we flew alongside an endless wall of ice and snow.

"That's the Wickersham Wall," Don explained from his plane, "longest continuous icewall in the world."

We flew high over the Peters Glacier then toward the East Face, dodging spires and peaks, crossing again from one glacier to another.

Then I saw what I supposed to be the three steps of the East Face. All of them vertical walls, each higher than the other.

"Can't get close enough to see," Don commented as I felt he was within wing-tip distance of the wall. "Down draft on this

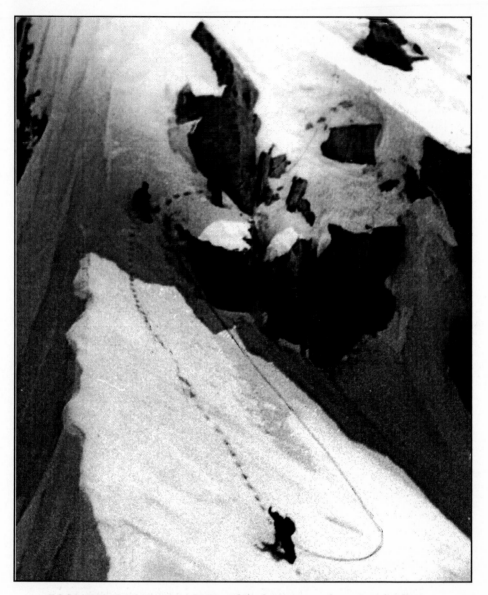

ZOOMING IN ON A GLACIER. This photo was made on your author's first flight to Mt. McKinley. It was made from Stu Ramstead's plane. Don Sheldon was hesitant about taking me up on a first flight. Perhaps he was testing me, or even trying to make me sick, so I would quit bugging him. We churned around and around and up and down, making eighteen air drops.

side. Makes permanent fixtures of guys who fly in too close. Getting low on gas. Best give 'er up for today. One more look and we head for home."

But we didn't find them on the next look so back through the canyons we curled. Rounding the East Buttress and dodging a spire, we burst through a slot into space again. Beautiful space ringed with jagged peaks like in the most fantastic science fiction.

"It's the Amphitheater of the Ruth Glacier," Don oriented, speaking to the Colonel, yet with the intercom open as if he were talking to me too. "You could throw the State of Rhode Island in it. We leave through the Great Gorge."

I was looking hard because I had studied Dr. Washburn's map well. As I tried to make sure of my bearings Don broke in again.

"Ask Mary if she sees that rotten hunk of granite to the left? That's what the German expedition is going to try to climb. A two-mile high hunk of vertical granite shaped like a tooth. That's the Moose's Tooth and nobody's ever climbed her."

Later I found out that it always looked darker than the rest of the range because its walls are so steep that snow and ice cannot cling to them. At the time it never occurred to me that later I would be landing on a ledge at a camp near the base of it.

By air the Moose's Tooth is about thirty minutes from Talkeetna, the Ruth and Kahiltna Glaciers, up which Don often landed with mountain climbers, thirty-four and forty minutes respectively.

By the time we reached the F.A.A. strip my stomach had almost stopped churning, and I was breathing more or less normally. As soon as we landed and I could jump from the plane I yelled, "WHOOPEE! FUN!" loudly enough for Don to hear me at the other plane, whose prop was already still. The Colonel who was crawling out looked as pale as I felt.

Don looked at me searchingly. "You mean you really liked it?"

"Loved it!" I said truthfully. "Loved every minute of it," I said without reservation, yet if I had been completely truthful, I could have said my knees were a little trembly. But at least there was no plane to clean up.

Don opened the door to the pick-up and invited the Colonel and me to hop in.

271

Not knowing that Don is one Alaskan who never touches a drink, the Colonel offered to "set 'em up."

Saying "Later," as he usually passed such invitations off, Don dropped the Colonel at the Rainbow Lodge and drove me to the schoolhouse.

"You'll do Kid," he said in the way of about the most appreciated compliment I've ever had from Don, "but if you're going roaring around that mountain you had better get some mukluks and fluffies."

Did he mean it? Was I really in? Did this mean he would fly me to the mountain himself?

"I'll have the story ready in the morning," I promised, "and the photos as soon as I can get them back. Maybe I'll just send one roll of film to each newspaper office. They promised to develop it if I get a real good story."

One more day of school. Who needed sleep? Mechanically I graded papers and averaged grades, but my thoughts were with the climbers on the mountain, especially the Alaska-Teton group, which Don always called the Blesser Expedition. Had they made it over the sheer East Face? Twice Don flew up to check and said he failed to see them, but more than likely they were just pinned down by weather.

Chapter 22

A Dream Come True

Saturday morning when Don came out of his own back-yard and saw Mildred and me sitting upstairs at our breakfast table, he stopped below our window long enough to ask how the mountain looked from our view. Never could the weather have been more beautiful. I knew he had flown to the mountain the day before, but he didn't say a word about it. He no doubt was trying not to disturb my last day of school. I was trying hard not to push my luck.

After grinding his toe into the gravel for a faltering minute, as if trying to make up his mind, he looked squarely at the up-stairs window and said to me, "Sharpen your eyeballs Kid, and put on your fluffies."

"You mean we're going? Did you find them? Did they make it to the top? Can I get a picture?"

"Holy Mackerel Kid, relax. We've got to find them before you get a picture."

"She'll be lucky if she finds her head," Mildred cut in. "See to your cameras. I'll tie up this box. It's finished except for the cookies I baked yesterday and the newspaper. You did say you wanted to send the last story you wrote about them, didn't you?"

In true Sheldon fashion, Don never mentioned sending me on my first flight to the mountain with Ramstad. He may or may not have done it to see if I would get sick, or he might have tried

273

to give me enough of the mountain in one big dose. One thing is true — we've never made so many air drops on one run since.

I don't know what Don was thinking as we started this first flight together. He was probably scared and telling himself he was a fool. I tried to leave him in peace. He didn't say a word until we came near the foothills.

"See all those tracks down there in the snow? Bear pulled down a moose. They're mean when they come out of hibernation. Look what a struggle! Tore up ten acres of snow. We could track him if we tried but the snow is up to your eyeballs here."

"What a battle for survival," was about all I could think. "There's tracks everywhere."

"But you see who won. Bear don't pull down moose except in the high country and at this time of the year when there's no other food. See his tracks leading off in that direction, all the way around the base of that hill. He's a monster."

After about five minutes of silence Don spoke again.

"This is the Great Gorge of the Ruth Glacier. Remember the Moose's Tooth? The Germans will be here next week to try to climb her. That's the Rooster's Comb to the left and Mount Barrille to the right.

I appreciated his being explicit.

"See straight ahead of us there? We're sailing out into the Ruth Amphitheater — west fork to left, east fork to right, McKinley dead ahead but you can't see her for the peaks between. I've been told you could toss Rhode Island into this Amphitheater as an appetizer, chew it up with the Moose's Tooth, swallow it through the gullet of the Great Gorge and spew it out and lose it in the great Alaskan wilderness."

Don had a unique way of telling anything. I know now that all his stories and comments should have been recorded, but he would never have gone for that.

Our plane seemed lost in the vastness of the Ruth Amphitheater, but Sheldon held his course and we headed through another canyon.

"Today we find them," Don said optimistically as we again neared the east face. Around and around and around we churned. Closer and closer and closer we came to that immemse forbidding wall. How could anyone climb it? It looked utterly impossible.

274

"They've made it!" Don yelled gleefully. "See there? They've dug their pickaxes into the ice right there. Right up over the tip of the wall! Maybe you'll get their picture."

But they weren't there. Only signs that they had been there. We couldn't spot them anywhere. The boulders were bigger than houses and the shadows around them dark and deep. Since no one had scaled the East Face previously, Don did not know which direction they would take. Maybe they were beneath an overhanging cornice, or tunnelling through a chimney. Everywhere there was case-hardened ice and rock, jagged rock and plenty of it.

We didn't seem to have searched too long when Don pointed and remarked, "We'd better get out of here fast!"

Clouds were boiling in below us and shutting off the mountain in places. As we sailed toward our previously smooth riding canyon the plane took the hiccups. Suddenly the bottom fell from beneath us and my head would have gone through the cockpit if my seat belt had not been fastened.

"Did you see that?" Don asked. "We were dropping at the rate of over fifteen hundred feet per minute."

I had no trouble believing him, although I could not see the instruments from the back seat of the Super Cub. It felt more like water than a hunk of air that we landed on. I have experienced a similar feeling when surfing in a speeding boat, climbing a wave and then dropping over the crest and splatting down — hard.

We were both pretty sick at not finding the climbers. Sunday she was all clobbered in again. On Monday Don said we would make another try. The weather was compatible, but the climbers just disappeared from the face of the mountain. Don was jubilant when we finally located their tent, just one day's climb, he thought from the top of the mountain. But they were not there. Around and around we sailed. No climbers. They had to be there but they weren't.

Back home again I telephoned my story to editor Dave Galloway, and the *Fairbanks News-Miner* gave us a full front-page banner headline. It read, "DRAMA UNFOLDING ON MT. McKINLEY" in the smaller head, "Searchers Fail to Spot Men Near Top." Then came my story which was published May 25, 1963:

Somewhere above 17,000 feet, six men are near the top of Mount McKinley, but a two-hour and twelve-minute search by this reporter and veteran glacier pilot Don Sheldon yesterday failed to reveal their location.

Weather permitting another reconnaissance will be made tomorrow in an attempt to determine whether they have made it to the top, or if they are in any kind of trouble.

These men, all climbing instructors, have been on the mountain thirty-one days. It was determined yesterday, although not officially confirmed, that these climbers are the first to scale the East Buttress. It is believed that they may also have reached the summit of Mount McKinley, since Sheldon spotted their tents above the third and most difficult sheer face.

The first mountaineers to conquer the East Buttress are Pete Lev, Boulder Colorado; Fred Wright, Burbank, California; Rod Newcomb, Jackson, Wyoming; Warren Blesser, Ft. Wainwright, Alaska; Jed Williamson, College, Alaska; and Al Read of Denver . . .

Before I was off the telephone I asked Dave Galloway a question — which I hated to — but one which never surprises an editor when a reporter goes after a story hard enough and long enough. Sometimes a newspaper gives a bonus for an exceptionally hard-fought story, but I didn't want anything for myself. I was thinking of the gas Sheldon had been out on this search, and the time. No one paid Sheldon for this. If we got a good story would the *News-Miner* pick up the tab? Dave's answer made me happy.

I don't think I could have lived until the next day if it had not been for the stories that flew from my typewriter.

"We'll go higher tomorrow," Don promised. "The climbers are bound to be near the summit. We'll go as light as possible. Only one camera and one roll of film. No extra gear and no food. Sharpen your eyeballs and get some sleep"

I was thankful school was out. Two days of flying the mountain with a third coming up! My stories were given banner spreads! The eyes of the world were with us. We had to find them!

Over and over Don's words kept coming to me. "We'll go higher tomorrow."

I couldn't sleep. I knew the flight into thinner atmosphere would be more hazardous than the others. If I dozed, the plane began falling. Yawning crevasses opened beneath us. Again we were falling fifteen-hundred feet per minute.

I crawled out of bed and wrote this little note to my daughter, Mrs. Frank Richardson of Houston, Texas:

May 24, 1963
Talkeetna, Alaska

To My Darling Daughter, Jeannie,

Tomorrow I am going to try something no woman has ever done before, fly over the top of Mount McKinley in a small plane with Don Sheldon, looking for lost mountain climbers.

If anything should happen, remember that I am doing what I want to do and must do as a writer. Life without adventure is not life to me. I know I'll come back to write the story, but in case we should have a little trouble, take good care of my darling grandbabies and Frank. He's the most wonderful son-in-law one could ever have.

God could never have given me a more precious daughter. I thank Him for all the wonderful things He has done for me and for letting me do what I love most, live the stories I write.

With all my love,
Mother Mary

277

Chapter 23

Over the Top

omorrow did come, and both Don and the weather were
"Go!" I was ready and watching as he finished preparations. I had assumed he would go in his Super Cub with ski-
wheels. Reluctantly he pulled more gear, including the survival
kit, from 39-Tango, his Cessna 180 on wheels. I had never seen
him take his sleeping bag from a plane in which he was preparing to make a trip. He checked to make sure I had no extra
weight and teased me about going on a diet.

Don started the motor to let it warm up.

"Have you noticed we're on wheels?" he asked. "Skis hold
you down. We have one bottle of oxygen between us. Are you
sure you want to go? There's no second chance in case anything
goes wrong. You still have time to think it over. Be sure before
you crawl into the plane."

For a fleeting moment I remembered the note to my
daughter, then said, "This is the greatest! Are we ready? Let's
get moving!"

Don wasted no time.

"How high can we go?" I asked as we sailed over the Susitna River and headed for McKinley. "Over 17,000? Above their
tents?"

"The ceiling on this baby is nineteen thousand—absolute
twenty thousand, but Might Mack is still higher. I don't know.

Again his eyes were on the mountain. He had been studying it even before we took off.

"See that umbrella over the peak?" he asked. "That cloud that looks like a tilted umbrella?" he explained.

I saw but didn't understand. It didn't look mean to me, not like the boiling clouds that had dropped us from eleven thousand to nine thousand feet in one-fourth of a minute the day before.

"Looks like a rising thermal," he said. "If we can just ride her up! We may be able to catch the tail end of it!"

Ride a cloud? Ride on that little umbrella angling up and over the mountain?

I looked at the phenomena so hard that I swore it disappeared right before my eyes as we came nearer.

"Can't tell," Don encouraged. "We're too close to see her now, but we'll know pretty soon," he yelled back at me over the roar of the plane's engine as we burst from the canyon of the Great Gorge into the Ruth Amphitheater.

"What a tunnel," I remarked, looking back at the jagged Rooster's Comb on the left and the Moose's Tooth towering two miles almost straight up to the right.

"And what a theater," Don added. "I doubt that there's another this large, nor half so spectacular in the world. Too bad there are so few spectators," he lamented as we sailed into space. (Later after Don's death, this amphitheater was named for him.)

Suddenly our plane, which seemed to fill the canyon with thundering defiance of wing-tip imprisonment, flew like a bird set free from a cage. Up! Up! and up we soared, higher than surrounding peaks now, heading straight for the mighty one.

Floating over a rim, I looked down into the deepest basin I have ever seen. An avalanche crashed to the bottom, churning as in a mixing bowl for the world.

"That's Thayer Basin," Don began his commentary, "elevation 12,000 at the base and 17,500 at the rim. There's an airliner down there, permanent fixture with seventeen persons aboard. Bored into the rocks. Could see the tail for a while, but she's covered now."

I wondered how many thousands of feet of snow were filled in at the bottom of this basin, deeper than Grand Canyon from

279

rim to base. I wondered if throughout the centuries it would fill. It was hard for me to realize even though I had studied Dr. Bradford Washburn's unusually fine map for hours and hours during the long winter nights, that Mount McKinley, turned upside down, would be over four times as deep as the Grand Canyon, her own canyons and walls and spires in like dimension. Rising from near sea level Mount McKinley towers higher from her base than any other mountain in the world.

Don's voice brought me out of my reverie.

"Look! See that! Look at the altimeter!" He pointed excitedly at the gauges. "We've hit it! We'll sail around and come back for another lift."

I could hardly grasp the meaning of what was taking place. Were we really being lifted? Were we riding the cloud? On the second pass there was no doubt about it even in my mind.

"Keep your eyeballs peeled," Don reminded as we hit the 17,500 foot level near where we had spotted their tent on a previous flight. Up and over the rim of Thayer Basin again but no sign of the climbers.

"They must be higher," Don surmised as we again circled. Up again past eighteen thousand and around the rim of the South peak. Don skirted her wide on the lee side. Again we hit the rising air and gained elevation.

"Watch Denali Pass between the North and South peaks, and keep your end of the oxygen tube in your mouth. But don't inhale too much or you'll get giggly."

I was wondering why Don came so close in on the east side of the mountain and gave so much birth to the west face so I asked him.

"Got to watch her every minute. What lifts you up on one side of the mountain will slap you down on the other. These down drafts can make permanent fixtures of you fast."

Again we hit the rising thermal. Up she inched past eighteen thousand feet. Eighteen twenty-eight, eighteen fifty . . . up . . . up . . . nineteen thousand.

"Ceiling," Don yelled. "Keep your eyeballs peeled. We'll ride her to a Mexican standstill."

"WHOOPEE! 20,320!" Don let out a big yell. "Watch for the climbers. Next time around we'll sail right over the summit!"

Contrary to my previous opinion there was nothing but ice and snow on the summit. The sun hit it so brightly that it sent spangles skyward, like the top of the world sending out light beams.

As we circled for the last climb I saw a lot of huge granite boulders sticking up in Denali Pass, but no climbers.

"The wind might have them huddled under a boulder," Don reminded, "or it might have blown them right off the face of the peak."

Almost every time he opened his mouth to comment the oxygen tube fell from between his lips. Finally, he kept it clinched between his teeth as he talked. I had to keep reaching for my tube too. We had left the masks behind because of their weight. The single tube coming from the bottle of gas was a long "Y," a slip-tube affair from which each of us sucked the clean tasting oxygen. One camera was all the weight I had been allowed, and only one roll of film. I chose black and white naturally for the newspapers. I grabbed the camera as we reached the summit.

"No! No! Look now and shoot later when we find them!" Again and again we roared over the summit.

I don't need to know what eternity is like. I saw it.

"That's Cook Inlet," Don explained as we circled above the south side of the peak where we did not expect to find climbers.

"It's over 150 miles from here . . . and you can see right over into Canada. See that peak," he pointed as we again reached the east side. "That's Mount Logan, the one on the far horizon. It's in Canada."

Suddenly we were laughing and singing. I started on a crazy little ditty, "On Top of Spaghetti, All Covered With Cheese," a parody someone had written to "On Top of Old Smoky," which was quite popular at that time.

Don tried to join me or say something and the tube fell from his mouth. I fumbled underneath the front seat for it, where it seemed to have lodged. Don looked toward the back trying to help me.

Suddenly I realized Don's lips were as thin as paper and he looked blue. Although I felt quite exhilarated when I saw his face I realized we had gotten too much oxygen, or not enough.

281

"Your face is blue!" I said in alarm.

"And yours is green! We'd better go down for a breath of air."

At fourteen thousand feet we sort of regained our senses. "If you're game Kid maybe we should look her over once more near the top of the wall. The wind might have kept them pinned down and they couldn't crawl out of their hole in time for us to see them. By now the Yetis have heard us and will be out. We have a little oxygen left. What say?"

"Go!"

Again we were sailing out over Thayer Basin, heading for the top.

"Holy Mackeral!" Don ejaculated. "Look! Snowshoes! Right there! On the second ridge above their tent. They're above eighteen thousand!"

Again we tried to hit the rising thermal, but it just wasn't there. We saw tracks but no climbers. We made her up a little past nineteen thousand, and she all but stalled when Don tried for more altitude. We never made it over the top again that day. I doubt very seriously that we'll ever make it again.

Circling at 17,500, we took a good look at their camp. Could they possibly have made it to the top and be on their way down?

"I see their trail!" I yelled just as Don spotted the climbers. Jubilantly we sailed past, but caught a glimpse of only three men.

"We'll take a second look. They must have been pinned down all this time. Did you see any of the others?"

For a moment Don fretted, then concluded:

"No, they're the best. We'll turn around and take another look. You can see they've been doing a lot of stamping around. Maybe they're relaying."

His assumption was correct. This time we saw five of the men, but we knew all was well because they pointed toward the summit.

"Jeez they're still climbing," Don marveled. "This group just doesn't give up. They'll make her all the way!"

We made another pass and saw all six men. I snapped a shot as they waved and was jubilant because I had a picture for the

Climbers on glacier wave at pilot Don Sheldon and photographer Mary Carey as they do a fly-by to check the group's progress.

newspapers — mountain climbers in action taken from a plane. If my shot was good it would be the first such news picture made of climbers on Mount McKinley. I had my story, headlines.

"But we can do better," Don promised as if reading my mind. "We'll catch them at the top tomorrow. I'll need to make a mail drop to the Zogg-Liska group on the West Buttress. What if both groups reach the summit at the same time from east and west buttresses? What a picture! We'll have a field day!"

But the next day it was raining in Talkeetna, and the next and the next, as it sometimes does especially in the spring. Visibility wasn't far beyond the end of your nose. It rained all week.

After ten days, it finally cleared, when there were two more groups of mountain climbers in Talkeetna waiting to be airlifted to the glaciers. We had no way of knowing whether the Alaskan-Teton and Zogg-Liska groups had reached the summit.

"Load up with goodies and ice cream." Don Sheldon advised on the following morning as I was over at the hangar getting stories and pics of the newly arrived climbers, twelve in the Dick McGown group and four in the Canadian.

I ran to the B & K Trading Post, and here I guess I may as well confess that I did run, literally. That's how I got my Talkeetna moniker, "Running Mary." There were three Marys in our village, Red Mary, Black Mary . . . and because I ran so much, I became Running Mary. Jim Beaver, one of the biggest pranksters in Alaska, gave me that name and it stuck.

I bought carrots, celery, apples, oranges, and even rutabaga turnips. Tomatoes and bananas just wouldn't stand the drop, nor my pocketbook the price. I bought a head of lettuce for ninety cents. The apples and oranges were twenty-five cents each. With six in the Blesser group and seven in the Zogg-Liska bunch it soon added up. Then came the ice cream but that was some of the best money I ever spent.

None of the new mountain climbers particularly enjoyed seeing me take off with Don and all of them still waiting on the ground. But Don wasn't sure of the weather — nor that we could even reach the climbers. The Alaskan-Teton group had been on the mountain forty days, and we knew they needed food.

However heavy the load this time didn't matter. A few miles north of Talkeetna we did get a bit above the overcast and could see the top of both the north and south peaks. Never was McKinley more beautiful.

Up and over Thayer Basin to look for the climbers. Don knew they had probably made the peak already, both groups, but we had to be sure. The tents of the Alaskan-Teton group were no longer at the 17,500-foot level, nor were they at the next lower camping level, 14,000-feet, so out we sailed over the glacier.

Don gave a whistle and pointed excitedly. "They've already made it and are down the glacier. See what they have stamped out!"

"PICK-UP" was tramped out in huge letters in the snow.

"They've made it!" I yelled as I grabbed for my camera. Before I could get them into focus they had vanished. How Don kept that mountain straight I'll never know. I'm still turned around and sometimes upside down when flying it, even though I should be somewhat of a veteran.

Before I could even get my bearings, we were zooming down over them again. This time we came quite low and they gave the victory signal. Don let out a war whoop. I must have let out some sort of screech that let them know a female was aboard, because one guy in red underwear, who was probably soaking up a little sun, headed for a tent on the double.

We circled again and Don looked over the area for a possible landing. No dice! They were still too high on the glacier.

"Quick," he said, "scribble a note. Tell them I'll be back and pick them up at the eight thousand-foot level on the park boundary."

I scribbled like mad and stuck the note through all my tightly tied strings into the box I had ready to drop as we circled.

"Bombs away!" Don shouted as we came in quite low again.

I did better than I thought.

Back in Talkeetna I became totally engrossed with the story. Eagerly I told of the forty-day saga of the six-man team of climbing instructors who had apparently reached the summit of Mount McKinley via the previously unscaled East Face and of their waiting to be airlifted by Don.

Carefully I reconstructed the story from the day they were ferried in on April 19 — how it was determined by photographic reconnaissance that these climbers had become first on a new route, of the unsuccessful flights, and of the May 29th flight when we spotted "PICK UP" stamped out in the snow.

Meanwhile Don managed to pluck three of the six climbers off the glacier. Then the weather closed in, but I was too busy with interview stories to worry much — not for a while anyway. Rapidly I wrote:

> Three of the six climbers who scaled Mount McKinley by the East Buttress this month, a route never previously traversed, are resting in Talkeetna today and waiting for bush pilot Don Sheldon to fly their companions off the mountain.
>
> Sheldon returned Jed Williamson of College, Alaska; Al Read of Lakewood, Colorado; and Rod Newcomb of Jackson, Wyoming, to Talkeetna Wednesday.
>
> Still on the mountain and waiting for the weather to clear so Sheldon can fly in to pick them up are Pete Lev of Boulder, Colorado; Warren Blesser of Ft. Wainwright, Alaska; and Fred Wright of Burbank, California.

This fiftieth anniversary story was picked up on the wires:

285

Three mountain climbers trapped at the eight thousand-foot elevation on the Ruth Glacier by seven feet of fresh snow, and a lone bush pilot waging a continuing battle against the elemental wilds of Mount McKinley, marks the fiftieth anniversary of the first successful assault made by the Stuck-Karstons Expedition of June 7, 1913.

The climbers, three of a six-man team and first to scale McKinley by the treacherous East Buttress who have now been on the mountain fifty-two days, are Warren Blesser, Fred Wright and Pete Lev.

The lone pilot, termed 'proprietor of the mountain' in the May issue of *Reader's Digest* and the *Alaska Sportsman*, has had this proprietorship contested daily since May 29, when, after lifting three of these climbers off the mountain, one at a time, weather closed in . . .

Then I told of the three rescued climbers. How finally after over a week's wait and an overdue induction notice from Uncle Sam, the waiting trio gave up the vigil, trusting their ill-fated companions to Sheldon's skill.

One of the boys on the mountain however would have a nice surprise when he finally did get back to Talkeetna. Pete Lev's father, Lester Lev, an attorney from Fullerton, California, had flown to Alaska to congratulate his son on the successful climb but needed a longer arm — about seventy miles longer.

During this period Sheldon did manage an air drop on June 4, but could not land. A strong tail wind might have caused him to overshoot the tramped-out runway in the snow, thus causing the plane to plunge into a huge nearby crevasse.

Dropping the men a note Sheldon asked that they stamp out a new runway leading past one side of the crevasse. When he finally found a hole in the weather three runways had been stamped out. Two new ones led past the crevasse on either side, yet landing conditions were not favorable.

Getting these climbers off the mountain and others on is an extremely precarious operation. The only way Sheldon can operate at all in such soft wet snow, is to undercoat his plane's skis with axle grease, about one inch thick. Although he has tried all kinds of ski waxes, none adhere to the bottom of his metal skis as well as plain old axle grease.

286

On every trip now he faces the possibility of either getting stuck in the snow or being weathered in. But it is hoped that these weather conditions cannot last much longer.

The fiftieth anniversary of the first successful climb finds at least fifty persons either on the mountain, trying to get to it, or trying to get away from it.

If Archdeacon Stuck were to observe the great commotion raised by the thirteen expeditions fluttering to and from the perilous peaks, the impact would at least raise one of his saintly eyebrows.

Since telling of these expeditions would fill a book within themselves, we will be forced to skip most of them which grew in number for the following eleven years, and take time to rescue only those we have on the mountain thus far.

After the clouds finally lifted, Don went into a Talkeetna-McKinley orbit, making twenty-three round trips without rest.

The remaining members of the Teton-Alaskan expedition had been without food for three days. They amused me by telling of the turnips and carrots which I had dropped to them the day before the more fortunate half of their group was airlifted from the glacier, ten days prior to their long awaited departure. They threw away the peelings from their oranges, carrots, turnips, and a few outside lettuce leaves at their upper camp, before we wrote them the note asking them to move three thousand feet lower and tramp out another runway. During the ten-day wait they went back up to the old campsite, dug the peelings from the snow and ate them.

Chapter 24

Arctic Air Lift

The summer of '64 was well spent before I could get around to filing my homesteading claim, September 9, 1964. Meanwhile, through the Alaska Press Club, I received three top honors at the annual awards dinner. Shortly after this an invitation to participate with other members of the press media throughout the world in Arctic Airlift week in October. This included many Alaskan activities, topped off by a flight over the North Pole to Sonderstorm, Greenland, to Dye Base No. 1 and Dye Base No. 2 — Who could resist such an invitation?

In Anchorage we had a full round of briefings and luncheons and intros to VIPs, as well as a trip to the Nike Missile Site and Mount Summit.

There was also a most enlightening review of the Biathlon Skiers, Olympic champions who demonstrated many of the techniques developed for Arctic warfare. I could have enjoyed watching these skiers without rifle-firing from the standing, kneeling and prone position, but it was all part of the course.

One highlight during this time was my meeting Alaska's first glacier pilot, Bob Reeve, now owner of the Reeve Aleutian Airways. Another was getting to know Col. Bernt Balchen, who wrote *Come North With Me*. When I expressed my disappointment about the bookstores being sold out of copies, Colonel Balchen said be believed he could take care of that problem. To my sheer delight, on the night of the banquet in his honor, Colonel

Several Arctic aviation notables were honored by the Alaskan Air Command at a commemorative dinner during Arctic Aviation Week. Shown above are, from left, Ray Peterson; Jack Jefford; Bernt Balchen; Noel Wien; John Cross; Lt. Gen. R. J. Reeves; Robert Reeve; Jim Dodson *and* Maj. Gen. James C. Jensen, *air command commander and host for the dinner.*

Balchen walked up to me and said, "I haven't forgotten your request."

I just couldn't believe it. With the big brass bowing and scraping, here he comes with the book I had wanted so badly. What makes a great man great? I sometimes believe that a prime prerequisite is humanity to man — a quality which, if lost, may well lead to decline.

The story of our North Pole flight, and of our reliving Colonel Balchen's epic rescue on the Greenland Ice Cap during the early days of flying, was written by newsmen from throughout the United States to Norway, Colonel Balchen's boyhood home. These stories can be read elsewhere, and certainly anyone wishing a good picture of the Arctic should read Colonel Balchen's *Come North With Me.*

I guess I'll just have to blame my offbeat Arctic Airlift story on being a female. Why don't I tell the truth? Statistics and defense mechanisms leave me a little cold. These highly precisioned instruments of defense are beyond my own comprehension, much less trying to explain them to others. Incapable of writing the big stories, I wrote about what I did understand and feel, an act of kindness as we started our flight, which showed me that the military has a heart.

My story did not make headlines, but it was published in the *Fairbanks News-Miner* and in the *Frontiersman*, a weekly newspaper in Palmer, the agricultural heart of Alaska. It was captioned "Talkeetnan is Arctic Airlift Guest" and I quote in full, with the permission of publisher Bill Snedden of Fairbanks and Mayor Theodore O. Schmidtke of Palmer, editors with whom I have enjoyed working.

I felt pretty small as I watched a snow plow and a jeep loaded into the C-130 in which we were to ride. I wondered what it would be like inside the plane when we were handed ear plugs. When we were given seats which pulled down from the side of the hull and faced the inside of the airplane, I felt this must be more or less the way paratroopers ride. Certainly we encountered that which I did not expect. Here is my story.

> To aid a man who needed surgery, a C-130, in which newsmen from Europe and the U.S. were riding to view Top of the World Airlift capabilities, diverted its course and dipped four hundred miles southward, from the Nome area to Kenai, on a mission of mercy. This is the 17th Troop Carrier Squadron of Elmendorf Air Force Base, Alaska.
>
> To show the vital role which Arctic Airlift does, and must command over 58,000 square miles of our virtually uninhabited northern frontier, representatives from the news media were flown to Alaska to view and parcticipate in demonstrations and Polar flights during the last week of October. This is the Alaskan Air Command.
>
> To demonstrate the all but incomprehensible speed and efficiency with which the Military can strike, units from the U.S. Army and U.S. Air Force joined King Crab VII exercises and Arctic Airlift Week activities, Oct. 25-30. Major General James C. Jensen, Commander of the Alaskan Air Command, was aided by Major General Ned D. Moore, Commander of the United States Army, Alaska, and the 452nd Troop Carrier Wing, a Continental Air Command reserve unit of California, in airlift activities and in transporting news media to Alaska. The 17th Troop Carrier Squadron for Elmendorf Air Force Base, Alaska, hosted the press on flights via polar deployment to Sonderstorm Air Base, Greenland, and to remote Early Warning Radar and White Alice sites in Alaska.

Paramount among the observations made by this reporter is the fact that no task is too trivial nor none too staggering for the Alaskan Command. Big men stoop to serve, small ones to conquer. We saw retiring Major General Ned. D. Moore share the first cut of a cake baked in his honor with a child. We saw the eyes of Eskimo children brighten as G.I.s approached with bulging pockets. In our own heart we felt more secure when the huge C-130 Lockheed *Hercules*, in which we were riding, changed its course to aid P.F.C. Mike Stischak, an M.P. from Toole, Utah, who is now recovering from an emergency appendectomy at the U.S.A.F. hospital in Elmendorf Air Force Base, Alaska.

The Alaskan Air Command plays an integral role in our lives. Previously the meaning was vague. Now we know that every man, woman, and child in the U.S.A. is dependent upon its efficiency and maintaining of the lifeline to our scientific and defense installations in the frozen north.

A joint paradrop involving the Alaskan Air Command and the U.S. Army, Alaska, was staged at Claxton Drop Zone, Fort Richardson. Airborne personnel and five C-130s from the Alaska Air Command's 17th Troop Carrier Squadron, commanded by Lieutenant Colonel John H. Statts of Elmendorf, was joined by the 172nd Infantry Brigade of Fort Richardson under the command of Colonel George W. Bauknight. Some 234 parachutists from the 4th Battalion of the 23rd Infantry made the jump.

A team of Air Force paramedics parachuted to a simulated accident scene, gave first aid and hoisted the victims into an H.21 Helicopter of the 5017th Operations Squadron which hovered under simulated firing conditions.

Although awed by the sky spectacular, amazed by the split second timing, half blinded by smoke signals and dazed by continuous firing as chopper after chopper churned overhead, we were thankful that it was only simulated warfare. We do not deny that in our own heart there was a continuing and non-suppressible prayer that it never happen, not literally.

There is little doubt that the realization of the Air Command's complete ability to retaliate almost immediately anywhere on the face of the globe. In a way we are all dependent upon the Alaskan Air Command's newest unit, the 17th Troop Carrier Squadron, which is the lifeline of the two Distant Early Warning radar sites on the Greenland Ice Cap and remote

291

A&W radar sites in Alaska. The 17th maintains Sonderstorm Air Base, Greenland, and is also responsible for search, rescue and air evacuation of the North Atlantic area.

Our personal thanks to information officers Lieutenant Colonel Elmer F. Edwards, U.S. Army Headquarters, Fort Richardson, Alaska; Major Robert H. Reed, director of Information Headquarters, Alaska Air Command, Seattle; and Captain John Walton and A/1C Stan McDonnough, Information Division Headquarters, Alaskan Air Command, Elmendorf Air Force Base, Alaska.

To the C-130 crews who flew news media on various missions; to the Anchorage Chamber of Commerce and the *Anchorage Press,* which hosted us for luncheons; to Major General Ned Moore of the Army; to Colonel Bernt Balchen, Air Force, retired; to Major General James G. Jensen, Commander of the Alaskan Air Command; to Betzi Woodman, Anchorage writer and former president of the Achorage Press Club, who offered this freelancer her seat on a plane; and to many more persons whom we should like to recognize and the nameless thousands participating in Arctic Airlift Week activities. Our most sincere desire is to reward your efforts by transmitting these activities to the press.

Chapter 25

Polar Bear Hunt

W inter came, but I was too busy to notice. Much of my time was spent in organizing centennial committees throughout big borough with a very small population. Although larger than most states, our borough has a population of 6,000. Most of these persons lived in Palmer or along the road between Palmer and Talkeetna, and I kept it pretty warm. Each community along the route was planning for the Alaska Purchase Centennial in 1967.

Yet I had newspaper deadlines to meet, too, and all these things had to "go" despite the fact Talkeetna was engulfed in a five-day white-out. Knowing that several downed pilots were waiting it out at the Fairview Inn, I canvassed it for column material.

When in need of any sort of advice or information, there were always plenty of views at the Fairview, where world problems are solved and dissolved daily at the bar. This time I struck it rich.

Things were more interesting than I had even anticipated. With my editor's permission, let me quote this particular column, "Talkeetna Topics," in full, because it does present a fair picture of a problem faced by pilots and guides at the time.

Fairbanks, Feb. 16, 1965
It's a poor white-out that doesn't force some interesting

293

person down in our village. This time there were several: two helicopter crews, one enroute from Elmendorf to Fairbanks for Polar Strike, another from Fairbanks headed for the Chulitna River bridge site where they are drilling for abutments and piers, and incidentally, where this columnist has homesteaded.

Among those forced down in planes were Bob Cooper of Cooper Flying and Guide service in Fairbanks, and Roy Stoltz, of the Missile Club at Clear, who seems to have fished every stream in this area. But three feet of snow on the ground and a white blanket extending skyward was not the proper setting for an angler. It seemed more conducive to thoughts of polar bear hunts, and Bob just happens to have a big one coming up the last day of this month.

Previously this columnist has felt nothing but sympathy for the polar bear, with planes tracking him down and landing within a few hundred yards for the kill. What chance does the bear have? His tracks are exposed for miles and a plane can close in on him within minutes. There's no hiding. He's dead — he and the rest of his clan until man has sent him the way of the sea cow, the whooping crane, and the bison.

These were our thoughts. Now we're confused.

When two of the greatest pilots and guides of the north-land speak, one listens. Perhaps Don Sheldon and Bob Cooper are right. At least we believe these pilots more qualified to express opinions than one who reads a book and/or periodicals, as we have done. Perhaps their deductions are even of greater merit than those of bar boozing specialists who solve world problems daily.

Our opinion, for what it is worth, is perhaps as valid as one who shook hands with Einstein in his day, thus declaring himself an expert on third dimension. But these facts become self evident:

A man with the means to hunt polar bear is not looking for bear meat — this he gives to the natives. What's more, he is not looking for a sow with a cub, but a trophy. His selectiveness, sharpened, curtailed and controlled by the game laws, causes him to pass many a tempting target.

The hunting range of a small plane over the huge polar ice cap might be compared with one placing a dime at the base of the Empire State Building and saying he will step from it to the top. The poor polar, which we thought had no respite, happens to have the largest uninhabited area on the face of the globe as his retreat.

Unless proven false, we'll take Cooper's word for it. Small plane penetration over ice cap is nothing in comparison to the all-over size. The polar bear population could never be depleted by this method of hunting.

We'll accept Sheldon's theory, too, that more polars are ruthlessly destroyed off the shores of Norway and Sweden from whaling vessels and fishing boats than will ever be taken by plane. A hunter in a plane is very limited, both in range and poundage. Hunters aboard commercial or pleasure craft cruising in icy waters are not so limited in range and tonnage. Many hunters are aboard. Polar hunting from a luxury liner is now a fad in the Eastern Hemisphere. All a tycoon has to do is come to the rail and shoot when a bear is spotted on an ice floe.

Although we sat and talked of polar bear hunting for a long while, I never realized why Cooper was discussing all this, and perhaps he was just talking it over with the others because the Alaska legislature was trying to stop polar bear hunting from light planes. Too many persons thought it inhumane. Cooper, as well as the other guides, had several hunts coming up and was afraid they would shut the season down, thus causing all of them to have to cancel hunts.

"We need help on this matter, and we need it bad," Cooper commented as he sized me up like a computer, probably wondering if I could take it. "Would you be interested in going and bringing your cameras and typewriter?"

He couldn't mean it! A polar bear hunt? At the topmost point of the continent? Surely he must have forgotten.

"But I'm a grandmother," I stammered.

"That hasn't stopped you from flying with Don nor over the North Pole with the Air Corps, has it?"

"But what would the big game hunters think?"

"It doesn't matter what they think, so long as I ask you along. There'll probably be seven of them. They'll probably appreciate a few photos and a story themselves. Should get a good magazine article as well as newspaper material. Are you game? Do you want to go? Are you chicken?"

I hesitated.

"Of course," he said with a wink at Don, "you'll be expected to sleep with all seven men every night, melt snow for cooking and dishwashing, skin out the bear and do a few little chores."

Bush pilot Bob Cooper, a bear hunting guide who told his passengers while en route to Barrow, "When you're flying 'dead reckoning,' if you reckon wrong, you're dead."

"You're faded," I countered. "When do we start?"

"Meet us at the Nordale Hotel in Fairbanks on the night of the 28th of this month — and be sure to have eiderdown underwear, camera, film and typewriter. And watch that weight! We're in small planes."

I still couldn't believe it, but nevertheless I wrote all the advance publicity I could and looked up game and fishing laws and studied the legislation before the house. I had to know what I was fighting, if I chose to fight for these guides. Cooper had been fair enough. He said I could write it as I saw it, that I didn't have to agree with him nor any of the guides. I was on my own and owed them nothing. He just wanted someone who writes to see firsthand. I was flattered, of course, and felt this would be one of the biggest assignments ever.

As usual, all those who read my columns knew what was up,

and I promised to keep them informed. I never missed a column. Sometimes they were written from Texas, on a plane, or from New York City while visiting the World's Fair, but my followers seemed to share my adventures eagerly. With permission from editor Ted. O. Schmidtke of *The Frontiersman*, perhaps this story is best told as the continuing story in my "Talkeetna Ticky-Tac" column.

On the first day I wrote:

Just our speed! Your columnist is headed for a polar bear hunt out of Barrow, and the only strange animals we have seen so far is a live pig and a dead pheasant in a Fairbanks cafe.

But we have faith, lots of it, otherwise we wouldn't have paid Koslosky's forty-seven bucks for a suit of underwear — and no black lace! Yet we're told that eiderdown and eiderdown only is recommended for going down on ice floes, in polar pursuit. Maybe it's because a mouthful of feathers frustrates bruin's chewin'.

We'll keep you informed — via bottle a la bobble from an open lead on the Arctic ice cap. In case "Ticky Tac" fails to show in the newspaper for one week, hold your breath. If we fail to sound off for a second consecutive week . . . you can relax.

A jet has just juggled a couple of hunters, Bernard McNamara and George Brittin, in from Minnesota. One of our guides, Mike Ehredt, who has a charter plane service in Barrow, brung 'em to the Nordale where we are waiting for heap big hunter Bob Cooper to show with more Knights of the Nimrod. One local hunter, Don Obray of Anchorage, got polar fever last season when bit by a cub, and is back for a larger dose. We understand he gave the cub to the Seattle zoo.

Since yours truly is the only Cheechako on the hunt, we'll wait until we get to Barrow to harrow you with our tales of frozen toes and nose on the ice floes. And just think, yesterday morning Alice Powell invited "Ticky Tac" down to the new cafe and dining room at the Talkeetna Motel where she went to a great deal of trouble preparing Eggs Benedict. Guess we'll just have to savor the flavor as we flow out to sea.

Although we knew none of these hunters prior to their arrival in Fairbanks, we have every faith that they will be gentlemen enough to shoot that bear before his breath frosts the lens of our camera. On the other hand, Cooper and Ehredt have mighty good reps as pilots and guides, and we don't believe

297

they would let them open season on a shutter clickin' grand-ma. But come to think of it, maybe we'd best shush with the mush or they just might. We were invited along to take pictures and write. We'd never tell that we've tucked a tag in the bag because we have every intention of getting our own polar, and legally. This news we'll break to Cooper gently, while he debates with the hunter as to whether the bouncin' bruin below is Boone and Crockett. For your columnist, most any polar would do. Now we could wish for a cub to bring home as a pet for our grand . . . shush, Mary Carey, you're always getting carried away on some tangent . . . on with the news.

Then I brought in a little local news which I gathered on the train ride from Talkeetna to Fairbanks, about persons very near and dear to the columnist.

Seeing Lloyd Wohlgemuth on the train did our heart good because we were not so sure but what he had taken his last ride when he went to Seattle, where he has undergone intensive treatment for cancer. The miracle of modern medicine has enabled him to return to his family. In fact his wife, Dorothy, met the train and taxied us to our huntin' headquarters. Lloyd and "Dotty" were our neighbors in Talkeetna for two years, and their son, Gayland, was one of the charter members of our first high school, composed of eight students and yours truly, as the total faculty. That was in 1962-'64. Didn't know how difficult your columnist was to replace. It took four teachers. Of course we admit that the new road, forty-seven students, and a new building might have a little bearing on the situation.

But we loved it, and perhaps no other instructor was ever so effective in teaching Independent and Dependent classes. Remember, Gayland, those implicit instructions I gave you when you were having difficutly? The clauses in your sentence were joined by the coordinating conjunction, 'but'. I had told you several times that if a clause made sense by itself, it was independent. You hesitated. Then I came through with our never to be forgotten, "Go ahead, cut off your 'but' and see if it makes good sense."

En route to Fairbanks I was looking through the newspaper when I saw the smiling photo of Dorothy Marie Jones. I was so proud of Dorothy that I just had to comment:

298

Our Queen from Talkeetna, insofar as we are concerned, won the highest award at the Fur Rendezvous in Anchorage. Although Dorothy Marie Jones did not become "Miss Alaska," she was named "Miss Congeniality." This title, which is bestowed by the other pretty queen contestants, is for the one among themselves with the best personality and just plain old get-along ability. Anyone who knows Dorothy Marie would applaud their choice. Dorothy was also a charter member of our first high school class and we are justly proud.

SO THIS IS THE YUKON

On March 1, as planned, we started our flight for Barrow. Perhaps it would be more nearly correct if I said we started on a Cook's tour of Alaska, with Barrow as a final destination.

From the time I read my first novel I became enthralled with works of Jack London and Rex Beach. Few names possess the romance and legendary quality of the Yukon. Now I was to see the river which is three miles wide when it reaches Fort Yukon, hundreds of miles from its mouth. This mighty river was impressive enough when I saw it in Canada, at Dawson City. Now I was to see what this Amazon of the north was like where it wound its way seaward.

For two days we flew on dead reckoning across tundra, through mountain passes and over contorted deserts of ice along the Yukon. In Canada and in the eastern part of Alaska, one can follow the winding, narrow and treacherous road from Dawson City to the Alaskan border, with a mighty river a mile below. And believe me, there are places along that hairpin where, if a motorist rolled over, I feel he might never be found. But where we are now flying the river spilled all over the country in ox-bows and braids.

We accepted Cooper's explanation of "dead reckoning." "When you're flying 'dead reckoning,' if you reckon wrong, you're dead," he said as two planeloads of us began a tour of Alaska. We could have reached the "Top of the World" in half the distance and time, but all of us, of course, wanted to see Alaska, the part which was like she was during gold mining days.

Some two hundred miles west of Fairbanks we made our

first landing on the Yukon at Ruby, a fabulous old gold mining center where there is still a little mining, considerable fishing, some trapping, and a little prospecting going on. Although Ruby roared during gold rush days, the village in the cleft of a mountain has settled to a complacent hum. Frozen fish wheels, sled dog trails and log cabins were a strange contrast to our aircraft landing on the frozen river, which must have looked just as it did during the days of Robert W. Service. We visited Jeannie's Cafe, which is reminiscent of her more picturesque days.

Only thirty mintues west of Ruby, we landed at Galena, where, if we had not seen Uncle Sam's huge radar domes and put our wheels down below our skis for landing on the long paved strip, which would have accommodated anything from a Cub to a C-133 *Hercules,* we could have believed ourselves in Robert Service's Alaska. Most of our time was spent in the Yukon bar, where one felt as if drinks should have been paid for from a little poke of gold dust.

The bartender, Hobo Joe, for whom there could have been no other name, was as colorful a character as they come. As Cooper, Brittin and McNamara repeatedly rang the bell to buy the house a drink, the crowd increased, and tales of the Yukon began to match the size of the sixty-two-foot mural of the "Shooting of Dan McGrew," which stretched around the walls.

"The dents in the bell," explained Hobo, "were put there last month by a crazy pilot — I won't mention his name, but it wasn't Cooper — who left forty-two bullet holes in the wall. He really tied a good one on. After the second fifth the only way he would ring the bell was with his pistol.

"After polishing off the third fifth he got mad at me and said: 'You so-an'-so. I'm going to shoot your teeth right out of your mouth.'

" 'Not while they're in,' I told him as I grabbed the upper bridge, which I acquired after a fist fight, and threw it into the air. That damn plate hit the floor in three pieces."

Bullet holes back of the bar confirmed the shooting, to say the least.

Meanwhile Hobo Joe had sent for Singin' Sam to serenade us. Strumming his guitar like a wrangler, Sam sang in everything from his native tongue to English and Spanish. He had picked

300

up melodies and lyrics from wayfaring strangers throughout his thirty-one years, and it was his birthday. He had triplets and was expecting twins. Although Sam was already the father of eleven children, his wife was only twenty-six years old.

The singing was unexpectedly good, and a beer would get you any number, until Sam got a little too close to Cooper's ear with the volume revved up and asked for a request.

"What about 'Silent Night,' Western style?" Bob asked.

Singin' Sam faltered. Frustrated for a few seconds while you could see the wheel turning, Cooper prodded with, "You bastard, you said you knew all the songs."

Immediately an Indian version wailed through the smoke rings.

Quite a contrast to the local coloring was Yvonne Worthington, a freelance artist of Anchorage, who was free-handing the last verse to "The Shooting of Dan McGrew" in Old English with a print so perfect that one would not have believed without seeing. Formerly a graphic illustrator from Boeing in Seattle, Yvonne says: "Have brush, will travel."

So personable her character and intriguing her work that hunger was forgotten until Leonard Veerhesser walked in and announced that Betty had our steaks ready at the Yukon Inn. What chow! Real Alaskan-sized T-bones—off Texas steers, no doubt — along with baked potatoes and the works, except for salad. That and milk are harder to find than gold nuggets, and probably worth more. Thus far we had found neither.

As the DEW Line domes and multiple spires of White Alice communications faded behind our prop wash on March 2, we left the Yukon River and headed up the Koyukuk River, into the vast, uninhabited waste of a new world. Flying over valleys pocked with spruce and loaded with moose — McNamara counted 32 — we saw little else of life, except for one herd of caribou, for some 250 desolate miles.

Kotzebue was a different story. Here, although the Eskimo women fished through a hole in the ice for shee fish and Tom cod by jiggling a barbless treble hook from a line maneuvered in a sort of dexterous knitting motion which dropped or took on line. Hotel accommodations at the Arctic Inn were modern. Here, too, T-Bones, overflowing huge platters, with all the trim-

301

mings except salad, were served at the immaculately clean Field's Cafe.

During our day in Kotzebue I met Jack H. Jonas, a strapping six-foot grandson of Colman Jonas, founder of the Jonas Brothers in Denver. Jack, who was stalking his own polar bear as well as seeking pelts, deduced that this writer was interested in native crafts as well as hunting.

"There's a place down the beach that just opened today," Jack suggested, "where they do their own carving and lapidary work. Would you like for me to introduce you to Mr. Spikes?"

My parka was already on, so I flipped up the ruff. I had wanted to see Eskimos carve ivory since I arrived in Alaska, almost three years before. Thank you, Jack, for this introduction.

Inside the S & S Crafts shop a native named Joe was etching as well as carving. John Spikes was utilizing some beautiful lapidary equipment in an anteroom. Huge saws with diamond-edged blades for slabbing the native jade — which came from nearby Jade Mountain in the Kobuk River area — hummed as they consumed electricity from a city plant. Vertical lapidary units, with sanding wheels with graduate from coarse to fine sandpaper until the stone is finally ready for buffing with jeweler's rouge on leather, stood ready to receive and polish cabochons. I was in a strange, yet familiar world, having been a rock hound for several years.

As hand-carved ivory bracelets, polar bears, seals and birds tempted me to rob the cache which must carry me through a bear hunt, I compromised for a ceremonial mask. This small, translucent mask, in the form of a pendant which was made from a caribou hoof and inlaid with gold, dangled from a delicate chain of gold. Matching earrings were irresistible.

Ivory birds perched on a terra-cotta rookery revealed the ingenuity of these craftsmen. A bit of worm-eaten driftwood cast upon the beach was transformed into a work of art.

Constant callers were almost as interesting as the craft. There was "Mr. Reindeer," Dick Birchell, who was in the area to inventory, protect and help the Eskimo with his herd. Out of Kotzebue there were seven herds, and the results were not as good as hoped. Often the Eskimo did not keep close watch over the herd.

There was B. N. C. Robert Trammell, with the Coast Guard, whose duties ranged from teaching the Eskimo how to vote, to giving instructions on safety requirements for boats. Even the Eskimo must register his boat and carry life preservers.

"Registering a boat and giving it a number is not difficult," says Trammell, "but did you ever try to describe them? They think I'm sort of nuts when I say 'skin upon bone and skin upon skin.'"

A man, very great of stature, who I thought must wrestle polar bear with his bare hands, walked in. Imagine my surprise in finding that "Old Red," as Mr. Richmond called himself, wrestled with bipeds rather than quadrupeds. The son of this school principal, David, was learning to carve ivory.

Mr. Spikes began pulling artifacts from beneath the counter, explaining their use and the area where they were found. Soon Mrs. Spikes — Ada — came home from the hospital where she was employed as a secretary. Together they gave me a verbal tour of the Kobuk River. Both of them had worked with the Bureau of Indian Affairs for five years as teachers and counselors. In my mind's eye I saw real, native Alaska, where the tallest tribe of Indians lives completely away from civilization. I was assured there was much jade in the area.

"I found a pair of mastodon tusks," said Spikes, "and this summer, when Dr. Dorothy Jean Ray, an anthropologist who has been digging in the area for some time, comes back, we are going to unearth them."

"You would enjoy Dr. Ray," Mrs. Spikes remarked, "and she is one of the greatest. Would you like to come along? Bring your sleeping bag, rock hammer and down underwear. The temperature may hit 90° during the day but it gets mighty cold at night and we will be sleeping in tents."

You can bet I boiled with anticipation. To go where white man has seldom trod, to visit remote Indian villages, to hunt jade and artifacts, as well as to have an anthropologist along with a treasure of the ages waiting to be unearthed. Accept such an invitation? Who could resist?

Mrs. Spikes suggested that I see the mineral collection of another rock hound, Evan L. Nelson, an engineer at the Kotzebue Hospital. She asked if I would mind walking a few blocks. In Kotzebue everyone walks, almost.

I thought Mr. Spike's drawl was unmistakable, so I asked him.

"You bet I'm from Texas," he replied. "Waco. I barnstormed all over the state and did wing walking on planes when flying was young."

Before we reached the Nelsons, Ada filled in a few details. Major Spikes had been a meteorologist in the air force. His specialty was long-range weather forecasting.

"And tomorrow," I asked, "will we take off for Barrow?"

"It will be fair," he predicted.

At the very comfortable apartment of the Nelsons there was running water, wall-to-wall carpeting, and in fact this very pleasant and modern unit was as comfortable as one would find "stateside." Mr. Nelson was at a Boy Scout meeting. We had coffee while we waited. No one calls to announce visits in the Arctic, but one is always welcome and time is of no great importance.

When Mr. Nelson returned we went to the basement, which was also heated, where he had a shop. For thirty years he had been collecting rocks, beginning while prospecting in McKinley National Park.

"You collected in a national park?" I asked in amazement.

"Under permission granted by the U.S. Senate," he replied.

I asked about some carnelian agate and a thunder-egg. "Are they from the park?"

"No," he answered with a slow grin, "they are from the Talkeetna Range, right under your nose. You did say you live in Talkeetna?"

I felt like a fool, but not quite so badly when he said the only way to get into the area was to fly in.

"That's the story of stone, ivory, and artifacts in Alaska," he made comment which I have found quite true. "You take a boat to where there is no dock, or a plane to where there is no landing strip."

It was getting late. Tomorrow, if the forecast of Major Spikes was right, our party would be flying. Again, according to our pilot and guide, Bob Cooper, on "dead reckoning." Yet, having flown the Yukon River with Cooper for three days there was little worry insofar as I was concerned. Tomorrow, if Spike's weather forecast and Cooper's flying were both as good as I believed, we would be landing at the "Top of the World" for a polar bear hunt.

304

As predicted, the morning broke clear. Eskimo women were already fishing through holes cut in the ice before our planes got under way. The temperature stood at -34°.

As the menfolk refueled and warmed up the motors of the Cessna 180 and the Super Cub, I observed the ancient method of fishing used by the natives, and of course I kept clicking and grinding away with the press and movie cameras. Through the hole in the ice, which was about three feet thick and used as a runway for several light planes, the woman maneuvered the line much as one would knit and purl, by a dexterous movement of two sticks notched at the end. The catch, which she shook from the barbless hook, froze as it fell to the surface of the ice beside the sled upon which she sat.

I wanted to watch longer, but purring motors told me it was time to start on the last day's journey northward, to the "Top of the World" for a polar bear hunt.

Previously, little time had been spent in observing the flying techniques of our pilot and guide, Bob Cooper. Having landed on glaciers in the Alaska Range to cover mountain climbing stories and rescues, this reporter is not the squeamish type.

The Delong Mountains were a different story. Flying through a pass we hit squirrely winds, down drafts and some zero-zero visibility. At times we lost sight of the plane flying alongside. When we glimpsed it now and then it looked as if an invisible rat terrier had caught a mouse and was giving it the works. Our pilot was talking into the headpiece, but we could not hear what he was saying.

We hit an airpocket, then our dropping Cessna hit hard on a squirrely current. Cooper did not seem in too great a sweat. As big and sturdy as they come, he seemed as well in control of the situation as the elements allowed. One of the hunters looked a little green.

Just as one of the Chechakos from the East asked if it would be wise to turn back, Bob broke through and over the mountains to the frozen Chuckchi Sea. Below us lay Cape Lisurne. Bob looked for Mike. We did not see him.

"I told him we would land here for refueling," Bob explained. "We'll find a smooth spot beyond these pressure ridges and bring her down."

We were over two hundred miles north of Kotzebue. Although the Cessna in which we were riding might have flown the six hundred miles to Barrow without refeulling, the Super Cub was only good for about four and a half hours. We were hardly out of the plane before Mike came sailing through the clouds. Bob motioned for him not to land too near our plane — "too much weight on one cake of ice is not too good," he explained.

As they refueled I took a look at the strange Chuckchi Sea. Smooth in some spots, as where we landed, yet broken and contorted pressure ridges around us spoke of the endless struggle of the restless water below to escape the ever-hardening encasement of ice. I wondered how it would sound to hear the sea break through the ice, and how high she would spew house-size blue-green boulders. How long would it take, if she split, for the non-relenting cold to seal these breaks, which ran farther than the eye could see? Someone said the temperature was -42°. I could have believed -62°.

I was suffering. I just had to relieve myself, and it may have been half a mile to the nearest pressure ridge. There was absolutely nothing to hide behind except the slender body of the plane. I was sure the men must have relieved themselves on the opposite side of the Super Cub. But I had to squat. I had no choice. I got as close to the side of the plane as I could and unzipped three layers. Cold! I forgot I was in the prop wash and I don't think my rear end thawed out for two days after we reached Barrow. I'll swear it was 100 below in that wash. Blown past the tail of the plane, amber icicles clinking to the frozen sea taught me what not to do.

Lifting from the ice of the Chuckchi, we headed up the coastline for Barrow. Determining where land and sea met was difficult. We followed what Bob said was a spit of land for over 150 miles. From Naohok to Icy Cape, a deserted military installation, we saw little sign of life. Suddenly there were many tracks and wallows on the tundra. Then they were below us, hundreds and hundreds of caribou.

Nearing the village of Wainwright, we saw many heavily-loaded dog sleds headed homeward. It was not difficult to guess what they were carrying. Our pilot circled to give us a better look. Outside every hut many dogs were staked. Our guide said

Award winning photo by author of an Eskimo women fishing through a hole in the ice with a barbless hook. After shaking the fish from the bait she wound the fishing line on a notched stick with a sort of weaving motion. Note the fish in the foreground and the clothes she is wearing. Her traditional parka is worn fur-side-in, her fur mukluks are homemade and the small sled on which she sits will be used to pull her catch back home, as is being done by the Eskimo in background.

307

it was caribou we saw stacked on top of their houses — where it was kept away from the dogs in nature's deep-freeze.

We would have liked to stop, but we had no choice other than making Barrow before nightfall. Bearing inland again to the northeast, we flew over Skull Cliff and Peard Bay. Our guide told us that soon we would be passing the Wiley Post-Will Rogers memorial. Flying so low that we could have read the inscriptions, it wasn't difficult to imagine obituaries being written here.

Again there were caribou below us.

"About five minutes out," Cooper remarked, "there's Barrow."

I could have believed we were at the end of the world rather than the top of it. In relief against a red sky, the radar domes of Point Barrow marked man's last outpost. Communication spires were suddenly above us and wires barely below us as we came in for a landing. Barrels by the hundreds were scattered over the barren landscape. Before I could ask why, lights blinked on down the snow-covered runway.

We were landing in Barrow. The temperature was -34°, but it didn't matter. Tomorrow we would go polar bear hunting.

BARROW, THE TOP OF THE WORLD

Could this be Barrow? This hovel of plywood box houses, with caribou and reindeer carcasses on flat roofs, and sled dogs staked out without shelter, for the most part, in the granulated snow? Shy children with big dark slanted eyes and oval faces peeped curiously at strangers as they passed, but said nothing.

To get anywhere, we walked. There was one taxi in town, but it was broken down at the moment. We always walked down the middle of the street, and were rarely challenged for this advantageous position, except when a military jeep came in from Point Barrow. But Barrow was off limits for the military, and it didn't take me long to know the reason.

As we walked toward town Cooper pointed toward a plywood structure not too far from the end of the runway, saying, "That's the Bore's Den, where the menfolk stay. I've made arrangements for Mary to stay at the Top of the World hotel.

There was a hotel with bath and running water in Barrow, but it burned to the ground last year. There's nothing to be afraid of or worry about, Mary. I know these people here and they'll take good care of you. I brought you here for you to make up your mind about polar bear hunting. You don't have to take anything off anybody. You're here to write and you're on your own."

I didn't see how anyone could be much more fair.

The lobby of the Top of the World, an unpainted shotgun affair, must have been 10' x 12' or even 12' x 14'. It was furnished with an old divan and one table and four or five chairs. One corner was blocked by a counter which served as a desk, and there were stairs leading to a second floor, where I never visited. One floor was enough. But the proprietors were kind, especially the ladies, who were sisters, I think.

I was shown my room and the bathroom, if one speaks benevolently. Although there was steam heat, and my room was always quite warm, there was no room in the room. What little space there was was usurped by bunk beds, upper and lower, against one wall, and a night stand upon which was a pitcher of water and a wash pan. Since the stand was not large enough to accommodate my typewriter, I asked for a table. The card table which was brought to me would hardly squeeze between my bed and the next wall. The bunk above mine, a real head banger, served as a storage spot for my miscellaneous gear.

The bathroom was of the variety which I have never seen before and hardly wish to visit again, although far preferable to the prop-wash on the Chuckchi Sea. It had three enclosed stalls, each with a regular commode seat on a square, or rather oblong, base. Below the seat was a five-gallon "honey bucket," as they called the removable containers. These were collected weekly and replaced by empties, much as garbage is collected in cities. There was running water in the wash basin, from an overhead tank. Paper towels and running water were luxuries; for them I was thankful.

The drinking water in the hotel, as in cafes, was something else. It was stored as cakes of fresh ice, usually outside the front door, until needed. Some places kept it covered, but for the most part these cakes of fresh water must have made some good stand-ins for city fire plugs, insofar as the roving malamutes were concerned. They could never resist hoisting a leg. These canine-flavored blocks, when brought inside, were rinsed off and dumped into containers to melt. In the hotel they used a five-gallon insulated tin and zinc water barrel, with a large pull-open lid at the top and a push-in spigot at the bottom. I had seen many of the same type used by oil crews out on the Texas plains for keeping their drinking water iced.

As Cooper promised, before leaving to help Mike get the fellows straightened out at the Bore's Den, they came by and picked me up for dinner.

The cafe, I've forgotten the name, wasn't bad. The waitress, Elizabeth Thibadeoux, was most attractive and seemingly well-educated. When I asked her for water she suggested that I just drink coffee or hot tea. No one drank water, and she didn't have to tell me why. Those who did not drink coffee disguised the flavor with Kool-aid or some sort of powdered drink mix.

I found out later that Elizabeth's husband, who was a pilot and guide, had been lost on an ice floe while on a polar bear hunt, and never found. Part native, Elizabeth had chosen to stay in Barrow to raise her children, one of whom was in college, although Elizabeth was only in her thirties. Her children were beautiful, native and French. I believe she told me her husband was from Evangeline country in Louisiana, although I am not sure.

The food, which was served in generous quantity, was fair, about like that of an average cafe except for lack of salad and milk, which was understandable. Only liquor and staples seemed precious enough to be flown in on the one Wein airliner which arrived daily — at least once a week — if weather conditions were right, which they usually weren't.

"If the weather is right, we fly tomorrow, but the taxi should be in operation and we'll come by for you, so don't worry," Cooper admonished as he and the hunters said goodnight at the doorway of my hotel.

But the weather wasn't good, so I visited the school. The school and church were the only attractive buildings I had seen in Barrow. In fact, the school looked much like any other from the outside, and I was quite surprised to learn that, despite the fact that the children go to and from the school in total darkness most of the winter months, the percentage of attendance in Barrow was the best in the United States. Perhaps warmth, cleanliness, free hot lunches, and absolutely no place else to go were contributing factors.

You can imagine my surprise when, walking in to the attractive hallway, the first thing which I saw was a bulletin board featuring bluebonnets and Texas Independence Day, March 2. It could have been on any Texas bulletin board at this season, but here — surely there must be teachers from Texas. There were, a mother and daughter, and the music teacher and her husband, who was scout director. I made photos, but much to my chagrin, have misplaced that set of notes.

I went to the principal's office, explained my mission, and was given a cordial welcome, as well as an attractive high school girl as a guide.

The only green thing I saw growing while in Barrow was in the Texas teacher's room, where plants of various varieties were thriving under a flourescent light. The children, fourth graders, were most proud of the vegetation and overcame their shyness in their eagerness to tell me the names of the plants. It helped, too, when their teacher told them that I, too, was from Texas and had seen bluebonnets grow.

They called me "Missie Carrie" and I spent half a day with them, enjoying every minute of it and amazed at the high scholastic standing maintained in their school. Their teaching and learning experiences were very similar to those of fourth graders I had taught in Wichita Falls, Texas, before my late husband and I moved to Dallas, where I was employed as a journalism instructor at North Dallas High School.

Since the wind was still blowing hard and visibility low, I accepted an invitation to lunch in the cafeteria. Here they had milk, made from the powdered product, but it tasted good. All vegetables were from cans, but they were much the same as children ate in school cafeterias throughout the nation. We had chocolate pudding for dessert.

After lunch I visited the teachers' lounge. It was much like any other, with one exception. It, too, had "honey buckets" in the restroom.

I expressed a desire to visit the other teacher from Texas. I

311

could have found her without a guide, except for the fact that she was in another building. As we walked down the spacious hallway, strains of "Home on the Range" greeted us from an open transom. My guide introduced me to the music teacher, who in turn introduced me to the children, telling them I was from Texas. They delighted in singing cowboy songs. "These are their favorites, anyway," explained the teacher as they swung out on "I'm an Old Cowhand, From the Rio Grande."

After school I went to the scout meeting, and then I knew beyond a doubt why school and its activities meant so much to these children. It was their life and they were making the best of it. I fully believe that when this generation has grown up, living conditions in Barrow will be much better. The school was new, and their mothers and fathers, who grew up during territorial days, knew no such luxury — as indeed it was for Barrow and the Eskimo.

The next day it was still blowing hard and white-out conditions prevailed, so I wrote.

On the third day there was still no change, but I was never one for staying inside. I had heard of a local missionary and her husband who had built a youth center in town and were doing a great deal of good work in Barrow, as they had done in other outposts where they had built missions, chiefly from their own funds and whatever they could raise.

Mr. Kenneth Garrison was out of town on business, but no one could have been more gracious than Beatrice Garrison, who was a teacher in the public school, giving everything which she earned to the furthering of Christianity. She and her husband had furnsihed most of the funds for the youth center, which she showed me. Her husband had directed and done a great deal of the building himself, here and elsewhere. When they have finished a building and have trained local converts to take over, they move to a new territory where there is no mission.

I accepted her invitation to come back during the evening for Bible study. I was amazed at how much the natives knew, especially about the New Testament. Once, during high school days, when I had stars in my eyes, I had dreamed of the mission field — even thought of studying for it.

On the fourth day in Barrow it was still blowing, but on the

312

fifth day, March 9, the wind had subsided and it was clear. Surely this was the day we had all been waiting for. Perhaps what really happened can be told no better than at the time through my column, "Talkeetna Ticky-Tac," from which I quote:

After five days of wind that slapped canine flavored ice particles into the ruff of my parka, however tightly I drew it around my eyes and nose, it let up and yours truly was exuberant. Surely, now, the day had come for a polar bear hunt. Offshore winds brought huge open leads to within seeing distance of Barrow. This would be the day. At 9:00 A.M. the town taxi would pick me up for the hunt. This was the standing agreement for pick-up time, if flying weather came.

At ten I was still at the hotel. The sun was shining. What a rare sight! I tried to overlook the fact that it was a little white seaward, and that black steam was boiling off the open leads. But it was quite clear overhead and the sun was really bright. Perhaps the only taxi in Barrow had broken down again or would not start because of the extreme cold. By now the planes should be warming up.

In near panic, "Ticky-Tac" pulled on the feathers (our apologies to Koslosky for complaining about paying $47 for a suit of down underwear, with no black lace), parked parka overall and headed for the airfield, about three-quarters of a mile from the hotel.

Before I got there my ruff, which was wolverine and not supposed to frost, did. The planes lay half buried in the snowsand. The cemented white stuff sounded hollow and I made no tracks. I hardly knew which way I disliked the Arctic snow the more, blowing or so cold and crusted that it had to be cut with a knife before melting, if you wanted water.

"Unable to feel my feet, I debated walking to the hotel again without warning them. The menfolk, I knew, were at the Bore's Den, just off the end of the runway. It was really Mike Eherdt's place, built to accommodate hunters. I stubbed it down there, hoping they were not still sacked out. They were.

"Female," I sang out hopefully as I banged at the door.

"Come in," came the reply, but there was no one in the . combination living, dining and kitchen area which was centered by a big, warm stove.

"Are we going out?" I asked of the surrounding walls.

313

"And why did you think we would go out this morning?" growled a voice which I recognized as that of Bob Cooper. "Don't you see that layer of white stuff out past the steam boiling off that open lead? You think you could see a bear through that?"

Feeling pretty small and talking to the wall, I tried to make amends by offering to make a pot of coffee and wash yesterday's dishes.

"Warm yourself and get back to your Tee-Pee. It's -43°. We'll send for you when it's flying weather."

Then came a pounding on the plywood walls separating the bunk rooms. "Larry," Bob boomed at the taxi driver who also stayed at the Bore's Den. "You have a passenger."

My eider-down feathers seemed a little warm, even singed.

TROPHY POLAR BEAR BAGGED

On the following day the taxi did arrive and I was never more excited. I must have looked like a stuffed Teddy bear with my feathers on under my parka and all the other rigging I could stuff on. But I wasn't too warm, not a bit, even though the fellows teased me and called me "fatty." To make things worse, my camera cached underneath my parka to keep the lenses from frosting made me look as if I were overdue at the maternity ward. I guess the fellows couldn't help but howl.

"Christ," Cooper kibitzed, "do we bring back a bear or a bare baby?"

The guys were still laughing and George asked to feel it kick as we sailed out over the frozen sea. Below us on a point of land, northmost on the continent, lay the military base, Point Barrow. Domes and radar and communication spires were quite a contrast to the cracker box houses of Barrow.

A few miles farther north over the broken and contorted frozen waste, then nothing. It was impossible for me to distinguish sea and horizon at a distance. It was difficult to believe the frozen mass was the Arctic Ocean. Below us, pressure ridges and open leads ran for miles and miles.

George Brittin and author kneel on skin of prize Polar Bear which he shot.
Barrow pilot Mike Ehredt, left, *and Bob Cooper,* right.

"Look at the seal," Cooper observed as we zoomed in lower. "Good sign. Keep your eyes peeled. Polar bear are a pale yellow against the snow."

"Stop!" I yelled, trying to get my movie camera from beneath ny parka to zoom in on the seal.

"In midair," Cooper teased as he circled.

Zooming in with the plane aroused more than the seal.

"Bear!" George Brittin yelled. "Behind that ridge."

Never was I more excited. I heard them debating the size of

315

it, and Cooper saying, "No," but I guarantee that bear sure got shot with my zoom. Seeing him swaying as he ran beneath us was worth the full trip.

Farther out we sailed. For an hour we saw no sign of life except seal, and very few of those. The cold came right through the thin skin of the plane. The thermometer on the wing read -54 degrees.

"Mike has spotted one," Cooper sang out as the red Super Cub dipped its wing. "He's circling it. Look the way his wingtip is pointed."

"Christ! It's a monster!" Cooper observed in a most enthusiastic tone. "Mike will keep circling him while I look for a landing area close enough to bring it down. Are you ready, George?"

George Brittin had been ready since the bear was spotted.

"When I land, jump from the plane. I'll try to get within range."

We did get within range, but barely. George didn't bring the rapidly disappearing monster down without difficulty and a full volley of rifle cracks, first behind, then leading the bear until he had dead aim.

The bear went down, but George had to pump another slug into the brute when he reared as we edged toward him.

"Wait," Cooper warned as I went plowing through the snow with them toward the bear. "You can't always tell."

Crimson spreading over the snow dulled my enthusiasm a little, but not enough to keep me from heeling in. Cooper watched both me and the bear, but it seemed to be dead and he relented, after he had poked it with his foot, rifle ever ready.

I had never seen anyone skin out a bear before, nor did I realize it could be done so fast. Bob and Mike were experts. I wondered why Bob had bound a package of twelve pairs of gloves together and brought it along, but I soon found out. The blood would freeze on their gloved hands and the gloves became so stiff they would have to be thrown away. We were all excited. Perhaps this polar was a record. We measured its paw prints and took photos. The guides measured its head, as is done for Boone and Crockett, but no decision could be made officially until the skull was sent in. We would not know for some time, but I had my story — more of a story than I thought

316

when we landed and found out other hunters might be in trouble. I wrote this story:

One of the largest, if not the largest polar bear on record was taken today by George Brittin of St. Paul, on the first hunt of the season, some twenty-five miles north of Point Barrow. Piloting the plane was Bob Cooper of Cooper Flying and Guide Service, Fairbanks.

On March 10 and 11 it was -54 degrees and blowing like hell. March 12 was beautiful, but cold. Cooper made two trips but came back without a bear. No one else got one either. We did spot three, a sow and a cub and perhaps an eight footer. These were spared because Bernard McNamara was trophy hunting. We came back empty-handed. The plane, in which this reporter rode, a Cessna 180, was flying cover.

March 13 was an exceptionally clear but cold day. Two trips over the ice pack of the Arctic Ocean netted two polar bears, both of them good but not of trophy size.

Figure the odds yourself, twenty-three hunters, ten days, three polar bears, and six days unfit for flying. Match this against polars which have never been counted on the largest uninhabited wasteland of the earth, the polar icecap, and do your own deducing. Personally, I was beginning to wonder what the big squawk was all about. If we want to protect the polar, why don't we look to the East where the hunter is allowed four bear per season? Some form of conservation which would regulate more than one portion of the icecap would present a more logical answer.

And then the winds came. She blew and blew and blew. On March 14, 15 and 16 she blew. On St. Patrick's Day it was still blowing. This was a white-out of the meaner type, not snowing, just blowing snow. Stark little stems of stunted grass stand naked on the barren tundra, breaking beneath your feet. White dunes rise wherever obstacles block the flying mass. Everything would be buried except for the fact that it's too arid for that much snow to fall. Flying weather didn't come.

Suddenly I realized I wanted to return to Talkeetna. This was spring according to the calendar, but there was nothing except granulated snow in Barrow. In Talkeetna the snow would be melting, and green peeping through. What's more, I was being a poor president for the Matanuska-Susitna Centennial

317

Council. I had postponed a meeting to come to Barrow, and set one up for March 30. This was to be a joint meeting, and the state director, as well as representatives from surrounding towns, were to join us. We were planning a May Day Centennial Caravan from Anchorage to Talkeetna. I had worked it out with community and committee heads and with Carl Sullivan, Centennial director for Anchorage. Potentates from Anchorage would get the caravan rolling, and it would snowball, picking up more cars and Centennial boosters, all the way into Talkeetna. Bumper stickers were printed.

On March 25 I wrote:

Who wants a polar bear? Not "Ticky-Tac," not if it isn't gotten before the next plane leaves out of here. In so far as I am concerned it can stay on the polar icecap forever.

The things your columnist wants most are: a bath, a drink of clear pure water, a green salad and milk. Throw in a few green trees and the temperature above zero and we'll swear allegiance to the banana belt forever.

Your columnist called a meeting of the Matanuska-Susitna Centennial council for March 30, and we plan to make it. Polar or no polar bear, that May Day caravan will be coming your way."

I had no way of knowing whether my columns were being published. I was in a lonely world. The hunters who had gotten their bear had been stateside two weeks, and the others were growing impatient. I was beginning to fear pilots and guides might fly in doubtful weather if pushed too hard by man and nature.

Why did I want a bear? I loved seeing them in the open, but to have a rug to step on every night, or a trophy for my wall? I could shoot one, of this I felt confident. If I didn't bring him down the guides would finish him off for me, as in the case of other hunters. What would this prove? I had killed a moose. I didn't particularly enjoy it, except for sharing the meat. Bear meat was lousy, to my taste at least.

Yet I would get my polar, the next trip out. It was my turn, of this I was assured. Realization and materialization were within my grasp. The conquest had been great and an experience in

318

life which could never be taken from me. I had my photos and stories. The hunting season had been extended ten days, rather than curtailed, but I had little to do with the extension. In fact, at this time I didn't know whether I was being published or not. Mail is slow in getting to Barrow.

I love nature, the wilder the better. Anticipation had been great, yet somehow realization had lost its charm. Why kill that which I loved in its natural state?

On March 27 I crawled on a Wein Airliner, no doubt the one which had the spark plugs aboard. I arrived home a month from the day I had started. My reception in Talkeetna was great.

Chapter 26

Centennial Planning and
Homestead Cabin

I made that Centennial meeting, and many more. We planned for the villages throughout our borough, to commemorate Alaska's Centennial of Purchase from the Russians.

Before I realized what had happened, I got tangled up in so much civic work that I found little time for homesteading and working on this book. To make things worse, I started another newspaper column, "Along the Mat-Su Trail." Mat-Su is the short name I gave the real chocker, Matanuska-Susitna Borough.

This new news column, covering activities in our borough, gave me plenty of news coverage for my new project, Centennial planning. Although half the size of the state of Texas, our borough still had less than one hundred miles of pavement. Our borough cannot be crossed in any direction on a roadway. When the Anchorage-Fairbanks highway is finished, it will bisect the borough, north to south.

I was greatly concerned when that portion of the highway north of Talkeetna was not let in time for the construction season. The two-million-dollar Susitna River bridge of which we were so proud would be idle a second summer. I asked why, extolling the merit and need of such construction through my columns. I was assured by highway officials that the bid would be let later in the summer, so I turned to coverage of mountain climbers. Already the season was well in progress.

Most of my summer was buried in Centennial planning and trying to get a cabin built at my homestead. I did a very poor job of covering the '65 mountain climbing season.

The eleventh hour had come for building my homesteading cabin.

Building where there is no road and no landing strip does present a few problems. Just getting the material to the homestead would be difficult, to put it mildly.

A new hunting and fishing guide in Talkeetna, Ken Holland, had a long river boat. He believed he could get all the material, which was now delivered and stacked on the bank of the Susitna River, up to my homestead in three trips, provided it was done immediately, while the water was still high. Nothing could have pleased me more, but I needed someone to do the building too.

Luck was with me. I hardly knew Don Bennis, but Alice Powell of the Talkeetna Motel recommended him highly, so I hired him. Without his help I'm not so sure that cabin would ever have gotten off the ground. I admired this fine-looking and well-educated man from the first time I saw him. The longer I have known him, the greater my admiration. But back to the business at hand.

Up the river we started — Ken, his wife Doris, Don Bennis, and yours truly, all perched on top of plywood sheets laid across and over a boatload of two-by-fours. The thirty-one-foot river boat was completely covered, except for pilot space in the stern, which Ken needed to man the huge outboard motor.

The current was swift and our progress slow, despite the fifty horses. We did quite well, however, past the swells at the confluence of the Talkeetna and Susitna rivers, until we hit that mile-and-a-half-wide stump yard where the Chulitna and Susitna join. It seemed to change channels every time it rained. We lost it. The river was cold and swift and laden with glacial silt. If you capsize in this river, your chances of getting out alive are about as good as that of a condemned man arguing with his executioner, as Don Sheldon would put it.

The water is so murky during glacial run-off that it is sometimes difficult to tell whether you have eighteen inches or eighteen feet boiling beneath your boat. Suddenly, as Ken swerved to miss a floating log, we realized it was nearer eighteen inches when the prop snagged, *zing-zing-zing*, against the rock bottom. We sheared a pin and the propeller stopped zinging. Powerless, the boat was caught by the current — goodbye boat and lumber.

Having grown up around boats, I read Ken Holland's mind. He went over the stern; Don and I went over on opposite sides of the bow, just before she hit a snag. When the waves tried to inundate the boat from one side, Doris tipped it the other way.

When we maneuvered the boat to where it came underneath the high end of the snag, rather than lodge against it crosswise, Doris and I both grabbed. The current was deeper here, and it's a good thing that both Ken and I were swinging on to the boat.

"Jump in and hold on!" Don yelled as my feet were washed from beneath me.

It wasn't easy, with no footing and trying not to tip the boat, but with one arm swinging on to the limb and the other on the boat, I bellied up.

"We've got her!" Doris screamed as she caught her breath. "Do you have an extra shear pin?"

As Ken got a leg into the boat, we hung on for dear life, with thirty-one feet of boat swinging behind that limb like a lure working on a swivel.

Ken dug into his tool box for a shear pin and raised the motor. Far out he leaned over the now horizontal shaft, inserting the pin. I was never so glad to see a cotter key go into place in my life.

"Hold on until I get her started," Ken yelled as we took on another dip of water over the side, "and don't let go until I'm under power."

These instructions were a little unnecessary for either Doris or myself, for neither of us had any intention of letting loose until the nose was splitting the current.

After dodging a forest of stumps, Ken managed to beach her on an island. Don was off the boat and pulling her up by the rope on the bow. He was making sure that the current didn't catch her again. A goodly portion of my homesteading cabin was aboard. We all crawled out, and for a few minutes none of us said a word.

"May as well start bailing," I said as I got up on unsteady pegs. "Got to keep your lumber dry!"

Mechanically, we lifted off the plywood from the top of the boat. Those 4 x 8-foot sheets had made the trip doubly dangerous. We bailed her out the best we could, from either end, without removing the 2 x 4s stowed in the bottom of the boat.

"From here we go into the canyon," Kenny said, "and there's no danger of losing the current, but there are a few boulders and the current is mighty swift. Just watch and sing out if you see a rock."

One ride like that was enough. White water and sheer canyon walls above us made for spectacular scenery and thrills and chills. Here and there a waterfall spilled over the cliff above. The rock strata was almost vertical, for the most part. The old earth really heaved and strained here at one time. I hardly had time for thinking I would like to check a dyke and contact zone for possible quartz veins, because all eyes were needed to watch for boulders which might be cached just below the undulating current. More than once Bennis sang out, just in time.

I just can't imagine Doris not wanting to go back home by boat. She and I stayed with Jay and Vicki Cornell while Ken and Don brought in more lumber. They had better luck on the next trip. I selected a cabin site on the first rise above the moose flats along the river. There was a good view and a crystal stream of water.

It took a while to cut a trail through the willow flats to get to the side of the hill, but it was an adventure like I had never lived before. If there was a neighbor within a hundred miles to the north, I didn't know it. I couldn't see the Cornells' place from mine, but just knowing there was a cabin down that unbridged river helped.

"You just keep working," I told Jay Cornell and Don Bennis. "I'm quite capable of carrying these two-by's." And I did. I'll have to admit that I needed help with the plywood sheets and the door, but the rest of it I tugged up the hill while they were felling huge spruce for the foundation and clearing some cottonwoods which were in our way. My job lasted four full carrying days, and there were blisters on my hands, but I kept ahead of them, even to the roofing, and this made me quite happy.

It was such a little cabin — 12' x 16' — but completely

323

wonderful and doubly insulated against the cold. Jay and Don teased me about the windows and the glass in the front door. They said it was just right for bears to break in, but I said it was just right for seeing Mount McKinley. To date a bear has never tried to break in, although they sometimes fish where my little stream joins the river. One little blackie has raided my garbage pit now and then. If he gets too bold, I'll have that bear rug yet.

The cabin was hardly finished when bad news came. The bid for highway construction, which would bring the new highway to my homestead, was not let.

To me this was a triple blow. There would be no pavement leading to some of the villages where I was doing Centennial planning and there would be no road to my homestead the following year. To solve this problem, I bought a Super Cub, N-9471-Delta, and resolved to learn to fly.

But this would not help with my clearing problem. With no road to my homestead the following year, there would be no heavy equipment in the area. How would I get my clearing done? Ordinarily, construction companies cooperate with homesteaders in virgin areas by renting D-8 Cats with operators by the hour.

My loss would be minor, of course, in comparison to what the delay in construction would cost the borough and the state. Maybe there was still time, if I gave her full bore through my newspaper column, for the governor to reconsider before the 1966 construction season.

At the time, I was writing four newspaper columns for the Fairbanks, Palmer and Anchorage papers. If two of these columns, "Mat-Su Menu of the Week" and "Alaska Recipe Round-up," hadn't been menu columns featuring Alaskan-grown products and foods, I would probably have tried getting a few blows in through them too.

Although I was disappointed when the federal funds for new construction were used for reconstruction after the earthquake, the reason was apparent, imperative, and understandable.

Yet, since federal funds were again allocated, I could see no reason for the bid not being let.

Vainly I sought the reason through the highway department and the governor. No answer was given. For several months I challenged through correspondence and through newspapers.

324

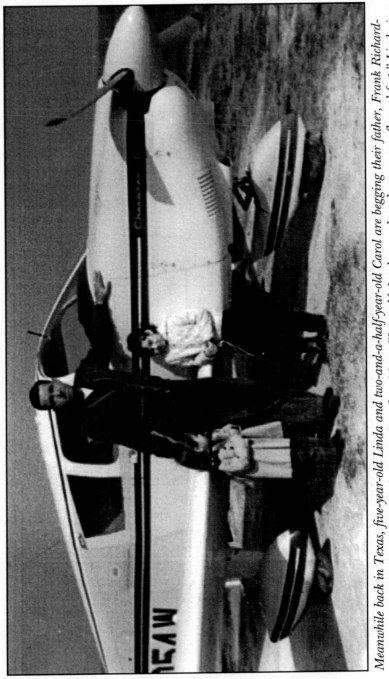

Meanwhile back in Texas, five-year-old Linda and two-and-a-half-year-old Carol are begging their father, Frank Richardson, why he doesn't fly them to Alaska to see Grandma Mary. "It wouldn't take very long because you fly real fast," Linda insists. "Me fly, me fly," chimes in Carol. "Me go see Grandma Mary too. Me go, me go!"

325

The Anchorage-Fairbanks highway was Alaska's greatest undertaking since statehood. Over five times the purchase price of the territory of Alaska had already been spent on it. Why work suddenly ceased along this portion of the blueprint highway seemed a mystery. I tried to awaken the citizenry through articles like this, published in *The Frontiersman*, February 11, 1966:

If Alaskans understood the vital effect which the Anchorage-Fairbanks highway, now under construction, will have on the state's economy and realized that this construction actually brings prosperity to us because Uncle Sam foots 95 per cent of the total cost, perhaps they would realize that Alaska's most important undertaking since statehood is jeopardized.

Nothing under construction will mean as much to the citizenry of Alaska as a whole and to the projected influx of tourists as completion of this sixty-five miles of highway, which would cut about one hundred miles from the distance now traveled between Anchorage and Fairbanks by the motorist. This would mean a direct truck line from the docks at Seward to Fairbanks, with connecting links to all major towns in south central Alaska. It would open a circular route for the tourist whereby he could visit the more populated areas of the state without doubling back. It would give both the Alaskan and the tourist a close-up of magnificent Mount McKinley and the virgin wilderness, with its vast potential, which would encourage economic development.

In so far as the tourist is concerned, we could probably plant daisies on either side of any pavement we now have and he would still consider it "lousy" in comparison to what he has at home. According to a graph compiled by Alaska's Tourism Department, eighty per cent of the persons questioned listed the nation's tallest peak and scenic wilderness as Alaska's top attraction. Why not give them McKinley? A good highway through this area is of inestimable potential. A short cut between Alaska's two major population centers has long been needed.

Here I will not bother to quote the cumbersome figures which I used in my articles showing how much money had already been spent on various segments of the road. It may be of interest, however, to know that by 1970, the cost was estimated at

The Susitna River Bridge at mile 104 on the Parks Highway is still the longest open-deck span in Alaska. It is 1,050-feet long. It is some eight miles southwest of Talkeetna where the Chulitna and Talkeetna rivers merge with the Susitna. This bridge was in place when the 1964 earthquake hit, but was not damaged.

$147 million. There are many places along the route which cost over a million dollars per mile. The most difficult stretch of road thus far completed, a distance of 4.8 miles through Nenana Canyon, cost $6.7 million. But again we are jumping ahead in our story. Back to our newspaper articles of 1966.

Do we leave the $35,722,500 already expended, lying practically useless in so far as most Alaskans and the tourist trade are concerned?

The magnificent two-million-dollar bridge across the Susitna River west of Talkeetna remains useless for a third season. Already the 28.5 miles between the unused bridge and the projected Chulitna River crossing has been cleared twice. Will it be left to vegetation and erosion? If the bid for this job were let as soon as September this year, construction season would be over. The first projected completion date of the highway was 1967. Will Uncle Sam continue to bear with us indefinitely and allocate more money as we lag years behind projected schedules for which the federal government absorbs 95 per cent of the cost?"

This and similar articles brought assurance from the highway department that the bid would be let. I fully believed it would be let in time for the 1966 construction season. I was so busy with Centennial planning and the homesteading and writing that I was temporarily quieted, more or less, by the promise which invoked this truce.

I was so proud of the work being done by my Centennial committees throughout the borough. Talkeetna was planning a museum; Willow, a replica of a gold mine; Montana Creek, Houston and Big Lake, adequate camper parks; Sutton, re-opening an old gold-rush trail; Palmer, a log cabin tourist center; and Wasilla, the restoration of Old Knik, Alaska's chief seaport on Cook Inlet before Anchorage, where they began anchoring huge ships across the bay, bringing it to life as a tent city during World War I.

My Centennial groups worked hard, and I especially want to thank the following leaders, who, as chairmen of the community committees, traveled many miles at their own expense over a two-year period of time: Curly Sutton, Palmer; Mrs. Dorothy Page, Wasilla (who refused to give up hope and carried on for this author when all hope seemed lost); Mrs. Helmi Blank, Big Lake; Mrs. Bernice Sellens, Willow; Mrs. Hazel Silfven, Mrs. Carol Sik and Mrs. Minnie Swanda, Montana Creek; and the Talkeetna workers. Let's not forget Carl Sullivan, the Anchorage Centennial head, or Bob Arnold and Herb Adams, Centennial coordinators for the state of Alaska, who were helpful not only with organizational planning but attended meeting and pre-Centennial functions as well. To each and every person who helped, and there were hundreds, our sincere thanks.

In January of 1966, my Centennial castles toppled — because our hopes for the new highway were taken away. Federal funds allocated for this project were transferred by the governor to other construction projects.

To say I was unhappy is putting it mildly. I fired this and similar missiles at the governor through the Anchorage, Fairbanks and Pler papers one week, then declared war on him and his administration the following week.

This particular letter to the editor appeared in the *Anchorage Daily Times*, March 1, 1966. Similar ones were sent to editors throughout Alaska. It was headed, "AMBITIOUS UNDER-TAKING SCUTTLED."

Dear Editor,

Anchorage has been robbed of Centennial tourism in a steal so clever that many persons are yet unaware of the fact.

The Anchorage-Fairbanks highway was first projected for completion in 1967. From 1960 to 1964 it was given highest priority. During those years we have spent over five times the purchase price of Alaska on connecting links along this route from Palmer to Nenana.

Then, suddenly and without apparent reason, work was stopped on the south end of this route. The $2 million bridge across the Susitna River, over which heavy equipment was to troll northward to join the 65-mile stretch with Cantwell and the Denali Highway, has remained idle since the last span was bolted into place in 1964.

Without any apparent reason, the governor of the state of Alaska has failed to answer any of the questions repeatedly asked by this reporter concerning delay in construction on this "high priority" route, projected completion date — 1967.

Without any apparent reason, the long delayed bid for the twenty-eight-mile stretch north of the new Susitna River bridge failed to appear on the list of those let for bid last fall.

On January 14, the reason became very apparent to this writer. This bid, which Governor Egan evidently held up in hopes of talking the federal government into letting him spend the money elsewhere, was the sacrifice now on the altar for "half-soles," patching sub-standard highways.

Last fall I challenged the highway department, the governor or anyone in authority for a reason as to why the bid was not let with the others, but received no answer.

There was no answer. It is my belief that this information was withheld from the public because those in authority knew a howl would go up from those who would suffer most by the loss.

I further believe that the "Centennial" soft soaping issued simultaneously with the announced "transfer of funds," which the governor states in a four-page telegram of explanations to the newspapers, "but until rather late in 1965, the Federal Government would not agree that the work involved (evidently referring to maintenance and "half-soles" for existing highways) qualified for funding under the Federal Aid Highway Act."

329

It is apparent to this writer that Alaska's most ambitious undertaking since statehood has been scuttled. It is up to the people to figure out why.

Practically every person in the Matanuska-Susitna borough was backing my fight — yet no response came from the governor. I may as well have been non-existent, insofar as getting an answer from him was concerned. I was completely ignored. This made me madder. This was an election year. If I couldn't defeat the governor of Alaska one way, I would try another. One of my editors, Theodore O. Schmidtke of *The Frontiersman* in Palmer, seemed without fear, so we lowered the boom.

Chapter 27

I Declare War on Alaska's Governor

I n a full-page spread, February 18, 1966, I declared WAR on Alaska's Governor William A. Egan, and all those in his administration who had been responsible for robbing the Matanuska-Susitna borough of federal funds allocated for highway construction on the Anchorage-Fairbanks highway. My publisher used the map given by the highway department showing the sixty-five mile gap where there was no construction activity. It also showed the parts paved and unpaved along the new route. Below it was a petition signed by residents of the borough.

On the following week, February 24, there was a full-page petition signed by residents, and another full-page which I had written explaining the situation quite fully. This is taken from *The Frontiersman*, February 24.

To the Honorable
WILLIAM A. EGAN
Governor of Alaska

We, the taxpayers and voters of the Matanuska-Susitna area, feel that your recent decision, transferring federal aid funds allocated for highway construction in this area to maintenance in other parts of the state, should be reconsidered.

We do not dispute the fact that a certain amount of repaving is necessary and desirable, but to sacrifice earliest possible completion of the direct Seward-Anchorage route to Fairbanks is unnecessary.

We believe that this decision, if allowed to stand, will work irreparable economic harm, not only to the Matanuska-Susitna Valleys, but to the entire state of Alaska.

We, the undersigned, petition you, the Governor of the State of Alaska, to restore federal aid construction funds allocated for the stretch between Talkeetna and Cantwell, thus allowing continued progress from both ends of this new route which will cut approximately one-hundred miles off the motoring distance from Anchorage to Mt. McKinley National Park.

Signatures poured in. Petitions were placed throughout the borough. Here's the full page story which followed:

"For want of VISION a VALLEY is lost,
For want of HIGHWAY the TOURIST is lost
For want of TOURIST the STATE is lost."

One who has never flicked a switch to illuminate his home does not miss the miracle of electricity.

One who has never seen Mount McKinley except from a distance does not experience the electrifying grandeur of nearness.

Endowed with an intimate knowledge and respect for the nation's tallest peak, this writer would be doing an injustice to fellow Alaskans, the tourist and posterity if failing to present potential within our reach.

Only sixty-five miles of construction is needed to close the gap which will cut approximately one hundred miles off the motor route from Mt. McKinley National Park from the south. Another hundred miles would be saved between Mt. McKinley National Park northward, to Fairbanks. Thus saving two hundred miles between Alaska's two largest cities.

Yet construction from the Anchorage end of the new highway is halted because federal funds allocated toward completion of this miracle of modern engineering have been transferred to maintenance or so called "half-sole" jobs on existing highways, thus prolonging the delay and hastening economic disaster for the Matanuska-Susitna area.

332

Mary Carey declares WAR on Governor Egan in 1966, showing him where the shoveling should begin to finish the 65-mile gap on the Parks Highway.

The plea for continuing construction from both ends of the route stems from more than love of a mountain. It is an acute sympathy for those along this promised highway who have been forced to give it up. It is an admiration for the stamina and courage of those who have stuck it out long after the "blueprint" highway was scheduled to reach them. It stems from the utter tragedy for those who have stuck it out this long only to find that the roadway which was cleared when his child was born will not be passable when that same child is of school age.

333

"For want of a ROAD his CROPS were lost,
For want of a SCHOOL his HOMESTEAD is lost."

My sympathy is with the farmer of the luxuriant Matanuska and Susitna Valley area, robbed of the magnificent highway over which his produce could flow, at reduced trucking rates, to existing and potential markets. My sympathy is with every Alaskan who must pay more for the necessities of life for years to come because of this delay.

"For want of a ROAD the MARKET is lost,
For want of a MARKET the ECONOMY is lost."

Yet this is only the beginning of a chain reaction. My sympathy is with the school board of the Matanuska-Susitna borough, because, after being robbed of the promised highway, some means must be devised for getting children across the Susitna River where the useless $2 million bridge terminated in swampland. Only very strategic moves thwarted the building of a schoolhouse. My respect goes to those who were clever enough to import one woman from across the Susitna River into Talkeetna, a woman with a college degree and several children in school, a homesteader who is now on half-day assignment.

For a borough with a sagging economy which already gives twelve of every fourteen tax mills to school support, this was a very strategic move. Half-a-day's teaching compared to that of a full-time teacher and building a new school is a real saving for the interim — until a school bus can roll across the new bridge into this area. But the road was scheduled to reach this area two years ago.

What will you do now? Sacrifice educational opportunity which is proposed for students in larger communities for a few in the bush who have no school at all? At the present rate of delaying action, there will be no road for at least two years to come.

A teacher at the time, this writer attended a school board meeting where a study was made of the cost involved in flying these children into Talkeetna daily. This was BEFORE we were robbed of funds for building the new highway upon which you depended.

Since the borough could not afford such expensive transportation at that time, two years ago, for what was considered or hoped to be a one-year interim . . . what can it do now? The cost of building and maintaining a one-teacher school across the Susitna River from Talkeetna alone would offset the $200,000 which is the projected five per cent the state would have to pay for construction of the adjacent twenty-eight miles of roadway. This is the section of the Anchorage-Fairbanks route, for which Uncle Sam allocated federal funds which were transferred by the governor for maintenance.

"FOR WANT OF A ROAD,
A BRIDGE IS LOST."

By the time the bid (for which federal aid funds were allocated and transferred) is let, there is the likelihood of every business and every homesteader along this route, from Palmer to Cantwell, being frozen out. This is the land of PROMISE. The land where promises never materialize.

"FOR WANT OF ECONOMIC OPPORTUNITY,
THE MATANUSKA-SUSITNA VALLEYS ARE DEAD."

Continuing work on the new highway will bolster our sagging economy. Stoppage hastens our economic death.

Half sole, if we must, but remember, the new highway symbolizes our seven-league boots. Our next giant step will cut one hundred miles off the motoring distance from Anchorage to Mount McKinley, an eternal attraction for all mankind.

If such consideration is not given, I, Mary Carey, backed by those petitioning said restoration of funds, hereby challenge the Honorable William A. Egan, governor of the State of Alaska, to public debate on the Senate floor in order that the people of the Matanuska-Susitna area, who have no senator to represent them, may be heard.

As I stated earlier, this was election year. In the same February 24 issue of *The Frontiersman*, from which I have just quoted, Wendell P. Kay, for many years a prominent practicing Anchorage attorney, who was running against Governor Egan for the Democratic nomination, came out with this statement which was given a banner headline:

It is unthinkable that the so-called "planners" of the state administration could spend over $35 million of our tax dollars on a major project and then suddenly decide it is not important enough to finish now. This vital artery should be completed and in use by the 1967 Centennial Year!"

335

Kay listed the advantages of the new highway and urged Alaskans to make a determined and concentrated effort to convince the governor to "reverse his stand before it is too late."

Republican hopeful Walter J. Hickel also used completion of the Anchorage-Fairbanks highway as a campaign issue. I was pleased when he asked me to organize campaign tours for him in the Matanuska-Susitna borough. Hickel not only won his campaign for the governorship of Alaska, but he later became secretary of the Interior for the United States of America.

The governor did relent, on the very next day, February 25. Jalmar Kerttula, state representaive from our area and Speaker of the House, announced that construction on the highway would continue.

This was good. The road would soon reach the long suffering '59'ers, and the children could be bussed to Talkeetna to school.

I have always appreciated Representative Jalmar Kerttula — "Jay," as I came to know him — since the year I arrived in Alaska. He wrote me several times during my long bout with the governor, although he was a strong Democrat and backed Governor Egan all the way. Jay and his wife, Joyce, who was on the school board before our borough was formed, helped me to get books and desks for our eight-pupil pilot high school in Talkeetna. Later our area did gain a seat in the Alaskan Senate, and in 1975, when Kerttula was majority leader of the Senate.

Retrospect is a great crystallizer. In 1966 it was difficult for me to see, but I know now that our former governor always worked toward what he thought best for the majority of Alaskans. The longer I know Governor Egan, the more I appreciate this truly great statesman. He is a kind man, a selfless man, a man of fine and unquestionable integrity. Even at the time I felt no elation when he was defeated in his bid for a third term for the governorship.

It was not until October 14, 1971, at the ribbon-clipping ceremonies of the new highway, that William A. Egan, who was again our governor after being out of office for four years, told me how proud he was of the new highway, that it was he who initiated construction of the new route, during Alaska's territor-

336

ial days. He said that no one, not even Mary Carey, could be happier to see this artery opened. There were tears in my eyes, and his were misty too.

Although every word I said and everything written was true, I did have an ulterior motive, my homestead. For this I wish to apologize, but not for my feeling toward the importance of this highway to the State of Alaska.

Perhaps, in time, I can even ask Uncle Sam and the Good Lord, Himself, to forgive me for gaining federal land under false pretense. I never wanted to farm at all, but I did want to share Mount McKinley with the world, and this was my only way of procuring the best view of the most magnificent mountain on our continent. Later both the State of Alaska and Uncle Sam saw they had erred by not embracing the southern view of Mount McKinley. By 1970, Denali State Park engulfed my homestead. By 1975, enlargement and proposals for extending Mount McKinley National Park to join Denali State Park on the southern approach had been made and were soon finalized. In case you don't know the meaning of the Indian word, "Denali," it means "Great One," as Mount McKinley was once called.

Chapter 28

House Warming in the Sky

*M*eanwhile, much was happening in Talkeetna. A daughter, Janice Holly, was born to Don and Roberta Sheldon on March 26. Don was so happy that I believe he could have topped McKinley without wings. Mrs. Campbell swore he was going to land the mountain climbers on the moon.

Don had been flying high for some time and building castles in the clouds. Perhaps it would be more factual if we stated that for months Sheldon had been flying building materials to the 6,000-foot level of the Ruth Glacier, where he was building a glacier chalet, and not a castle in the clouds.

At the starting point for many climbers of Mount McKinley, Don was building a refuge. The glassed-in hostelry would also serve as an observatory and headquarters for skiers, those who wish a twenty-mile course.

Aided by a Talkeetna resident, Chester "Chet" Price, Don built a hexagonal observatory on an outcrop of rock on the moraine of the Ruth Glacier. This outcrop, jutting some 1,500 feet above the glacier floor, gives a close-up of Mount McKinley which can only be experienced by one who is actually on the mountain.

To get to the glacier house one must climb a steep snow incline from the landing area below. When reaching the top, it is quite startling to realize that the next step could be 1,500 feet down. Sheldon had this area roped off, but I was wondering how many such missteps one might encounter while climbing McKinley. Sometimes I think mountains are made to look at, not to climb. McKinley's treachery was not fully realized at this time, certainly not by your author, who has thrilled to glacier landings and frolics. It was not until 1967, when eight climbers lost their lives, that I realized how fully cruel and how cleverly "Denali" caches her traps.

I am glad these tragedies were still in the future on May 11, 1966, when the "Grand Opening in the Clouds," as I termed my story, took place.

Perhaps there has never been a party like this one. The decor was furnished by nature, an extravaganza of dazzling peaks and frozen rivers of time, as if in a different world. On the day prior to the arrival of thirty-nine guests of note, Sheldon, with the help of world-adventurer Lowell Thomas, Jr., who later became lieutenant governor of Alaska, airlifted a six-man instructor squad, led my Hans Metz, atop the glacier observatory, where they remained overnight.

Six sled dogs were used to pull supplies up the hill to the glassed-in cabin. The only furnishings in the 16' x 16' hexagon were the six bunks around the wall and a central heater. Nothing else seemed needed; the bunks served as divans, the stove for cooking. Outside, a little ways down the hill, was a Chick Sales, the first such wooden structure upon Mount McKinley. Built in full half-moon glory, with a Sears Roebuck catalog hanging from a chain, the nostalgic effect made one forget the snow below.

Throughout the following morning guests were shuttled in from Talkeetna and Anchorage. I was happy to see so many of my friends at the grand opening, and to become acquainted with a few persons whom I had wanted to meet ever since coming to Alaska.

Betzi Woodman, president of the Anchorage Press Club, who offered me her seat on a polar flight during Arctic Airlift Week, was there. Carl Sullivan, Anchorage executive, who had helped me organize the Mat-Su Centennial Council, was present. Both Carl and Betzi were among those who had traveled in my May Day Centennial Caravan from Anchorage to Talkeetna.

Don Sheldon's mother-in-law, Mrs. Tillie Reeve of Aleutian Airways — whom I had come to love through her visits with Roberta and Don in Talkeetna — was there, as well as Roberta's sister, Janice Reeve. Roberta was not there, and with very good reason, a new baby. Dr. A. Clair Reen, obstetrician from Anchorage who had delivered Roberta and Don's firstborn, said she was reveling in nature's white rather than the white of the maternity ward.

Herb and Miriam Hilscher, who had co-authored a book, *Alaska, U.S.A.*, which I had faithfully studied before heading north, were there. I had read and reread Hilscher's chapter on an upcoming young businessman, Walter J. Hickel, whom they predicted "the most likely to succeed." The book dealt with Alaska as she was in the year of statehood, 1959. Now this man, whose ability was lauded seven years earlier, was a Republican candidate for the governorship of Alaska. I have since wondered whether they were surprised when President Nixon appointed him secretary of the Interior.

Among the persons whom I recognized from Hilscher's book was "Muktuk" Marston, founder of the Alaskan Scouts, who later gave me an autographed copy of his book, which I cherish. Muktuk, who reportedly got his name from eating whale blubber with Eskimos during his younger days while organizing and training Eskimos to defend Alaska, was as colorful as the Hilschers pictured him.

Lars Johnson, director of the State Division of Aviation, whom I knew through the Press Club, was there, as well as Martin Ridener, ski editor of the *Anchorage Daily Times*, and free-lance writers John Grady and Jim Balog.

Two men whom I had known or read about many times, Dr. Rodman Wilson and professional photographer Paul Crews, no doubt relived a less-pleasant experience on Mount McKinley in 1960. Both had reached the summit on May 17, the same date as the John Day Party. They followed the four-man-on-a-rope fall which broke John Day's leg. Helgo Bading's high altitude sickness, led to the seemingly impossible rescue and care of the sick and injured by these men. This was when Don Sheldon made the highest fixed-wing landing ever recorded. This rescue was discussed earlier in this book in conjunction with the account of Don Sheldon being down.

Adding color and beauty for the photographers were two Reeve Aleutian Airline hostesses, June Stanford and Toni Abbott.

Appetites were sharpened by the clean, crisp air. Huge "wolverine" steaks, as Don called the Alaskan-sized sirloins, with baked potatoes, barbequed beans, and salad, were served out in the open. There's little dust and no smog in Alaska. On the mountain you breathe deeply of the cleanest air on earth.

There were many VIPs, photographers, and friends from the news media with whom I should like to have visited, but I kept thinking that this was Wednesday noon and that if I could get back to Talkeetna and get my photos developed and my story into the Palmer paper, which was a weekly, I might get a scoop because the other reporters planned to stay throughout the day.

Lowell Thomas, Jr., had a dinner engagement in Anchorage to show film on his Alaskan adventures. I got this bit of information from Mrs. Miriam Hilscher, who said her husband was riding out early with Mr. Thomas.

What if I could get back ahead of the other reporters? I wanted a "scoop" for the Palmer *Frontiersman*, which had backed me so faithfully in my war for continued highway construction.

"Do you have room for another passenger?" I asked of Lowell Thomas, Jr., as he and Hilscher headed for the plane.

"Why would anyone want to leave this party?" Thomas asked. "You're not ill, are you?"

"Oh, no! Just anxious," I confessed, blurting out my desire to get a scoop for a weekly newspaper.

Fortunately enough, Hilscher had once worked for a weekly. "Give Mary my seat," he responded graciously. "My appointment is of the 'if I can get off the mountain in time' variety. It can wait."

Thanks to Herb, Miriam and Lowell, I did get that scoop, but not without added excitement.

As we tried to take off from the wet, sticky snow on the glacier, the skis on Lowell's plane failed to shake loose. The further we plowed down the glacier the deeper they seemed to dig. When Mount McKinley holds you down, you're stuck.

I feel that Lowell Thomas, Jr., could have lifted without

additional weight, and he probably would have lifted with my added weight, but he just isn't a pilot who takes unnecessary risks. Already we were beyond the strip used for landing. There were snow bridges and crevasses on this glacier, and no one was more acutely aware of this fact than Thomas. Cutting the motor, he said he would ski down in front of the plane to check.

Having been stuck on glaciers previously, I crawled out and started tramping down a runway in front of the plane's skis. Hopeless for one person without snowshoes, but one has to try to help, to say the least.

Lowell must have been a half-mile down the glacier when I looked back toward the glacier house, wondering if they realized we were in trouble. Soon I saw specks gliding toward us, six of them. Hans Metz and his ski instructors were en route. They reached us shortly after Thomas got back. He was shoveling snow from the plane's imprisoned skis when the men on the board offered helping hands—and feet—as we tramped out a runway. This was fun. I thought back to the time I had joined the Frenchmen in tramping out a runway for the previous year, when Don brought me in for a story.

Thomas said there were no crevasses ahead, but he doubted that he could take off in the sticky stuff with additional weight. He said he felt he could make it by himself if I didn't mind walking back to the better packed runway at the observatory.

Of course I didn't mind. I had always wanted to take a long walk on a glacier. I sank mini-skirt deep in the snow, but I didn't mind since I was wearing ski pants—without skis, darn it. I must admit that the melting snow clogged inside my boots taught me what kind of footgear not to wear on a glacier.

I must also admit that I was pretty happy to see Carl Sullivan bringing snowshoes for me. How wonderful! It must have been well over a mile back.

The gang at the glacier house had set up a ceremonial ribbon for me to cut at the goal line, just for me. They gave a rousing cheer when I made it, huffing and puffing. I'll never make a mountain climber, not even a snow bunny, so help me!

Our second try for takeoff was more successful than the first. And to top it off, I need not have worried at all, nor rushed, for the others got closed in by a white-out and twenty-five of the party remained in the 16' x 16' overnight. Oh, well, that's what comes of sticking to duty, always missing fun.

Did I forget to tell you how scared I was when our plane failed to take off? Excuse me, but I wasn't. Not at all. We simply failed to lift. If there had been a crevasse in front of us large enough to trap a plane, Thomas would have seen it. If we had hit a snow bridge, the wings would no doubt have spanned it. We weren't even in danger of tearing out landing gear. Sorry, folks, but our position was less precarious than if we had been in a car stalled on a freeway, and it was much more exciting because I admire Lowell Thomas, Jr., greatly.

I had my scoop, but the editor had a story, too, which began thus the previous day:

> For those still listening to radio reports on Don Sheldon's glacier party on Mt. McKinley, *Frontiersman* columnist Mary Carey is back in Palmer with the first pictures to be published on the world's most unique "Grand Opening," even though she gave listeners a few suspenseful hours while stuck on the Ruth Glacier in a plane piloted by Lowell Thomas, Jr. of Anchorage.

Chapter 29

Up The River in D-8 Cats

*A*ccording to federal land laws, homesteaders must clear and cultivate 20 of the 160 acres, as well as build and live on the homestead, before applying for final proof of possession. Since I filed as a widow of a veteran, the terms were a little more lenient, in so far as the amount of time I had to live on the land is concerned, but I still had to clear and plant 20 acres within the first three years.

Despite winning "the war," the new highway would not reach my homestead in time to be of help in so far as bringing in heavy equipment was concerned. Furthermore, I couldn't homestead in the bush where there was no communication whatsoever with the outside world and keep four newspaper columns.

My first editor, Dave Galloway of the *Fairbanks News-Miner*, suggested I keep my column, "Talkeetna Topics," which I had written for five years, turning it in whenever convenient. This I am still doing.

After writing farewells through my other columns, which had become an intimate part of my life, and explaining how impossible it would be to keep them while homesteading in an isolated fly-in area near Mt. McKinley, my thoughts turned to the seemingly unsolvable problems at hand.

Imagine clearing and planting where there is no road and apparently no feasible means of getting equipment into the

344

area. This law is as outmoded as a reindeer for transportation in Alaska. When a homesteader has cleared and planted his twenty acres, how does he get his crop to market, if there is no road? Invariably the consequence, unless he has a fortune backing him, is going broke.

If I had my way, the last choice for use of the land in this magnificent wilderness area where I homesteaded would be to push down the tall virgin timber for farming. But homesteading laws must be obeyed. I had to homestead, as well as file an eighty-acre Trade and Manufacture site, to have enough acreage to reach the top of the butte where I want to put a Mt. McKinley Observatory. Yet, without these homesteading laws I could never gain this land. I am humble for this opportunity to try for it, even though I complain of outdated laws which I feel should be amended.

To get a D-8 Caterpillar into this virgin wilderness to clear land, and put in an airstrip — since the road would not reach it for the next two years — seemed a virtual impossibility. Yet nothing smaller was capable of handling this type of work. Size of equipment was really no factor since there was no road and no bridge across the Chulitna River, anyway.

I had a problem. No one seemed eager to risk such an expensive hunk of equipment as a D-8 on such a "damn fool adventure" in the Alaskan wilderness. I had little choice. Now I must buy a D-8 Cat, which I couldn't operate, to add to my Super Cub, which I couldn't fly, or give up homesteading. Never had any sense, anyway, so I found a second-hand Caterpillar and started looking for operators.

Fortunately I found a man, Jack Silfven, who said he would risk his Cat since I would have another along. This was great. Finally I found four men who believed they could walk two D-8s up the twenty-eight mile clearing, if you could call it that, which would later become a part of the Anchorage-Fairbanks highway. They would have to cross the unbridged Chulitna on the winter ice. Could they make it?

There was eight to ten feet of snow on the ground. No highway equipment had been on the road clearing since last fall, when a D-8 broke through the muskeg and sank to her stack. The operator managed to get a cable around the blade and hitch the Cat to a large spruce tree. This cable and stack were the only reminders of the depth of the muskeg, fed by warm springs, which we would have to cross. How well I remembered, from way back in 1962, when the first clearing was done in this area. The construction crews laughed about a swampy area, rightfully named Rudy's Lake, because a very determined cat-skinner named "Rudy" sunk three mechanized monsters there before making it through the muskeg to higher ground.

It was a terrible chance to take. Such an odyssey had never been attempted previously, but I had to try.

With much foreboding and fear, I plunged my life savings into a seemingly impossible dream in the Alaskan Wilderness. A huge, twenty-one-foot sled was built and loaded with twenty-four 55-gallon drums of diesel, two drums of aviation fuel, and ma-terials for building another cabin on my homestead, this one for hired help. Cached between the fuel and lumber was a sleeping-room-only area, which was covered with a plastic tarp and warmed by a small heater. Here the four men, Jack Silfven, Earl Ray, Gene Richardson, and Jim Sibert, Jr., would sleep.

Since the blade on the machine which Earl Ray was operat-ing had a higher lift than that of Jack Silfven, Earl was to break trail and Jack would pull the sled. This wasn't as simple as it sounds. Twice Earl was stuck in areas where warm springs kept the muck soft all winter. Much cable and time was expended ex-tracting the Cat from such wallows. Always there were snow bridges to be filled in over open streams by the lead Cat. These bridges had to be substantial enough not to wash out nor break through before the Cat pulling the overload sled could follow.

It took the men eleven days to make the first twenty-two miles. Temperatures ranged from ten above to minus twenty de-grees. I became desperate.

Nothing could hold me in Talkeetna any longer. Although it was against his better judgement, I persuaded Don Sheldon to fly me in. We saw the Cats within three miles of my cabin. They seemed to be making good progress along a windswept ridge. I asked Don to land on the river bar below my cabin, so I could walk back to meet the men. Landing here was less dangerous in winter than in summer. I would never have attempted such a landing myself . . . never did. It is precarious enough, flying

346

down this canyon, any time of the year. Yet in winter, if you overshoot the postage stamp bar below, you will at least skate out over the drink rather than being dumped into it.

Knowing I'm nuts, Don didn't argue. Down through the chute we fluttered, landing like a duck as the skis skimmed the snow. He argued with me in silence, as he sometimes does, while I reached for the snowshoes.

"If you just have to go," he finally relented, "maybe you'd best carry my rifle."

"Why? We didn't see a thing except moose and they were concentrated below, on the willow flats. We flew up the clearing and I can see all the way back to the Cats from the top of the ridge."

"Okay, kid. You'd probably shoot a toe off anyway."

As Don took off I saw him flying low over the trail, again checking and perhaps routing any game within hearing distance of the plane's roar. Bear had long been in hibernation and moose didn't care for deep snow. If I met a cow and calf, which I surely had sense enough to watch for by now, I could get out of their way faster than the cow could get to me, since I was on snowshoes. Moose have a great deal of difficulty "swimming" in waist-deep snow and avoid doing so, sticking strictly to well-beaten paths most of the time.

I was so happy when I made it back to the Cats that the fellows probably thought I was some type of idiot or that I had gotten "cabin fever," as one sometimes does in a frozen world away from civilization. I later learned that Gene Richardson, whom I hardly knew at the time, said, "Good God, not a woman! What will we do with a woman?"

At this time I had every confidence that the men would make it to the cabin. It was 10:30 A.M. and shelter was less than three miles away.

It is quite evident that I did not know what was involved in those three miles. Earl Ray invited me to climb on the lead Cat with him in order that I might make photos fore and aft. The big blade bit into the deep snow all the way, and pushed or pulled it to the side. Once when we stopped, I forgot and jumped from the Cat without snowshoes, and sank waist deep in the fluffy stuff.

We came to a grade which seemed insurmountable. Thirty-four passes were made upgrade, dragging back a snow fill. The

347

incline was so steep that Earl stopped and suggested that I ride on the trailing Cat. Its long cable, which was attached to the lead Cat for extra pull and protection, in case either machine should plunge out of sight into soft muskeg or into a snowbridged ravine, was now disconnected. The grade was so steep, it was explained, that the front Cat might slip backward, as it had done on previous inclines.

It would be difficult for me to speak my admiration for these men. There are more kinds of pioneering in Alaska that is done by dogsled or plane. My prayers must have helped support the Cat. With each drag it made to the side, I was sure it would go over the cliff and plunge into the river, which we now paralleled. On the thirty-fifth drag back, Earl made it to the top. Triumphantly the big Cat held its footing as it clogged in reverse to the rear Cat.

Downgrades were worse than upgrades. The sled back of Jack's Cat kept sliding down and bumping into his D-8. The heavy guard rail which they had built in front of the sled was not heavy enough. Fuel barrels were punctured and lumber and materials toppled overboard with terrific impacts.

Adding to these delaying miseries, some of the longer two-by-fours had to be sawed off because they extended too far over the rear of the sled. When turning a corner they would bang into trees. When crossing a narrow ravine, the 2-by's bridged it and seemed to suspend the whole sled. There was little or no fill along this part of the clearing and there were dropoffs where streams cut through.

The nearer the river, the steeper the downgrades. The men put on snowshoes and walked to the top of the final ridge. It was too steep. They backtracked, then walked down a ravine to the river. They drilled the ice with an auger brought along for this purpose. It seemed thick enough to support the Cats. Eighteen inches of ice will support a lot of weight, but each Cat weighed about twenty-four tons, and that sled was no feather.

By pushing over a few trees, the fellows deduced we could reach the river by heading straight down the ravine. From there we would go upriver the rest of the way on the ice. There was open water in places along the river where the current was too

Bush pilot Cliff Hudson of Talkeetna sees D-8 cat in trouble and runs across Chulitna River ice to see if he can be of assistance

swift for the clutching fingers of ice. We would have to chance it; there was no other possibility for making it, and this was not a crew for turning back.

I thought I had been quite a few places and done quite a few adventuresome things, but nothing like this. Going down the steep ravine, the only way I could stay on the bulldozer was to swing to the crossbar overhead. The temperature was dropping and my gloves seemed to give little protection against the sticky-cold iron. Earl gave me some heavier gloves, which I pulled on over mine. They helped.

When we finally reached the river I held my breath as we inched the iron monster out on the edge of the river ice. It held.

Gene Richardson took his turn on the snowshoes, as he and Jim Sibert had done all along, leading the way. The snow was not so deep on the windblown river ice and the going was much easier. Ahead of the Cats, the fellow kept the ice auger in constant use whenever the ice looked thin. Again the gigantic invaders were coupled together by cable. This time the span was lengthened to avoid putting too much stress on the ice in a concentrated area. We were almost within seeing distance of my

cabin across the river, but getting to it would be a different story. There were open spots in the river, and overflows. She was
too deep and swift in this canyon area to freeze solidly all the
way across. If she did freeze, the current would cut away under
the ice until it escaped and overflowed. On up to where the glaciers had done their own bulldozing, the river was wider and not
so deep. Ahead, the nation's tallest peak loomed closer, pinker,
and colder as we trespassed by virgin southern flank with clank-
ing iron monsters.

It was -22°, and late in the evening when we made it to
where the men thought we might effect a crossing. The ice was
thinner, but there was little choice. Earl sent me to the back Cat
again. They were roped with a long, black cable, like climbers on
a mountain, just in case.

Earl seemed to be doing so well, when suddenly, down the
Cat plunged! There was slack in the cable, and we hardly felt the
lurch as the front end of the lead Cat slid into the water. We
yelled and waved at Earl Ray to jump, but he rode her down,
scotching the brakes before swinging on the overhead beam and
leaping to the shattered shelf ice which had broken away from
the rest of the pack.

It was a strange, as well as a horrible, sinking feeling, seeing the motor of the Cat underwater almost to the stack, yet
hearing the motor *put-put* as it kept running. The back Cat
would not budge her.

"Quick, the chainsaw," Earl directed, "the blade has caught
on shelf ice and she's holding. If we can cut an ice ramp, maybe
I can back her out, if she keeps running."

I had not realized that the Cat was suspended by the huge
blade which bit into the ice and held as the motor sank. A test
made with a steel rod carried for this purpose showed fourteen
feet of water underneath the blade. If the ice gave way, no
more Cat.

Ice and snow flew as the men sawed through the frozen
shelf and kicked it down on a firmer footing. Water sloshed up
and froze on their gloves and clothing. They would surely freeze
to death. I had been no colder in the prop wash on the Arctic
Ocean. This was it!

Our drama was so intense that we hardly noticed a plane

350

circle overhead, until it landed. The men did not have time to stop work. It was Talkeetna bush pilot Cliff Hudson who saw the predicament we were in and landed on the river to see if he could be of possible aid. It was getting late. Although it was twenty-two below, the men were working so hard and fast that they were wet and sweating despite the ice which clung to them where it did not get knocked off.

Cliff offered to take a chainsaw, but Earl thought it would be of more help if he flew me back to Talkeetna, where I should stay, sending back dry socks and gloves for them while there was still light enough for a landing. If they got the Cat across, they would stay in my cabin.

My spirit was lower than the Cat. My feet had long since ceased to have any feeling, and I wondered if one could tell when one has frozen toes. The meat had been frozen in the sandwich which I had eaten for lunch, and my stomach felt as if the meat never thawed up. Yet I didn't want to leave.

"We'd better hurry," Cliff encouraged as he offered to help me through the snow to the plane. "The trading post will be closed and it will be too dark for me to get back."

The store was closed, but I managed to buy eight pair of gloves from Carroll Close at the Roadhouse, and a jug, of course. Quickly I begged socks from anyone I could find.

Mrs. Christine Flescher was headed toward her home down the runway. Knowing how precious minutes can be in case of emergency, she didn't let me look elsewhere. Like the old pro which she is, she same up with the goods immediately.

I ran with my contraband for the plane, which Cliff already had revved up. He took off in the gathering gloom.

I returned to Christine.

"Sit down and warm yourself and relax," she invited. "Cliff should be back within forty minutes. You'll be right here on the runway to hear the news."

"But it will be dark."

"He's landed in the dark before. In Alaska one does what he must."

Mrs. Flescher made me a little ashamed of my own anxiety as she talked of her fishing days in Ketchikan, when she had owned

351

her own fishing fleet of four boats, as well as a charter cruiser. She knew what it is like to be in trouble, especially in the water.

It was difficult for me to imagine her in such a role, so immaculate her dress and so soft her speech.

Soon after dark I heard the drone of a plane. I rushed to the airstrip. Before the prop stopped turning, Cliff climbed from the plane and beat me to the draw by asking:

"What's the matter, Kitten, worried about something?"

"Tell me," I pleaded.

"They're O.K. The Cat's out of the water. They're headed for your cabin and I bet there'll be a little party tonight."

I could have cried with joy and admiration.

There was no doubt in my mind now that the necessary clearing would be done. The worst was over.

Chapter 30

I Break My Back — Twice

S uddenly it was fall and I was back in the schoolroom. It was good, being back home, and all went well until February 8, 1970, when I fell and fractured a couple of vertebrae. This time Don flew me to the hospital rather than to the mountain.

A friend of mine, Miss Sharon Pace, who was my student teacher in Naknek, had been to Talkeetna that very afternoon to see me. As coincidence would have it, she had just finished college and was looking for a teaching position. Since she graduated at midterm, no opening had presented itself. I couldn't resist the temptation.

From my hospital bed, after I had been put into traction, I called Sharon and asked her if she would like to have my teaching job.

"Where are you, Mary Carey, and what are you talking about? Have you lost your mind?"

"One question at a time, please. I'm here in Anchorage, and I wondered if you would like to start teaching for me, tomorrow. I haven't lost my mind, but I do have a slightly broken back. Not bad; the cord's not severed, just sort of cracked up."

"Oh, no! You've got to be kidding. You couldn't even be in Anchorage this soon. I just got back a few minutes ago myself. You're in Talkeetna. Are you drinking? You're loaded!"

"No, but it sounds like a good idea. Maybe you could sneak a little nip. Room 512, Providence Hospital. I am a little shook."

"You idiot!" Sharon all but screamed into the receiver. "You can't fool me! I'll find out!"

Within a few minutes she was at the hospital.

"You fool," she blubbered, "you didn't have to break your back to give me a job."

"Just want to make sure my students don't get a better teacher than I am. That could be tragic since the doctor says I'll have to be out for some time. Why don't you have the nurse bring that telephone back? We'll call my principal."

Just like that. I'm in the hospital, my student teacher is with me. There's no housing available in Talkeetna, but the new teacher could move into my cabin — and be my nurse when I got out of the hospital.

"Always an ulterior motive," Sharon smiled as she gave me a peck on the cheek. "And if I'm going to be your nurse there'll be no drinking! Not anything except doctor's orders."

And believe you me, she meant it. I gave her my job, and she gave me hell. A cast on my back was bad enough, but the hammer she held over my head was worse.

The doctor said I should not try to go to the bathroom alone. Sharon hid my crutches and told me to pee in the bed if I had to go before she got home from school. But she, or a student or a friend was always there with me. I was seldom alone, even for a few minutes. They pretended not to be organized, but some woman from our Homemaker's Club or the church just happened by every day, while Sharon taught. Of course there was a telephone beside my bed. Getting to the bathroom wasn't quite so easy. Sharon had to help me to the restroom so often that she began calling me "Honey Bucket." In case you are not an Alaskan, a honey bucket is a portable potty used where there are no sewer lines. Sharon was so mean and strict with me that I began calling her Mafia. Finally we agreed that if we ever came through it together we would write a book entitled *The Honey Bucket and the Mafia in Alaska*.

I didn't get back into the school room that spring, but I did get to my homestead, on crutches, when the second temporary bridge went in.

Determined to have more comfortable living quarters. I bought a trailer house, *with a bathtub!* It was one of the first things across the temporary bridge. What a luxury! I had gravity flow water from a spring-fed creek right into my trailer house.

With a road and a bridge, I needed a car, not a plane, so I sold it and bought a Jeep Wagoneer — to pull the steep grades. I wanted to work on my book — this book — but I had to figure some way of earning a living. Had it! I would put in a gift shop and package store. Not many of the construction workers would be looking for gifts, but as Will Rogers commented, "Alaska is the longest bar in the world."

I got my license and was busy converting the cabin I had used previously for hired help into a little store. Of course I was not supposed to drive while in a cast, but I did, to bring in supplies. Big Jim Christianson, the bridge contractor, didn't enjoy seeing me drive across that temporary bridge, which had no railing, but he was nice enough to turn his back.

I had just gotten in my last load of contraband and was ready to open shop when the rains came . . . and came . . . and came. A creaking and grinding and crashing sound in the night told the story. The bridge washed out . . . the second temporary bridge was gone. My new Jeep was trapped on the wrong side of the river.

Weeks passed. The river remained high. Fortunately for the workers, the skeletal ironwork for the new structure arched 190 feet above the raging current.

My food supply was nearing exhaustion, but I had plenty of beer. I made a big sign: LET'S SWAP BEER FOR BREAD! Soon I was the best-fed person around.

In July I was to get the cast off my back. What a great day that would be. Earlier I had rented my own little homesteading cabin to one of the workmen who wanted to bring his wife out. She volunteered to drive me to Anchorage. Since my orthopedist, Dr. William J. Mills, had told me not to drive, I thought this might be wise.

It couldn't have happened, not under these circumstances, but it did. She rolled the car and I got two more fractured vertabrae.

I never saw a madder doctor in my life.

355

"Mary Carey, what in the . . . blankety-blank-blank have you beeen doing?" Dr. Mills stormed as he reached the emergency room. "I told you not to drive in that cast."

With that he left the room, and I wasn't too sure he would return. My friend, who had been doing the driving, thought it time to confess. Fortunately she was not injured in the accident — mostly shook up over my complications.

As for myself, I felt it was nothing short of a miracle the way my old sacroiliac hung together. I tried to soft-soap Dr. Mills by telling him what a good patient I had been, and how the cast he had made for me probably saved my spinal cord from complete severance. The latter statement was sincere, but Dr. Mills would never buy my being a good patient. Wonder why?

I've seen him work with children, as gentle as the breath of hope, yet I've seen him so mad at grown-ups that one would think a prized Rembrandt had been destroyed. And that is my opinion of the way he feels about bones. You can bet he made a believer of me the second time around.

Dr. Mills is the meanest orthopedic doctor in Alaska — perhaps in the world — when you fail to obey his instructions, but he's one of the best, the very best. His medical accomplishments have been recognized nationally and internationally. He walks on an artifical limb himself, but how this came about I do not know — probably never will. But I did learn about something that happened in Vietnam. Dr. Mills would never give out such a story, but it seemed to have leaked out in the form of a news item.

Forgive me, Doctor. I could tell a more authentic story if I had a few details, but you would never tell, so I'll do the best I can.

If I understand the problem correctly, a soldier was brought in with a live mortar shell in his back. Anyway, it was something which could, and proably would, explode. You had the room sandbagged, ran everybody out, then proceeded with the operation, very successfully.

As I was saying, Dr. Mills can be pretty nice with other people, but the second time around he tried to hang me. Weights on my neck and weights on my feet. He threatened to put me in a cast with a Queen Elizabeth collar, and leave me there forever.

"Because of my age" he finally relented and put me in a body brace instead.

Since I had six months of previous training, I was a real pro on my crutches. My back did not bother me so much as my hands. Now that I was set to write my book, I couldn't push the keys on my typewriter.

Back to the doctor I went. He sent me to a therapist who worked with my hands and showed me several exercises to practice faithfully. Dr. Mills said if this didn't work, he might be able to relieve the pressure by an operation on my spinal cord, near the base of my neck. This was really frightening. I thought I had been scared after the wreck, when my left arm and leg failed to function for a short time, but this was worse.

I determined not to have that operation. My hands had to work. I had to finish this book. There had to be a way. I was never dependent upon others, and I wouldn't accept such a sentence now. I could take care of myself.

My first home therapy was quite unique, to say the least. For several years I had extolled the merit of a spring tidbit, called Fiddle Head Fern, which grew wild on my homestead.

Beginning in 1969 and really taking hold by 1970, Sigmund Restad, head of the Institute of Agricultural Sciences in Palmer; Charlie Marsh, research economic; and Mrs. Marge Sumner, in charge of processing and preparing the fern for the table, began marketing the fern in an experimental program. They were paying people thirty cents a pound to pick the fern, which was a real bonanza, especially for the children of the Talkeetna and Trapper Creek areas. One can gather several pounds within an hour and it grows in great abundance.

I thought it over. I could at least try. Putting on rain pants and a jacket, I tucked a duffle bag underneath my crutches and climbed the gentle side of the slope across from my trailer house. Sitting down and dragging my crutches behind me, I slid down the steeper part of the hillside, picking Fiddle Head Fern all the way. When I reached the bottom I would dump the fern from my duffle bag into the spring box, which I had used to keep my food cool before getting a refrigerator which used bottled gas.

Much to my surprise and delight, Mrs. Marge Sumner wrote

encouraging notes, commenting on how fresh and firm and clean my harvest was. I worked harder. Soon I became their star picker.

I've never told anyone previously how many times I climbed and slid down that hill, nor how painful the picking really was. I forced my hands to work. No wonder my fern was clean. Much of it was bathed in tears. But "Therapy Hill" was my greatest ally. It still means more to me than any other spot on my homestead, and I still check it faithfully each spring for the first violets and the first mess of fern. I serve it at my lodge and people enjoy this new gourmet delicacy. If those eating fern only knew how much this little plant did for me in 1970, therapy-wise and economy-wise, perhaps they would understand my extolling its praise.

Since Uncle Sam lopped off funds for this and other experimental programs, I have been working with those who did so much to advance Fiddle Head Fern as a food source for coming generations. By putting in a small processing plant, I hope to provide employment for school children of the area while developing a new food substance which is here for the taking. Why neglect that which God has so freely set on His table before us when we know we must face a hungry world?

Chapter 31

First Woman in World on Mt. McKinley in Winter

(Article by Art Davidson)

*B*rian Bartlett, a young medic recently returned from Vietnam, wanted to be the first person to climb McKinley alone in winter. Although he had reached the summit previously in summer with other mountaineers he seemed determined to make this winter climb, alone.

For several years the Park Service would not agree to anyone attempting such a climb in sub-zero temperatures and long hours of darkness. There had been trouble enough in 1967, when eight tried and one died in the first winter assault, discussed earlier in this book. The odyssey is written in book form, *Minus 148*, by one of the three climbers who reached the summit. The other two, Ray Genet and Dave Johnston, are now my neighbors. Ray operates the only licensed guide service on Mt. McKinley and had reached the summit 19 times by 1974, but this is getting ahead of our story. Dave became a park ranger and is bringing up a family in the shadow of "The Great One."

Finally Bartlett wrangled permission from the Park Service to make the solo winter climb. I never saw a climber with so much gear. He hoped to carry a pack on his back and pull a sled behind him in the case-hardened snow. He wanted Don Sheldon to air-lift him to the six thousand-foot level on the Kahiltna Glacier, where he would begin his climb.

If Bartlett was fool enough to attempt such an ordeal and

Don agreed to put his little yellow snow bird on the glacier in mid-winter, I was fool enough to want to go along for the story.

Again Don was hesitant, but finally agreed that if he could get Bartlett and half his gear in the first day, he would take the remaining gear and Mary Carey in the next. Never was a photojournalist happier. **The first and only woman on Mt. McKinley in winter — and to cover the first and only solo winter climb!**

Sheldon did take Bartlett in. Although the weather looked a little doubtful the following day, Don said we would try, if I put on enough clothes. I stacked on three layers, a face mask, and gloves with liners. Even though I insisted my bottom layer was the eider down I had gotten for the polar bear hunt in Barrow, and my parka was sealskin, Don hunted up some snowmobile coveralls and helped me inside — so I wouldn't come apart in the middle. We headed for the mountain with three hundred pounds of gear.

"If we can make it off the Talkeetna strip with his load," Don commented with his usual grin, "then we can hope to make it off the glacier, when she's three hundred pounds lighter."

We did make it off the strip and for a long while both of us remained silent. Mt. McKinley in winter is the most beautiful sight on earth, in my way of thinking. I was wondering if I would feel the same about her tomorrow, if I had a tomorrow.

"We'll see how much headway Brian's made with his relay," Don commented as we sailed in at ten thousand feet.

Don's low whistle of surprise was my first clue that all was not well.

"Not a sign of him," Don puzzled as we sailed down the glacier toward the six thousand foot level where he had deposited the climber and his gear the previous day. "Jeez, look how it's snowed," he observed before I realized the trouble, "not a sign of my ski tracks."

"That will make a good photo," I called as I saw Brian in front of his tent, waving.

"Put down that camera and tighten your seatbelt," Don commanded as we skimmed, then submarined through the whiteness. The suddenness of our stop and the settling of the plane told me that we were in soft, very soft snow. I had thought it would be crusted in mid-winter.

"I can't move," came Bartlett's plaintive greeting as Sheldon opened the door, probably to see whether we were right side up or upside down. We seemed right in the middle of a snowball and it was good to see the wan light of the winter day.

"I want a photo," I urged as I slid from the plane and sank miniskirt deep in the fluff.

"No story. No photo," Bartlett insisted. "I've let myself, my sponsors and my friends down. I can't move, much less climb and pull a sled. Take me back to Talkeetna."

"Holy cow!" Don commented. "I can't. I'll do well to get off the glacier with the load I have. Tell you what. I'll take Mary

Your author shares food with Jacques Batkin and fellow mountaineer on a previous and happier expedition. Early in the Centennial Climb a snow bridge gave way with him, plunging him over 50-feet into a crevasse from which his body was recovered.

back, unload, and come back and pick you and the rest of your gear up. But be ready. The wind's coming down off that peak."

Just like that, without even being given an opportunity to snap a photo, I was ordered back into the plane.

Don revved her up, but she didn't budge. He tried again, no progress. He motioned for Brian to push on the strut. Again the engine roared, but the little bird was trapped.

"Let me out," I suggested with a sigh, remembering the times I had been stuck on this glacier before with the French Expedition and when Don had "Open House." Tramping down a runway is not child's play. It takes hours — and hours — for several persons.

"One more try," Don shouted as he pointed toward the other strut.

I made connection as quickly as I could swim around the plane. Again, Don revved her up. With her tail in the air and a mighty roar and shuddering sound, as if the little plane were trying to pull up the whole glacier with its skis. The Super Cub lurched and I fell forward into the snow.

As I dog-paddled my way and blinked some of the snow from my bewildered eyes, the yellow bird was disappearing down the glacier — and I was trapped on the mountain.

Realization! The plane would never have lifted under existing conditions, with me and that load. Don would have to fly back to Talkeetna, unload the plane, and then come back. This would take up to two hours I knew but would the weather hold? I glanced at the peak. The snow plume seemed lower.

"We'd better get out of the wind," the young medic advised through his snow-clotted face mask. "Here, let me dust you off a bit. Leave your mask on until we get inside."

Both of us! Inside that pup tent! However small, you can bet that I lost little time wiggling my way inside. There was hardly room to sit upright, but we were out of the biting wind. Brians' sleeping bag on which we sat took most of the room. A little primus stove with a flicker of light and a pot melting snow on the smallest burner I have ever seen promised tea. This was heavenly, I thought, but the wind whipping the tent was a grim reminder. I asked how cold it was.

"Not bad," he replied, "only 60° below but the wind is blowing and that puts the chill factor down."

Half sitting and half lying down in the cramped quarters I hoped that Brian would talk, but he was in no mood for anything except bemoaning his fate. The unbelievably heavy snow had tried to bury him and his tent during the night. Of course he had no sleep because he had to keep digging out and trying to keep his gear from disappearing beneath the unrelenting white ocean throughout the long winter night.

Since he was in no mood for talking, and more or less saying that he had rather die than see his trip ended so unsuccessfully, I began to worry. What if neither of us got back to civilization?

I tried to tell him that his failure was no disgrace, that no other man since time began had even attempted to climb Mt. McKinley alone in winter, when daylight hours are short and the temperature ranges from 20° to 148° below zero. Sometimes it takes courage to know when to quit. Maybe the good Lord had sent the soft snow to stop him before it was too late.

I was not doing too well and changed the subject. He was pretty unhappy with what had transpired in Vietnam and greatly disturbed about world conditions in general. Earlier he had said he needed the solitude of the mountain for meditation and writing his memoirs. Now I wondered if he even cared whether he returned. I talked, and he balked, at any subject.

I was beginning to think it might be a rather long solitude for us both unless I could bring about a change in his mood, fast.

"Maybe we had best dig a snow cave," I suggested as the wind gave a stronger tug at our tent. "Don won't be back for some time, and we'll be in pretty bad shape if the tent goes." Any activity helped. Soon we had a nice cave scooped out with the little shovel and again retired to the tent. Hot tea and frozen candy was welcome.

"Did you know there are yetis on this mountain?" I asked. "I don't know whether there are now, but there were at one time." I related the story of the battered French expedition, the first to climb Mt. Huntington. Their leader, Lionel Terray, fell and dislocated a shoulder.

Don left me on the mountain for an interview while he flew Terray to the hospital. Did you ever try to interview seven

363

Frenchmen, none of whom could speak English? It wasn't too difficult. One of the group, Jacques Batkin, who later fell to his death during the group winter climb of 1967, did understand, and spoke few words in English. Sign language worked beautifully. They pointed out where Terray had fallen and indicated that they would resume the climb when he returned. They did, but before they reached the summit, one of them went snow blind and had to be carried most of the way down. Fourteen thousand-foot Huntington had taken a terrible toll, so Sheldon rigged up a yeti party and we were waiting for them when they reached their base camp on the glacier.

Roberta Sheldon dressed in wolf's clothing, Dorothy like a bunny, and Baverly Garrett in a hula skirt over long red underwear. A hula on the mountain seemed hilarious to me and to the Frenchmen, but it hardly provoked a smile from Brian.

As Don flew part of the group out, I told of how those remaining on the glacier cleaned camp. They had built an igloo — the only one I have ever seen since coming to Alaska — and stuffed all their empty boxes and excess debris inside and set it on fire. As it burned one of the Frenchmen jumped on top of it, danced a jig and sang the only word he probably understood in English. "T-A-L-K-E-E-T-N-A! T-A-L-K-E-E-T-N-A! T-A-L-K-E-E-T-N-A!" And oddly enough, this word is not English but the Indian name for our village, meaning "River of Plenty." But we all understood.

Now I understood how that poor guy felt, and wished I was in Talkeetna.

Eternity dragged by in an hour-and-a-half. Not too much daylight left. The wind grew stronger.

Something else bothered me. No matter who you are nor where you are, nature eventually calls. My eyeballs were floating. I drank only one cup of coffee before leaving Talkeetna, but was regretting that. The tea was great, but it, too, added to my misery. I had to go! In hip-deep snow? With the wind blowing? Impossible!

There must be some alternative. No, that wouldn't do; it would freeze down my pant leg. Just a cup full? No. Once I started there would be no cut-off valve. I couldn't relieve the pressure that way. Maybe mountain climbers had some way of going inside the tent. No, not a female. I could never get into position to go inside that tent, not even if Brian sensed my dilemma and excused himself.

I pulled on my face mask and heavy gloves. "Excuse me, I'll be right back," I said as I crawfished toward the door. Evidently Brian understood and made haste to get the tent flap unfastened.

Wallowing toward the rear of the tent I wondered how it would feel to have my own rear buried in snow as I relieved myself but it didn't matter. Getting ready to go was something else. First the coverall zipper, and the whole darn mess had to come down before I could get to the next pair of pants. Now the third. Surely I couldn't have on four layers of clothing. But I did and that last layer hung in my nylon pantyhose. Now what? No damn fool would wear . . .

I couldn't wait. Not one second longer. Yanking the zipper open I squatted in the snow, hardly feeling it. Suddenly I realized my right hand was bare. Shoving it beneath my fur parka, I finished the most imperative business. W-A-T-E-R R-E-L-I-E-F!

Now for my glove. There it was! A big ball of yellow ice, right underneath me.

There was no humor in the situation, not then. I knew my hand would freeze in seconds.

With my left hand I struggled with the zippers. The first was broken. I was terribly clumsy with my left hand, especially so with it in a glove and liner. Only then did I realize that my nylon liner was still on my right hand, but it was so numb I couldn't feel it. I had to make it work, but it wouldn't. Only one thing to do. Forget the underpants and my pride, zip up the coveralls and get inside the tent. I could work with the zippers when my hand thawed out.

Just as I got the outside zipper up and asked Brian if he had an extra glove, I heard — or saw — a speck moving up the glacier. The little yellow bird.

Quickly Brian began pulling the tent pegs. All other gear except the minute stove with the cheerful little flicker and the sleeping bag was packed.

"HURRY!" Don shouted as the prop of his plane created another snowstorm. "Can't you see how low that wind is on the peak? I'll do well to get both of you out. Flag your gear Brian. I'll come back and pick it up later, if the storm doesn't blow it right off the mountain. Crawl in the plane. Mary, back in the boot. I've got to get you both out. Hurry, Mary, hurry!"

I was trying, but my feet and legs didn't cooperate. I couldn't step up. My right hand had no grasp and I couldn't pull myself up. Three pairs of trousers bagged around my . . . shall we say . . . knees?

"HURRY! What's the matter?" Don shouted as he held the door open against the wind.

Suddenly Brian grabbed me around the legs and shoved me into the plane like a stick of stovewood. I managed to wiggle and push myself to a lean-forward position in the tail of the Super Cub. Rarely was the rear seat in place in Don's yellow bird. Took too much space where he could stack gear.

From the mountain to Talkeetna there was no chance to zip back up, not with Brian more or less in my lap as we sat on the floor with our feet stretched on either side of the "plane driver's seat." Don always called himself a plane driver.

A more embarrassed reporter was never landed on the Talkeetna strip and poured from a plane.

That was my first, last and only trip I ever plan to Denali in winter, no matter who tries to climb her.

Chapter 32

Don Sheldon Dies

*A*lthough it was expected, it is hard to realize that Don Sheldon is no longer waging his battle with the wind. I have seen a few brave people in my life, but none as brave as Don, unless it is his wife Roberta. I visited with her after Don all but lost the battle for life in 1972 when he underwent two major operations. At this time it was hard to conceive of a comeback for Don, much less a major victory. I was doing a pretty poor job of trying to express my sympathy and concern. Roberta wanted neither. She never talks much but what she does say bears a great deal of thought.

"God has given me nine beautiful years," she said pensively, "and three wonderful children. Without Don I would never have known any of this. I thank God for every hour and every minute we had together. I am indeed fortunate."

Don had a real soldier by his side. Together they fought for time. In my way of thinking they won the battle . . . two extra years.

In face of death — his own — Don flew thirty-four groups of climbers to McKinley in 1974, more than in any previous season. His comeback was more spectacular than his rescues, so quiet and convincing that those near him could not believe what they feared was true. He worked so endlessly and so patiently that everyone was surprised to hear he was back in the hospital Christmas Day 1974. He died January 25, 1975.

Alaska's Governor Jay Hammond a bush pilot and guide himself, asked the federal government to name a natural feature near Mount McKinley in honor of Sheldon. The resolution met with favor in the Alaska legislature, which was in session.

This is fine. I feel the amphitheater south of the peak should bear Sheldon's name, and a monument placed near his glacier house but I hope this is only the beginning.

I think it would be greater yet if Washington, D.C. sees fit to grant Don Sheldon's request, that "Denali," the Indian name for Mount McKinley, meaning "The Great One," be restored to the nation's tallest peak. This to me seems fitting and proper since President McKinley never came to know Alaska and the peak named in his honor.

I should like to turn my homestead into a memorial site for Sheldon and for Robert (Bob) Reeve, our first glacier pilot. Both Don and his father-in-law are makers of Alaskan history. Bob is still going strong at seventy-three; Sheldon died when he was only fifty-three. I feel that Don must have had visions of the day when his son, Robert Don—who was not yet four years old when his father died—would work in the office as Bob Reeve and son Richard do now, keeping vigil over Alaska's toughest terrain.

Now I think back to that day over twelve years ago when I finally bugged Don Sheldon into landing on a boulder bar in the Chulitna River canyon. For months I had been talking about homesteading and putting in an observatory on a two thousand foot point which we had flown over several times checking the view.

"Homestead?" Don pondered as he studied the ruggedness of the foothills. "You'll do well to climb it, much less homestead and put in an observatory. NOT FOR A WOMAN!"

Seems to me I had heard this phrase before, when I began my harrassment to fly Mount McKinley with him for news stories.

Women can dream. Sometimes these dreams materialize. My homesteading is completed and I do have a lodge with a glassed-in view of Mount McKinley. This year I am doubling its capacity and putting in a conference room where Anchorage press and rock clubs can meet, joining hands with their Fairbanks counterparts at a midway stop.

I am in the process of donating ten acres of land on top of the butte to the University of Alaska, where President Hiatt and journalism head Chuck Keim hope to put in facilities for students where they may study the aesthetics.

From Inspiration Point where I hope to put in that observatory, one can see right into eternity. To the northeast lie Mts. Deborah, Hess and Kerr on the Denali Highway, to the east Mt. Logan in Canada, to the south Cook Inlet and Mt. Susitna, to the northwest the whole Alaska Range stretches with Mts. Foraker, Hunter, and Denali at your fingertips.

It's a dream, a big dream, but I can see it very clearly. I wish to share it with the world from generation to generation.

Robert Service and Jack London must cross this stage hopefully with fairly authentic representation. We want the good as well as some of the none too reputable characters — gold seekers and chorus girls. We want the Eskimo and Indian, the railroader and trucker, the driller and the North Slope.

When we come to such persons as Tillie and Bob Reeve, we'll want scenes reproduced as authentically as the living can direct, right down to the good Alaskan furniture made from wooden crates which once protected 5-gallon cans of aviation fuel.

For Roberta and Don Sheldon there must be an old rinky-dink piano. Although Mrs. Campbell and I often listened as classical music poured from the baby grand in the Sheldon living room, I can still see the gatherings as they were at the Rainbow Lodge and Fairview Inn before a road was punched into this wilderness area. Don would fly across the Susitna for Shorty Bradly, Jess Beech would bring his hand-crafted violin, and Jim Beaver his harmonica. Roberta led with the piano as Don sat with his accordion squeezing it for all it was worth with tongue protruding to the corner of his mouth, vigorously tapping out the rhythm with his foot.

"Let's run that old bear through the blueberry patch once more," Beaver would say as Roberta swung out with the rinky-dink.

The coliseum must be large enough to house everything from Boy Scout jamborees to church, lodge and political meetings. Alaska needs such an edifice, in a central location, and such entertainment.

We need more. Somewhere there must be a workshop housing lapidary equipment, where people can learn to work with stone as a hobby or a profession. There must be beautifully white kitchens with ample refrigeration, for those who wish to work with fern and berries. There must be fields of transplanted fiddlehead fern bordered with fireweed, which I feel should be Alaska's state flower. There must be a gift shop where people can earn as they learn to work with and appreciate that which nature has so bountifully bestowed.

In summer hiking trails and bridle paths, bordered with wild flowers must enhance streams, rivers and lakes. In winter there must be dog-mushing and skiing. Of course there must be a lift to the top of the butte, where Denali in her soft pink ermine will continue to challenge and bring out the best in man throughout the ages.

Alaska must and will become a winter wonderland for sports. This is part of her destiny. Oil must flow from the North Slope and agricultural products from her fields to provide energy and food for a cold and hungry world. Majestic beauty and solitude must radiate from her peaks, providing inspiration and food for thought to a harried world.

This is my dream. That of a woman.

God has given the mountain. Bob Reeve and Don Sheldon have perfected glacier landings enabling the daring to set foot on rivers of time. Man has built a highway bringing Denali into year-round focus for the motorist. Previously a close-up was limited to the summer months for those who had time and money. The sixty-eight mile drive to the scenic viewpoints in Mt. McKinley National Park is limited chiefly to shuttle buses. But now we have a year-round highway with a close-up of our mountain majesty for the poorest comer.

God has given us Denali. This is my prayer:

"Grant, Lord, that I may help preserve, share and perpetuate that which You have so bountifully given and that which such men as Reeve and Sheldon have enhanced and immortalized. Amen."

Chapter 33

A Lodge Filled with Laughter

I n 1971 when my lodge was finally finished, I thought life might be pretty dull. Much to my surprise I found it a different adventure to any I had experienced previously. Helping to make it more exciting were the help, the guests and the oil boom. And please don't let me leave out our twin black bear cubs, Slew Foot and Sargeant Pie, who adopted the lodge.

Oil had been discovered on the North Slope in 1968. The new highway, for which I had declared war, was dedicated in October of 1971 but was not kept open in winter until 1972. My lodge was finished and open for business when Alaska became Boom Town, U.S.A.

With the opening of the Parks Highway came a flood of traffic mostly trucks in winter, big eighteen-wheelers. The new highway was so much better and so much shorter than the old route to Fairbanks that practically all Prudhoe Bay freight was routed my way. Soon the truck drivers became my mainstay especially in winter.

While Mary's McKinley View Lodge was still in its swaddling clothes, my sister Lela Lloyd of Cisco, Texas was spending her first winter in Alaska with me. My sister had never lived where public utilities were non-existent.

There was no electricity in the foothills of Mount McKinley where I homesteaded in 1964. There were no electric lines along-

371

side the new highway in the seventies nor the eighties, and may be none in the nineties. (Ed. note: To this date, there are none.) Since my homestead is now an island in Denali State Park created in 1971, it is unlikely to be electricity there soon because all lines will have to go underground. This is fine with me; never enjoyed electric poles ruining good scenery. But since there is no land available for homes, there is little prospect there will be electricity in the foreseeable future. When I put in my lodge I had to have electricity, and the only way to get it was to install a generator, a great big expensive one. Moreover I was the one who had to baby sit that miraculous monster.

I've never been mechanically minded, but I certainly learned to check and change the oil in that generator. It was our lifeline. Without its running we had no lights, no water, no appliances, no anything electrical that would work. Unfortunately my first winter at the lodge was the coldest. It got down to 40° below zero and hung that way for three days and four nights. On the fourth night the lights in the lodge started dimming soon after Sis and I had retired. The lights grew dimmer and dimmer and the motor seemed to be running only by gasps and spurts.

Quickly I put on my Arctic gear, grabbed the heavy duty flashlight, a butane torch, and made my way through the miserable cold down the precarious trail to the generator house. And I do mean precarious; one step off the packed trail and you were hip-deep in snow.

Once inside I quickly pulled the plug on the electric heater which had kept things from freezing thus far. Now there was hardly a glow. I had to take the load off but that wasn't enough. The motor was still coughing.

"It must be that small copper feed line," I said to myself. *"I'll just run the torch up and down it a few times. If it works I'm back in business."*

It did work for about an hour. Past midnight the lights started dimming again. Why didn't I think to take the kerosene space heater out with me? The line must be freezing again. Reluctantly I crawled from beneath my warm blanket for another seance with the rebellious monster.

It would take a while but once I got the generator house warmed up there should be no more trouble . . . But I couldn't stand out there in -40° waiting to make sure the line didn't freeze again. As soon as the generator got going good again I could use both the electric and the space heater. But once back in the lodge and warm I fell asleep.

That poor little space heater made it almost. But when that generator changed tunes I jumped up from my chair realizing that I had gone to sleep without returning to plug in the electric heater.

Again I was putting on woolens and down, and probably making a few unkind remarks about the iron monster letting me down when my sister walked in saying;

"Please don't go back out there," she begged. "You'll freeze to death. Come crawl under the ELECTRIC blanket with me."

When I explained the facts of life, where everything convenient depends upon a functioning generator, she vowed I could not go back without her help. She could at least hold the light while I worked. This gave me a vague feeling of uneasiness, but she's an older sister who wanted to be helpful and was in an unconventional situation. But in Alaska the unconventional must be dealt with quite often.

We were less than a third of the way down the narrow path when she stepped a little wide and went almost to her hips in snow. Before we could get out of the trap the generator had quit completely. We had just made it back to the door of the lodge when I heard an eighteen-wheeler applying air brakes as they usually did coming around the curve and on the down-grade near the river and my lodge.

"Get inside!" I commanded, "I've got to stop this truck."

Waving the flashlight up and down rather wildly I guess to make sure it was noticed, I skidded across the plowed drive toward the oncoming truck. Soon not one but three big Sea-Land trucks came to the rescue. Pulling out their space heaters, they soon had the generator perking again, and said it was safe for me to put on the coffee pot.

"Your trouble," said Jack Steele, who checked the thousand-gallon tank, "is that your fuel has jelled. We left our heaters near your flowline but that will clog up again. Is there anyone you can get to help at this time of night?"

"There is a homesteader Ben Bendix, who lives between here and Trapper Creek who I might be able to get."

"Then I suggest you try because fires should be kept at each end of the tank until it thaws. If he can't come I'll call you back on the C.B."

Ben did come and he did keep a fire at each end of the tank until it was fluid. I must admit the fires scared both me and my sis, even though we both knew diesel oil is not as volatile as gasoline.

With the coming of summer customers mushroomed and I needed more help than I could draw from Trapper Creek community eighteen miles to the south, and from the village of Talkeetna, forty-nine miles further down the road. I was too far from Anchorage to try to explain the joys of wilderness living to a prospective employee who might pale at the thought of no telephone, no bus and no entertainment. About the best I could do was put a "HELP WANTED" sign in the window.

It was one of those busy times when I first began catching tour buses, that I noticed a couple of young ladies sitting on the patio. After the crowd cleared a little one of them walked into the cafe and said, "I see your 'HELP WANTED' sign in the window. When you are not too busy would you talk with me and my friend? We will wait on the patio. The scenery is absolutely out of this world."

When I finally got to them I was greeted with, "This is my friend, Julie Bowles, and I am Mary Malpass. We're run-away mothers who want to earn our vacation here in Alaska."

"What do you do? I need a back-up for the cook and another waitress."

"Actually we're teachers," Mary explained, "but I have cooked a little on a shrimp boat and Julie can wait tables. We're rapid learners."

A few days after they started to work Mary Malpass asked if I would mind if they got a little exercise.

"Maybe you would like to climb the 2,000-foot butte across the highway if you're not afraid of bears," I suggested.

"A hike is not exactly what we would like to do," Mary confessed. "You see Julie and I are belly dancers. I told you the truth, we do teach. Julie teaches kindergarten and I teach belly

374

dancing. If we could just get a little exercise in the bar before it opens or after it closes, then we could use the records we brought along."

They were good, really good. Mary was a much better belly dancer than cook. Soon the help and the curious were peeping through the windows.

It was my custom to give a party every year for the old timers of Talkeetna. The following week would be Rocky Cummins' 86th birthday, and I asked the girls if they would dance for the party.

The house was packed. As requested Julie and Mary danced closer and closer to Rocky dropping a few veils.

Rocky was entranced. Suddenly his shoulders started shaking as he laughed whole bodily. Finally gaining control he commented, "Oh me lasses! If I were only eighty-five again."

ORAL ROBERTS IN THE BAR?

It was not long after my first lodge expansion when a couple of 'city dressed' fellows walked in, ate and then stood out on the patio for some time admiring the Alaska Range and my blaze of tuberous red begonias.

Then they walked back into the restaurant and one of them remarked, "I've never seen a mountain so beautiful as McKinley. The view from here is breathtaking. But we haven't seen it from the national park yet. We're on our way there now, scouts for the evangelist Oral Roberts. We're going to do an 'Oral Roberts in Alaska' show."

"Really? That's great! But to tell the truth I think the view is better from the south side. That's why I homesteaded here. But in 1917 when they established Mount McKinley National Park (now Denali National Park), they did mighty well to reach interior Alaska at all. At first there was less than ten miles of dirt road inside the park and horse drawn carriages. Then when the Alaska Railroad was finished in 1923, people came by rail and a few more miles of graveled roadway were added. There's not much roadway yet, less than a hundred miles for an area larger than three of our middle sized states put together, but you will always remember the spectacular view. Nothing like it absolutely nothing. What a glorious setting for such a show."

Five days later the men returned.

"Did you pick your spot for the 'Oral Roberts in Alaska' show," I babbled.

"Is it always this beautiful here?" one of them asked as he gazed at the nation's tallest mountain through the picture window.

"Not always not by any means," I answered truthfully, "but it's out a lot more from this south view than it is from the national park."

The men sort of looked at each other again and the spokesman added, "We were wondering on the way back, wondering if the show could possibly be done from your viewpoint, that is if Oral Roberts agrees. How many people can you accommodate?"

"With only ten rooms to let," I stammered. "Not many. How many will there be of you?"

"There are fifty-six in the chorus, but if you could accommodate the Oral Roberts family, that's his wife, their son and his wife and baby, and the cameramen and staff. If you could take care of them as we were talking on the way back, then the chorus could be bussed out of Anchorage."

Tentative agreements were made. The only way I could feed them all would be with a buffet luncheon. In this manner I could still take care of my other customers. Weeks and weeks went into the planning. It was an exceedingly busy and most exciting time at the lodge.

The "Oral Roberts in Alaska" T.V. show was being filmed at my homestead and on Mount McKinley.

The Oral Roberts' family and the staff were our guests. The others were being bussed 135 miles from Anchorage for the filming. We were literally bursting at the seams. There were "Oral Roberts" signs everywhere.

Outside a helicopter kept shuttling back and forth to the mountain as part of the filming was being done from a glacier. People were everywhere. None of my guest rooms were large enough to accommodate the make-up artist while getting ready for the show. Only the bar was large enough. It seemed a sort of sacrilege to have it opened anyway so I closed it down. I suggested it be used as a make-up room.

My parking area was large and all morning a chopper shuttled back and forth, landing in a roped off area. Lowell Thomas, Sr., of Tibetan fame was working with Rev. Roberts on the glacier. Back and forth and back and forth the chopper flew.

Finally I managed to get my buffet out and was trying to protect it from the dust as people continually left the doors open. Another tour bus pulled up as the chopper took off again kicking up dust. To protect my lavish buffet I appointed a doorman to keep the doors closed during landings and take-offs.

Just before lunch another tour bus pulled in and people kept pouring in.

"Oral Roberts!" one of the female passengers beamed. "You mean Oral Roberts is here in Alaska? I've got to see him! I've watched him all these years and helped support his T.V. services. I simply have to have his autograph."

"Not now," I blurted, trying to push my way through the mob to close the door. "He's in the bar."

"In the bar? Oral Roberts in the bar?" she screeched in astonishment. "I don't believe you!"

All eyes seemed trained on me. I was speechless.

Fortunately Oral Roberts opened the bar door himself, just as I was confronted. Make-up kits not glasses were much in evidence.

The woman waved her notebook wildly begging for an autograph.

"Come in," he invited as he pushed a make-up kit aside to make room for autographing.

Then he turned to me and asked if I was ready to go with them to the field where the filming was being done. I was to be interviewed in front of my little homesteading cabin with McKinley in the background naturally.

My greatest hope was that the make-up artist who had done my face did a good cover-up, one good enough to conceal a very red flush.

By 1976 we were so busy at the lodge that I was delighted when my niece Mary Jane Little, and her husband Bobby both

377

Texas teachers agreed to a working vacation at McKinley View Lodge, if I didn't mind having their five-year-old daughter LaDawn on the premises. Because of the bar she was told where she could not go first, then informed that so long as she behaved properly she could sit at a certain table in the dining room where the help ate when we were not running a full house.

Although she was only five LaDawn could read children's books quite well and did a commendable job of entertaining herself. Her mother told her she believed it would be better to sit on the patio than crawl underneath the table to read.

Then as summer was in full swing and the buses started hitting two and sometimes three at a time, LaDawn was pretty much on her own. As I lectured to various groups about Alaska I noticed LaDawn standing on a chair on the patio talking with first one cluster of people and then another.

When we finally had time to catch our breath she came back in with her pockets jingling.

"Where on earth did you get that money?" her father asked. "Did you earn it?"

"People gave it to me for lecturing," she answered.

"Lecturing! What did you tell them?"

"Just the same as Aunt Mary," she answered coyly. "All about Alaska."

A few days later after another hard run, we were trying desperately to close the dining room when another bus pulled up right at 10:00 P.M. LaDawn came running into the kitchen announcing, "Oh! My God, . . . more cussomers."

"To bed!" her father ordered. "You've been listening to the dishwashers."

"I know I should blister her," her mother commented, "but I feel just the same way myself."

Then there was the summer when my daughter, Jean Richardson and my granddaughters Carol and Linda came to vacation with me and mostly worked.

Carol was too young to work as a regular employee, but she was always ready to take cash when we got swamped. The unsuspecting customers were cooperative perhaps thinking they were dealing with a child. Maybe so but in size only. When only twelve years old Carol represented the City of Houston in scholastic competition in math. She was still in junior high when she came to visit in Alaska. When Carol was behind the register she had to use a stool to stand on to reach the keys. But she was better and faster on the "bandit" than I was, and she made fewer mistakes than the rest of us.

At times when we were really pushed, I was delighted when Carol snaked her way through the crowd to the register. This was after my first book, *Alaska, Not For a Woman*, was off the press and several persons were waiting for autographs. The driver of another bus who came in as the first group was leaving had told his passengers that I would lecture.

"Go, Grandma Mary," Carol beamed. "I'll take over here."

The waitresses were too busy and too polite to walk in front of me as I lectured, so we often put the pie and coffee customers on 'scout's honor.'

A fine looking gentleman, who seemingly enjoyed talking loudly enough for everyone to hear, beamed down at Carol and asked, "Honey, how much money do you want?"

Ann Rendall, author's sister, in charge of kitchen, declared that the back kitchen door was to remain locked after Sgt. Pie reached around her, swiping a freshly baked pie from the cooling rack.

Cub bear up a tree as sketched by Alaska's foremost wildlife artist, Doug Lindstrand, who illustrated four of the books your author has written.

379

"Mister," Carol beamed back in her loudest voice and broadest smile, "how much you got?"

THE SAGA OF SLEW FOOT AND SARGEANT PIE

What to do with the garbage when I opened the lodge was a very good question. Not only was there no delivery service available so far out in the bush, there was no garbage pick-up either. About two hundred yards downhill from the lodge was a pot hole that I would like to have filled in. A natural garbage pit, a place where it could be dumped and covered by a D-8 Caterpillar before freeze up. This worked for a while then bears appeared.

This was not too bad for the first two years because they were so far from the lodge that they were rarely noticed. On the third year the sow let a cub come with her to feed, but it was difficult to get near enough for a photo even with a zoom lens. But on the fourth year things changed. The sow appeared with the cutest twin cubs you can imagine.

Evidently the sow herself had become less afraid, or had little fear for the cubs because she didn't always take them with her when she left the dump. The cubs ventured closer. Then when they found a huge tire from an 18-wheeler about halfway down the hill, they took possession, jumping up and down. Soon they were shadow boxing. This delighted the tourists who could see this far down the hill, and very often they would sneak down for photos. I was afraid the sow would appear, but she never did. Then I began wondering if their mother was still alive because we never seemed to see her anymore. The cubs were a great tourist attraction.

The following spring when they came out of hibernation, my how they had grown! My sister, Ann Rendall, of Cisco, Texas, had come to manage the kitchen for me during the summer. Her first encounter with one of our yearlings wasn't the greatest.

The outside door to the pie room, as we called the addition to the kitchen where I made pies, was standing open. Ann rushed in to take a pie from the cooling rack to serve. Just as she reached for the pie a large, black, hairy arm reached around her and one of the pies disappeared as she screamed bloody murder.

"I've told the dishwashers not to feed pie to those cubs," I said loudly enough to be sure all the kitchen help heard.

Then the cook added her ultimatum. "As long as I am in charge of this kitchen there will be no feeding of bears. Furthermore, the back doors are to be kept locked."

All went well until the day there came a knock at the kitchen door. It was a hitch-hiker asking for a handout. Good kind-hearted Annie, she could never refuse anyone. Quickly she wrapped up some sandwiches and was reaching on the pantry shelf for pie when . . .

"WHOOOF!"

"Bear!" screamed the hitch-hiker as he fled down the highway. We never saw that hitch-hiker again that summer, nor the bear either. I often wondered what happened to the cub. He like his mother had just disappeared.

Ann went back to Texas in the fall to return with the seagulls the following spring. Those seagulls were something else. I didn't even know they were migratory until one with a broken leg returned every summer for seven years with her new brood. The gulls loved pie too and announced their arrival with loud squawking as they circled the lodge several times. Finally they zoomed in on their favorite feeding spot, where I tossed grain and food scraps near the lodge in order for the tourists to enjoy them.

Once when I had to be away for a couple of days, we ran out of rhubarb pie. One of the cooks decided to surprise me with having the pies made when I returned. We had lots of rhubarb on hand but no rhubarb pie.

I rarely wrote out a pie recipe because I was the sole pie-maker at the lodge. But that day the cook decided to surprise me. He knew I put cornstarch in most of my pies, but he didn't know how much. He literally cemented those rhubarb pies with cornstarch.

When I returned everyone was still having a ball watching the seagulls trying to fly off with unbreakable hunks of 'lead pie.'

As usual both cubs and seagulls made their debut as the

381

snow gave way to the first fiddlehead fern of the season. How those cubs had grown! Right away we noticed that one cub was limping badly. Evidently he had been caught in a trap . . . and thus derived his name, "Slew Foot."

Ann was back and all went well for a while. Then suddenly one day, while the dining room was filled, an off-duty waitress who was sunbathing on the upstairs patio came screaming down the fire escape. Of course everyone in the dining room expected to see a man chasing the bikini-clad beauty.

"It's a bear!" she yelled. "He was in my room looking out the window at me."

Armed with broom and mop, upstairs went the kitchen help to oust the intruder. We had little trouble intimidating the invader, who we knew was Slew Foot from his decided limp.

By this time everyone except the cashier I hoped was upstairs. Employees were checking rooms. Evidently Slew Foot had investigated everywhere he found an open door.

"Help!" screamed a waitress. "He's been in my room and left his calling card."

"Murder!" the housekeeper cried in vexation. "If Slew Foot is going to live here, I do wish someone would show him the bathroom."

The following summer the cubs were almost grown, and I think they must have spread the word that the chow was pretty good at Mile 135.

A bus load of Japanese were in the dining room. I thought I saw Sargeant Pie ambling toward his favorite haunt, but I was too busy to go scare him away from the back door, which we always kept closed because of prior incidents. Not noticing him return to the dump, I thought I would shake a broom at him when the house cleared.

A sudden scream and flying dishes electrified the place. The bear, not finding pie elsewhere, sneaked around the corner, probably unnoticed, reared his full height outside the window where two Japanese women were eating. Tea and pie flew.

"It's O.K. It's all right," I tried to assure everyone as the help rushed in for the clean-up and to bring more pie. "I'll just go out and wave my arms at him and he'll go away."

But somehow I didn't trust my own statement too much.

382

That bear didn't look too much like Sargeant Pie. I was hoping someone would come to the rescue before I was mauled too badly, if the intruder resisted eviction. I screamed my very loudest and waved my arms threateningly. For a second that lasted an hour, the bear just looked at me undecidedly then turned with a disgusted grunt and walked away.

"That does it!" I declared later. "I'm driving into Talkeetna this very day and call Fish and Game. They've got to tranquilize those bears and get them out of here. Furthermore there will be no more dumping in the pot hole. I can get a man with a trailer to haul out garbage regularly. In fact he said he would start Monday when I talked to him last week. But we've got to get the bears out of here before someone gets hurt."

But before Fish and Game arrived we had another incident. My sixteen-year-old granddaughter, Linda Richardson, was again visiting and working as a waitress on the evening shift. After the dining room was closed she filled the salt and pepper shakers, cleaned the place mats and set up the tables.

As Linda worked Linda danced. Around and around the tables she flew with dark swirls of curls floating around her shoulders.

Earlier in the day Linda had confided, "Grandma I'm afraid of bears and I don't want to go outside that door after dark."

"Of course," I answered, "and why should you want to go out that door after dark?"

"The night cook sometimes sends me out to the outside store room after something."

"Don't do it, honey," I answered.

At this time of summer darkness doesn't come until between ten and eleven after the front door has been locked and the late shift is busy with cleaning and mopping. Usually I stayed downstairs until everything sparkled, but I was hot and wanted to get upstairs, get off my girdle and crawl under the shower, so I just took the day's receipts up with me to check after getting comfortable. I had just gotten into my pajamas when I thought I heard a woman scream for help.

Thinking of what Linda had said about bears, I bolted downstairs yelling, "Stop the music!"

383

Startled poor Linda rushed to turn off the hi-fi and looked at me like, "Poor Grandma, she's finally flipped."

"Did you hear someone scream for help?" I asked.

Before she could answer there were more screams and a loud pounding on the back door.

"Help! Let me in! There's a bear out here!"

Both the cook and the dishwasher rushed to unlock the back door.

"Didn't you hear me screaming?" the cook's wife shouted. "The bear was looking through the glass window in the cabin door. He was pushing on one side and I was holding on the other. I screamed and screamed until he finally went away."

"Get your gun, Paul," I ordered. "This is too much." The rest of us grabbed brooms and mops and cautiously followed him outside in the gathering gloom. Finally we spotted the bear. It was up a tree. It was afraid to come down.

"Why, Honey," the cook teased his wife, "aren't you ashamed of yourself? You've scared that poor little cub half to death. He may never come down."

Without another word Lenora Preston, the cook's wife who took cash on a day shift, went back into their cabin. In so far as I know Lenora didn't speak to Paul for the next two weeks. It was a good thing Lenora worked behind the cash register and Paul managed the kitchen, otherwise we would all have needed to learn sign language.

Needless to say I again drove into Talkeetna, and was very explicit in telling Fish and Game that I wanted them "NOW." Not only were our tame bears still around, they seemed to have brought their cousins and a new generation to the picnic.

I lived at my homestead from 1965 until 1981 when I sold the lodge, and never had any real trouble with bear encounters. In so far as black bears are concerned, I believe that it is the ever-increasing public encroachment upon their territory and leaving food within the range of their keen noses that brings about misunderstanding.

I felt as if it were I who was the culprit as Fish and Game tranquilized the bears and moved them to a deeper wilderness location. Certainly I wish them well in their return to nature as it should be.

384

Chapter 34

Cat Train

*Y*ou'll not find the meaning of 'Cat Train' in the dictionary. It's coined, perhaps in Alaska where colorful words and expressions are born of necessity, describing a new world of oil exploration in the Arctic.

A cat train is a long assembly of housing units, supplies and heavy equipment, mounted on skis and drawn overland by Caterpillars, not the fuzzy kind, but the iron monsters called D-8's and D-9's.

Cat trains are found only in the Arctic. Few people have ever seen one, and fewer yet have ridden on this non-passenger type locomotion. Usually the personnel is composed of Wagon Master, drivers and crew as it crawls across white space to a designated drilling site. Upon arrival it is broken down into city-long blocks soon to be occupied by the full construction crew.

While en route a few of the housing units as well as the office, diner, and bath facilities, are kept warm by generators, which are an integral part of such mobile camps for heat, water and electricity. The train is a 'cook and sleep as you go' facility. Upon arrival at the drilling site it is broken into the block-long units connected by utility lines. This camp housed 426 men and eleven women.

To join this train my photographer Jean Petersen and I left Anchorage on a jet-liner for Lonely, a communications and sup-

*There's precious little time for photo taking during the long Arctic night, es-
pecially at a distance. This is a block of housing units pulled in by the Cat
Train. Wind-blown woman in foreground is photographer Jean Peterson.*

ply base near Barrow, the north-most city in the world. From
Lonely we took a smaller plane loaded with construction workers. We were to join "C" Train near its destination Lisburne, the
name given to a drilling site so remote that it required its own
medic. Later we would visit "Fox" Train, where gas wells were
being drilled and a six-inch pipe line was being laid to supplement the natural gas flowing to Barrow, the largest native village
in Alaska.

Jean and I were the only females on the plane. We were
guests. As reporter and photographer we wished to share this
experience with the world. We waited several months for clear-
ance through Arctic Slope/Alaska General and Husky Oil. Arctic
Slope/Alaska General was doing the groundwork, Husky would
do the drilling. This was part of a five-year exploration program
on the twenty-three-million-acre National Petroleum Reserve,
commonly known as "Pet 4." The entire program is being carried out under the auspices of the U.S. Department of the Interior. Jean and I are freelancers on our own as photographer and
writer.

386

As explained to Roy Cheney, president and general manager of Arctic Slope/Alaska General Construction, the work on the site was behind schedule because the winter was warmer than usual and the ice on nearby Betty Lake was not thick enough to accommodate heavy planes, the vanguard of such operations.

To remedy this situation lighter planes were flown in and holes were drilled through the ice to pump water from underneath the ice for a build-up of ice on top of the lake ice. For a landing strip a 48-52 inch thickness of ice is needed.

We were met by Cat Train Master Bob Alexander, without whose help and guidance we would not have known what was going on half the time. And believe me it took a lot of his time and patience for such explanations. Sometimes a different kind of smile, a funny little quirk at the corner of his mouth seemed to appear involuntarily when we asked stupid, female-type questions.

We were told there would be running water in the bath houses, but not in the commodes. Of these we must be very careful. The waste is consumed by a chemical fire. One of the girls would explain such operations to us. Of necessity men and women used the same bath house, but the commodes were enclosed and the showers were curtained stalls.

The twin beds in our room were clean and comfortable. There were two small closets, a small night stand with a mirror above, a table, two straight backed chairs, two empty three-pound coffee cans and a crowbar over by the door. Since we found no coffee and no pot, we thought the last three items must have been left in the room by mistake, but we learned when the nearest bathroom is almost a block away down a long string of housing units, and it's 60° below—you learn.

Our room, a portion of one of the mobile units on skis, was warm except for when the door had to be opened. On the first night we learned why the pry-bar was left near the door. It froze closed on the outside while we slept warmly on the inside. There was no way to call the office, and no passer-by heard our knocking. All sounds were muffed by the pulsating of the nearby generator our lifeline. When our joint efforts of pushing the door with our buttocks failed we almost panicked. Then came the dawning . . . the crow-bar. It worked!

Cat Train housing is far from luxurious, but the food is super, geared for energy as well as a morale builder. The pleasant diners, two of them were open around the clock with steaming coffee, milk, fruit juices, fresh fruit, and all sorts of baked goodies always available. And the meals they served! Several kinds of appetizing salads, two or three kinds of meat, vegetables, hot bread, and a variety of desserts. On Sunday New York steak with lobster with all the trimmings, all you could eat of either or both.

Where men work 7-10's (ten hours per day seven days a week), nutrition is a major factor. Neither man nor machine works efficiently when it dips past 40° below. That's when men are called inside, but the machinery must be kept running twenty-four hours per day, every day or it freezes up and fails to start.

We were told that working ten hours a day seven days a week serves and saves in many ways. The job can be handled by a smaller work force requiring less housing. There are fewer idle hours, where no recreational facilities are available as in larger and more permanent camps. Longer hours and overtime days mean greater financial remuneration for less time on the calendar resulting in longer stays at home. Air transportation is provided free of charge to the larger cities in Alaska and most Arctic construction workers get to spend almost as much time off the job as on it.

All sorts of unfamiliar vehicles and construction work was in progress seemingly in all quadrants. Ice roads were being laid for immediate use. A herc (Hercules Cargo Plane) strip was under construction for year-round use, a rock-crushing plant was in operation for gravelling needed summer roads, and a drilling pad (platform) where a rig (derrick) would be erected.

Alongside the air strip under construction were stacks of styrofoam so big that from a distance we first thought they were buildings. Later we found styrofoam was to be laid on top of a gravel base to prevent frost action from breaking the paved airfield.

At a distance there was blasting. This we were told was where the drilling platform was to be built, the second location. The first one had to be changed because artifacts were found. Conservation and preservation are ever governing factors.

The vehicles used in this Arctic world of construction were

388

strangers for the most part. Our limousine was a "Snow Crawl-er," with tracks controlled by more 'elbows' than a centipede has legs, which needed no road. The huge Magnum Four is a truck but one like we had never seen before. It is built specifically for the Arctic, has 28-ply tires, carries a seventy-ton load and is cap-able of reaching speeds up to twenty-three miles-per-hour, no doubt after shifting all eight speeds forward. The Delta-3 is a water tanker but one like few people have ever seen. Less than one hundred of them were built.

Imagine our surprise when we saw a charming young woman driving this monster, which inhales and exhales 5,000 gallons of water several times daily, thus laying down ice roads. The driver was Kate Cotten, the only woman in the world driv-ing such a rig. Jean and I rode out fourteen miles with her to Py-ramid Lake, so called by the shape of a nearby mountain, to a pumping unit for a load of water. Along the way Kate pointed out the apple orchard, orange grove and banana thicket, where fellow workers had tied fruit to the few stark bushes that dotted the area. We also stopped to feed an Arctic fox. It was not tame but it did know where its next meal was coming from. It re-mained at a safe distance, not approaching the food until after we left.

All the while we were in touch with the main dispatcher at camp. All the vehicles we saw were equipped with C.B.'s (Citizen Band two-way radio units). The Delta-3 was really geared for survival. Inside the cab there was unbelievable luxury and warmth. There was a small refrigeration unit for food storage, supplementary heat, music, magazines and a full-sized bed, just in case an Arctic storm zoomed in with zero visibility (where you can't see your hand in front of your face) and hurricane force winds, burying the vehicle in snow. Traveling in the Delta-3 made us realize how far man has come in his never-ending quest for oil and his non-relenting battle for survival in the Arctic.

We visited only two of several such trains that Arctic Slope/Alaska General had in operation, but it doesn't take a long time to gain a healthy respect for the companies and the men and women involved in this type of exploration.

Chapter 35

The Longest Night

Not all adventures are planned. Sometimes they stem from misadventure. Perhaps the longest night of my life was spent with the mother of children, lost children, when the temperature was well below zero. This happened shortly after I sold my lodge, on the never ending night of January 7, 1982. I was at home alone on the Talkeetna Spur road, when I received a call from a former employee at the lodge, Verjean Davidson, known as "Little Bit." Although it had been dark for some time, the evening news was just over and I had returned to my typewriter when the telephone rang.

"Mary, this is Little Bit. Are Marsha and Steve at your house? They left home about noon and planned to ski across the Susitna River to Talkeetna to see friends. They had a picnic lunch along."

"No I haven't seen them. Is there something wrong?"

"They were supposed to be back before dark," she said with a great deal of uneasiness in her tone.

"Maybe they've just stopped off to visit with friends. You know how kids are."

"But we've checked every place they might have stopped in Trapper Creek. I was just hoping that because it got dark so soon they might have stopped by your house and asked you to drive them back because it was so late."

390

"Would you like for me to check on this side of the river? I'll call everyplace I can think of, maybe they stopped to eat."

Time passed. No one, absolutely no one had seen them. Little Bit's son John and a friend had taken lights and skied across the river; they found no trace of them.

State troopers were alerted. Friends and neighbors were combing the neighborhood. Prayer groups gathered on both sides of the river as the thermometer dipped to twenty below zero.

Again I talked with Little Bit. They had sent to Anchorage for a bloodhound. She was having difficulty keeping her fourteen-year-old son, John, Jr., from dashing into the wilderness to find his sister. "I don't know if I can hold him back much longer."

"I'm on my way," I answered. "I will pick you and John up at the Big Su Cafe where you are calling from. If they are lost it seems the only sure way for the children would be to head downstream to the bridge." I did not say that it was doubtful that anyone could live through a night like this without shelter. I did say, "My T-Bird has a good heater and a C.B. I plugged it in when you first called. It should give no trouble starting."

It was midnight when the bloodhound and handler arrived from Anchorage. The wind gusts were so high that rescue planes and choppers did not get off the ground. No one wanted to say that the chill factor was probably down to forty below. They called all local help off for fear they would mess it up for the dog. Some of the searchers had been walking in knee-deep snow for over six hours. The Cache Creek Lodge served free food all night for those joining the search. Carol Seik, a '59'er made coffee and drove around all night. Those who could not join in the search put candles in windows and turned on every light possible. All prayed.

Throughout the long night we drove up and down and up and down. Listening for fragments of news, hanging to the faintest thread of hope. Little Bit was the bravest and calmest mother I have ever seen under such stress.

But this is Marsha Moore's story. This is how she told it from her hospital bed:

"Hello. I'm Marsha Moore, a 16-year-old junior in the Susitna Valley High School near Talkeetna, Alaska. This story

391

comes from my heart, not from my pen, because I am in Providence Hospital in Anchorage and have no feeling in my hands.

The first thing I want to do is thank some very special people who risked their lives out hunting all night for a couple of foolish kids, lost with the chill factor about forty degrees below zero. If it wasn't for them I wouldn't be here telling this story because my younger brother Steve and I would probably be dead. But on the night of January 7, 1982, I didn't want to live to tell this story. I just wanted to die.

Maybe Alaskans are a little different especially teen-agers. Who else would want to go skiing and on a picnic when the schools were closed down because of the cold and extremely high winds. Maybe I had best start my story at the beginning.

Early Thursday morning we were listening to the news reports and waiting for announcements, like we always do when it's really nasty outside. The newscaster was giving it to us full blast: power lines down, winds gusting up to seventy-three miles per hour slapped together high voltage lines at a Palmer substation, cutting power to 800 homes and businesses in the Matanuska Valley . . . In the rural areas of Willow and Talkeetna, minus forty-four degrees was reported. Roads were blocked by blowing snow . . . no school today in Palmer, Wasilla and the Talkeetna area.

That was the announcement we were almost sure we would hear. There were four of us kids at home. For a while we were happy enjoying our Christmas games, but even those you play on the T.V. screen get a little boring after so long a time.

By mid-morning the wind was dying down a bit and the temperature warming up. My fourteen-year-old brother, John, Jr., had gone out and he and his friend, fifteen-year-old Harlow Robinson, were playing football in the snow. My twelve-year-old step-brother, Steve Howington Moore, and my eleven-year-old sister, Donna Jean, were at home with our mother, Lynn Howington Moore. My father, John Moore, Sr., was gone. He had flown to the village of Stebbins to install a big, round dish-like thing which he sells. It brings television into some of the more remote areas of Alaska besides bringing it in better at home.

We live in a real neat log house in Trapper Creek, a

wilderness area near the base of Mount McKinley. When the snow is deep the only way we get around on foot is with snow-shoes or skis.

By noon the temperature had warmed up to about zero and the wind wasn't bad. That's when I more or less announced to my new mother that I was going to ski across the river to Talkeetna, and that Steve wanted to go with me. I'll be seventeen in May, and I guess I'm terribly independent. I grew up that way. My mother and father have been divorced since I was eleven. I never went much for minding babysitters; they're gross.

I don't know why but my new step-brother and I became very close. He isn't quite big enough to be accepted by the older boys, so he is in my room most of the time and we read and play lots of games together. I do have an eighteen-year-old sister, Tina Louise Moore, but she stayed in Kenai to finish her senior year in high school there when we moved to Trapper Creek. Can't say I blame her. She's an honor student, a star in basketball, and wants to earn a scholarship to college. After all my new mother and my father had been married only four days when this happened. Thank God my father and Tina didn't know, not during the longest night of my life.

Like I was saying, Steve and I were bored so I just decided we would go for a picnic and ski. I started throwing sandwiches and fruit and other goodies into the neat little backpack my real mother Verjean Davidson had given me for Christmas. I made sure I had a new pack of cigarettes (I'm ashamed to confess) and three lighters, just to make sure I would have one that would work in the cold. Then I threw in a flashlight like we always do in Alaska. I don't know why there's really no place to spend it out here, but I threw in my billfold with the $100 bill my father had given me for Christmas.

I could tell my new mother didn't like the idea of Steve going along, but he is all boy, energy and appetite. He was hollerin' to go about ninty miles per hour. Where I go he wants to go. Like the native children, we get used to the cold and play outside a lot. Really zero feels pretty warm to us in winter, especially after a storm.

So Steve and I started out right after lunch. It's almost three miles from our house to the river crossing, so we stopped by the Bailey house to warm up and visit our classmates, Pam and Tommy. Soon Tommy, who was playing outside with a friend, came into the house and announced, "Your car just went by and your little sister, Donna was driving it."

We laughed. "Impossible," I said. "Donna Jean is too young to drive. That was my new step-mother, Lynn, driving. She's probably taking Donna and Junior over to visit with our mother and grandmother. They only live a mile down the river road. Lynn's good to us," I added with a little twang of conscience, remembering how I had marched out of the house without permission.

How wrong could I be? I found out later that when my brother John Moore, Jr. returned to the house with his friend Harlow Robinson and found out Steve and I were skiing across the river, he began begging our stepmother to let him follow us. Since Lynn was probably concerned about Steve and me, she said Junior and Harlow could follow us provided Harlow could get permission from his parents. Harlow's father Pete is a mountain climber and a park ranger. His mother Nancy was a teacher when they lived in Talkeetna. Harlow knows the area real well since he has lived on both sides of the river; besides he's fifteen.

Since it was nearly 1:30, and it starts getting dark around 3:30 at this time of year, my stepmother drove them to the river crossing, telling them to look for us all the way over and back.

Unfortunately we were still in the Bailey house and didn't notice Lynn driving back without the boys. Pam was telling me, thank goodness, that a scarf wasn't enough that I should have a hat on my head, so she loaned me her new wool cap warning me not to lose it. Besides that I had on long johns, a T-shirt, a sweat shirt, a heavy wool sweater, and my favorite Normandy Rose jeans. We both had on two pairs of socks. Steve's were wool and I had on one pair of thin socks and a pair of wool ones over them. We both wore ankle-high ski shoes.

It was a little colder when Steve and I got to the river, but I thought we could still make it over and back before dark. The wind was beginning to pick up just a little, but it was to our back, so we started out on the trail full speed ahead.

We couldn't see Talkeetna because of the islands with trees. There are lots of islands, sand bars and stump piles. This is where three rivers come together, the Chulitna, Susitna, and Talkeetna. We followed the trail around one tangled island then another and another. We came to a place where

394

the trail split and talked it over. Steve had just pointed out the Talkeetna railroad bridge a few minutes earlier, which was to our left. It's a big black bridge with lots of ironwork overhead. Since it was to our left and Talkeetna is a little to the right of it, we took the trail angling to the right when we should have taken the one angling to the left.

It was getting colder and the wind was blowing harder, but we were sure to see the lights from Talkeetna soon. We hurried. We talked about turning back but didn't. After all we could call our mother from Talkeetna if necessary, and she would come and pick us up. It's thirty-one miles from our house to Talkeetna by road, but only six or seven when the ice is strong enough to cross the river on the ATV (all-terrain vehicle) trail. That's what we were following when we got lost, a three-wheel ATV track to the right.

"I thought you said it was just a little ways," Steve grumbled. "I'm cold and I don't want to freeze to death. How come we can't see the lights from Talkeetna? How come Marsha how come? We must be lost."

I didn't answer so we kept going. The wind kept getting stronger. It was whipping the snow and stinging our eyes. The snow kept curling around over the ice and the trail was hard to see.

"I'm turning back," Steve said, but the wind caught him full blast in the face. He fell down on the glare ice and was having a hard time getting up. He turned back toward me and started sobbing. "It's getting dark and the moon's not up yet. Mom's really going to be mad at us. We're lost!"

"Be quiet so I can think!" I yelled as we huddled behind a stump pile. If I had been thinking about setting the logs on fire then, rather than wanting a cigarette we would have been rescued much sooner, but at that time I didn't think we were lost. It would be embarrassing to have a search party looking for us. What would my friends think? My hands were already numb through my mittens, but Steve knew what I wanted and fished through the backpack until he found my cigarettes and lighter without my having to take the pack off. After several tries, and his helping me we got one lit. Steve ate part of a sandwich while I smoked.

Of course we didn't know what was happening back home, but we were told that when Junior and Harlow got back and reported that they didn't see us anywhere, the whole area was alerted as well as the state troopers. Trooper DeHart was almost fifty miles down the highway near Willow and off duty, but he was driving in to meet Trooper Corporal Wadman at Mile 115. A search should be organized.

All I knew at the time was that I was very cold and that we should be seeing the lights of Talkeetna by now. We hurried but in the wrong direction. It was getting late, I don't know how late but the moon was up and the wind was blowing harder. It was cold, real cold, and Steve kept complaining about being lost.

"You're right I agree, we're bound to be way down past Talkeetna by now. We took the wrong trail but we can't turn around; the wind's too strong. Let's keep going downstream to the Susitna River Bridge," I suggested. "It's just ten miles from Talkeetna to the bridge and we've come a long way."

We talked about getting to the bridge, going to the Big Su, an all-night cafe at the end of the bridge, warming up and eating a big hot meal while we waited for Lynn to come pick us up. Mom would be mad for sure, but she was probably getting pretty worried about us by now. The only way we could keep from being really lost was to head for the bridge. There would be lights at the cafe and we would be able to see headlights. Eighteen-wheelers cross the bridge all night heading from Anchorage to Fairbanks.

We tried to hurry, but the wind was so strong it blew us down and took our breath away even with our backs turned. Sometimes we were on glare ice and sometimes we couldn't see the trail at all. Then the ice got real rough and broken. We could see steam rising to our left. This meant open water. Big icebergs stuck to the top of the ice where there had been an overflow, making it rougher. The trail was gone. We could no longer follow the river so we headed for the bank. We were on jagged ice and fell often. There was little or no feeling in our feet and hands. Our ski poles did help us to stand up but our skis were just in the way, especially when we made it to the bank so we took them off and carried them. The bank was too steep to crawl up so we walked till we found a gully. There was loose snow, stumps and devil's club but we made it.

We stopped long enough on the ridge to catch our breath and to put our skis back on. It was warmer under the trees than on the river ice, but the snow was only knee-deep and we kept getting our skis tangled in alder roots and brush. Long

396

fingers reached out from every stump, roots I guess, but they kept grabbing at us. There were all kinds of noises. The wind sobbed and moaned and limbs snapped and trees cracked against each other like devils dancing in the sky.

"When will we get there?" Steve kept bugging. "How come we can't see the light at the bridge. I thought you said it was only a little ways. I'm going to cut across the river to the side the cafe is on."

"Go on if you want to but I'm not going to fall through the ice. I'm going to walk across the river at the bridge." Steve trailed.

"I'm freezing to death. I can't feel my feet," he kept on like a broken record. "I'm too young to die."

"HUSH! Listen! It's a plane!"

"It's a plane," Steve yelled. "Maybe they're looking for us."

We screamed and yelled and waved our arms, but the plane flew on over.

"It's coming back! Marsha, it's coming back! Let's signal."

I fumbled in my knapsack. My fingers were numb but I recognized the shape of the flashlight. I tried to turn it on to signal, but it wouldn't work. I guess the batteries were frozen or the switch was stuck. I tried . . . and I sobbed, mad because I couldn't feel the switch with my hands. We would have to start a fire. The pilot could never see us in this mess of trees.

The wind kept getting higher but the plane kept flying up and down the river. We had to get a fire started! None of my lighters would work. We HAD to get down to the river quick! We made it down but the plane was gone.

We didn't know it at the time but the pilot was Jim Okonek, who was given the "Helicopter Pilot of the Year" award in 1980 by the International Helicopter Association. Now I understand why. When other aircraft were grounded, he took off by himself from an unlighted strip on a frozen lake near Talkeetna to look for us. He's saved lots of lives. I just didn't know men could be so brave.

But while he was still flying around we were still trying to get back down on the river, where he could see us signal in the bright moonlight. We got down to the river, and waited . . . and waited. The wind was so strong it kept pushing us out toward the open water in the current. We couldn't stand the wind any longer so we clawed our way back up the bank, fell

397

over a big log and just lay there. We were both crying and I was shaking so hard I just couldn't do anything. We fell in a sort of sheltered place. I kept crying and shaking. I was so cold I just couldn't stand it any longer. After the plane left I just wanted to die, but I couldn't. I was shaking too much.

Then I thought of the silliest things. I kept wanting to plug in the electric heater under the log. Then I wanted to set it on fire but I knew I couldn't. The wind screamed at me and I screamed back. I just wanted to get it over with.

Steve roused and begged me to rub his feet. I don't know how I got his shoes off or if he did. I couldn't feel anything, I was shaking so bad. I tried putting his feet between my legs and hugging him. Maybe if I could protect him he might live. It was all my fault. I wanted to die.

"I'm sorry Junior, I'm sorry. I didn't mean to get us lost."

"I'm not Junior, I'm Steve," he mumbled. "Rub my feet harder, I'm freezing to death."

"I'm sorry, Junior. I'm sorry."

"I'm not Junior, I'm Steve. Are you crazy? Don't you know the difference between me and your own brother? I'm freezing to death. I'm too young to die."

"I'm sorry, Junior, I'm sorry."

"You are crazy and I'm freezing to death. Rub harder."

The more I told him I was sorry the more he fussed because I kept calling him Junior. If I wasn't so cold I might get my head together. I needed a cigarette.

I don't know how long we huddled under that log. Forever almost. Finally Steve told me he was going to sleep. Something told me he might not wake up. My brother was really freezing to death and it was all my fault. I wanted to die but I couldn't because I was shaking too hard. I kept shaking harder and harder until my whole body was just jumping around.

I thought I heard a snow machine and voices. Maybe. Maybe it was just the wind. The wind kept screaming and crying and long arms kept reaching for me. Why couldn't I die?

Them some warm air blew in my ear. Was it a moose? I didn't see one. I thought I saw grizzly tracks earlier but I didn't want to scare Steve. The warm air kept blowing in my ear. My brother was asleep . . . or WAS HE DEAD? I was still shaking so it was hard to get up, but I had to wake him.

"Junior! Junior! Wake up! It's daylight! We've got to keep moving."

398

"I'm not Junior. I just want to s-l-e-e-p."

"Junior! Junior! Get up! I hear noises. If you don't come on I'm leaving you," I think I said as I gave him another good shaking.

Slowly he got up and followed. My mittens were frozen so solid that I couldn't bend them aroung my ski poles, so I threw them away I think. I guess I must have kept my hands under my wool sweater all night, or under my arms. If not I wouldn't have any hands. Later we were told that Steve had chewed the thumb right out of one of his mittens and had thrown it away.

All I knew then was that I kept hearing noises, then they would come and go away. Then I heard snow machines and planes, or was it a chopper? I had been hearing noises all night, but this one wouldn't go away.

"Junior! Junior! It's a chopper! Over here! Come on!"

I started out with all my might following the chopper, but Steve went the other way.

"No, Marsha, over here. It's a dog. No it's a snow machine. Come on!"

"It's a chopper!" I screamed. "Come back! Don't leave us again please. I'll pay. I have $100. Please come back."

I am told that I almost plunged right over the cliff into the river ice below. Steve LaLime a neighbor caught me just in time. He put his coat around me and pulled off his gloves and put them on my hands. I grabbed my stepbrother and we were hugging and crying. The dog was rubbing its nose up and down my leg. The men said they would help us down to the river where the chopper was waiting on the ice.

Later I learned that the man with the dog was its trainer Tim Taylor of the Anchorage Police Department. Winds were so high that he couldn't be flown in so Tim drove the 117 miles with his K-9 Shultz. When he got to the Cache Creek trooper station at mile 115, Lynn was waiting with my night-gown and bra and Steve's dirty socks for Shultz to sniff. By then our trail was ten hours old. Steve LaLime our neighbor who had just returned from an earlier search, turned right back around and went with Tim and Shultz. Steve walked fifteen hours in knee-deep snow.

By daylight which comes about 9:00 A.M. now, there were three planes searching all from Talkeetna. There were still hurricane-force winds in the valley between Anchorage and

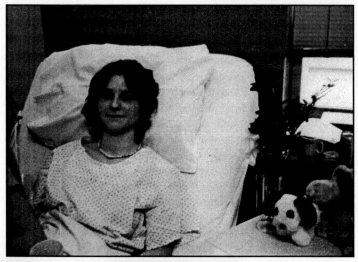

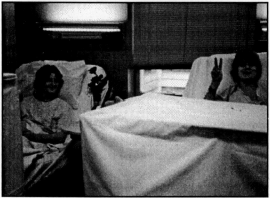

From her hospital bed, 16-year-old Marsha Ann Moore tells of her grueling experience while lost with her 12-year-old stepbrother, Steve, for almost 20 hours as the temperature hung around -40 below zero.

Talkeetna. But Jim Okonek was up again this time with his son, Brian as spotter. David Lee the pilot with Akland Helicopter, Inc., of Talkeetna was alone, searching from his plane. Bert Hales was piloting his own plane with Jay Melville as spotter.

The wind was still high and battering them around but the pilots around here are a different breed. They fly Mount McKinley, our nation's tallest peak, and she's a real killer. Knowing the area helps but our pilots are just plain crazy when someone is in trouble, real trouble.

I am told that David Lee spotted us on the bluff and flew back across the Susitna, where he crawled in a Chopper with Dennis Brown, owner of Akland, who had the whirly bird warmed up and waiting. They say the wind was so high that Mr. Brown almost crashed twice while he was trying to land on the river ice below us.

David Lee climbed up the bluff to help Tim Taylor and Steve LaLime get us to the chopper. I am told that I said, "Boy, am I glad to see you," to Mr. Brown.

We were flown back across the Susitna to Akland, where they had to cut my long johns and jeans off of me because they were frozen to my legs. While they were trying to warm Steve up and check for frostbite, he started hollerin' he was hungry and gobbled down two peanut butter sandwiches and a cup of hot chocolate while everyone watched in amazement.

The only thing I remember wanting was a cigarette. Now I understand why E.M.T. Dorothy Jones yelled, "NO, ABSOLUTELY NOT!" when someone offered to light one for me. In our area where we're a hundred miles from the nearest doctor, the folks really take Emergency Medical Training seriously.

Suddenly there were lots of people around. Everybody was petting the dog. My own mother Verjean Davidson and Junior were there. Our neighbor E.M.T. Lynn Turner who, in so far as I know, was the only woman who was actually out with the search party looking for us was there.

The next thing I remember they were putting us back into the chopper. My mother was telling us that our friend Mary Carey was driving her to Anchorage and she would meet us at Providence Hospital.

Fortunately Dr. Mills was waiting to receive us. About all I remember after arrival is being dunked several times in a thermal bath. I am told that each time they raised me, photos were made showing the change of color in my skin. I'm glad I didn't know then that my toes would soon be turning black.

After that they put us in the room where everyone wore masks, blue paper caps, gowns, and shoes. My father got there and they let him in. He looked strange in the blue shower cap and mask. I drifted off . . .

I don't remember much until I wound up in another ward in the hospital. Steve was in the bed across from me. There were huge white things on our feet and big white tent-like guards around the foot of our beds.

"I need a cigarette. I want a cigarette real bad," were my first words after coming out of isolation.

From the look on my nurse's face you would think I had just smashed a Rembrandt . . . I may as well have asked for a revolver in so far as getting my wish was concerned.

"One puff young lady," came the firm voice of Dr. Mills who was entering the room and evidently heard my request, "one puff while suffering from hypothermia could mean the difference. It could induce pneumonia if you do not have it already. You are scheduled for X-ray and smoke clouds a lung X-ray and gives a false reading. If you want to come out of this hospital alive forget smoking. Understand?"

Little did I know at the time that I was talking with the top authority in the whole world on hypothermia. It was Dr. William H. Mills, Jr., who established this the only such thermal unit in the United States. Smoke in this ward would have been

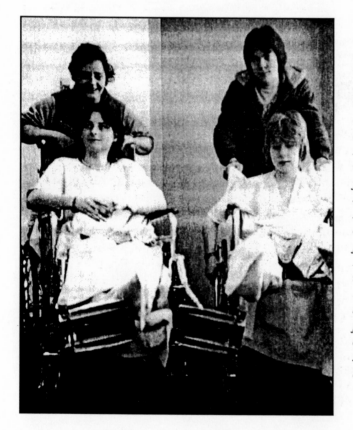

Times were happier when the children were able to be pushed to therapy. Marsha's mother, Verjean Davidson, pushes Marsha's chair and a friend, Robert Hamilton, pushes Steve. Note the big, white footies worn by both Marsha and Steve.

more devastating than a revolver. If it had not been for this doctor and his knowledge I would not be telling this story.

Ten days later, I was allowed visitors. My own mother entered the room with our friend Mary Carey who wanted my story for a magazine article . . . when I felt like talking, of course.

But what I wanted right then was for mama to fill in the gaps on the side of the story I didn't know.

"It's a night like I hope no mother will ever have to face again," my mother related. "It was a night when friends actually held me back when I was sure I could find you. It was a night that will haunt us for a lifetime. Ask Mary; she was with us, hanging on to me and both of us hanging onto John, Jr. I just can't talk about it."

"It was a night when all hearts beat as one," came Mary Carey's summary. "A night when prayer groups were organized on both sides of Talkeetna River. A night when many people who never pray, did and lit a candle. The night when many persons we know and many we don't know by name laid their lives on the line with little thought of personal safety."

Again Steve flipped his television button.

"Stop that!" I griped. "Can't you see we're trying to talk. All day you've been spilling Coke, ringing for the nurses and flipping that television control about ninety miles per hour."

Flip! Flip! Flip!

"Steve, if you don't leave that television alone I'll come over there and clobber you!"

"Oh, yeah! You can't come over here. And just because you can't use your hands doesn't mean I can't use mine. How come you keep telling people about the brave things you were doin' when you didn't even know what you were doin'? You were crazy, man, crazy. And how come you kept callin' me 'Junior'?"

"If you mention that once more I'll come over there and I'll . . ." At that moment Dr. Mills walked into the room. We both clammed up. Mom and Mary were polite enough to leave the room during his examination.

"No cigarettes?" he asked with a wink and a smile. "I thought you would be here much longer than Steve, but you are doing so well that maybe, just maybe . . ."

403

I wasn't sure Dr. Mills was convinced, but as he was leaving the room he turned back with a sly grin, commenting,

"It's a miracle, but I think that both of you will leave this hospital with ten fingers and ten toes each . . . if we can get you out of here before you tear each other apart."

Chapter 36

The World's Only Fiddlehead Fern Farm

y beloved lodge became such a busy place that it consumed me. I wanted to go on new adventures and write but lacked the time. My new book was doing beautifully, and the second one came about in a most unusual manner. It must have been in 1977 when a very timid young man came into the lodge and waited for an opportunity to talk with me.

"I'm Doug Lindstrand," he introduced himself. "And I sketch animals," he added haltingly. "Do you think you might be able to sell some of my drawings?"

"Well, I really don't know," I answered. "Suppose you bring them in and I'll take a look if you have them with you."

His sketches were amazingly good.

"Certainly those will sell," I encouraged. "Be sure to check back again soon with more of your work."

When Doug again checked all his work was sold. Then I sold more and more of his sketches. Once when Doug came with replacements, he hung around and I could tell there was something he wanted to talk with me about.

"Are you thinking of expanding?" I asked the young Vietnam veteran.

"Well, since you write and I sketch, I was wondering if you would write a book for me to illustrate?"

"That's the best offer I've had yet," I replied sincerely, "for

Mary Carey picks Ostrich Fern fronds to be used as greenery for wildflower arrangements which she always keeps in her shop. She takes time to tell patrons whatever they want to know, from common to Latin name of each plant.

I believe you will soon become Alaska's greatest wildlife artist. What would you like for me to write about?"

Doug hesitated . . .

"You do animals so well and I see you have added Eskimo children. Would you like for me to write about them?"

"Yes that would be fine," he stammered. "Want me to check with you when I come back?"

"Sure," I answered. "Since winter is settling in I should have some time available. I should come up with some idea soon for your approval."

A few months later he returned and asked if I had come up with a subject.

"My part of the book is finished," I replied. "I had part of it written before you asked. It's about fireweed."

"FIREWEED!" Doug exclaimed in astonishment. "I never drew a flower in my life."

"Well you're just fixing to expand your territory. It's about fireweed and an old prospector. I've entitled it *Fireweed Philosophy* and it's poetry," I added quickly half afraid he was going to faint. "Don't read it now, take it home with you. If you don't like it we'll try something else. But the fireweed is so beautiful I think it should be our state flower."

"Why?" he gasped.

"Because it and the fiddlehead fern are the first plants to come up as the snow goes. Many a prospector has used them as his earliest greens. Then in the summer it is so pretty. I use it for bouquets here in the lodge and I also make honey from the fireweed and clover blossoms. That's an old homesteader's trick. My patrons can hardly believe me when I tell them that I made the honey they have just eaten. Some day I am going to write a recipe book and you can illustrate that too."

Doug was still a little too overcome to speak, so I continued.

"And that's not all I like about the fireweed. It doesn't get its name from its color. That name was given because it grows like a weed and is the first thing to come back after ground cover has been disturbed or burned over. It's a real tourist stopper. When I first came to Alaska I stopped all along the way making photos of fireweed. It grows beautifully in the bar ditches along the roadside. I love fireweed and I just wanted to write about it through the eyes of an old prospector," I added before he completely revived.

As of now Doug has illustrated four of the eleven books I have written including that cookbook.

But we are still a long way from learning why I put in the world's only fiddlehead fern farm. It's been a real adventure, stemming from a misadventure, a near tragedy when I whacked my back twice in 1970. This was the year before I started work on the lodge.

The Palmer Agricultural Experimental Farm was paying children and adults to pick Ostrich (fiddlehead) Fern. By 1969 I had finished my homesteading requirements and gone back to teaching in Talkeetna to support the homestead at least until the highway was finished and I could make the homestead support me.

The fall of 1969 promised a very exciting school year. The big new beautiful consolidated high school at the Talkeetna "Y" on the Parks highway was scheduled for completion that fall, but like most Alaskan construction it had fallen behind schedule.

I kept thinking of my earlier teaching in Talkeetna, when I had only eight students in the one room down at the end of Main Street, no books and no desks. I really believe that was the most challenging year of my teaching career. But the next year was very promising. My high school enrollment had more than doubled, jumping from eight to seventeen. A new teacher was added. Mrs. Campbell and I lived in the apartment on the second floor of the red schoolhouse which is now a museum. Then the grade school and high school overflowed with the coming of the bus students and the opening of the spur road in the fall of 1964. A new school was built just off the spur road before you get into downtown Talkeetna. Soon this was housing both the grade school and the high school. It even had a full gynmasium and a library. We were really uptown, and I guess we can say that literally. Talkeetna's population had grown from 76 when I first arrived to 414. A new fire station, our only fire station, was put in across the parking lot from the new schoolhouse. A new lodge, the Latitude 62, was built just across the highway. The number of air services had doubled, from two to four. Besides the services belonging to Cliff Hudson and Don Sheldon there was Talkeetna Air Taxi belonging to Lowell Thomas, Jr., our former lieutenant governor, and Geeting Aviation belonging to Doug Geeting, Talkeetna's young stunt pilot who added suspense to every occasion with his aerial acrobatics.

Akland Helicopter Service was also in swaddling clothes. Unfortunately this service went under but fortunately it brought into our village another V.I.P., Jim Okonek who also saw opportunity with the mushrooming mountain climbing expeditions. He and his wife Julie put in their own Air Service, K-2. Because of his almost unbelievable exploits while a chopper pilot in Vietnam and his daring rescues on Mount McKinley, Okonek was named "International Helicopter Pilot of the Year" in 1980.

But back to 1969. Our new schoolhouse in Talkeetna, the third one in which I taught was full to overflowing and the high school students were to be moved to the new building at the "Y," which was to have been completed earlier.

The new expanded high school, which would have more teachers than I had pupils when I first started teaching in Talkeetna, would be ready for occupancy about mid-term early in 1970.

Just before we moved from the old schoolhouse, if you could call it old, to the new I slipped on the steel-rimmed concrete steps laced with ice, and broke my back. Fortunately the cord was not severed but I was out of commission. Some months later while going to Anchorage, I was involved in a car accident and cracked four more vertabrae. This time I was out of commission for months.

As the days and weeks passed my back did not bother me so much as my hands. With six months previous experience I was quite a pro in a cast and on crutches, but now my fingers failed to grasp. Dr. Mills sent me to a therapist who worked with my hands and showed me several exercises to practice. He said that if this didn't work he might be able to relieve the pressure by an operation on my spinal cord near the base of my neck.

This was frightening. I was determined not to have that operation. My hands had to work. I didn't have the money to go to Bellevue in Washington as Dr. Mills wanted me to do for the special therapy. I wanted to build my lodge and to write books. My hands had to work. There had to be a way. I was never

409

dependent upon others, and I wouldn't accept such a sentence now. I could take care of myself.

My first home therapy was quite unique. For several years I had extolled the merit of a spring ostrich fern delicacy called fiddlehead fern which grew wild on my homestead. I began eating it in the spring of 1965 when the nearest super market was almost a hundred air miles away. Preparing to homestead I checked every book I could find on edible plants that I might expect to find. Fiddleheads are the very best and most delicious. Ostrich fern grew in the Matanuska and Susitna River valleys. If they grew that near, surely they would grow in the nearby Chulitna River valley also.

I found the Ostrich fern, and being an adventuresome soul, I started experimenting with it. I found the fresh fern good in salads, casseroles, and sautéed in butter with fresh wild mushrooms. Having no refrigeration, I wondered how I could preserve some of these delicious greens throughout the winter. They canned beautifully if not over-cooked. I had written a great deal about them in my news columns.

In 1969 I was really delighted when Sigmund Restad, head of the Institute of Agricultural Sciences in Palmer, with Charlie Marsh, research economist, started studying the Ostrich fern. By 1970 they started marketing it very successfully. They were paying people thirty cents a pound to pick the wild fern. This was a real bonanza especially for the children of the Talkeetna and Trapper Creek areas. I had already learned that one can gather several pounds of fiddleheads within an hour, and it grew in great abundance on my homestead.

The more I thought about it the more I was determined to make it work. How wonderful the spring air, much better than that of a hospital room. Wild violets were more exciting to me than floral bouquets. How I missed my fiddlehead fern patch. That was it! I could earn money doing my own therapy rather than going into debt in a strange hospital.

Putting on rain pants and jacket, I tucked a duffel bag underneath my crutches and climbed the gentle side of the slope across from my homesteading cabin. Since I whacked my back the second time in February, and May was almost gone, walking was no real problem. I only used crutches to guard against fall-

410

ing. The real problem was getting my fingers to work. I could handle my crutches between my forefingers and thumbs, but I still couldn't sign my name. That's why I had to resign teaching; I couldn't write and deep in my heart I wanted eventually to do more than grade school papers, I wanted to write books.

Getting up the hill on the easy side wasn't too bad, but getting organized to slide down the steep side picking fern all the way and hanging onto my crutches and duffel bag, wasn't too easy. I slid the crutches in front of me, sort of pushing them into the bank as my security blanket. At first I had to sort of snap the heads off between my forefingers and thumbs, but little by little my fingers began bending ever so slowly it seemed, and with many an outcry of pain. Day after day I picked. Each day the experimental farm sent trucks out to pick up the fern in Talkeetna and Trapper Creek. By then there was a temporary wooden bridge across the Chulitna River. A friend working on the new bridge faithfully picked up my fern each evening and delivered it to the pick-up stand in Talkeetna.

Much to my surprise and delight, I received a note from the experiment station saying mine was the nicest, cleanest fern of all. I worked harder. Soon I became their star picker.

I never told anyone previously how many times I climbed and slid down that hill, nor how painful the picking really was. I forced my hands to work. Small wonder my fern was clean. Much of it was bathed in salt tears so I guess it was seasoned, too.

"Therapy Hill," as I called it was my greatest ally. It still means more to me than any other spot on my homestead and I still check it faithfully each year for the first violets of the season and the first fern.

For ten years I served Ostrich fern at my lodge. I served it as hors-d'oeuvres at the bar. It made a fun guessing game. Deep fried in a beer batter they were sometimes said to taste a little like oysters. I think this was more or less a figment of the imagination when I fried the buttons only. If I left a little of the stem on they looked like fried shrimp but would never pass as shrimp. To me the fern tastes more like asparagus than any other vegetable, but really has a distinctive taste of its own.

In 1984 I sold my lodge to Gary and Linda Crabb. I never wanted to sell my business. I wanted to put in a chair lift up the butte as I had planned so I could share my mountain with young and old alike winter and summer. But when they created Denali State Park, I lost the land I had filed on across from my homestead as a Trade and Manufacture site. I had materials for two cabins air lifted in by chopper and had a swath cut through the alders for a ski run. I had big dreams but never had the money for the lift. I couldn't borrow it because I didn't have title to the land, and they would not give me title without the lift I had said I was going to build. Thus I lost that land and was saddened by the fact I could never realize my dreams completely. They were big — like a multi-story hotel, a theater-in-the-round, and a convention center on my twenty-acre field I had to clear and plant.

It was a big dream too big for me to handle and I wasn't getting any younger. Besides I had two books off the press and wanted to write more. It was then that Gary Crabb, my neighbor about a hundred miles to the north who owned Mt. McKinley Village and North Face Lodge, began begging me to sell to him. He and his wife Linda were much younger, had proven their capabilities with the two places they had, and would follow through with my plans even to the chair lift if the state would lease the land.

I just had to get writing and travel. I had never been out of the Western Hemisphere. Now I have been to all the continents except Antarctica, and I really don't care to go to see the hole in the ozone. Unfortunately we may be developing one or two of our own near the North Pole.

But back to our story. I did write and I did travel. It took me two years to write my next book, *Green Gold in Alaska*, which was about my homesteading and fiddlehead fern.

Unfortunately the more I wrote about the fern the more I realized I had in no way fulfilled the debt I owe this gourmet delight. I missed the lodge and believe it or not, I missed my patrons, even though I visited the lodge.

Fortunately I kept a portion of my land there, Therapy Hill naturally. Going back and picking fern gave me a contentment that nothing else could. But it also reminded me of my unfulfilled commitment.

That's when I decided to put in a fiddlehead fern farm at

my new home, Mile 1 on the Talkeetna spur road just one mile from the Parks highway. I would transplant fern, have church groups, Scouts and Brownies pick fresh fern and bring it to me. This I did in 1983, when, *Green Gold in Alaska* which Doug Lindstrand illustrated came off the press. I would work with fern and sell books during tourist season, and go on more adventures and write more books in winter. This vow I have found no trouble keeping. My fourth book, *Let's Taste Alaska*, was also illustrated by Lindstrand, and is now in a third edition.

nfpw

Leadership Service
certificate

NATIONAL FEDERATION OF PRESS WOMEN, INC.

Mary Carey

in appreciation of service on the NFPW leadership team

Charlotte G. Schexnayder
President

*Perhaps this award from the National Federation of Press Women means
more to me than any other. Your author put two years of planning into it, beginning with smaller quests for free transportation, then for harder ones. My
first request honored was for a free West Tours bus ride to where the press
women would see the terminus of the pipeline. The second was from Princess
Tours to Talkeetna for a free wild game dinner. The third request honored
was by ERA Helicopters to land guests on a drilling platform in Cook Inlet.
The biggest request, one which may never have been granted except for my
hard-working committee, was a free 56-place plane to Prudhoe Bay, honored
by Wein Airlines.*

Chapter 37

Prudhoe Bay

fter fern season ended in 1989, I took off on two adventures. One was again with my constant ally Mrs. Oro Stewart. The fact that we were both now widows didn't mean that we no longer love our seven-league boots. The adventure of July 1989 was far from how it was planned, but you can't win them all.

Our Chugach Gem and Mineral Society of Anchorage had a rock hunt planned as far as the Yukon River on the Haul Road to Prudhoe Bay, but Oro Stewart had no idea of stopping there. While her husband Ivan was still alive, they floated down from Circle City in an amphibious car to where the Yukon bridge is now located. Many were the eyes that popped when they came merrily floating down the Yukon in a car. This had never been done before.

Now there was a new challenge for Oro, putting the amphib car in the Koyukuk River running alongside the road and floating toward the Arctic Ocean stopping at some native villages. This was for me but we never made it.

We did join the rest of the club members at the Yukon River bridge and we did go the rest of the way. But not in the amphibious car. It wouldn't stay afloat. The seals so recently checked and resealed didn't stay sealed. The amphib wouldn't float not for long, so it had to be left behind. There were five of us who planned to go on the float trip. This included club members Butch Rudowski who was going to drive the amphib car, Andy Hersha a master mechanic, who was going to handle the speed boat with extra fuel and supplies, and three females, Oro Stewart, Dee Crume and myself.

The three ladies were going to ride in my "hippie van," as I called my Dodge Prospector, because it had a bed, a refrigerator, and loves to go. We all had sleeping bags along but Oro, Dee and I decided we would sleep in the van. The chairs let all the way back, supplementing the bed for sleeping. We used our sleeping bags so we had no beds to make. This way we never pitched a tent as we planned to do alongside the Koyukuk River. Admittedly sleeping quarters in the van were a little confining, but it was warm and we felt pretty snug. No worries about grizzlies. Butch and Andy camped out part of the time, but found the camper on the back of the Stewart truck more comfortable on the colder nights.

Our first night after leaving the rest of the club members at the Yukon River bridge, we camped at an abandoned Haul Road site where there was water flowing from two artesian wells. Several road-maintainance vehicles came in and filled with water while we were there, including water trucks which sprinkled the dusty road to keep the fine glacial flour from penetrating vehicles and nostrils alike. Air conditioning made little difference; the dust was our first unpleasant encounter. More about these later.

I had been to Prudhoe Bay by air during her hay-day. How wonderfully comfortable on a chartered plane with the presidents of the Women of the Press from almost every state in the union. I spent much of my two years after selling the lodge in coordinating this trip. It was my turn. I was free. Thus I began with the easier targets first. I went to American Bus Tours and asked if they wouldn't like to send the press women to Talkeetna on a free charter to a wild game dinner. This wasn't too difficult. Then I went to Westours and Alaska Sightseeing, asking for free charters to Valdez and Kenai. This was a little farther but the season wasn't yet into full swing, so they gave way to

416

"Look at the free publicity you would get in almost every state in the union."

I went to ERA Helicopters of Anchorage asking if they couldn't furnish chopper service to an offshore drilling pod, reminding them of the many times our rock club had flown with ERA. This was a little much but if I could get them to the beach landing strip near Kenai they would make two trips in and out to the Grayling platform, which happened to have four legs. There were other offshore sites which were smaller and were only monopods or tripods. But the larger pod had a bigger landing and recreational area. This was very exciting.

With these victories we began dreaming of another and greater one. Why not try for a Wein charter to the North Slope? Things were really booming and exploration going full tilt. There were two women on my committee who worked for Arco. We could try, but previous victories were not repeated too easily. First we were defeated by a vote of 4-2. We gave it another try and came out with a tie. As I waited those last few weeks I was very busy with alternate plans for a trip to Fairbanks if the North Slope deal fell through.

At the last minute they gave us a fifty-six-place Wein charter free of charge. We were never more jubilant. Certainly the National Press Women would have a tour of a lifetime all free of charge. I could never have made it without the finishing touches from my hard-working committee members and without exercising every "con" tactic we could think of. The red carpet was rolled out for us all the way.

In Prudhoe Bay two small buses and a Limo awaited our arrival. We were shuffled to headquarters, where we were given a kit with much printed matter about the North Slope and what we were about to see and hear. We were taken into the control room which had more gadgets, panels, etc. than I ever expect to see again in one place. We were taken to the motel dining room where we lined up as the workers did, but I do know that steak, lobster, shrimp and most of the more expensive food items were served. The game rooms were something else. There was everything from pool tables to saunas, and a tree was planted in the glass-fronted lobby.

We were bused from drilling rigs to tank farms and always

with a knowledgeable guide. Prudhoe Bay created a very glowing spot in our hearts that really whetted our journalistic appetites.

But the trip by auto in 1989 was something different. One must have a permit to drive past the Arctic Circle. This Oro Stewart managed calling ours a writer-photographer expedition. But driving to the Arctic Ocean along the only road leading thereto is another story. I can see why uninformed persons want to drive there but now I understand why the public is denied admission.

Anyone who had driven the Alcan Highway, twenty-five years ago encountered some of the problems faced on the highway to Prudhoe Bay in 1989. It's dust, mud, or big trucks flying past. Add to this no service station, no cafe, no restroom, and no bush big enough to hide behind for miles from Coldfoot to the Arctic Ocean, and you begin to get the picture, if you've added in the mosquitoes.

Ever since they put in that one and only road to the Arctic Ocean, I had wanted to drive it, especially during oil boom days when it was called the Hickel Ice Road. It was difficult for me to imagine the trucks loaded with pipe and supplies crossing rivers on ice bridges, though that's how rivers are crossed in the Arctic in winter. I wanted to travel this North Slope Haul Road to the Arctic Ocean after the mighty Yukon River, Mississippi of the north, was bridged, but was always too busy serving those who drove the road hauling pipe and supplies. Besides there was little time for pursuing journalistic dreams during my lodge days.

Then in July 1989 my dream materialized. As planned we met other club members at the Yukon River bridge, fifty-six miles north of Fairbanks. This within itself is quite an experience, a very enjoyable one. The bridge which is half a mile long is quite a masterpiece of engineering. Bringing our club train near, the group feasted on grayling caught in nearby streams. The rock we found wasn't that great in so far as being pretty is concerned, but the gold found in this area is something else. From the Yukon River Inn to Coldfoot, 175 miles of graveled roadway, there were no facilities. True there were many names of mining towns and abandoned highway camps along the way but no services.

Being rockhounds, we naturally left our graveled roadway for more challenging paths leading to such historical sites as Prospect and Wiseman. Before reaching the Yukon we took a side road to Livengood where our travel guide proclaimed we would find a cafe and a service station. Not true. This all-but-a-ghost mining town is a 'must see' stop along the way, but the only public services are now a liquor store and a gift shop. It's the type of liquor store where you go in and lay your money down and leave it because the attendant is usually not present. The gift shop is the type that when prospective customers pull up the owner comes and opens it. The gift shop is delightful, filled with truly Alaska-made handcrafts. The people of the deserted village, the three men we saw and talked with, are quite colorful. Two of them were goldminers and they told us there were twenty-six miners and prospectors in the area, but they were out on the creeks or at their diggings doing their thing.

In Prospect and Wiseman there was no one to talk with. Mostly, "Keep Out" signs and deserted buildings greeted us. In Wiseman we did see much evidence of mining but little appreciation of our presence. I was very anxious to interview Jack Bullock, who caused the haul road to be re-routed, but there was no sign of him. In the 1960s I did news stories of him and his partner blocking the Koyukuk River crossing, the river which we wanted to float in Oro's amphib car. When we came back through we made another try. This time we found Bullock's partner Harry Leonard but his niece had just brought him back from a nursing home in Fairbanks for some memorabilia. Unfortunately his memory was gone; I found nothing about Jack Bullock. I had waited too long for a follow-up. Mrs. Stewart thought she had friends living in Wiseman too, but Leonard could tell us nothing about them. We did learn from Leonard's niece that there was still mining being done in the area and that several of the houses in Wiseman still housed miners. Unfortunately we got to talk with none of them.

Coldfoot was a different story and our most exciting stop. Dick Mackey and his son Rick has run the Iditarod every year since it started. It was son Rick who pulled me from a snowbank in Grayling in 1984 the year he won the Iditarod.

Dick and his staff were most gracious, and for the Arctic

419

have a very luxurious establishment, this including a service station, gift shop, restaurant and a rather large motel. Father of the "Coldfoot Classic," Dick takes pride in showing his kennel and huskies to summer tourists who are allowed to drive this far, even 38 miles farther to the Arctic Circle, without a permit. Just beyond the circle there is a guardhouse where John Q. Public is allowed no further without a pass. Now I truly understand why. No facilities not even an outdoor potty between Coldfoot, mile 171, and Prudhoe Bay, mile 414.

At mile 221 we found black marble with white calcite veins, but it was of poor quality. At mile 255 we came to the farthest north spruce tree. From here to the Arctic Ocean there was no bush large enough to hide behind to relieve yourself. Just millions of mosquitoes waiting for the first show of bare flesh. Soon we were climbing up and up on grades steeper than allowed on freeways.

The view from Atigun Pass, elevation 4,800 feet was breathtaking, the most spectacular view along the Dalton Highway, if indeed it could be called a highway. From this summit pass of the Brooks Range it was hard to realize that throughout the ages of time this mountain range, Alaska's oldest, has eroded to about half its estimated height. From the summit of Atigun Pass to the Arctic Ocean the roadway loses altitude until it reaches sea level. Most of the loss of altitude comes immediately after reaching the summit. Then comes what is know as the roller-coaster area, where the road goes up and down so suddenly that one gets the roller-coaster feeling in the pit of the stomach.

Keep in mind that the Dalton Highway follows the pipeline to the bay. At mile 269 we reached the pump station with the highest elevation along the route, 2,760 feet. When we reached a lower elevation where the North Slope desert was almost flat, I was told that the zig-zag was put in the line to eliminate the possibility of all of it being bombed along a straight line. There were places too, where the line went underground.

Although there is only desert north of the Brooks Range, it is criss-crossed by many all-but-bankless streams. This is an area where the fisherman's fly is almost an unknown factor to the grayling, which can be seen peacefully swimming or resting in the crystal clear water. Keeping Andy and Butch away from these tempting spots was difficult. In fact all of us had fishing

420

fever but the mosquitoes and the fact that there was usually no place to pull off the road became dictator. Perhaps this is one of the reasons the public is not invited. There is only room for trucks to pass each other, so a car parked just over a rise which could become a real hazard in case two trucks met near the same spot. There would hardly be room for braking. Trucks do not stop easily, especially when loaded. Besides there's always the possibility of getting a rock through the windshield. Along this route I did get two headlights knocked out and one rock in my windshield, but fortunately it did not come through.

At mile 301 we had a good view of Slope Mountain where reportedly we would see Dall sheep, but we could not find them, not even with binoculars. At mile 376 we did see a very large pingo. A pingo in this area is usually formed by ice wedges. Freezing water rises above the surface, sometimes for several hundred feet. Here the summers are not long enough or hot enough to melt such huge blocks of ice. Blowing glacial silt covers the ice, and vegetation, mostly mosses and sedges, take over. Like sand dunes covered with vegetation these are not likely to go away.

Often we saw a few caribou or a single, standing underneath the pipeline. Whether they liked the shade the line provided, or possibly fewer mosquitoes and graveled repair roads alongside, this seemed to be the only place we saw caribou. True they were not yet gathering by the thousand, yea tens of thousands as in the largest herds.

More and more shallow ponds and more and more water birds nested in the tundra where the ice never thaws over a few feet below the vegetation. Water stands everywhere. Jaegers patrol the area feeding on the young. This area is also noted for its support of many hawks and waterfowl on the endangered species list, one the peregrine falcon. In one area the pipeline had to shut down one of its small air strips because of numerous collisions of birds and planes.

When we saw the Franklin Bluffs to the east of the road, we gave a cheer knowing that within less than fifty miles we would reach the Arctic Ocean. We wanted to hunt rock in this area, but all of us were working folk pressed for time. Soon we could see buildings and oil field equipment across a lagoon. At mile 414 we hit a check point, which was alerted the minute we left the checkpoint just north of the Arctic Circle. We had made it but did not feel too welcome. This was really no place for us to be. Because I was working on this book, I did not want to be announced as the press club was ten years earlier, when we were given a Wein charter free of charge. I wanted to see what it was really like now, now that the construction boom was over.

It did not take too long to realize that Prudhoe Bay was no place for a tourist on his own. We saw only two service stations, no grocery stores, no shopping area, no gift shops, and no cafes. The big hotel at Deadhorse was closed, as were other lodging spots around the bay. There was no waiting Limo to take us to the plush Arco camp where the Women of the Press were treated so royally a decade earlier.

We found there were only two relatively small hotels where we might find food and lodging. Both were made up of mobile camp units. One was run by a native corporation and completely filled, but we could find food there. But we wanted to get a bath and some of the ingrained dust off if possible. At the other hotel we did find one room available, a double for $185. A bathroom even though it was down the hall, was a real luxury. Here I must admit that we did a little cheating. Dee Crume stayed with Oro Stewart and me, and the men sneaked down the hallway for a bath without anyone noticing. How sweet it was!

Food was no problem at the hotel so long as you didn't mind paying $15 per meal. But the food was good and well worth the cost. Soft drinks were free. You helped yourself from nearby refrigerators filled with everything from milk to juices. There was no intoxicating drink for sale. Beer and cocktails are not served and the reason is apparent. Prudhoe Bay is a work place not geared for parties.

Everywhere we tried to go by auto in the Prudhoe Bay area there seemed to be a private road with a guard at the entryway. This too is a must I am sure because of the nature of the oil business. Cigarettes alone could create a disaster in some places.

Uninvited, unannounced and simply in the way, it did not take us too long to realize that the tourist is not welcome. Most of the places which were open during the height of the construction boom were closed. We seemed in the way in the town and on the highway. In fact we were a hazard, at least along the highway. There's no time nor place for sightseeing and very few pull-offs where one can stop for a minute's rest or a picnic, and there are no facilities for this. Along the haul road to the North Slope one could easily get a bashed skull from flying rocks from eighteen-wheelers. Every time they see a tourist vehicle they slow down, but they no doubt do not appreciate doing so often because they are paid by the load, not by the hour. Then if you have trouble, you're really in trouble. No repair shops for autos.

I loved my first visit; it was loaded with glamour. But on the second one it became quite evident that the public is not welcome and is only in the way of those who have a job to do. For entertainment, go elsewhere.

Chapter 38

Alaska Rock Hounds
Circle Australia

Since foreign trips with the Chugach Gem and Mineral Society of Anchorage have become such an integral part of my life for the past twenty-two years, perhaps we should enter at least one chapter on my favorite continent to visit, Australia.

Our leader, Mrs. Oro Stewart, has led the Alaska gem society on seven trips to Australia. I have been on three of them. The first was to Sydney, thence westward through the Blue Mountains to Lightning Ridge, where we hunted for black opals. On my second trip we entered at Carins, on the northeast coastline along the coral reef, then westward on the narrow gauge railroad to central Australia, thence southward to Alice Springs and Ayers Rock. Then to Coober Peady, the underground mining town, where we explored milk-opal mines. But on our third trip, we circled Australia. Now for a different adventure!

For thirty-two years, Mrs. Oro Stewart of Stewart's Photo in Anchorage has led rockhounds from all over the U.S. and parts of Europe on international gem tours. To the best of our knowledge this is an undisputed world record for such leadership, and judging from the group, the most outstanding ROCKS!

In 1995 we doubled up on our foreign trips, since some of us are getting older and feel that the best way to keep from feeling older is to live every minute to the fullest. In the fall of 1994, we visited Brazil, Argentina and Chili for a second time. In the spring of 1995 we visited Hong Kong, China, and the fall trip of 1995 was to Turkey.

But it is Australia we wish to share.

On October 1, 1992, a rockhound migration from Alaska and several Western States converged on the shores of San Francisco. From the Golden Gate to Hawaii, their flying carpet was labeled "Quantas." Then on to Australia in search of their soul food, "ROCKS."

Time jumped. We gained a day crossing the International Date Line. After refueling in Brisbane we flew down the East Coast to Melbourne.

Getting through immigration a little ahead of the others, our leader suggested your writer go on outside in search of our next magic carpet, a Koala bus. It really wasn't too difficult to spot a shining yellow and blue bus with a Koala bear painted on the side. A handsome man, perhaps in his forties, stood primly beside the door. He wore the traditional coachman's coat, with braids and stripes signifying his rank. When he saw me closing in on him he jumped in surprise. Is my countenance that startling, I wondered?

"Are you our coachman?" I asked.

"If you are with an American group of rockhounds, I am," he answered in a Scottish-Australian accent as he regained his composure. "I'm Douglas Gunn."

By this time a batch of our group spotted the bus and were closing in, all but stopping traffic as they dodged across the street to the esplanade. After the proper intros and stowing away of a McKinley of luggage, we were off for our hotel. En route Douglas identified buildings and places of interest in true coachman style.

When Oro Stewart and I were alone in the hotel I commented, "I don't know about this driver. He's mighty formal and as nervous as a volcano. How is he going to cope with our informality?"

"Give him a chance," she answered in her quiet voice. "We've had such good coachmen on previous trips, we're spoiled."

"I know, but we have to live with this bloke twenty-two days, and he can make or break a trip. You should have seen how high he jumped when he saw me."

A quirk at the corner of Oro's mouth made me change the subject, fast.

That night a "Welcome Aboard" wine and cheese party was hosted by Ed Romack and Von Baxter. Ed is the outgoing president of our National Gem and Mineral Federation. He is from Idaho Falls, Idaho. Von, who owns the J.C. Morris Insurance Agency, lives in Anchorage. There were several new ones aboard and this was our first get-together. The guest list was complete when Mr. and Mrs. William Hall joined us in Australia after their seventeen-hour flight from Vancouver. Truly dedicated rockhounds, they remained at the helm of the Northwest Federation Show until it was over. Now all thirty-one of our group were in tow.

Throughout the evening I noted that our coachman seemed relaxed and rather human. But every time he glanced or spoke with me that strange and puzzled look came into his eyes. It wasn't sex. I'm eighty. But why was he so startled when he first saw me? I found out on the last day we were together, but without his confession it would have remained a mystery. It took me three weeks to find the answer, so I'll be derned if I tell before the end of the story.

October 5. On our first full day in the "Land Down Under," we were greeted by the Gemological Association of Australia. We were shown what kind of specimens we could expect to find and what gem material. Recently Australia became the world's largest diamond producer, with the Argyle find. She produces 75% of the world's sapphires and has long been the leader in opals. After a tour of the facility and a most informative program, demonstrations were held in various rooms, depending upon individual interest. After "high tea," which is usually a full buffet luncheon, came a very enthusiastic rock swap.

Each of us was given a plastic bag containing collector specimens of smoky quartz, pyrite, and a small piece of Andamooka opal from the mine on our schedule for October 9. These prized specimens were compliments of Ralph Smith, president, and the local club.

October 6. Rain! Rain! Rain! It was raining while we were in Melbourne, and it was raining as we left, aboard our luxuri-

426

ous coach, for Adelaide. Natives were complaining of the rain and cold, but we were warm and comfortable. True, this is not the weather we had expected, and those of us who had been to Australia previously failed to bring foul weather gear. But who cared? The panorama which we viewed through glassed-in comfort is unforgettable. Soon we were passing through millions and millions of brilliantly colored flowers, most of them the cultivated variety. Victoria is called the "Garden State of Australia." Gradually the scenery changed from flowers you would like to pick to mountains you would like to climb. Unfortunately the gold mine we were supposed to visit out of Ballart became a NO! NO! because the unpaved roads became rivers of mud. Gold was discovered in this area in the 1850s. The strike was so big that it drew prospectors from throughout the world. Leaving this fabled area, we passed through Stanwell and Bordertown as we headed for Adelaide down a very long grade.

Because we had to drive some 500 kilometers through the rain and because of imperative stops, it was past dark when we reached our hotel and unloaded. Doug had called ahead to our hotel and they waited dinner. While we ate he called the rock club and explained the reason we were so late. Despite the fact that we were almost two hours late, they waited. Even sent an escort to lead Doug through the downpour to their enviable building, a real lab for rock enthusiasts. What a spread they had laid out for us! Remember, when you are in Australia, never eat before attending a high tea. We loved the ladies who came to our bus and told us about the work their club was doing while their husbands guided us to the meeting place. After displaying their lapidary lab, we gathered for a rock swap. One lady, who was not a lapist, used different colors of birch bark to do miniature scenes which she cleverly encased in such things as bracelets and necklaces. What entrepreneurship!

October 7. A free day, and we needed it. Despite the continual rain, our coach captain took us on a good city tour, visiting the water front and many rock shops. As we drove alongside the beautiful Murray River your author could not help but think of when Mark Twain rode on this river at the turn of the century. He declared himself amazed that he should find, half a world away in the Murray, the mirror image of the mighty Mississippi.

427

If he had been with us he would have seen the Murray bank to bank with floods threatening.

It rained and rained. Perhaps getting up earlier than we had planned would help our coachman stay ahead of the predicted flooding. It was too wet to enjoy a side trip to Eyre Peninsula, as scheduled, to see kangaroos, koalas, emus, and other wild animals and plants not yet caught with our cameras. And that includes rocks, too, enormous granite and limestone cliffs.

October 8. Today we stay ahead of the flood, almost. In places the water comes right up to the pavement. Salt lakes, long since dry, stretch for miles. Our coachman and guide, Douglas Gunn, lives in Mt. Culah, Australia. Soon we realized that he not only had a keen sense of wit, but an encyclopedic as well as personal knowledge of his homeland. His hands seemed to wrap around two luggage handles as easily as around the steering wheel. No wild animal nor rare bird escaped his view, and he knew them all well. Maybe he wasn't such a "bloke" after all. He kept us all comfortable, safe and laughing.

From Port Augusta on the southern shore of Australia we turned north toward the Red Center. We passed through Woomera, where atom bombs were tested, then on to Roxby Downs, where we would spend two nights. Roxby Downs was as modern as it was young. Not like most mining towns at all. Built as a home for Olympic Dam workers, it was only twelve years old, and laid out beautifully.

Our hotel was something else. The complex was built around a spacious swimming pool and garden. The great white dome which sheltered it could be seen for miles. Our rooms were beautiful, each with a sliding glass door and balcony overlooking the pool. Only one glitch in our secure haven. It was still raining. This would not cancel our trip to Olympic Dam, but the trip to the Andamooka opal field was out. An act of God, we were told.

Certainly the newspapers backed this claim. The *Adelaide Advertiser* headline read: "BIG WET HITS THE PLAINS." A Bureau of Meteorology spokesman called it the most rain and worst flooding in over a hundred years. People had to be rescued by boats and choppers. Livestock drowned in the fields. Homes, businesses, and ranches were all but floating in the sea of rainwater. Going to the Andamooka opal fields out of the question.

428

But not for our leader. Mrs. Oro Stewart had been there previously, this being her seventh trip to Australia.

"What do you mean, out of the question? I've been there before. They have rigs that can make it in any kind of weather. The ground is flat. It's not floating there. Besides, it's supposed to start clearing tomorrow. Call them. I saw four-wheel drive rigs on the road."

Then came the long flab. I admired our leader's guts, but questioned her judgment. But of course I hadn't been to these mines before, either.

The powers that be met in conference. It was finally decided that if the weather improved our own coach would take us as far as the driver felt it was safe, then he would call for their vehicles to pick us up. HOORAY FOR ORO!

Like magic the weather cleared overnight. The sun was shining as we toured the Olympic Dam complex where gold, siver, copper, and uranium were all mined. I thought I had seen dams, but nothing like this. We were told that it could furnish two-thirds of Australia with water. There were twenty steel gates weighing 95 tons each, used to control the flow of water, which ran underneath, not over, the gates to control the silt. It was almost too much to grasp. There was a second dam upstream in the gorge for security storage, 800,000 gallons.

There were just too many divisions of the complex to count, and their operation certainly too complex for this writer to explain. Monstrous ore trucks belched from the bowels of the earth and dumped their loads into strings of gondolas on a railroad track. This railroad is owned by Hamersly Iron.

The trains are pulled by three diesel electric locomotives hauling 210 ore cars each. These are the heaviest and longest locomotive trains in the world. But the trip to the Andamooka opal fields comes up this very afternoon, so we do not linger.

We slip and slide along a red, red road before Douglas figures the bus can't swim in deeper water. He calls ahead, and 4-wheel drive vans are waiting for us. The water was deep in places, but we never slid off the road, not once. The sun shone brightly and we were fairly well out of the mud as we entered a small town with no paved roads, and as we were told, no taxes, no central water supply, no electricity, no governing body, and no police force. It was as different from the Olympic complex as a pick and shovel is from a computer, and that is just what many of these folks used for mining opals. The houses had no bathroom facilities. We carried a picnic lunch with us and ate out under some trees. Some of us sat at a crude table in a clean but Spartan one-room board cabin which once served as a miner's home. There was a bar in town, and to the best of our recollection, this was the only indoor toilet in the community. There were plenty of clean outhouses and the modest homes seemed clean. We visited a couple of rock shops and were given an opal cutting demonstration.

Then we went fossicking for opals. None of us made any spectacular finds, nor did we expect to. We searched in tailings. Then we visited the most unique home and mine I have ever seen. It was dug into the side of a hill. It was a nice house, and quite clean. But upon opening either of the back doors you found yourself in a maze of tunnels.

We were shown how mining was done in the tunnel, mostly by hand. We were told that one miner found an opal which he sold for several hundred thousands of dollars. What did he do? Where did he go? He went right back to digging. Maybe Robert W. Service was right when he wrote in his Alaskan ballad that it's not so much the gold as the finding of the gold.

October 10, 11. Saturday and Sunday were mostly spent on the road. We saw lots of emus and stopped now and then to gaze at the amazingly blue-green Indian Ocean, with its great white cliffs. During one such break Virginia Murray found what we thought was an iguana, but Doug identified it as a blue tongued, shingled lizard. It looked fierce, but Doug picked it up by wrapping his right hand around its back, just behind its head. With his left hand he started picking ticks from underneath its shingles. "Now you'll feel better," he explained as the reptile stuck out its blue tongue.

October 12. On Monday we reached Kalgoorlie, where gold was discovered in 1902 by an Irishman, Paddy Hannan. Of course we visited what is known as the "Richest Square Mile on Earth." The tailings piles were as far as eye could see, and seemingly endless, but neat and trim. We were told that every bit of this earth would be recycled for fine gold and then all tunnels would be refilled. It was a massive project.

Finally, getting past the tailings, we came to Hannan mine. It was no longer operative, but restored and now mining tourists. After walking down a rail track we came to a mine shaft. We were given hard hats and an operator dropped us down a 140-foot shaft much quicker than we can tell about it. Talk about that funny feeling in the pit of your stomach! Courteous and friendly guides explained how the mine functioned, showing us drill holes where dynamite was used to speed up the digging. We followed the narrow rails through tunnel after tunnel as they snaked, following quartz veins once heavy with gold.

Back to daylight, we followed a siding to a tent, similar but much larger than those the miners first used. Inside, an animated Paddy Hannan told us what it was like during gold rush days. Then back to the office and gift shop where several of the group bought gold nuggets.

October 13. Today we reached a different world, Perth, on the Western coast of Australia, where we will spend two nights. The approach to the town with almost a million people defied the urban masses, but the skyscrapers seen across the tranquil Swan River and six-lane traffic spoke the truth. Here we would attend the West Australian Lapidary and Rock Hunting Club. Again we were late, but the miles seem endless in Western Australia. The meeting was in progress when we arrived, but afterward we were served high tea, then an enthusiastic rock swap and a tour of the facility.

"Wouldn't it be great if we had such a lab in Anchorage," Vi Susky remarked.

October 14. What a beautiful day for sightseeing in Perth. No more rain. Beautiful sunshine and it was warmer. Originally known as the Swan River Colony, Perth was settled by the Hollanders.

First settled in 1829, Perth boomed as gold was discovered in Kalgoorlie, and thirty years later in Boulder. Then iron was discovered in the north. With the building of dams and water pipelines, the boom continues. Although Perth has some of the most beautiful white sand beaches in the world, we were quite anxious to get back to the Swan River, to get close to the black swans we only glimpsed while on our way in. What fun! The river was a paradise for fish and fowl. Flowers were everywhere. Film burned as shutters clicked.

October 15. Again we are on the road, this time headed for Nambung National Park. From a distance we saw the Pinnacles, and some of our group hit the sand running. Thousands of limestone pillars rise out of what was once a sea-bed. Erosion took away the sand, leaving the rock formations which have puzzled onlookers since Dutch sailors saw them from the sea and thought they were the remains of an ancient city.

Before getting back on the bus for another long stretch of road, Earl Kelly came hustling from the men's privy with a stick to which a vicious spider still clung. Earl exhibited it proudly, explaining that it would not give up the toilet seat to a stranger. Hustling outside, Earl found a stick to champion his cause. The spider, as big as a tarantula, clamped onto the stick, refusing to retreat. No one disputed its right and left it with the stick, figuring it'd rather bite than fight.

October 16. While on the lonely road to Carnarvon we met a roaring monster which came too close for comfort as the two wide vehicles passed.

"Here we call this 62-wheeler a 'road train.'"

At the next oasis one of the group spotted a brochure which explained precautions to be taken when passing a road train. To begin with, you would need about a mile of straight-of-way with no other traffic in sight . . .

As we drove across the Murchison River bridge, the water just disappeared. We were told that during the dry season, when the water level drops, it keeps flowing, but underneath the sand. Everything alongside the river was irrigated. We made a pleasant stop at a banana and papaya plantation where we were given an excellent explanation as to how it was done and how such industries were blooming in this area, anywhere there was water. Given a taste of fresh frozen chocolate-coated bananas, we all indulged. Some bought enough freshly dried banana chips to keep our potassium high the rest of the trip.

October 17. Heading northwest from the coast, the land is known as the Pilbora, where the rocks date from 3,500,000 years ago, the oldest in Australia. Since they were formed before there was life on earth we would find no fossils, but vast deposits of iron.

The further north we rolled the hotter it got. Soon we were

432

crossing the Tropic of Capricorn. No one had to tell us we were in the torrid zone.

October 18. Leaving Tom Price, named for an American engineer who gave his life helping develop this vast iron area, we crossed the Hamersley Ranges to Whittenoom, built in 1947 to mine blue asbestos. The mines were closed in 1966 with the big asbestos cancer scare. It was a ghost town, but had a very good rock shop, and the motel where we spent the night was comfortable. We found plenty of blue asbestos at the local mine, but since it is barred from entry into the U.S., we dared not try to get it past customs.

October 19. This is the day we visited Marble Bar, noted as the hottest town in Australia. It lived up to its name. It was so hot that some of us hesitated about leaving the air-conditioned comfort of our coach. The marble we picked up burned our hands. The good stuff was too hard to get to. We did, however, enjoy watching those swimming in the cool green pool far below where we stood on the bluff. We left this climb to the long legs of Joe Blazek, Jim Thomas, Von Baxter, and our scout, Jack Simmons. Earlier, when we picnicked in a park, Joe was spotted working out on the monkey bars.

October 20. Today we head down the long hot road for Broome. In mid-afternoon things became so quiet that Doug put on one of our favorite tapes, "Waltzing Matilda." Our mischievous one, Jane Pattison of Anchorage, winked at yours truly, slid into the isle, and danced. Up and down the aisle we waltzed on that long straight-of-way. That woke them up for our visit to a pearling farm.

The walk to the pearling area was a short but very precarious one, over slick, rounded rocks that were under the tide twice daily. As we gathered around, the master of the farm pulled a narrow, oblong wire cage from the water, which imprisoned six saucer sized oysters. He explained how they underwent implants yearly, which would become luminous pearls within twelve months, when the implant was removed, followed by two implants the second year. The third year, three implants. The fourth year, after removal of the three pearls, four would be implanted. Then the shell was crushed and the fragments used as mother of pearl. The life of an oyster didn't sound too exciting. We'd prefer a rock, with a lot of geological background.

433

October 21. Turning inland again, we headed for Fitzroy Crossing. What a bit of "out back" this was. The motel rooms were on stilts. We assumed this was to keep out creepy, crawly things, but it didn't deter a hoppy critter. What Mark Twain could have done with this frog story! But let's hear it from Ed and Von.

"When I ventured into the semi-dark bathroom, luminous eyes stared at me," Von explained. "Turning on the bathroom light, I saw a big green frog had beat me to the seat. I called Ed to come see our new roommate."

"Flush it, quick!" he admonished. "I did, but it came swimming back up, made a big leap and almost hit Ed in the face. We chased it around our bedroom in quite a game of leap frog. The frog won. We couldn't find it, not even in our luggage. It had escaped. But the next morning we found him . . . sitting on the toilet stool again."

Well, Boys, I guess the frog was there before we were. So were Aborigines, but in this part of Australia, at least, they seemed to practice segregation. There was no other establishment within miles; the dining room was closed and we were thirsty. Out back of the building which housed the dining room we saw Coke and beer signs. We heard lots of strange yelling, too, but more like from the bottle. We saw none of the noisy ones, but several men stood outside the building, which may have been a barn at one time, downing a cool one. Determined to see what Australia is all about, Rachel, my roommate, and I walked bravely toward the group. Evidently those at the bar didn't see foreigners too often. This off-the-beaten-tourist-path was certainly no tourist trap. We hesitated, then two fine looking men emerged and introduced themselves.

"We are travelling police, out of Darby," the younger man explained. "We range over a vast territory. This is the chief of police, and I am Tom Troani, a detective," he said, handing me his card. "May we buy you a drink?"

As we walked to a picnic table on the porch, the place seemed to quiet down a bit. We didn't get to see any of the local lore at all. It came from a room inside. But the company was charming.

Just as we had a good thing going several of our group

came trooping to the rescue, darn it. We never saw who was inside the bar room, but as the place grew quieter we noted a few Aborigines walking away. We were never close enough to see inside any of their homes nor learn what their life is really like. We're rather sure this is a fault of all tourism groups. You never get to know the true natives of any land you visit, especially where you don't speak the same language. You see what they want you to see, and are always pushed for time. But there is a flip side of the coin. If we lingered we would never see many of the places that we travel around the world to see.

October 22. What a wonderful day this was! Cruising through Geikie Gorge is on the scenic highlights of Western Australia. This is why we were off the beaten path. We came to Fitzroy Crossing especially for a boat trip downriver through Geikie Gorge. There's no way to really describe what we saw without writing a book and that wouldn't do it justice. Limestone cliffs of the Devonion age loomed thirty meters above our flat-bottomed boat carrying about fifty passengers.

These cliffs were formed before there was life on earth. Now fresh water crocodiles, a wealth of birdlife, and strange fish from ages past intrigued us. Bats hung upside down from trees, watching for small fish and insects. Crocodiles cruised below, waiting for a bat to dive for food.

We would love to have gone spelunking in many of the caves, but this area is so pristine that no one is allowed on the banks of this gorge.

October 23. As we retrace our steps before heading for Kununurra, we stop at a huge Boab Prison tree. We had been hearing about prison trees for a long time, where Douglas said they really held prisoners overnight. This we had to see. It was a huge tree, mostly hollow, with very few branches. This one must have been thirty feet in circumference. Several of the men crawled inside, and it would probably have held all thirty-two of us. A hole at the top enabled one to see skyward. We couldn't help but wonder how many prisoners had been held in this tree in bygone days.

Cruising northward to within 12 degrees of the Equator, we wondered if it would be hotter than the 120 degrees we encountered at Marble Bar. It wasn't, and we thought how pleasant our sunset cruise would be on Lake Kununurra.

It was a fantastic cruise. Our captain told us briefly of the Northern Territory and how they hoped to become a full-fledged state. "God gave us the sun and soil, now man has harnessed water. We can grow any kind of tropical fruit or vegetable, and we will when our land is fully irrigated."

Again we saw fresh water crocodiles and birds by the thousand. He told us about the construction of the big dam that would hold water from monsoon to monsoon, and of the territory's dream. Of course, there were thirty-one affirmatives when he asked if we would like to visit the Zebra Rock cutting and polishing center.

Zebra rock is found only in this area, insofar as has been determined, so we came home loaded with it, everything from spheres to cabs and bookmarks. Much raw stone was purchased by those in the group who do cutting and cabbing. What a great family-run shop this was, out in the middle of nowhere, away from all roads, with only boat traffic to support it.

October 24, 25. Here we will dispose of all small talk and spectacular scenery in between and get to the grand finale of our tour.

Never have we seen anything to compare, not even the Johannesburg Diamond Mine in South Africa. Few people have seen the Argyle Diamond Mine because of its remoteness, its inaccessibility, and because the massive complex was not opened until late in December 1985.

Here let us fill in with a brief orientation. Prior to the Argyle find a few diamonds had been found in Australia, but in the traditional host, Kimberlite. In 1979 geologists working in Smoke Creek near Argyle Lake found diamonds in lamprolite. This find sent geologists from around the world scampering back to areas they had previously discarded.

Soon the Argyle find was determined the largest in the world. Here diamond pipes were exposed near the surface, where they could be mined from open pits. Not only did they find the traditional sparklers, but brown, amber and rare red ones as well. The amber and brown ones are called "Champagne" and "Cognac." The red diamonds are the most expensive diamonds in the world.

Our flight to the diamond mine, the only way it can be

436

reached by tourist groups, was worth the $250 dollar tab. This is the ony way to get to see all of Argyle Lake, which has a capacity of 5.6 million cubic meters, covers 740 kms, and is eight times the size of Sydney Harbor.

The Argyle is one of three dams in this watershed; the other two are Ord and Olympic. Streams and smaller bodies of water seem everywhere. But the three dams mentioned above reportedly hold enough fresh water to last a drought stricken Australia four years. Of course, irrigation ditches and water pipelines are much in evidence. A water pipeline ran alongside our highway for over 535 kilometers.

Landing within a few miles of the complex, we were bussed past company housing and to the cafeteria where we dined sumptuously, as was always the case in Australia. Despite the fact that we were in a desert, the man-made garden walk to the front entrance was enhanced by an Australian-long fish pond, complete with exotic fish and lilies and bordered by flowering shrubs and trees. We created no sensation, since employees, pilots and tour groups are fed here daily.

The cafeteria resembled many of those in our country. From the cafeteria we were escorted to the large processing plants. En route we were warned by our new guide that once we de-bussed we would be under constant scrutiny. Bend down and you would be in real trouble. As in the iron mine, rails, dumping areas and various plants and facilities were everywhere.

Believe it or not, since we were rock hounds, we were invited into the heart of the complex. Here we viewed the computerized operation of the entire mine. On the television screen we saw huge shovels mounted on giant cranes dumping multi-ton bites into trucks which would dump their loads at a processing plant. Here, from plant to plant, other valuable minerals would be extracted through separation after separation tanks throughout the complex. If anything went wrong anywhere throughout the mining area or in the processing plant it would show up as a blinking red light on the graph of the complex. The monitoring engineers could shut down any machine for repair, or the whole complex. It was difficult to believe what we were seeing. Not even a mouse could have entered this complex without being detected. What miracles man has created!

Of course we knew televised eyes watched as we entered the display room. Here multi-million dollar sparklers were only inches away, enclosed in glass. This included the Hope as well as other fabled diamonds from throughout the world.

The colored ones were different from other diamonds. Most of them were smaller, as well as more expensive, especially the red ones which are extremely rare. Best of all there were graphs and charts with the Argyle displays.

Climaxing the tour, we flew over part of the 3,000 kilometer Bungle Bungle National Park. This is not a park with roads and housing. It is one of Australia's natural wonders. Endless stacks of layered formations carved by erosion. Man is the park's worst enemy. The striped rock formations have a thin outer layer of black lichen and orange silica. If the the skin is broken, torrential rains speed erosion. The deep gorges and towering cliffs are awe-inspiring. Some of the gorges have inviting pools of emerald water. Bungle Bungle fan palms can be seen clinging to the face of virtually vertical cliffs. How we would like to return some day and see it all over again.

On our return flight the pilot flew low over the Argyle Dam and nearby points of interest. Below us lay Kununurra, our overnight home. Small wonder Chief Kununurra fought so hard to preserve his homeland. Some day we hope to see Tunnel Creek and walk through the long limestone tube which was his last hiding place as he and his Aboriginal tribesmen lost their lives protecting this beautiful and unexploited homeland.

October 25. Today we must push many, many kilometers to reach Darwin, a city we hope to see on our next trip. It was hard just to think about leaving so many wonderful friends until next year, when Oro will again lead us to another wonderland half a world away.

Yet one thing still puzzled your writer. Our coach captain, Douglas, had gained our love and respect and we bestowed the honor of "Fellow Rockhound" on him at dinner. He no longer got that puzzled look in his eye when he saw yours truly. He had confessed. The reason he jumped so high when he first saw me was because he thought I was his mother, whom he thought was hundreds of miles away in Scotland.

"Why apologize?" I asked. "I would be proud to have a son like you."

October 26. This was our last day in Australia. We would no longer be together as a group. Three of the group would catch a plane to Alice Springs. The rest of us would fly to Carins, on the East Coast, before splitting. Eight would continue the adventure by flying to New Guinea. The rest of us would be heading for the good old U.S.A. Our Coach Captain would be retracing his steps, over 10,000 kilometers alone, back to the East Coast.

As Mr. Douglas Gunn unloaded our baggage at the airport, terminating our trip with him, your writer stuck out a paw and said, "Goodbye, Son."

Leaving the bags lay, he gave me a hug and peck on the cheek, saying, "Goodbye, Mom. I'm proud to be a rockhound."

Chapter 39

The Glory Road

S
ixty years have passed since I tried to take my own life. The farther down the road, the more glorious life becomes. My cup runneth over!

Jean, that prisoner's daughter, has been a constant source of inspiration. Before she was born I feared she might not be normal because of malnutrition. She's not. She's far above the average "norm." In her graduating class of over 6,000 students at the University of Texas she finished in the upper one-half percent. All the way through school she was an honor student, yet she like myself was all but an outcast in our own home town.

Things have changed. Now we are honored. Jean has seven books off the press and I have twelve. Now I can see that much of the credit goes to so-called "Society." You made it so tough on us that we had to prove ourselves worthy citizens. Thanks!

During the Depression when we were starving I never dreamed of having a car and anything I wanted to eat, much less owning three businesses, all of which are doing quite well.

But best of all is my wonderful family. Thanks to Jean and her fine husband Frank Richardson, I now have three grandchildren of whom I am justly proud. Linda, the eldest, has far outstripped her infamous grandfather in becoming a doctor. She wants to be an orthopedist because she loves working with children. Carol Ann, my second granddaughter, went right off the scale when given I.Q. tests. When she was five she cried of frustration because her little fingers would not span enough keys for playing classical music. As a twelve-year-old she represented Harris County, Texas, in math competition. Now through college, Carol is working for an oil company and climbing. Joe Frank Richardson, my only grandson, is not yet through college. When he was fifteen years old he won the world championship in B.M.X. bicycle racing. His last two summers have been spent in Alaska. He is a great lover of nature. Now, Jean, Frank and Joe are all working toward making "Grandma's" dreams materialize.

I am forever grateful to my incredible mother, whom I once thought I hated, and my father, who never gave up believing in me. Without them I could never have made it through. My mother was the strongest woman I have ever known, and my father the most trusting and encouraging man. My older sister, Lela, who has six books to her credit, turned ninety-one on January 30, 1996, and is still writing books and making public appearances. Our sister Ann, now deceased, has enough wonderful children, grandchildren and great-grandchildren to make up for me having only one daughter, our Jeannie, whom we have always shared as our very own. Of my five brothers, all of whom made good in the oil field, two are still alive. They and their families have helped to make this world a better place to live. Thank you! What a wonderful heritage.

In 1970 when I broke my back, my daughter asked, "Mama, have you ever been sick a day in your life?"

"I don't think so, Darling, not really sick. This is the first time I've been hospitalized. You were born at home, not in a hospital, and it cost $35."

"Am I worth it?" she asked.

Throughout my life something good always seemed to have been born of tragedy. The year I broke my back is also the year I began working with Ostrich (Fiddlehead) Fern and building my lodge near Mount McKinley. My lodge and homestead are now engulfed by Denali State Park. But thankfully, my "grandfather rights," or should I say "grandmother rights," were honored and I was not forced to sell. I still bill it as the best roadside view of the nation's tallest peak and those who gaze at it through the cathedral-like windows of the lodge agree.

441

In 1983 I started the "World's Only Fiddlehead Fern Farm" and my second gift shop at Mile 1 on the Talkeetna Spur Road. As of 1997 the lodge, the Fiddlehead Fern Farm, both gifts shop and my daughter's and my books are doing quite well. My greatest desire is that the fern farm will be a boon to posterity and help feed a hungry world. I fear that with war and famine and the greenhouse warming trend, ours will be a hungry world. Perhaps my greatest tool for fighting famine is not my typewriter but Ostrich fern, which has survived since the age of the dinosaur. Better yet it is one of our most delectable and nutritious vegetables. It requires no planting or fertilizer and grows wild throughout much of South Central and Southeastern Alaska. Already I am sending fern by air cargo to Glacier Bay and to the Fiddlehead Fern Restaurant in Juneau, our state's capitol.

Just seeing a child's eyes light up when he knows he has really earned his first money, or teens picking fern rather than passing pot on a street corner, is reward enough. But many seniors also pick fiddleheads. It gives them extra pocket change as well as good bending down exercise in some of the cleanest, freshest air on earth. Yes I am thankful that mine, the World's Only Fiddlehead Fern Farm and other dreams are materializing too.

Today my daughter and I work as a team, writing and making public appearances. Yet it was not until that prisoner's daughter was well on her way to success in the writing world that I am revealing her father's real name Roy King in this book. She was afraid her children would suffer as she had suffered through man's inhumanity to man. To those who read the fictionized versions of my catastrophic earlier life, *Fugitives* and *How Long Must I Hide*, only through publication of this book am I revealing true names. In those publications Roy King was Roy Gregg, Jean was Carolyn and I was May Gregg.

Why tell all now? Because life can be beautiful, if you have the guts and determination to stick in there and fight even though the odds are overwhelming.

We belong to a good world. A just society does not demand that breaking the law of man be passed to the second and third generation. If we are strong our mistakes and failures become stepping stones. Roy King was not strong enough to resist narcotics, and he paid the price. Now I realize I owe him a great

442

deal too. His weakness made me strong. His daughter is my greatest joy in life.

No doubt there are many persons today who face unknown problems which seem insurmountable. Each time I speak I want to cry out, "Look, it can be done! Have faith and the determination to start over and over again even though circumstance has pushed you to the brink. The underdog fights harder. Each victory is one more step along the glory road."

My first book was written with a cast on my back in front of a wood stove at my homestead on a manual typewriter because I had no electricity. It took me five years to finish *Alaska, Not For A Woman*. Soon after its publication in 1976, it was lauded as a best seller by the publisher. It won first place awards in both Texas and Alaska. It is now through a fifteenth edition.

To those who think they are too old to start a new career, I was a grandmother before I came to Alaska and a senior citizen when my first book came off the press. Jean waited until her children were assured of a college education before beginning her career as a writer. Now she has seven books off the press. Best of all, her first children's book, *Tag-Along Timothy Tours Alaska*, did so well that the publisher asked her to do another, letting the little rabbit, Tag-Along Timothy, tour Texas. Now it is suggested that she do forty-eight more, letting the rabbit visit state and national parks throughout the nation. It has been suggested that these books serve as a child's encyclopedia to state and national parks.

My life has reached full circle. How sweet it is! Deep in my heart I have always felt God had some mission for me as He held my hand through the depths of despair. If stumbling and picking up the pieces to fight again gives inspiration, I have achieved my mission.